ORALITY AND LITERACY
Reflections across Disciplines

Orality and Literacy

Reflections across Disciplines

*Edited by Keith Thor Carlson, Kristina Fagan,
and Natalia Khanenko-Friesen*

UNIVERSITY OF TORONTO PRESS
Toronto Buffalo London

© University of Toronto Press Incorporated 2011
Toronto Buffalo London
www.utppublishing.com
Printed in Canada

ISBN 978-0-8020-9826-9

Printed on acid-free, 100% post-consumer recycled paper with vegetable-based inks.

Library and Archives Canada Cataloguing in Publication

Orality and literacy : reflections across disciplines / edited by
Keith Thor Carlson, Kristina Fagan, and Natalia Khanenko-Frieson.

Includes bibliographical references and index.
ISBN 978-0-8020-9826-9

1. Oral tradition. 2. Literacy. 3. Language and culture. I. Carlson, Keith Thor
II. Fagan, Kristina Rose, 1973– III. Khanenko-Friesen, Natalia

P35.O73 2011   306.44   C2010-904479-7

University of Toronto Press acknowledges the financial assistance to
its publishing program of the Canada Council for the Arts and Ontario
Arts Council.

 Canada Council   Conseil des Arts    ONTARIO ARTS COUNCIL
for the Arts   du Canada   CONSEIL DES ARTS DE L'ONTARIO

University of Toronto Press acknowledges the financial support
of the Government of Canada through the Canada Book Fund
for its publishing activities.

This book has been published with the help of a grant from the Canadian
Federation for the Humanities and Social Sciences, through the Aid to
Scholarly Publications Programme, using funds provided by the Social
Sciences and Humanities Research Council of Canada.

Contents

PART THREE: GOING PUBLIC

PART FOUR: SUBVERTING AUTHORITY

PART FIVE: UNCOVERING VOICES

Acknowledgments

The authors and editors would like to thank the administration, faculty, and staff at the University of Saskatchewan and St Thomas More College for supporting this project, and in particular Professor J.R. Miller who through his Canada Research Chair in Native–Newcomer Relations covered the majority of the costs for the original symposium at which the authors were able to come together to share the results of their research. The symposium was co-hosted by the Prairie Centre for the Study of Ukrainian Heritage, St Thomas More College, the Humanities Research Unit, the Department of History, and the Department of English at the University of Saskatchewan.

We are also grateful to the various graduate students who volunteered their time to make that symposium such a success, especially MacKinley Darlington, Heather Watson, Chris Clark, Byron Plant, Christine Charmbury, Paget Code, Tasha Hubbard, and Joanie Crandall. We also thank Carey Tufts, who created the symposium website. We are grateful as well to both the University of Saskatchewan Faculty Club and the Bessborough Delta Hotel for their wonderful meals, accommodations and service. Likewise, we thank Maria Campbell and Brenda Macdougall for preparing and hosting a wonderful traditional Métis feast at Maria's house at Dumont Crossing; Sherry Farrell-Racette for sharing her knowledge of Métis history, the staff and management at the Batoche National Historical Site for opening their facilities and sharing their knowledge.

We owe a special debt of gratitude to graduate students Mandy Fehr, Ana Novakovic, Katya McDonald, Sarah Nickle, and Lesley Wiebe for assisting in tracking down stray footnotes and in other ways helping to fix the manuscript. And of course, as editors, we are especially thankful to Teresa, Steve, and Tim for their patience and support throughout.

Selected Place Names Appearing in Volume

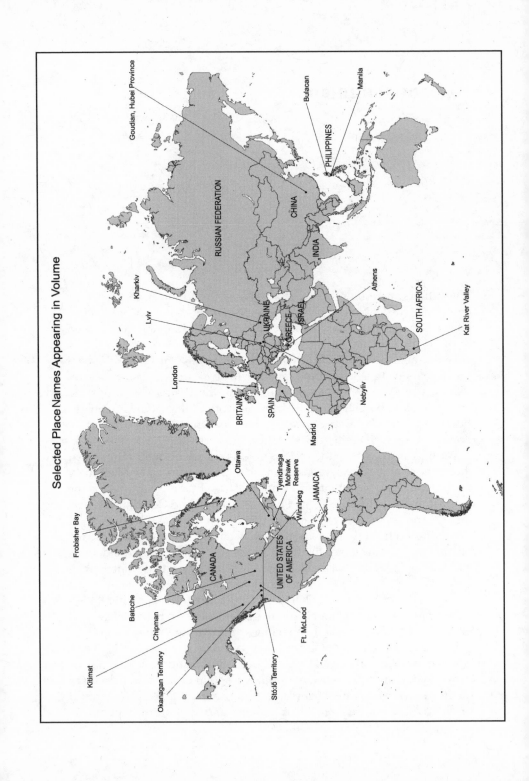

ORALITY AND LITERACY
Reflections across Disciplines

Introduction

Reading and Listening at Batoche

KEITH THOR CARLSON, KRISTINA FAGAN,
AND NATALIA KHANENKO-FRIESEN

The wind was constant and cold on that October day in 2004 as we walked across the open Canadian prairie toward the little graveyard on the banks of the South Saskatchewan River. The Batoche cemetery still sits where it did when the conflict between the Métis, a people of mixed Aboriginal and European descent, and the Canadian military forces raged over its grounds in 1885. As we made our way into the burial ground, bending our heads against the stinging gale, we paused to examine a tall monument listing the names of those Cree and Métis who fell in the battles of Batoche, Fish Creek, and Duck Lake. We studied the names carved in stone and we thought about their meaning.

Each of us in the group was, in a sense, a professional thinker about meaning. Twelve scholars from different disciplines – anthropology, folklore, history, literature, and sociology – with diverse ethnic backgrounds and from different parts of the world, we had gathered for an invitational three-day symposium to talk about how we interpret the different ways that meaning is communicated through, and across, the spoken and written word. None of us specialized in prairie Métis history or culture. Our excursion to Batoche was primarily a social one. We had not come with the intention of formally examining the historical conflicts and tensions between Aboriginal people and the Canadian state, although as organizers, we did hope that we might see and experience some of the theoretical issues we were engaging at the conference being played out in a real world setting – and in that desire we were not disappointed.

Though the Battle of Batoche looms large in Canadian history, it does not necessarily resonate in Canadian popular consciousness – let alone in the minds of people living elsewhere. What is known about it – or at least what is communicated through history texts – describes a conflict that was ostensibly over land, governance, and identity. What we observed that day suggested that it was also, in a fundamental sense, a conflict between literacy and orality. The Canadian military came armed not only with Gatling guns and artillery but with documents and maps asserting title, proclaiming law, and declaring legislative authority. The Métis responded with bullets, and, when those ran out, they reloaded their rifles with rocks, nails, and brass buttons from their coats. But behind their powder and shot were oral traditions that spoke a counter-narrative, in which title emerged from relations with the land itself and the spoken words of God resonated in the ears of Louis Riel and those who followed him.

As we stood with our faces to the wind, studying that seemingly simple text carved on the Batoche monument, we were reminded just how complex communication is. Those inscribed names were mnemonic devices that triggered a symphony of layered stories, stories of individuals, families, and nations. All these stories pushed in different directions, highlighting the slippery middle ground in the contact zone between orality and literacy.

Immediately prior to visiting the gravesite we had shared steaming bowls of soup, plates of bannock, and saskatoon berry tarts at Maria Campbell's home. Maria, perhaps best known as the author of the 1973 autobiography *Halfbreed,* is a descendant of Gabriel Dumont, the Métis military commander in 1885. Her house is on the riverbank on the site of Dumont's old home. Over that wonderful meal, Sherry Farrell-Racette, a Métis scholar, shared with us what she knew to have happened at Batoche and what has happened to the Métis people since. Some of her accounts came from her family, part of a living oral tradition. Others came from digging up written archival records. She blended these, weighed evidence, contrasted accounts and motivations, and created a story that was both hers and a community's. She passed quickly over the battle, which for her was but a moment (admittedly an important and tragic one) in the Métis story. The battle did not define the Métis people. Sherry spoke more about what they did after it. Hers were principally stories of survival.

As we departed Maria's house on our way to the Batoche National Historic Site, we were warned to be sceptical of the 'government version' of the story. We arrived at the federal interpretive centre and were ushered into a theatre to view a multimedia show about the history of Batoche. The presentation began with a quotation from a song titled 'Maria [Campbell]'s Place' by Canadian folk singer Connie Calder:

On the South Saskatchewan River
There's a crossing and a bend
That they call Batoche
And on the banks of that river
A battle was won
And a people were lost.

'A people were lost.' It was clear that we were going to hear a very different version of Batoche from that told in Maria's kitchen. Indeed, what we watched was a detailed story of the battle – a story that stopped when the battle was over. It left us wondering what happened next: what did it all mean? Then the lights came on and we met our tour guides, a young Métis man and a woman from the local French-speaking community. As they spoke enthusiastically about the land that we stood on, it was clear that for them, the story did not end in 1885. We were told, for instance, about the bell from the Batoche Catholic church that had been taken 3,000 kilometres back to Ontario as a war trophy by the victorious Canadian soldiers. After sitting behind glass in a central Canadian veterans' Legion Hall for more than a century, the bell had recently disappeared. With a twinkle in their eyes, the guides explained that witnesses had reported seeing an old pick-up truck bearing a Saskatchewan licence plate speeding into the night the evening before the 'theft' was discovered. And yet, while our guides provided glimpses into the ongoing oral traditions surrounding Batoche, they also referred to a government-composed interpreters' manual that gave them the 'official meaning' of Batoche, a meaning that did not include things such as stolen bells. Clearly, once again, both written and oral traditions were at work in dynamic tension.

So we stood in the graveyard with a variety of stories pushing against one another in our minds. And, of course, we also brought our own stories with us. Those of us born in Canada reflected on what we had earlier learned, or not learned, in school, as we contemplated the meaning of a government heritage site that commemorated that same government's military alienation of Métis lands and the supposed destruction of Métis governance. And language made a difference. Some of the names were Cree and few of us could penetrate their meaning. One of the symposium participants, however, was looking at the name of his Cree grandfather on that monument. His story was surely a complex one. Others in our group were not from Canada, or had never been to the prairies before. For some of these visitors, the English names were just as foreign. Surely they were sorting out a different set of stories (perhaps having to do with Canadian winter weather).

The graveyard at Batoche is layered with stories: some written, some oral. Some have the authority of government manuals, others of archival documents, still others of family connection and intergenerational memories. They make different and sometimes conflicting claims about Batoche and they require different kinds of interpretation; some provided space for counter-interpretations, and others were polemical. And it was not simply the messages that were in tension but also the media. Oral and literate sources competed for legitimacy, each citing different criteria for authority and each received differently. Some listeners/readers were predisposed to privilege one over another, but as we said, we were all, in a sense, professional thinkers about meaning, and so we paused to reflect on what we brought to the stories and what we were going to take away.

In trying to figure out these kinds of tensions and differences, early and influential theorists of orality and literacy – such as the 'Toronto school' of Harold Innis, Marshall McLuhan, Eric Havelock, and Walter Ong – tended to assume that oral cultures and written cultures were essentially, inherently, and universally different, both psychologically and culturally.[1] The culmination of the Toronto school is found in the seminal writings of Walter Ong, who claimed that 'fully literate persons can only with great difficulty imagine what a primary oral culture is like.'[2] The oral–literate epistemological chasm was nearly impossible to bridge, Ong argued, because writing was 'a technology' that literally 'restructured thought.' So profound was this transformation that within oral societies thought functioned in a manner that to the literate mind appeared 'strange and at times bizarre.'[3] Once transformed, literate people's minds worked in a new and distinct way, as reflected in Ong's list of binary divisions: oral peoples tend to aggregate knowledge, speak repetitively or redundantly, think conservatively and empathetically, and reason situationally. Such characteristics contribute to the saliency of words and thereby enhance the memorability of utterances. Among literate peoples, in contrast, knowledge tends to be analysed, thought is innovative, ideas are objectively distanced, and reason is approached abstractly. Within literate societies words are not necessarily spoken so they will be remembered (written texts can always be pulled from the shelf and referred to when needed), nor are they necessarily meant for an audience that can respond immediately. While text relieves the need to memorize, it simultaneously creates a distance between writer and reader. This distance in turn facilitates the interiorization of thought, and when thought is interiorized people are able to situate themselves abstractly within time.

Considered in this light, the relationship between orality and literacy inevitably becomes characterized by a unidirectional displacement; literacy, once introduced into a society, becomes an unstoppable force, impelling orality to recede into darkness. Thus for Ong, just as a child exposed to literacy in the Western tradition ultimately and inevitably became a literate-thinking adult, so too civilizations and cultures transform, mature, and develop once literacy is introduced. For Ong and Havelock, literate thinking necessarily supplants oral thinking. As such, these theorists highlight that orality and literacy are not simply two ways of expressing the same messages; rather, as Marshall Mc-Luhan famously declared, the media themselves define and ultimately become the messages.

Running parallel to the Toronto school was the work of anthropologist Jack Goody.[4] Ethnographic evidence Goody collected among African tribal communities seemed to confirm the theoretical musings emerging from the Toronto school. Oral societies were 'pre-logical,' Goody argued, by which he meant that they lacked syllogistic reasoning (i.e., 'If A, then B; but not B, so therefore not A').[5] In addition Goody found that his study group lacked complex hierarchical systems for organizing information and therefore had trouble using visual representations to arrange conceptual data. Oral societies, he argued, might have arithmetic, but they inevitably lacked multiplication tables and as such the ability to develop organizing systems such as algebra, calculus, or trigonometry. In such societies, Goody concluded, knowledge could never be cumulative and therefore one person's reasoning could not be recorded and built upon by someone from the next generation – as occurred in classical Greece, for instance.

Though Ong concluded *Orality and Literacy* by asserting that neither orality nor literacy was superior to the other (p. 175), and Goody attempted to be cautious in assessing the broader implications of his case studies, the thrust of their overall arguments fit snugly into a stream of popular and political discourse that regarded western European society as not only unique but superior and exceptional. Critics latched onto Ong's assertion that 'both orality, and the growth of literacy out of orality, are necessary for evolution of consciousness' (p. 175) and Goody's contention that 'Cognitively, as well as sociologically, writing underpins "civilization," the culture of cities.'[6] The Eurocentric and evolutionary normativism informing such assumptions were plain to see, and if not explicit, the belief was that all societies would (perhaps should?) go through identical evolutionary changes as had Europe. Thus, whatever the merits of their analysis, those who followed Goody and Ong sought correctives that showed, for example, how orality had not always bowed to literacy, and how orality continued to inform literacy long after earlier scholars had dismissed its influence.[7]

Revisionist works that emerged over the past two decades have generally either sought historical examples of oralist achievements to challenge the supposed evolutionary rule (the Inca, for example, were oral and had yet built a nation state), or pointed to the veracity of oral forms within supposedly literate societies (the English written epics were largely products of oral thinking and representation;[8] oral communication persisted as the dominant vehicle despite the introduction and adoption of literacy in Malaysia[9]). One of the earliest, and most compelling, of these critiques came from Ruth Finnegan, who questioned the technological determinism that informed Ong's and Goody's work. Although literacy and its associated technologies could be credited with creating certain of the conditions that precipitated the rise of modern democratic institutions, scientific thought, and rationalism, they were not, she argued, their causes. Nor, in her opinion, did the introduction of literacy mean that an oral culture would necessarily abandon its traditions and embark down the path of Western rationalism and modernity.[10] Certain African tribal communities, for example, had oral traditions that matched the complexity of European literature. Among Maori orators she found clear evidence of oral–literate hybridity, and among Fijian oral historians she observed people who cared deeply about keeping narratives fixed and unchanged as they were transmitted across generations. Perhaps more important, however, Finnegan intimated that literacy's supposedly inevitable benefits were not so inevitable. Biblical authority, for example, could stifle intellectual enquiry, and divisions between literates and non-literates within a society could lead to deeper and reified social stratification. There existed no genuine 'great divide' between orality and literacy; rather what mattered was how the technology of literacy was controlled and mobilized within a society.[11]

The debates and discussions surrounding the orality–literacy divide continue. Rather than viewing orality and literacy as separate and opposite, the authors of the various essays in this collection take for granted that whatever meaning literacy and orality have are a product of their relationship to one another. Put another way, it is impossible to understand literacy outside the context of its relationship to orality, and exceedingly difficult to understand orality in isolation from literacy. Furthermore, most scholars today have become attentive to the sometimes subtle ways in which power shapes this relationship. It is unfortunate that the first scholars to explore the dynamics between these two forms of communication did so primarily through an evolutionary lens derived either from their understanding of the process by which western Europe collectively adopted literacy, or from observations of the equally culturally specific experience of a single child's transition from an oral to a literate state as he or she passes through the process of Western education. This legacy has been difficult to shake, as is apparent from the common and popular conflation of the term *non-literate* with both *preliterate* and *illiterate*.

Considering the history of Batoche quickly makes it clear that the relationship between orality and literacy has been shaped as much by power relations as by inherent differences in the media of communication. At its most simple level, the Battle of Batoche can be seen as a fight between an oral people (the Métis) and a literate people (the Canadians). The Métis wanted to create a community that conformed to the natural landscape of the river and prairies, in which each family's land would include a portion of the riverbank. The Canadian government sought to impose a written orderliness on the landscape. They wanted to discard the natural features in favour of a grid system consisting of quarter-section farms. The surveyed grid was based on, and in turn justified by, literate, paper-based mapping, land tenure, and ultimately governance. The Battle of Batoche was, then, the orality–literacy conflict writ large and in real, human terms. But it also took place in a world where Métis leader Louis Riel wrote proclamations and decrees and where many of the Canadian soldiers were themselves illiterate.

We can see the story of Batoche as a 'micronarrative' that complicates some of the 'metanarratives' which have dominated scholarly discussions of orality and literacy. Similarly, most of the essays in this collection investigate the intersections of the oral and the literate through close study of particular cultures at particular historical moments. This focus on culturally specific micronarratives reveals the powerful ways in which cultural assumptions, such as those about truth, disclosure, performance, privacy, and ethics, affect how particular cultures approach and make use of the written and the oral. Our efforts to ascribe value and meaning to written or oral texts is inevitably culturally determined. And as J.E. Chamberlin points out in his contribution to this collection, because of these cultural assumptions, 'the trouble is that one community's currency is often merely another's curiosity' (p. 21). The power imbalances that arise out of this trouble have often served to marginalize oral-based cultures in the face of societies for which literacy is the currency of power. Across the colonial world, for instance, oral forms of knowledge and interaction have been devalued by literate invading nations. A reading of the essays in this collection reveals connections and commonalities between societies around the world that have been disempowered in this way, from post-Soviet women in Ukraine to the First Nations of North America and to peasants in the Philippines. However, the essays also remind us that we must be careful not to overgeneralize the oral-marginal/written-powerful binary. Overall, this collection highlights the need for scholars to be attentive to the social and cultural contexts of written or oral texts rather than relying on universal generalizations about how literacy and orality function.

Diversity appears on many levels. It is unusual to find a volume in which Canadian Aboriginal communities and authors are discussed alongside Soviet women, ancient Chinese autocrats, medieval magic, Plato, Ukrainian immigrants, Filipino peasant romantic verse, and South African Khoikhoi tribesmen. We did not select these topics for inclusion because they reflect a suitable range of people, cultures, and times to reveal the workings of the dynamics between orality and literacy. Rather, as editors from three separate disciplines but working on the same university campus, we invited scholars whose ideas about orality and literacy we found stimulating, provocative, and insightful. The purpose of this collection, therefore, is not to focus on any particular cultural group but rather to raise theoretical issues about the interaction of orality and literacy through the exploration of specific cultural contexts. The collection is also cross-disciplinary, bringing together scholars who are pushing the boundaries of their home disciplines (while recognizing the value of a firm disciplinary grounding). Individually and collectively, these authors move beyond disciplinary boundaries and in so doing are seeking to redefine their disciplines as much as they are striving to reassess the topics of their research enquiry. We invite readers to engage these essays not as an introductory survey of orality and literacy, nor as a scholastic appetizer providing a taste of a particular methodology or approach to the study of orality and literacy, but as a sampler of the innovative research occurring at the intersection of orality and literacy across several disciplines, on several continents, and relating to different periods.

We begin with two challenging essays that we group together under the heading 'Questioning Truths.' These chapters set the parameters and establish the tone, tenor, and trajectory of the chapters that follow. J.E. Chamberlin's 'Boasting, Toasting, and Truthtelling' is a wise and wide-ranging essay and the only one in the book that does not undertake a close reading of a particular cultural moment. But it reminds us of the fundamental reason why such close study is essential. He points out that each of us essentially lives inside our own minds, gaining access to the outside world only through the lens of our own interpretation. Thus when we take in a work of verbal art – whether spoken, written, or sung – we look to our own learned methods of interpretation to understand it. But we may not know how to access and interpret another culture's messages and furthermore, intermediaries such as translation, transcription, electronic recording, and so forth may stand between us and the original message. We look to these works for truth, but our sense of what is true is largely determined by the form and style they take and the kind of pleasure we get from them. To understand the truth of a work we must learn to experience the kind of pleasure it can give. It is an assumption that understanding sophisticated oral traditions comes naturally to the sympathetic ear. It does not. Just as we learn how to read, so we learn how to listen. This kind of learning is the purpose of this collection.

Chamberlin's broad examination of truth within oral and literate media is followed by Keith Carlson's deeply focused essay, 'Orality about Literacy: The "Black and White" of Salish History.' Carlson's epistemologically sensitive study exemplifies the way that learning about specific interactions between orality and literacy can challenge many of our assumptions about them. By engaging Salish historical consciousness, Carlson turns the table on the postulation that literacy was a new arrival in North America, imposed upon indigenous orality. He reveals that Salish people claim the power of literacy as an indigenous practice that once belonged to them. Within legendary Salish stories of community origins and transformation and nineteenth-century prophetic narratives, and as revealed through ethnolinguistic analysis of the Salish words for writing, inscription, and ancient transformation, literacy is portrayed not as an outside imposition but as a tradition that can be repatriated. While historians have traditionally dismissed such claims about literacy as untrue, Carlson, as Chamberlin suggests, shows a way of listening to the kinds of truth that these stories of literacy can tell. In turning the usual idea that orality precedes literacy on its head, he disrupts standard Western notions of the evolutionary relationship between orality and literacy, and in so doing challenges us to rethink the our approach to the history of Native–newcomer relations.

Other essays in the collection find more subtle but equally nuanced ways to contest the idea that literacy necessarily supplanted orality. The next two, by Twyla Gibson and Susan Gingell, do this in a way we characterize under the heading 'Writing It Down.' Early communication theorists McLuhan, Havelock, and Ong argued that we could see Plato's writings as evidence of the 'great divide' in human history, when Greek society's primarily oral perspective (seen in Homer and Socrates) was replaced by a gaze that was fundamentally literate. This perceived rift between oral and written cultures has acted as a model for how theorists have understood other, more recent, meetings of the oral and the literate. Twyla Gibson invites us to revisit this long-held belief about 'the great divide.' In 'The Philosopher's Art: Ring Composition and Classification in Plato's *Sophist* and *Hipparchus*,' she provides a close reading of two of Plato's dialogues to reveal the degree to which they are structured around 'ring composition,' a traditionally oral technique characteristic of ancient Greek poetry. The dialogues, she argues, represent a blending of oral and literate traditions in which oral modes persist alongside and into written texts, and this has implications not only for the way we interpret ancient, orally derived works of history and philosophy but also for the study of current oral cultures.

Returning to Aboriginal content, Susan Gingell's 'The Social Lives of Sedna and Sky Woman: Print Textualization from Inuit and Mohawk Oral Traditions,' provides a thoughtful engagement with contemporary Aboriginal writers that makes a similar point to Gibson's about the blending of oral and literate traditions. Much like, and indeed perhaps because of, the Greek 'great divide' theory, the academic view of writing down Aboriginal oral traditions is that the writing process will help to salvage oral traditions as they die away, since 'the written supplants the oral in a linear development from the primitive to the more sophisticated' (p. 113). However, drawing on Julie Cruikshank's insight that Aboriginal people use oral traditions in a way that is suited to contemporary circumstances – that stories have a 'social life' – Gingell explores the ways in which two Aboriginal writers have drawn on ancient oral stories to express ideas about contemporary Aboriginal lives. Moreover, she illustrates that they have mobilized distinguishing characteristics and features of oral style in their writing. The stories continue to live and to change, moving into writing and, Gingell points out, back into the oral.

Like Gibson's reading of Plato, Gingell's engagement with the narratives .
reveals a complex intermingling of the oral and the written.

Along with their assumptions about the 'evolution' of literacy, the
Toronto school of orality theory emphasized that individuals had little
control over the ways in which literacy entered their lives and minds.
Literacy was regarded as a societal phenomenon: broad, unstoppable,
and all encompassing. The essays by Kristina Fagan and Natalia
Khanenko-Friesen, grouped together under the heading 'Going Public,'
show how this is simply not the case. Using diverse examples (Ukrainian immigrants to Canada in the former and indigenous writers in the
latter), they show how communities have deliberately and strategically
harnessed certain oral tales for written tellings.

Keeping with the Aboriginal focus of earlier chapters, in '"Private
Stories" in Aboriginal Literature,' Fagan explores the process through
which indigenous writers negotiate the move from oral, public communication to seemingly private reading and writing. This carefully
argued piece shows how Aboriginal writers have engaged with the
published and thus public written word while remaining conscious of
the oral value placed on privacy and reticence in communication. This
does not, however, mean that they are disinclined to disclose in print.
Indeed, as Fagan shows, Aboriginal authors have frequently used the
printed page as a place to share information not deemed culturally appropriate for oral transmission. Exploring a variety of works by Aboriginal writers over the past century, Fagan shows how the writing is both
shaped by, and sometimes deliberately against, cultural protocols.

Similarly, Khanenko-Friesen's folkloric study shows how Ukrainian-
Canadian narratives of migration have been shaped by oral traditions
and forms. In 'From Family Lore to a People's History: Ukrainian
Claims to the Canadian Prairies,' she shows how individual narratives
of migration have, over generations, been appropriated by entire communities to create synthesized, generic stories that are themselves
heavily influenced by even more ancient Ukrainian folk tales. She
traces the oral roots of current Ukrainian-Canadian community self-
representations to show that the resulting mediated master narrative of
Ukrainian history in Canada is intricately connected to oral traditions.
But she also shows how writing down these community stories in order
to legitimize them and make them more publicly accessible has changed
their form, eliminating some of their folkloric qualities. Like Fagan, she
emphasizes the ways in which the community has moved to write
down previously oral stories for strategic purposes, changing them

while remaining aware of cultural values and forms.

While Gingell, Fagan, and Khanenko-Friesen all find people from traditionally oral cultures moving to take advantage of the power and legitimization offered by writing, such is not always the case. As in the essay by Carlson, who shows how the Salish claim literacy as their own precolonial possession, the power relations between orality and literacy play out in very different, and from a contemporary Western perspective, non-intuitive ways in other contexts. Gary Arbuckle's and Frank Klaassen's contributions to this volume, collectively identified under the heading 'Subverting Authority,' remind us not to rest in the easy assumption that literacy is always a stable institutionalizing force while orality is marginal or subversive. In reopening the debate over the Daoist sage Laozi, Arbuckle's 'Literacy, Orality, Authority, and Hypocrisy in the *Laozi*' argues that a kind of 'fabricated orality' was promoted within ancient China in order to give legitimacy to Laozi's oppressive political program. Alongside this 'faux spoken style' (p. 210) Laozi wished to see a literary vacuum in which political analysis and protest could not take root and grow. Within Laozi's ideal non-literate world, a village would be 'a frozen dream, not a real place, and its imaginary population ... little more than a collection of waxworks' (p. 211).

Klaassen's sweeping engagement with medieval European manuscripts in 'Unstable Texts and Modal Approaches to the Written Word in Medieval European Ritual Magic' likewise reveals that literacy sometimes functioned within a theatre of ritual and discourse that ran counter to common assumptions about the relationship between literacy and orality. Previous scholars examining the medieval transition toward literacy have usually understood this move to be illustrative of literacy's reification as a static and standardized medium – a development reflective of society's increasingly rational and objective outlook. Within the dynamic realm of magical manuscripts, however, Klaassen finds that 'the intellectual culture surrounding the production of texts revels in, and self-consciously employs, the ambiguous or unstable features of the written word' (p. 219). Ironically from our present-day perspective, it was the oral utterances associated with the text that provided a level of stability and community to their readers.

If cumulatively the essays presented here hint at the depth and breadth of the complex power relations between orality and literacy, certain contributions remind us forcefully that scholars cannot exempt themselves from the dynamic. Academics and poets alike are often engaged in the process of 'textualizing orality' – recording, or encoding, oral creations on the page. Indeed, much of the work on orality is conceived of as an inclusive project to legitimize voices from the margin within officially construed Western – literacy-based – histories. Within this school of thought, writing the oral message down is meant to legitimize it. The final two essays in the collection, grouped under the heading 'Uncovering Voices,' deal with, among other things, the possibilities and limits of oral historical methods. Reynaldo Ileto's essay 'A Tagalog Awit of the "Holy War" against the United States, 1899–1902' looks at a handwritten version of a Filipino oral romance (an *awit*) composed by a member of the resistance army, in order to reveal the shortcomings of conventional oral historical methods. Building on the theory and approach pioneered in his seminal study, *Pasyon and Revolution*,[12] Ileto demonstrates the extent to which classic methods of engaging oral history are inadequate to the task of retrieving the 'language of popular mobilisation' from the distant past. Through this awit, Ileto derives an understanding of the history of resistance to imperial rule from below, a story that is not part of institutionalized literate Filipino history and yet is only available through literate sources.

Oksana Kis deals with the challenges of collecting oral histories in the present. Kis, a feminist oral historian from Ukraine, offers her critical assessment of post-Soviet Ukraine's first women's oral history project in her essay 'Telling the Untold: Representations of Ethnic and Regional Identities in Ukrainian Women's Autobiographies' and reminds us that even such supposedly neutral terminologies as 'cultural setting' and 'cultural context' can never truly be void of politics – especially in times of totalitarianism. In the Soviet Union, the official discourses, whether in politics or entertainment – were empowered by the written word. As such they became associated with the domain of literacy: a predominantly male and urban preserve. At the other end of this process of marginalization, unofficial counter-discourses, with their often rebellious testimonies, were routinely confined to the domain of oral circulation among trusted family and friends. As a result, Ukrainian women's oral autobiographies and testimonies rarely exited the intimate circulation of which they were a part. Once liberated from this context, Kis demonstrates, such testimonies illustrate the contested nature of privacy while providing historical insights that challenge both the old official Soviet line and the more recent revisionist interpretations of Western political historians.

While there are often inequities and tensions between modes of communication, taken both individually and as a whole these essays show that past generations of scholars were misguided to conceive of orality and literacy primarily as set in opposition to one another. However, our intellectual forebears did initiate the discussion, and without their work to build upon we could not have launched the symposium that led to this collection and that brought together voices from many cultural and disciplinary backgrounds. Our goal was to explore the ways that orality and literacy make meaning in complicated and intertwined ways. Insights inevitably emerge not from a study of one form of communication but from the cracks and fissures where orality and literacy give meaning to one another. It is appropriate perhaps that the Métis history we engaged at Batoche, the history of a blended people, introduces us to how oral and written traditions blend as well as how they contest one another. We invite readers to bring their own voices to the topics, themes, and theories raised here and to engage in a conversation that will help to move the discussion beyond where it stands today.

NOTES

1 See especially Harold Innis, *The Bias of Communication* (Toronto: University of Toronto Press, 1964); Marshall McLuhan, *The Global Village: Transformations in World Life and Media in the 21st Century* (New York: Oxford University Press, 1989); Eric Havelock, *The Muse Learns to Write: Reflections on Orality and Literacy from Antiquity to the Present* (New Haven, CT: Yale University Press, 1986); Walter J. Ong, *Orality and Literacy: The Technologizing of the Word* (London: Routledge, 1982).

2 Ong, *Orality and Literacy*, 31.

3 Ibid., 1.

4 Jack R. Goody, *Domestication of the Savage Mind* (Cambridge: Cambridge University Press, 1977); Jack R. Goody, *The Interface between the Written and the Oral* (Cambridge: Cambridge University Press, 1987); Jack R. Goody, *The Power of the Written Tradition* (Washington, DC: Smithsonian Institution Press, 200).

5 Goody, *Interface between the Written and the Oral*, 205.

6 Ibid., 300,

7 Myron C. Tuman, "Words, Tools, and Technology" (review of Walter Ong's *Orality and Literacy: The Technology of the Word* [New York: Methuen, 1982]), *College English* 45, no. 8 (1983): 769–79.

8 Adam Fox, *Oral and Literate Culture in England, 1500–1700* (New York and Oxford: Clarendon Press/Oxford Press, 2000).

9 Amin Sweeney, *A Full Hearing: Orality and Literacy in the Malay World* (Berkeley: University of California Press, 1987).

10 Ruth H. Finnegan, *Literacy and Orality: Studies in the Technology of Communication* (Oxford: Blackwell, 1988).

11 Among the most prominent scholars to challenge Ong, Havelock, and Goody were Jonathan Boyarin and Daniel Boyarin, *The Ethnography of Reading* (Berkeley: University of California Press, 1993); Among those who tended to support the literacy-orality divide were David R. Olson and Nancy Torrance, eds., *Literacy and Orality* (Cambridge and New York: Cambridge University Press, 1991).

12 Reynaldo C. Ileto, *Pasyon and Revolution; Popular Movements in the Philippines, 1840–1910* (Quezon City: Ateneo University, 1979).

PART ONE

Questioning Truths

Chapter 1

Boasting, Toasting, and Truthtelling

J. EDWARD CHAMBERLIN

Most literature, and all history, begins with boasting and toasting. Where truthtelling comes in is the subject of this essay. Boasting and toasting, of course, connect across cultures. When Muhammad Ali insulted his opponents and entertained his audiences with lines like 'I'll float like a butterfly, sting like a bee,' he was speaking in a tradition of exaggeration that was part of his African heritage, but also part of European, Asian, and Aboriginal oral traditions.[1] In fact, he sounded exactly like one of Homer's heroes, or any number of trickster figures boasting and toasting in the great storytelling traditions of the world.

Truthtelling is more complicated. It raises a very difficult set of questions, philosophical and political as well as legal and literary. It also involves deeply vested interests, and for this reason it does not always travel well through time or across cultures. Put differently, when we believe something to be true, we 'credit' it, accepting that it has meaning and value. That's what credit is all about; and the text, spoken or written, is like a form of currency. The trouble is that one community's currency is often another's curiosity. And even when we have agreed to accept each other's currency, to credit a particular coin or piece of paper or secular or sacred ceremony, to believe they have a certain value or a special meaning, this agreement is often accompanied by considerable scepticism.

That shouldn't be surprising, for the artifice of such belief is crucial, and it is closely linked to the artifice of listening and reading and of language itself. We learn to believe just as we learn a language; they become comfortable habits. Truth is a comparative latecomer on the linguistic scene, and it is certainly a mistake to suppose that language was invented for the purpose of telling it. When Umberto Eco brought the word *semiotics* into popular currency – the word comes originally from medical diagnostics, and simply means the interpretation of 'signs' – he argued that it is not so much the study of truthtelling as of everything that can be used in order to tell a lie. If something *cannot* be used to tell a lie, he suggested, it cannot be used to tell the truth; it cannot in fact be used to 'tell' at all.[2]

That's why forgery and fakery of all sorts are so fascinating, and so fundamental to our understanding of authority and authenticity, and of truthtelling. At the end of the day, some say, all we know is what *we* alone know, each of us, in our own individual hearts and minds.

Oscar Wilde used to insist that truth is questionable when more than one person believes in it; and any discussion of truthtelling has to begin with a question about how we know anything outside our own consciousness. In a famous attack on the metaphysics of knowing that drew on the most recent technology for its images, the British mathematician and philosopher of science Karl Pearson argued, in his *Grammar of Science* (1892), for the unknowability of things in themselves. In his account of human consciousness, he insisted that

> we are like the clerk in the [new] central telephone exchange [in London] who cannot get nearer to his customers than his end of the ... wires. We are indeed worse off than the clerk, for to carry out the analogy properly we must suppose him never to have been outside the telephone exchange, never to have seen a customer or anyone like a customer – in short, never, except through the telephone wire, to have come in contact with the outside universe ... The real universe for him would be the aggregate of his constructs from the messages which were brought by the telephone wires in his office ... We are cribbed and confined in this world of sense impressions like the exchange clerk in his world of sounds, and not a step beyond can we get.[3]

For many of his readers, these remarks recalled Walter Pater's grim description in *The Renaissance* (1893) of our 'whole scope of observation [being] dwarfed to the narrow chamber of the individual mind ... Every one of those impressions is the impression of the individual in his isolation, each mind keeping as a solitary prisoner its own dream of a world.'[4] It's not a very cheerful prospect, for in such a scenario the odds seem to be against knowing much at all, or of getting more than one person to believe in anything.

So let's begin with one person's story and see where it takes us. Since I am trying to establish a frame for truthtelling, I'll turn to the most untrustworthy of human exchanges, horse trading. And to the set of understandings and misunderstandings that developed around horses on the western plains. That's where Canadian history really begins. Horses were the reason the North-West Mounted Police were established in 1873, and it was on horses that they tried to get the plains Indians off theirs.

Actually, it was not the Indians' horses that bothered the NWMP. They admired their horses, and their horsemanship. It was their habit of stealing them. And then of boasting about it. Horse stealing had become a way of life for the Indians of the western plains, and a way of exalting the virtues of curiosity, courage, creativity, and conspicuous consumption. But horse stealing was also exacerbating old conflicts, especially between tribes that had long been in competition with each other for territory and trade; and as resources became scarce – the buffalo in particular, but also land – the habit of horse stealing spread. And with it, a proliferation of small but often deadly feuds.

When the police arrived, word went out that horse stealing was to stop. The Indian braves said nothing ... and went right on stealing horses. Even their elders told them to stop; but the youngsters did not listen to them, instead taking adolescent delight in defying their authority and displaying their stolen horses.

Boasting was as common then as it is now, or as it has always been. From Achilles to Muhammad Ali, from Zulu praise songs to Maori chants, from sports club cheers to national anthems, boasting and toasting abide. And from time immemorial, across all cultures, historians are the tribal toastmasters. Which is where horse stealing comes in.

My grandfather settled in Fort Macleod in the 1880s, when horse stealing was still a local custom. One of his friends was Crop-Eared Wolf, who later became head chief of the Blackfoot; but when my grandfather first knew him he was a young man, and he stole horses. He was very, very good at it; and he boasted about it. He sent my grandfather a message saying he had something for him. My grandfather hoped it might be a horse.

So my grandfather left Macleod for Stand Off, on the Belly River, where the Kainai – members of the Blackfoot confederacy – had retreated after a punishing decade of tuberculosis, treaties, and the disappearance of the buffalo. It was winter, and cattle were grazing the plains. The weather was very cold and fairly dry, as usual, with light snow covering the grass. The cattle could still scrape and snuffle their way through, like hungry children raiding a refrigerator.

Then came a Chinook, as surprising as a cool wind in the Kalahari. Except that Chinooks are warm, and quite common in the foothills of the Rockies. They work like a refrigerator in reverse. When westerly winds carrying moist air from the Pacific hit the mountains, the air cools as its rises, dropping rain and then snow. If the conditions are right, the now dry air will slide right down the eastern slopes of the Rockies, ten thousand feet to the plains below. Cold air heats up when it falls, because the air is denser and the pressure higher at lower altitudes; and dry air warms twice as fast as moist air. The warm air pushing out the cold creates the wind called a Chinook, signalled by a wonderful arch of cloud in the western sky. It can raise the temperature dramatically and melt an inch of ice an hour. Riding across the frozen river, my grandfather saw the unmistakable Chinook arch, and small splashes of water. A Chinook was always welcome in the middle of winter; but it was also a warning. If the Chinook melted the ice, he'd be stranded on the other side of the river for days, maybe weeks. He turned around. He would have to wait to see Crop-Eared Wolf, maybe later in the spring.

The cattle also sensed a change, a new lease on life. They wouldn't have to scuffle and scrape any more. They looked up to the sky in a moment of faith and stumbled on through the crud and the crust in a mellow mood. The temperature, which had been well below freezing that morning, was almost comfortable enough for shirtsleeves by now. The snow started to melt, and before long they could see the grass underneath the water that covered the land.

But this Chinook was short lived. The cold weather came again, hard and fast, and by the next day the water was frozen so hard that the cattle could not break through. It was much worse than the snow cover. All they could do was look at the grass a few inches below the surface of the ice.

My grandfather made it back. But thousands of cattle did not. They starved to death that winter, within sight of the food that would have kept them alive. Which is where some questions about stories and storytelling come to mind. If stories nourish the spirit as grass nourishes cattle, how important is the physical presence of the storyteller? Is listening to a story over the phone, or over the radio, or on a recording, like looking at grass under ice? And what about reading a story?

When my grandfather finally caught up with Crop-Eared Wolf, he did not get a horse; instead Crop-Eared Wolf gave him a story, a boasting story, in the form of a ceremonial riding quirt. It was made of a hard wood about eighteen inches long and two inches wide, in the shape of a small cricket bat, with figures that he had carved and painted on all sides. It had a braided leather tail about three feet long, and ornamental buffalo hide bound in at the end.

Along with a gun and a pipe, two men were represented on the quirt. One was probably Crop-Eared Wolf himself, while the other (in traditional Blackfoot iconography) was a person he had killed in battle or from whom he had taken horses. Maybe both. There are iconographic accounts on the quirt of several raids on enemy camps, telling of the capture of Cree and Crow warriors; and there are four horses, his most prized thefts.

Two of the horses have reins running down to the ground; they would have been especially valuable, attached by their reins to the ankle or wrist of the owner as he slept in his teepee with several dozen dogs outside. Crop-Eared Wolf must have had extraordinary skill as a horse thief. An ethnologist and an elder who read the quirt for me said that he must have had help. I thought they meant from within the camp. They laughed. From the spirits, they said, with the certainty of scientists.

The carvings and painting are precise; but the story, like all stories, has a number of uncertainties ... such as, what exactly happened on those escapades? The tradition of boasting complicates rather than clarifies things. And there is another complication. The ethnologist (Gerald Conaty, the best in the business, from the Glenbow Museum in Calgary) said that the quirt recorded things that had actually happened; the elder (Frank Weasel Head, a legendary Kainai storyteller) said that it recounted a dream of those things.[5] In his reading, the events themselves took place after the dream had been recorded on the quirt. This is a fairly basic difference. Either that, or it highlights an uncertainty at the heart of all storytelling. In the tradition of Khoikhoi performance in southern Africa, stories begin with a word, |garube (the| indicates a soft click made at the front of the mouth). It means 'the happening that is not happening.' *Did the Greeks Believe Their Myths?* asks the French classicist Paul Veyne in the title of his book.[6] Yes and no, he answers.

This brings us to another fundamental problem. Where *is* the story: on the quirt, or in the reading of it? And wherever it is, *whose* is it? Copyright in a letter is vested in the writer, while the physical letter belongs to the recipient. Is copyright located in the quirt, or in its story? Whoever owns a letter cannot quote it without permission from the writer. Can I tell the story written on the quirt? If I do, is it an original or a copy? And – assuming you believe what I am telling you – is it me you believe or the quirt? A lot more than we might think depends on the answers to these questions.

New recording technologies, about which I will say more in a moment, raise these questions even more awkwardly. What is a recording of a performance? Is it *another* performance? Or a dream of a performance, as Frank Weasel Head might put it? Glenn Gould might have put it that way too. But is not a recording also rather like a photograph of a performance? Or grass under ice?

With the quirt, we have a material record. It is a time-honoured artefact within a tradition of record keeping as venerable as that of any European archive. It may also be a spiritual record. But is it a record of what happened, or what Crop-Eared Wolf dreamed would happen, or some storied 'not-happening,' the stuff of boasting and toasting? Was it, for Crop-Eared Wolf, the record of the past or of the future?

Whatever the case, it *is* a record of something that took place when you and I – and Frank Weasel Head and Gerald Conaty – weren't there. The quirt brings us there, but only after a fashion. We sometimes say that this fashion began with printing, though forms of writing like the quirt belie that ethnocentric precedent. More recently, in what we sometimes call the 'modern' era, photography brought us another illusion of being there. Nobody was really fooled, but people were fascinated. They were also fearful. To take a picture is to *take* something, after all; and many people thought it might be something important, like their spirit. 'We only want to capture the moment,' explained the photographers, in another uncomfortable phrase. That may be why records like the quirt were often kept in medicine bundles. This one may belong in one, which is something I have been discussing with the Blackfoot elders.

Photography was something new at that time, and new things always make folks nervous. Something new also began with the telephone, and some of us grumble that something else is happening right now with the compact disc, the computer, and the cell phone. My grandfather listened to his family's friend Alexander Graham Bell make the first telephone calls from his summer home in Brantford, Ontario, in the 1870s, but like many people confronted by something radically different, he thought this newfangled device was little more than a neat trick.

By the 1890s, faster even than the computer, the telephone was taking over. It had established a place for itself in many big cities, and everyone was trying it out. Some, like Karl Pearson, were using it to make a point about how we know things, and what it is that we know when we think we know something. And Pearson raised another old question. How do we communicate with each other if we are all limited to the world of our own private consciousness? To complicate the answer, anthropologists and linguists of the time were reminding everyone that the way in which we experience the world – the way we think and feel and behave – may be strictly determined by our language.

All the old certainties seemed to be up for grabs. The telegram and the telephone; photography and film; wax recording cylinders and tape and disc recording, and then radio and television; electricity and all the wonders we take for granted in the twenty-first century: these came quickly, and came everywhere. They brought people closer together, but in a paradox that we still have not resolved, they also set them further apart. They changed people's sense of space and time, and they changed their sense of themselves and each other.

They also changed the ways in which people told stories. And maybe how – or in what sense – they told the truth. Art began to move toward nonrepresentation, which confused a lot of people who were accustomed to an imitation of reality. The riots that accompanied Stravinsky's *Rite of Spring* when it was first performed in Paris in 1917 are only one reminder of the concern this created. And consider the following three statements, made within twenty years. First, there is Matthew Arnold in the 1860s, proposing that the function of art and the criticism is inspires is 'to see the object as in itself it really is.' In the 1870s, Walter Pater changed this to 'know one's own impression as it really is.' By the 1880s, Oscar Wilde was insisting that the function of art was 'to see the object as in itself it really is *not*.'[7]

At the same time, science was revolutionizing the way people thought about the world, replacing material certainties with imaginative indeterminacies. The consequences of this were not lost on those trying to generate other revolutions. In 1908, Lenin spent a good part of a very busy year writing a book called *Materialism and Empirio-Criticism,* in which he launched a detailed attack on the 'idealist' science of Karl Pearson and Ernst Mach and other prominent architects of relativity theory and twentieth-century science. Around the same time, Wassily Kandinsky promoted the new non-representational or 'abstract' art in an essay called *Concerning the Spiritual in Art.* 'Whose spirit is this?' was the question many people would ask over the next century as they tried to understand how voices could come out of black boxes and people come to life on a silver screen.[8]

That question – whose spirit is this? – comes from one of the greatest modernist poems, 'The Idea of Order at Key West' by the American poet Wallace Stevens. It opens up questions like a Chinese box. 'She sang beyond the genius of the sea,' the poem begins, describing a woman singing a song by the seashore. It later adds,

> The song and water were not medleyed sound
> Even if what she sang was what she heard,
> Since what she sang was uttered word by word.
> It may be that in all her phrases stirred
> The grinding water and the gasping wind;
> But it was she and not the sea we heard.
>
> For she was the maker of the song she sang.
> The ever-hooded, tragic-gestured sea
> Was merely a place by which she walked to sing.
> Whose spirit is this? we said, because we knew
> It was the spirit that we sought and knew
> That we should ask this often as she sang.

Stevens accords his singer extraordinary power over the world of which she sings:

> It was her voice that made
> The sky acutest at its vanishing.
> She measured to the hour its solitude.
> She was the single artificer of the world
> In which she sang.

But ultimately there is something more, something that has to do with the transcendent power of the imagination, a fearful as well as fantastic power – and a truthtelling power. At the end of the poem, the speaker turns to a companion:

> Ramon Fernandez, tell me, if you know,
> Why, when the singing ended and we turned
> Toward the town, tell why the glassy lights,
> The lights in the fishing boats at anchor there,
> As the night descended, tilting in the air,
> Mastered the night and portioned out the sea,
> Fixing emblazoned zones and fiery poles,
> Arranging, deepening, enchanting night.

Oh! Blessed rage for order, pale Ramon,
The maker's rage to order words of the sea,
Words of the fragrant portals, dimly-starred,
And of ourselves and of our origins,
In ghostlier demarcations, keener sounds.[9]

The poem catalogues our ancient obsessions with beginnings and endings, origins and purposes, patterns and perspectives, conjuring up the
spiritual in the closing lines with words like 'enchanting' and 'blessed'
and 'ghostlier.' There is a celebration of the authority of the singer and a
set of questions about where her authority lies. Who, or what, underwrites
the sovereignty of stories and songs? Where is the truth in truthtelling? Is
it in the form or in the content? The style or the substance?

For all our modernist incompletenesses and indeterminacy and our
postmodern anxieties about them, we still have a fondness for truth. It
may be old fashioned, but it sustains our secular and sacred institutions, and preoccupies those of us in the business of reading or listening
and of speaking and writing. I spend a lot of my time paying attention
to poets, a human preoccupation for a couple of thousand years at least.
Not that poets always tell the truth. Indeed, like politicians, prophets,
and priests, they are routinely accused of lying. Plato called them un-
truthful, and therefore immoral. He especially distrusted the way in
which they spoke in other people's voices instead of their own. Others
have been even less generous. For the most part poets embrace these
accusations, welcoming them as a signal of their freedom from the distorting prerogatives of utility and morality.

But they never claim freedom from an obligation to tell the truth, insisting instead that they do so in their own way, with the authority that
comes from having nothing to gain or to lose. This element of disinter-
estedness is crucial to a whole range of oral and written testimony, and
it takes the forms of both immunity from compromise and what is
sometimes claimed (often by very political poets) as the impersonality
of great poetry. And yet our experience of listening to trauma testimony
has complicated this line of logic, as the personal becomes both the conveyor of truth and the guarantor of it, both the currency and the credit
upon which it depends. Or maybe it has simply returned us to the roots
of lyric. 'So much depends upon a red wheelbarrow,' says the Spanish-
American poet William Carlos Williams at the beginning of one of his
poems.[10] In the venerable convention of poetic discourse, challenging
such a statement is both a bad tactic and bad taste.

One of the reasons I think poetry is such a useful example is that all poems, like all linguistic performances, begin by insisting that readers and listeners suspend their disbelief. The question of what to believe, and whom, has preoccupied literary, legal, and ecclesiastical theory for a very long time. In different forms, it preoccupies members of every community every time it tries to determine the truth. And so communities establish certain criteria for passing judgment, and develop a consensus (or conspiracy) of sympathetic understanding. Sympathy and judgment are the points of reference here, though they are obviously anything *but* fixed. An uncertainty about whether we believe the singer or the song, the teller or the tale, nourishes this indeterminacy, as do the complementary conventions of naturalness and artifice that we associate with different kinds of truthtelling.

One of the oldest questions in human history is which came first, music or language. The eighteenth-century scholar and philosopher Giambattista Vico cut to the chase when he said that human beings danced before they walked, which (in his imagery) gives the nod to music. He also said that signs and gestures came before speech. Some modern scholars agree: the ethnomusicologist John Blacking, for example, argues that 'early human species were able to dance and sing several hundred thousand years before homo sapiens emerged with the capacity for speech as we know it.' Others have a more complex explanation. Susanne Langer, a formidable philosopher and critic, argued that the ceremonial dance and the creation of visual imagery supplied the conditions for language. In her opinion, not words but *phrases* – musical phrases or accretions of sounds – were the origin of language. Listening, in her opinion, first depended on recognizing a pattern, on distinguishing music and meaning from noise and nonsense.[11]

The Irish folklorist James Stephens once described how the legendary Finn McCool asked his companions what was the finest music in the world. First his son, Ossian, proposed the call of the cuckoo singing from the highest hedge bush; then Oscar, their comrade-in-arms, suggested the ring of a spear on a shield; and soon the others in the group joined in: the belling of a stag across the water; the baying of a pack of dogs in the distance; the song of a lark in the morning; the laughter of a happy girl; the whisper of one making love. Then Finn himself was asked. 'The music of what happens,' answered the great chief. 'That is the finest music in the world.'[12]

The happening that is not happening. Plato once said that if we change the forms of music, we change something fundamental in not

only the artistic and cultural but also the moral and political character of a society. Down deep, we all know this. It is why we react with
such initial outrage to each new musical style, like rock and roll or
reggae or rap. Could we say that bad stories give us noise? Or stories
badly told?

What then is the test of good and bad? And is it a test of truth? It may
be closer to this than we think. For many people throughout the ages
and across cultures, the test of truth is the same as the test of beauty and
of goodness. It is pleasure, *learned* pleasure, the sort of pleasure that
makes us say 'yes' to a carving, or a dance, or a story, or a song.

Pleasure may seem like a rather trivial test; or a very uncomfortable
one, since it suggests that we sometimes take pleasure in sorrow and
suffering. Well, we do ... at least in hearing about them. Many of the
greatest stories and songs, again across time and place, are incorrigibly
sad. But this paradox aside, pleasure forms the basis of many of the
world's great philosophical traditions. Feeling good is a touchstone of
truth as well as of beauty in a long line of Asian and African philoso-
phies; and in the ancient crossroads of Europe, the poet and philosopher Lucretius based his theory of the nature of things – *De rerum natura* – on the relationship between pleasure and truth, beauty and
goodness. David Hume underlined it again in the eighteenth century;
and his arguments became enormously influential, shaping everything
from social policy to physical science.[13]

Our modern test of truth and beauty and goodness is remarkably
similar. We still make pleasure the mark, though we sometimes mask
it in the language of costs and benefits. But when it comes to important
things, we go back to the basics. We tell our children that if they encounter a stranger or find themselves in an unfamiliar situation, or are
touched by Uncle Fred and it does not feel good ... then they should
run like hell. 'What is moral is what you feel good after,' says one of
Ernest Hemingway's characters.[14] 'I don't know much about art, but I
know what I like' is the aesthetic version of this. We all rely on it, no
matter how sophisticated we think we are. The first act of criticism, of
giving credit, is irrational. Sympathy and judgment are as inseparable
as form and content:

> The dreamer awakes
> The shadow goes by
> The cock never crew
> The tale is a lie.

But harken it well
Fair maiden, good youth,
The tale is a lie
But the telling is truth.[15]

Now I want to turn to a courthouse in northern British Columbia not so long ago, where a judge was listening to an Indian woman tell her story. Like many of us, he listened to stories for a living. And he was in the business of assessing the truth of what he heard.

This was a tale of ancient times, stretching back thousands of years to an age when human beings and animals lived in concert with the spirits of the place, and when conflicts were punished swiftly and surely. Hard to believe. Just like the Bible. The woman had sworn to tell the truth, backed by these same spirits; and so she told her tale not so much to the judge as to a group of older men and women, custodians of those traditions and agents of those spirits. These elders, like the judge, listened to stories for a living.

The woman knew that the judge wanted to hear her story because he was trying to piece together the history of her people, the history of what happened. Like most stories of the past, hers had long since broken into pieces ... people, places, events, words. But she was a good storyteller; and when she spoke, everything seemed to come together. The past became present, the present made sense, the pattern was revealed. When she spoke, everything she said was true. The elders believed her – she had been taught to tell these stories by them, after all; and many of the others who were listening believed her, except those who were paid not to believe. All societies have those sorts of people, and we should not mock them, for they constitute our sacred and secular academies. And while she spoke, the judge believed her too.

It was when she stopped speaking that the trouble started. The spell of her storytelling was broken. The story, too, was broken into the different pieces that different people remembered, for few in the audience had memories as well trained as the elders. Also, she spoke a language that was strange to many people there. In a literal sense, the judge did not understand a word.

But the judge was used to not understanding the languages in which people told their stories to him. He had learned to listen to Mandarin and Cantonese and Hindi and Farsi and Finnish and Portuguese and at least a dozen other languages, with a translation accompanying them. He would watch the speaker carefully for tricks of the storyteller's trade, trying to distinguish them from cultural traits that he might misunderstand: a studied deference, a sincere zealousness, a failure to make eye contact, an elaborate speaking style. Unordinary language and unusual ways of speaking were his business. He knew that for millennia people – including his people – had been organizing their lives around languages they did not understand, like the language of the law, or the language of the old Latin liturgy in the Catholic church. The key was that someone sanctioned such language, attested to its truth; and in this case, the elders were doing just that.

But translation always presents a problem, to legal no less than to literary listeners. Robert Frost once said that when we translate a poem, we lose the poetry. I am not sure, but I can see what he was getting at. Sound is central to poetry, and what literary critics sometimes call 'voice.' We lose this in translation. We cannot hear the rhythms and the rhymes, especially when we are translating between languages that are differently structured. We cannot hear the music. Even more so with translation from performance to the page, from listening to reading. The translation becomes a form of 'hearsay,' and hearsay evidence is routinely discredited in court.

The judge was uneasy about the degrees of separation that transcriptions generated, but he was usually able to make up his mind what to believe. And whom to believe, for that was an indispensable part of judging the truth. Indispensable, but independent. He had always been fascinated by the distinction between whom to believe and what to believe. Translation made it even more intriguing, especially in a case such as this when the witness was so compelling at the time, but not afterward, when he read the transcript. It no longer felt right. It was sort of like phone sex; not the real thing. Or maybe – to take a more judicial perspective – like the difference between evidence and opinion. While she spoke, she was giving evidence; but when she finished, it became opinion. For the judge, the truth of the woman's story disappeared as soon as she did. Reading the transcript, he did not believe it. So he said that he believed her, but not her story.[16]

Now, I believe both the Indian woman *and* her story. I have read the transcript, and I have heard a tape of her testimony. But I was not in the court. How much difference does that make? An entire music recording industry is premised on the fact that you *do not* have to be present; and yet we know what it is like to actually be at a performance by Neil Diamond or Neil Young. 'You had to be there,' we say. Our professional listeners – medical practitioners, confessors, counsellors, custodians of Aboriginal oral traditions, and of course judges – insist on this. And I *was not* there. So how can I dispute the judge's choice? One way would be to wonder whether there really *is* a choice between the story and the storyteller, and whether perhaps the credibility of a story, rather than being located in one place or another, instead hovers between the teller, the tale, and the audience.

A question remains, however. Is the centre of gravity different depending on whether the audience reads or listens? There is probably no single answer, for the situation varies between cultural traditions. But the question haunts us all.

It was another ethnic cleansing, another forced migration, another Trail of Tears. Arabs and Acadians and Cherokees and Choctaws and Japanese and Jews. It is a long list. This time it was Hottentots.

The government of South Africa had decided that the rich farmland of the Kat River valley in the Eastern Cape should be turned over to white settlers. The problem, of course, was that there were other people there, in this case the descendants of Khoikhoi – or Hottentot – herders who had been moved to the Kat River over 150 years earlier.

The Khoikhoi had been on the move for centuries, driven first from their ancient homeland in the Northern Cape by blacks migrating south from central Africa, and then by white immigrants from western Europe. The Kat River would be 'a place to collect the remnants of the Hottentot race, to save them from extirpation, to civilize and Christianize them,' said Commissioner-General Andries Stockenstroom, his intentions shaped by the language and the logic of the time, the time when Saartje Baartman – the 'Hottentot Venus' – was on display in salons, fairs, and animal acts in London and Paris.[17]

Within a few years of their arrival in the 1820s, the Khoikhoi surprised everyone with the success of their Kat River community. They had maintained their distinctive traditions of worship, having converted to Christianity some time before but still calling on Khoisan, or Bushmen, shamans to perform healing ceremonies and rituals to restore the natural rhythms of the land. They fought alongside the white settlers in a series of battles against the Xhosa, and later in both world wars, but some of them joined with other Khoikhoi in rebellion against unscrupulous lawmakers and landowners in the 1850s. Which is to say, they somehow remained themselves, even as they changed.

Now they were to be moved once more, all 6,000 of them. This was the 1980s, during the last days of apartheid, and at least three Cabinet ministers came to assure them that everything would be alright ... though they could not tell them where they were going, or why. But the legislation was passed, the laws enforced, and within months the Kat River community was no more.

It's an old story; except that this time there seemed to be nobody to tell it. Truth and reconciliation were not yet the watchwords of South Africa, and many people were very scared. Others were simply too tired. But scholars were sent by the African National Congress to document the removal as best they could and to record the testimony of those who would talk.

One of them, an old man named Piet Draghoender, spoke to historian Jeff Peires from Rhodes University. Peires listened to Draghoender tell how his people had come to be there, and how they had made a life that was strange to them at first, coming from the dry desert lands of the Karoo and the Kalahari. Soon it became the only life they could remember. Rooting themselves in the new land, they learned a new livelihood as farmers and became comfortable in a new language, trading what travellers called the turkey gobble of Khoikhoi for the pig grunt of Afrikaans (which had no written form until the end of the nineteenth century, when it began a fierce fight with Dutch for status as a 'real' language).

Seated under a tree, Piet spoke straight to the video camera. On tape, he looks like any expert on television. Except he is not skilled as a speaker. His eyes shift constantly, he licks his lips nervously, and his hands shake uncontrollably. Piet was nearly eighty when the interview was conducted, an old man, frail and fussy. But he spoke to break the silence, so that the history of the place would not die along with its people. He answered questions, awkwardly, about the past, the present, and the future of his Kat River community. He told the truth as best he could, with lots of backfillings and a good amount of gossip, the way we all do.

'Tell us about your neighbours, Oom Piet. What happened to them?' asked Jeff Peires. A startled look came over Piet's face, as though he suddenly realized the role he was playing. He stood up, and he began to speak in a quite different manner, with a different rhythm, a different rhetoric, and an almost delirious energy.

I have seen the videotape, which is of very poor quality, like one of those photographs taken right into the sun and out of focus that we used to take on family holidays and call a 'record shot.' On the grainy videotape his gaunt face is visible only in cartoon-style relief, and his voice is blurred, intermittently breaking up into bursts of sound. Watching it at first, it is easy to wonder what all the fuss is about. Even the question put to Piet about what happened to his neighbours is off-mike, so although we see and hear the change in Piet's manner, we are not sure what prompted it. His outburst has something of the character of an operatic ending, when the hero or heroine sings in full voice as they die of a terrible wound, or tuberculosis. And it is absolutely compelling.

Here is Jeff Peires' first-hand account of Piet Draghoender: 'All of a sudden the tone of his speech subtly changed. From a slow hesitant beginning, he gradually worked himself up to a fever pitch, speaking like a man possessed so that it really seemed as if the frail body of the old man had become a medium of the spirit of the Kat River itself.'[18]

'Whose spirit is this? we said, because we knew / It was the spirit that we sought and knew / That we should ask this often as she sang,' wrote Wallace Stevens. In literary language, Piet's outburst would be called inspired. In any language, his elegy for the loss of his land and livelihood and his family would be called poetry. And this is where the problem arises. For poets, as we have seen, do not always tell the truth.

And yet in the short time since it was recorded, Piet Draghoender's lament has become a central part of southern African literature, and in a place where the sorrow and suffering have become commonplace, it has become a classic.[19] A judge trying to determine the details of what happened would not be helped much by Piet's lament, and would almost certainly be put off by the notion that Piet was inspired, possessed by some spirit. And yet his testimony rings true.

Bearing witness is complicated. It is less a substantiation of verifiable events – less a way of seeing, that is – than a way of saying, a proclaiming, a music of sorts. Bearing witness always displays a tension with which readers of poetry will be familiar, a tension between intensity and nonchalance (for the speaker), or between sympathy and judgment (for the listener).

Here is part of Piet Draghoender's lament, as transcribed and translated by Edgard Sienaert (who first saw the videotape when he was director of the Centre for Oral Studies at the University of Natal in Durban), with help from Levi Namaseb (a Khoikhoi scholar from Namibia).[20] Sienaert immediately recognized in Piet's declamation not just a story but a storytelling style as old as human history, set down in a manner that displays the elements of its oral performance, something more than mere speech: the bilateral character of its phrasing mirroring the bilateralism of human beings; logic and rhythm becoming one; memory bringing into service the spiritual liturgies of faith and fury, both European and African:

then from here up   it is pure coloured people
but they are out like this   out like this
that they did not leave face first   they are out backwards
against their will

against their will
so as it went today   so as it happens today also
I must go   also today
against my will

but I say   I prophecy
not on earth   not on earth
I prophecy up
no one that did evil to me   who did sin against me
he will not live
he will not live on earth   and he will not have the privilege above
he will be punished above   and he will die here
and he will be buried   under the earth
this I prophecy   this I prophecy
prophecy it
should you prophecy   should you prophecy
you say everything that you speak   it happens as you said
because you ask this from your guts   this is what I ask from my guts

look how weak I am but now I have to go

But this is what I said to the Old Man   I say: I put up the white flag truly
and say: Peace   I ask peace
for everything that comes over me   keep me
just as a child   just as a servant of you
let not you leave me   let you not leave me behind
put me in a line of righteousness
all that I must speak today   I must speak
as long as I live in righteousness
This then is what I ask the Lord   nothing I want from another man
not a blue farthing   not a blue farthing
I don't want   neither a morsel of ground

Look these trees, look   these fruits, down there.
look   look these fruits of my uncle's son
this is purely why we say   for it is sad

it is sad for a man to plant   and you will not harvest it
and you will not enjoy the harvest   so I feel very heartsore

but I give this thing away   I give it away
to the greatest Boss there is on earth   the Boss who strikes where you
cannot see and say
so I put myself there 'tirely satisfied   I say to everyone
to the Devil or the Enemy   I am guilty for this reason that
with my ...
I am guilty

This land here was given away   for blood
the blood comes from my grandfathe   and after my grandfather
there comes a war   and we give three sons three
Isak, Klaus and Gert   three sons I give to the death
to make free   to make free this place
that it be free
they have taken these children   my children taken in war ...

There is a moment when Piet cannot remember his sons' names. On the
videotape, you can see how upset he is; and rather than break the rhythm,
he repeats Isak's name twice – 'Isak, Isak, Gert.' Edgard Sienaert has 'corrected' it on the page, but in performance it is both awkward and aston-
ishingly powerful ... and not just because we feel sorry for Piet. His entire
performance is full of stammering and stuttering, just like everyday
speech; and yet it flows like a river. Piet is not a good speaker, and he was
not known in his community as a storyteller. But he is taken over by his
tradition, and his memory of the Christian and African liturgy gives form
to his testimony. Maybe that is more important for truthtelling. Piet knows
the words to use, and (however awkwardly) how to use them. He knows,
as Northrop Frye once put it, that 'words can describe things only ap-
proximately; all they can do with any real accuracy is hang together'[21]
in rhetorical forms and figures of speech and the fictions of grammar
and syntax.

Piet turned to a tradition of lament that was both his own and as old
as humankind. It is in the Bible, and it is in the traditions of southern
African praise songs. It is in ancient Greek elegies and in the chants of
mourners in modern India. It is a tradition in which we speak with a

knowledge that is not necessarily ours, of events that sometimes have not yet happened, as though we had seen it all before, and yet are as astonished as if it were happening for the first time. Which it is, each time.

It is the most powerful of human performances, and maybe the truest. And yet it is all made up, and in this case even written down, with formulaic phrases and gestures and rhythms and rhetoric. These are forms of expression that give us a sense of being right there with the speaker, and with his or her subject ... even though we are not.

In one of his trademark witticisms, Oscar Wilde once said that 'truth is entirely and absolutely a matter of style ... It is style that makes us believe in a thing – nothing but style.'[22] And style, in this case oral style, is what all storytelling is about. It is style that certifies truth – not the subject or the sincerity of the speaker, except insofar as that sincerity is an element of style, as spontaneity might also be. Milman Parry, the scholar who brought oral traditions back into the centre of literary and historical study with his analysis of the oral style of Homer's epics, insisted that style, not language, constitutes thought in oral performance.[23] In the nineteenth century, they used to talk about virtue and style in the same breath, and so art critics would speak of the style, the soul, the virtue, of Renaissance painting.[24] In a nice turn that brings in the new technologies of oral performance, 'virtual' comes from the same root as 'virtue.'

This is the language of literary criticism, you may protest, which has little to do with historical truth. And yet we can take our cue from Jan Vansina, who has written with authority on oral history.[25] He suggests that history is simply a series of documents, all of which are lost except the last one; and that in order to recover the truth we need to re-imagine all the previous versions – all the other 'virtual' representations, with their characteristic and often coy stylizations – right back to the actual event. This is what truthtelling is all about.

NOTES

1 Viv Edwards and Thomas J. Sienkewicz, *Oral Cultures Past and Present: Rappin' and Homer* (Oxford: B. Blackwell, 1990), 100–11.
2 Umberto Eco's sly remark about lying is in his *A Theory of Semiotics* (Bloomington: Indiana University Press, 1976), 7.

3 Karl Pearson, *The Grammar of Science* (London: Walter Scott, 1892), 57–8.

4 Walter Pater, *The Renaissance: Studies in Art and Poetry* (London: MacMillan, 1893), 235.

5 These remarks were recorded in September 2002 for an interview of Frank Weasel Head by J. Edward Chamberlin for a BBC Radio 2 program, 'Another Country – As a Tale That Is Told,' directed by Kate McAll and broadcast December 2002.

6 Paul Veyne, *Did the Greeks Believe Their Myths? An Essay on the Constitutive Imagination,* trans. Paula Wissing (Chicago: University of Chicago Press, 1988).

7 Matthew Arnold, 'The Function of Criticism at the Present Time,' in *Lectures and Essays in Criticism,* ed. R.H. Super, vol. 3 of *The Complete Prose Works of Matthew Arnold* (Ann Arbor: University of Michigan Press, 1962), 258; Pater, *The Renaissance,* xxix; Oscar Wilde, 'The Critic as Artist,' in *The Artist as Critic: Critical Writings of Oscar Wilde,* ed. Richard Ellmann (Chicago: University of Chicago Press, 1969), 369.

8 Wassily Kandinsky, *Über das Geistige in der Kunst* (Concerning the Spiritual in Art) (Bern: Beteli, 1911) ; Vladimir Lenin, *Materialism and Empirio-Criticism: Critical Comments on a Reactionary Philosophy* (Moscow: Zveno, 1909).

9 Wallace Stevens, 'The Idea of Order at Key West,' *The Collected Poems of Wallace Stevens* (New York: Alfred Knopf, 1954), 128–30.

10 William Carlos Williams, 'The Red Wheelbarrow,' *Spring and All* (Paris: Contact Editions, 1923), 78.

11 Giambattista Vico, *The New Science of Giambattista Vico,* trans. Thomas Bergin and Max Fisch (Ithaca, NY: Cornell University Press, 1948), 231; John Blacking, 'Making Artistic Popular Music: The Goal of True Folk,' *Popular Music* 1 (1981): 9; Susanne K. Langer *Mind: An Essay on Human Feeling* (Baltimore: Johns Hopkins Press University, 1981).

12 James Stephens, *Irish Fairy Tales* (New York: Macmillan, 1920), 62.

13 Titus Lucretius Carus, *De rerum natura,* trans. R.C. Trevelyan (Cambridge: Cambridge University Press, 1937); David Hume, *Four Dissertations* (1757; reprinted New York: Garland, 1970).

14 Ernest Hemingway, *Death in the Afternoon* (New York: Scribner, 1932), ch. 1.

15 Traditional folktale ending.

16 Judge McEachern's comments are recorded in the transcripts of the Delgamu-ukw trial (1987–1991), finally decided (in favour of the plaintiffs) by the Supreme Court of Canada on 11 December 1997. *BC Studies* devoted a special issue to the trial and judgment; and a book of excerpts, cartoons, and commentary from the trial, compiled by Don Monet and Skanu'u (Ardythe

Wilson), *Colonialism on Trial: Indigenous Land Claims and the Gitksan and Wet'suwet'en Sovereignty Case* (Philadelphia and Gabriola Island, BC: New Society Publishers) was published in 1992. Leslie Pinder wrote a powerful monograph titled *The Carriers of No: After the Land Claims Trial* (Vancouver: Lazara, 1991); and Dara Culhane a scholarly study, *The Pleasure of the Crown: Anthropology, Law and First Nations* (Burnaby, BC: Talonbooks, 1998).

17 Andries Stockenstroom, quoted in Edgard Sienaert, 'Perspectives on and from an Oral Testimony: Piet Draghoender's Lament,' *Mosaic* 21, no. 2–3 (1988): 227.

18 Jeff Peires, quoted in ibid., 230.

19 See Michael Chapman's *Southern African Literatures* (London and New York: Longman, 1996), 35.

20 Edgard Sienaert and Levi Namaseb. Personal communication from Sienaert, in a new setting and translation to catch the bilateral rhythm of the oral performance.

21 Northrop Frye, 'Creation and Recreation,' in *Northrop Frye on Religion*, ed. Alvin Lee and Jean O'Grady (Toronto: University of Toronto Press, 2000), 39.

22 Oscar Wilde, 'The Decay of Lying,' in *The Writings of Oscar Wilde*, ed. Isobel Murray (Oxford: Oxford University Press, 1989), 227.

23 Milman Parry, *The Making of Homeric Verse*, ed., A. Parry (Oxford: Clarendon Press, 1971).

24 For example, as Pater does in *The Renaissance*.

25 Jan Vansina, *Oral Tradition as History* (Madison: University of Wisconsin Press, 1985), 29.

Chapter 2

Orality about Literacy:
The 'Black and White' of Salish History

KEITH THOR CARLSON

> The Great Spirit travelled the land, sort of like Jesus, and he taught these
> three *siyá:m*, these three chiefs, how to write their language. And they were
> supposed to teach everyone how to write their language, but they didn't. So
> they were heaped into a pile and turned to stone. Because they were sup-
> posed to teach the language to everyone and because they didn't, people
> from all different lands will come and take all the knowledge from the
> people – because they wouldn't learn to write they lost that knowledge.

Bertha Peters, Stó:lō Salish elder, 1995

Some indigenous histories not only challenge Western chronologies but
dispute Western ways of knowing. Indeed, a number of indigenous
stories circulating among the Salish people of south coastal and plateau
British Columbia challenge us to reconsider both the history of Native-
newcomer relations and our understanding of such core concepts as the
relationship between orality and literacy, and ultimately, our definitions of indigeneity.

If communication theory and ethnography have interpreted literacy
as a force capable of facilitating profound cognitive (and thereby assimilative) change in non-literate people,[1] as a colonial 'weapon capable
of inflicting damage' by relocating the sacred from local control and
into the public domain,[2] and more recently as a Western tool sometimes
employed by Aboriginal people to preserve their cultural and traditions against colonial assimilation,[3] certain Salish stories reveal that
other Aboriginal truths regard literacy as something indigenous that
was itself once taken away. In addition to Bertha Peters' story of the

transformed chiefs, quoted above, is the 'beginning of time' narrative shared by Harry Robinson, which describes Coyote's 'loss' of literacy, and also the thematically related oral tradition of a contact-era Salish prophet's use of sacred texts (and subsequent alienation by Catholic Church authorities) described by a second, unrelated, Bertha Peters. Considered together, as well as in relation to a countervailing Salish discourse that regards the process of 'keeping writing out' of sacred and ritualized ceremonies as an 'act of integrity,'[4] these indigenous historical narratives reveal the enigmatic role and place of literacy within Salish epistemology.

Within the oral traditions, literacy sits alternately at the centre of the Salish world and outside of it. It is simultaneously foreign and indigenous, threatening and protective; it is from the past as well as the present, and it looms large in the future. Literacy challenges orality, and therefore Salish notions of self, while at the same time these narratives reveal that literacy is implicitly regarded as something in need of repatriation: a repatriation that, once accomplished, will restore a balance that was earlier disrupted.

No matter how Salish oral histories situate literacy, it is always within a context of power relationships and a discourse that emphasizes the value of innovation and flexibility.[5] Presented here is a discussion of several Salish oral traditions that strives to situate literacy within an indigenous cosmology and thereby to begin the process of filling a void that Peter Wogan has identified as a serous impediment to our understanding of Aboriginal responses to European contact.[6] To accomplish this, I attempt to invert the now standard scholarly exercise of trying to determine the effect of literacy on orality, as well as the more recent efforts to assess the degree of 'orality in literature' or the extent of 'literature in orality.'[7] Instead, I turn my gaze to the indigenous orality *about* literacy.

A stream of scholarship led by Ruth Finnegan suggests that what Walter Ong and others identified as a qualitative cognitive difference between literates and non-literates is better understood as merely a social construct: a product of ethnocentric assumptions concerning evolutionary progress and development.[8] Support for this position has also recently emerged from historical studies of European literacy. Adam Fox, for example, has argued that pre-modern British ballads such as *The Ballad of Chevy Chase* were much more heavily influenced by literacy than was previously thought, just as early modern British literacy was in fact permeated with orality.[9]

Additionally, while communication theorists no longer necessarily interpret the relationship between orality and literacy within a strictly evolutionary developmental paradigm, suggesting a transition from primitive to civilized, nonetheless it is still a working assumption that orality antedates literacy, and that all historical movements between the two states (whether within cultures or across cultures) is unidirectional, with literacy following orality. Exceptions to this rule, if they existed, would signal a civilization's decay or a culture's decline. Within this context, literacy has been considered as either a gift of enlightenment bestowed upon North American Aboriginal people or as a colonial tool of assimilation imposed upon those same people.

Presented here is an effort to take indigenous historical understanding seriously, not necessarily because it helps to explain aspects of non-Native history but because it destabilizes mainstream understanding of and assumptions about history and therefore creates new starting points for cross-cultural dialogue. All of the indigenous storytellers discussed in this chapter firmly believed that there was a time in Salish history, no matter how fleeting, when at least a few of their ancestors had working knowledge of literacy that preceded, and was therefore independent of, newcomer initiatives and influences. They were literate because powerful forces from the spirit world had wanted them to be literate, and they would become literate again for the same reason. Literacy is not, according to this version of history, something imposed on or introduced to Aboriginal people as part of the colonial process. It is therefore not necessarily assimilative and presumably, therefore, it is not inherently a threat or a challenge to Salish people's sense of self vis-à-vis non-Native outsiders. The non-conformity of these beliefs in relation to Western historical understanding, as well as some contemporary Aboriginal political discourse, suggests a disjuncture between Salish and newcomer ways of knowing, which in turn collectively offer insights into the causes of the misunderstandings that have characterized so much of Native–newcomer relations.

Situating Literacy within a Salish world

It would be misleading to suggest that there was, or is, a 'Salish world' in which political and philosophical ideas were universally shared. The Salish people have never been politically united, and great diversity exists among the speakers of the twenty-two mutually unintelligible Salish languages. Culturally, the greatest division is between the seven

Interior Salish language groups, which occupy the Columbia plateau in British Columbia and Washington (and small portions of Alberta, Idaho, and Montana), and the fifteen Coast Salish language groups whose territories stretch, with interruptions, from the shores of northern Oregon to the mid-coast of British Columbia. Nonetheless, their shared linguistic roots suggest a commonality that is reflected in certain metaphysical beliefs. These are in turn accentuated in those regions where social relations were historically maintained.

The Coast and Interior Salish people of what is now British Columbia (my focus here) have long had significant social interactions. A series of communication corridors linked people east to west across the Coast Mountain range. Marriages aimed at cementing economic benefits and facilitating diplomatic relations were common, and the children of such relations appear to have been anything but systemically disadvantaged.[10] Moreover, even if scholars have failed to make it a focus of research, Aboriginal people identify a Coastal and Interior Salish metaphysical continuum premised on the shifting identity of the 'beginning of time' Transformer figures.

Among the lower Fraser River Coast Salish people (the Stó:lō) the central Transformer character is X̱á:ls – the 'Great Spirit' of Bertha Peters' narrative, whom she describes as having travelled Stó:lō territory 'sort of like Jesus.' In other Stó:lō discussions, such as those related to Franz Boas by George Chehalis in 1884, we are told that X̱á:ls was the youngest of the four children of Red Headed Woodpecker and Black Bear, who were collectively known as X̱e:x̱á:ls.[11] Their home was in the mountains near the north end of Harrison Lake (on the border of a principal travel route between the Stó:lō and the Lillooet Interior Salish people). Red Headed Woodpecker also had a second wife, Grizzly Bear, who was envious of Black Bear. In a jealous rage Grizzly Bear killed both her husband and her co-wife, Black Bear. Fearing for their lives, Black Bear's children set off from their home, and in the process became X̱e:x̱ál:s, the Transformers.

In the Stó:lō histories, X̱e:x̱á:ls are sometimes described in human terms and sometimes in relation to their bear-like characteristics. Together they travelled Stó:lō territory 'making the world right,' that is to say, they transformed people and things into their permanent forms, thereby creating the world we recognize today.

According to widely circulating stories, X̱e:x̱á:ls travelled down Harrison Lake to the Fraser River. There they turned eastward and eventually passed beyond the limits of Stó:lō territory through the Fraser Canyon.

The Stó:lō explain that they know little of the Transformers' activities immediately after they left the coastal region except that they eventually reached the sunrise. Once there, they travelled through the sky with the sun to the sunset, and in the process acquired additional miraculous transformative powers. From the sunset they travelled by canoe eastward, eventually reaching the mouth of the Fraser River, and from there they resumed their journey back upstream. As they travelled east to west across Stó:lō territory and back up the Fraser River they performed ever greater transformative feats, including punishing the three chiefs who refused, or failed, to share their knowledge of literacy. Eventually the Xe:xá:ls passed through the Fraser Canyon and beyond Stó:lō territory, 'never to be seen again.'[12]

According to some of the Nlakapamux people, who reside in what might be considered the transition zone between coast and plateau, however, Xe:xá:ls, and in particular the youngest brother, Xá:ls, did not necessarily disappear. Rather, they transformed from bear-like humans into coyote-like humans and became the Interior Salish Trickster/Transformer figures known as Qoa'qLaqal and Coyote.[13]

References to literacy, and in particular the loss of literacy, also feature prominently in the Interior Salish historical transformation narratives, thereby reinforcing the linkages between these two regions and peoples. In speaking with ethnohistorian Wendy Wickwire in the early 1980s, Okanagan elder Harry Robinson explained that near the beginning of time, as God was busy setting the world in order, He revealed literacy to Coyote and Coyote's twin brother. Then began Coyote's problems:

> He put the paper on the ground, well, just because he's God. And he find a stone. And he take stone and put the stone on the paper so it wouldn't fly away ... Went up to Heaven ... But these two [twins] still around ... And this younger one, he look at this paper lying there with stone on 'em. He thought, 'I take this paper and I hide 'em ...' And he thinks, 'This paper, He's going to give 'em to my friend because he's the older one. He's going to get this paper not me. And he's going to be the boss. And not me. But I take this paper and I hide 'em ... Tell 'em that the wind blowed.

> ... And that younger one, now today, that's the white man. And the other one, that's me. That's the Indian. And that's why the white man, they can tell a lie more than the Indian. But the white man, they got that law ... And [God] told him, 'That paper, it'll tell you what to do. But you have to tell the Indians.'[14]

As with Bertha Peters' narrative of the transformed chiefs, Harry Robinson explains that it was God's original intention that Salish people be literate. In both accounts, future generations of Salish people are denied literacy; through the failings of their own leaders in the former case, and through the conniving and selfishness of the white brother in the latter. The consequences are profound. Immediately after sharing her transformation narrative with me, Bertha Peters made explicit the ongoing historical significance of the loss of literacy:

> When the first white people came, a white man raped this Indian woman. And she got syphilis. Then, when her husband *went* with her, he caught syphilis too. But they didn't know about these sicknesses, and so the man went up the mountain to die. He was laying there naked and a snake came up to him and ate all the sickness off his penis, then wiggled away. Then it ate three types of plants and got well. So the man went and ate the three plants and got well. So they knew a cure for this sickness, but they couldn't write it down, so they lost it.[15]

For Bertha Peters, literacy was not necessarily a source of knowledge or power in itself. Rather, it was principally a tool for preserving certain kinds of knowledge that could have assisted Salish people during times of great distress, such as those associated with the arrival of Europeans. White people's mastery of literacy gave them an advantage not only in terms of preserving their own European knowledge but in terms of their ability and propensity to steal and profit from indigenous wisdom. For as Bertha went on to explain, 'This [white] man came to see me and he told me the Indians have a lot to be proud of because there are twenty-eight different types of medicine they use in the hospital which came from the Indians. That knowledge of medicine was taken away from the Indians by the white people because they didn't write it down.'

In a similar fashion, in a follow-up conversation with Wickwire, Harry Robinson outlined the consequences of Coyote's loss of literacy on Salish people in terms of alienated lands and governing authority. Long after Coyote's white twin brother had stolen literacy and moved to Britain, troubles began emerging as a result of the imbalance in the world between the literate white brother's children and Coyote's non-literate children. An 'Angel of God' then appeared to Coyote, bestowed additional powers upon him, and directed him to embark on a mission to England, where 'you and King are going to make a law for the white people and the Indians.'[16]

In Robinson's description of Coyote's adventures in London, the king of England is reminded that Coyote too is a king, and that as monarchs they together have the authority to make lasting laws for their two people, and in particular, to regulate relations between the two races. Such laws are necessary, Coyote explains, because the English king's children have started arriving in Coyote's country 'and they don't do good with my children ... They just don't care for them. They just go and claim the land and they just do as they like.' It was a serious matter, Coyote clarified, for when his own children tried to explain to the English immigrants, 'This here is mine,' the English settlers responded with violence and some of Coyote's children were killed.[17] Only a written law could ensure that the two groups of children would 'be good; not be in trouble, not be bad to one another.' Coyote insisted that the two sides would not have to fight if he and the English king 'marked down on paper a law, so it can be that way for the rest of time, to the end of the world. Because that's God's thought, you know.' Coyote wanted the Indian Law, which he referred to as the 'Black and White,' or 'the Indian Law,' to clarify the criteria by which Indian reserves would be defined, to set restrictions on the degree to which white settlement could 'crowd' the Indian reserves, and to entrench guarantees concerning the future inalienability of Indian lands. It was intended, in other words, to codify and regulate Native-newcomer relations.

In Robinson's narrative Coyote is continually stymied by the English king, who seeks ways to escape having to properly fulfil 'God's thought.' In the end, it is only Coyote's mystical ability to reveal to the English king a vision of an impending attack by an indigenous army that convinces the British monarch to agree to put pen to paper and create the document Coyote desires. Indeed, 'Coyote just forced him to do something he don't really like – and that idea is still the same right now ... [and that's why] they always try to beat the Indians, because the king is not really satisfied.'

So difficult is the task of composing the 'Indian law' (and so reluctant, it seems, is the king to work speedily) that the task cannot be completed during Coyote's visit. And so Coyote has to be satisfied with a point-form list and a commitment that 'when I leave you, then you can do the rest. Take your time and do the rest. When you finish, all the paper, that'll be the Indian Law; you give 'em to my children. Not right away, but long time from now ... You gonna give 'em to my children. By this time, my children, they can read. That's *their* law.'

Robinson explains that ultimately, 'the King, he didn't make that stuff.' Coyote and his people had to wait many generations before the English king's promise was finally fulfilled by one of the his successors – a queen. She was a good woman, according to Robinson, who took the promise of her ancestor seriously. She wrote the Indian Law and made copies, so there were four in all. One the queen kept in her London office; the other three she sent to Canada. Letters were attached to the books requiring that they be deposited in Ottawa, Winnipeg, and Victoria, 'til the Indians get to be educated so they can read.' A Salish man named TOM-mah was hired to guide the government official who carried the BC copy of the 'Black and White' through the mountains from Kelowna to Hope. Robinson explained that one night while camping the government official opened the Black and White and showed it to TOM-mah. Because TOM-mah couldn't read the government agent explained to the Salish man the book's contents. He also showed TOM-mah an illustration in the book – a photograph that showed the king of England in Buckingham Palace meeting with Coyote. TOM-mah told his people what he had been shown, and Robinson had met TOM-mah in 1917, when the guide was more than eighty years old. This, Robinson reasoned, meant that the Black and White was delivered about 1860.

Wickwire's published version of Robinson's narrative ends with Robinson explaining that he had himself seen the padlocked book of the Indian Law when he visited Victoria in the company of Aboriginal activists Andrew Paul and Tom Gregoire in 1947. The actual interview, however, goes on to describe how literacy came to the Salish people and how they used literacy to mobilize the power of the Black and White. According to Robinson, as Coyote's children became literate, they 'open[ed] the Black and White and read it and ... [thought] for themselves.' One of the first to do so was a Salish man named Edward Brett. Robinson remembered meeting Brett circa 1947. Brett's parents had died, according to Robinson, while their son was quite young, and so Brett had been raised at the Roman Catholic residential school in Kamloops. As a young literate man, Brett learned that the Black and White was locked in Victoria. After much difficulty, frustration, and personal financial sacrifice, Brett was eventually able to acquire a 700 page copy of the Black and White from a government agent, and 'he read that and he knew exactly what it said from the Queen and the King.'[18]

Upon returning to his community with his copy of the text, Brett is remembered to have organized study sessions every month or so to allow Salish people from a wide region to congregate to hear him read and translate a few pages at a time of the Indian Law. In this way, over the course of many months, the people from all around became familiar with the great book and its laws – with the Black and White. They came to know, in other words, what regulations had been established for Native-newcomer relations and were thus able to assess non-Native behaviour in relation to codified criteria. The conclusion was clear: non-Natives could not be trusted. Just as Coyote's white twin brother had stolen literacy, white settlers and the Canadian government were stealing land and Aboriginal people's dignity. For Coyote and his descendants, literacy was the key to accountability and the means of restoring interracial balance.

Throughout Robinson's narrative, literacy is shown to be a powerful force, capable of precipitating transformations in people's lives not unlike the transformative power associated with Coyote. After initially having literacy stolen from them, it is the absence of literacy that sets Native people apart from their English brothers. Coyote's desire to encode, standardize, and make predictable Native-newcomer relations through the repatriation of literacy and the Black and White should not necessarily be regarded as a sign of assimilation or weakness on the part of Salish people. Rather, it speaks principally of the extent to which Salish people perceived differences between themselves and the strangers who came to their lands from afar, while also illustrating that they anticipated a means of peaceful and prosperous relations. Indeed, it illustrates that Robinson considered Salish people and non-Natives to have a shared history of creation. As he explained,

> Now, they had them all finished ... that's the Indian Law. That's where the Indian's Law is, in that book. Nothing but the Indian Law and that's what they call the 'Black and White,' because whoever made that law, one he was black and the other was white. See that's the key ... that he was white. And Coyote was black: that was Indian. Black and white. He made that law. That the reason why they called that book 'Black and White.'

Prophetic Salish Literacy

Until relatively recently, it was an academic commonplace to assume that non-literates across time and cultures reacted to literacy in identical ways, in what former US president George W. Bush might describe as 'shock and awe.'[19] A counter-current of scholarship has posited that what was regarded as universal indigenous amazement was more likely a reflection of Western assumptions and arrogance on the part of literate observers and recorders. So pervasive is literacy's importance as a symbol of Western superiority that, as cultural theorist Michael Harbsmeier has observed, 'only modern European civilization came to make its own ... proper literacy, into the very definition of its own identity against the rest of the world.'[20] Along similar lines, Patricia Seed raises the possibility that 'the geographic diversity of reports of native "marveling" over several centuries of encounters with non-Europeans suggests not an implausible similarity among the Ibo, Tupi, Nambikwara, and Raratonga, but rather a historical continuity in Western expectations of the conduct of non-European peoples.'[21] The narratives of Bertha Peters and Harry Robinson challenge the notions underlying each of these observations in ways with which the existing scholarship on orality and literacy are ill equipped to deal. Their narratives of 'beginning of time literacy' (and in the case of Robinson, literacy's indigenous repatriation) suggest that at least some Salish people believe not only that their ancestors were not necessarily awestruck by the arrival of Western literacy but that they embraced it as part of their own historical identity.

To sift through newcomer biases it is useful, and revealing, to situate the accounts of ancient Salish literacy alongside what on the surface might appear to be rather distinct narratives of nineteenth-century Salish prophesy. For from the perspective of several Salish carriers of historical narratives, Salish literacy before the residential school era was not restricted to the ephemeral encounters of the three transformed chiefs or betrayed Coyote. These Salish histories also tell of pre-contact prophets who, within the context of Bertha's and Harry's accounts, might be thought of as having reacquired literacy directly from the spirit world, and who used this medium to prepare Salish people for the profound changes associated with European colonization.

Tucked away in the British Museum in London, England, are the restricted fieldnotes of the anthropologist Marian Smith, of Columbia University, and those her graduate students, compiled during their summer of ethnographic research among the Stó:lō in 1945.[22] A number of the entries were made during conversations with a Mrs Bertha Peters (whom I will refer to simply as 'Mrs Peters,' to distinguish her from the other Bertha Peters referred to above). Mrs Peters described the profound role that prophetic literacy played in nineteenth-century Salish-British relations.

She explained that her 'great-grandfather's great-grandfather' St'a'saluk had been a prophet. In and of itself, being a prophet was not necessarily considered remarkable among Salish people. As the anthropologist Wilson Duff, among others, has documented, Salish individuals with the power to see what was transpiring in other settlements, and who could foresee future events, have a long history that pre-dates European contact.[23] Indeed, among other things they played an important role in advising people about the potentially hostile intentions of those in other settlements. What apparently set St'a'saluk and at least one other nineteenth-century Salish prophet apart from others was less their ability to predict the future than their use of literacy to accomplish this feat. According to Mrs Peters, St'a'saluk acquired from God himself a piece of paper that foretold the future, including the impending arrival of white people. As a result, this paper was so valued that it was passed from 'son to son' and in that way continued to provide a valuable service to Salish people across generations.

Within Salish traditions, not unlike the practice of medieval European magic described by Frank Klaassen (chapter 8, this volume), rituals and incantations were carefully guarded and their secrets passed from mentoring ritualist to novice. Moreover, as in medieval magic, in which utterances in Latin were regarded as especially sacred and invested with power, Salish incantations also tended to be in an esoteric language (often described as 'the old language,' and sometimes as 'the high language'), which only the practitioner and his or her acolytes could understand.

According to Mrs Peters, on the sacred paper that her great-great-great-great-grandfather received from God were 'the fanciest capital letters' that 'only the old man could read.' In addition to foretelling the coming of white people and the imminent arrival of various Western technologies (including light bulbs, cross-cut saws, nuclear family housing, and glass windows), European stock animals, and domesticated fruit and vegetables, St'a'saluk's text taught a special creed to facilitate positive relations between Salish people and the European newcomers. According to Mrs Peters, he told them,

'They will be different. They will be white and they will give you anything you can get from them.' He begged his people, when these people come to be kind to them and treat them like their brother. He even mentioned the stock (animals). This was first time they ever knew how pigs looked like. (He grunted to show them). 'That will be your meat.' He got a sheet of paper.

No one ever saw such paper and it has writing on it. He told them that he got it from God. That is why they had to pray and fast for 40 days. He told them about vegetables. 'And the fruit will be growing outside your places.' On this paper it said you are not supposed to steal or kill anybody.[24]

The prophet read the special words on the paper and told the people that they should not fear the changes that were coming. Indeed, contrary to most other nineteenth-century North American Native prophecy movements (such as those associated with the Ghost Dance at Wounded Knee or even the neighbouring and historically associated Interior Salish 'Plateau Prophet phenomenon'), in which people were encouraged to reject whites and their new ways, the Coast Salish prophet of Mrs Peters' story encouraged Salish people to join in certain rituals designed to hasten the newcomers' arrival. 'One part of ceremony they danced with their hands over their heads and looking up begging God and the strange people to come,' she explained, and 'this is why he was making them pray, because they wanted these times to come.'

The point behind Mrs Peters' recounting of the prophecy narratives was not simply to show that one of her ancestors was a remarkable man whose prophecies had come true – although this was no doubt one of her motivations. Rather, the significance of the story lay in its power to link indigenous literacy with the alienation of Salish lands by European settlers. As she repeatedly stated to her Columbia University interviewer, the prophet's paper was 'the reason these people here didn't fight for their country when the white people came.'

To the Salish people's chagrin, the prophet's printed word revealed certain truths that ultimately led to their marginalization by the very people the sacred texts had encouraged them to welcome and make room for. Contrary to scholarly orthodoxy, the Native people did not lose their land in large part because they were non-literates who could be easily duped and manipulated by nefarious literate settlers and mendacious colonial government officials, but, ironically, precisely because they were literate! Within Salish historical consciousness the prophet is remembered as having prepared Salish people for the arrival of newcomers who he expected would bring positive change to a chaotic world in the aftermath of a smallpox epidemic. In a manner similar to what Elizabeth Vibert has documented in the context of the Columbia plateau prophecy phenomenon, the Coast Salish prophet was operating in a world devastated by recent smallpox epidemics, when people were desperate for new solutions to new problems.[25] Introduced epidemic diseases, which pre-dated European settlement and the imposition of colonial rule, had resulted in the Salish world being disordered, and (without sufficient context to link the diseases directly to Europeans) the Salish people interpreted smallpox as the product of a disruption in the spirit world: a disruption that needed to be corrected by new transformations not unlike those associated with the corrective transformative work of X̱á:ls, or Coyote.

While St'a'saluk's prophecies eventually proved correct – white people and their technologies did come – the newcomers themselves ultimately proved a disappointment. As in the Coyote story related by Harry Robinson, the whites who eventually arrived and confirmed the prophecies were not necessarily good people. They were, as one account of the prophet's teachings predicted 'half good and half bad.'[26] Unlike St'a'saluk, who was 'good and innocent enough for God to give him that paper,' the white people presumably possessed literacy because they had always had it. As a result virtue was not associated with their use of paper. Mrs Peters explains that St'a'saluk was pleased when white people started to arrive and thus fulfil his prophecy – until some of the newcomers began to challenge the authority and sanctity of his texts:

> When Catholic priests came they heard and told Bishop Durieu and he went against it. It was (the paper) handed down from son to son. The paper was put in a little house (miniature) and was put up a cedar tree ... The Bishop took the paper and burned it at Sk'welq. He was telling [St'a'saluk] it was the devil's work. As soon as he saw it, little house and all, he threw it in the fire. [My] mother saw him do it. She was 15 at the time.

So whereas the Salish who listened to St'a'saluk are remembered as not having fought the newcomers for their land because of the will of God as revealed through the prophet's paper, the white settlers ultimately used paper to dispossess Salish people of their land and resources. Where through these narratives Salish literacy is portrayed as legitimate and proper, newcomer literacy is described as illegitimate and corrupt. Just as the white brother stole Coyote's paper, so the prophet St'a'saluk's white counterpart within the Christian faith stole his paper.

The Question of 'Authenticity' in Historical Salish Literacy

Bertha Peters' story of the three chiefs who were turned to stone and Harry Robinson's account of literacy being stolen from Coyote by his white twin conform to all the standard criteria associated with a genre of Salish narratives commonly referred to by outsiders as 'legend' or 'mythology' with one exception – they appear to contain post-contact content.[27] While non-Natives have generally not been overly concerned with the historical legitimacy of Aboriginal legends and myths (if only because they assume them to be fiction),[28] they have been greatly concerned with their 'authenticity.' Stories that appear to have been unduly influenced or informed by post-contact European events and issues have long been discarded to the dustbin of scholarly interest. This prejudice applies equally to prophecy stories such as those shared by Mrs Peters in which the assertions of prophetic power are perceived by outsiders as being built upon information acquired in the post-contact era. That is to say, we have grown so accustomed to associating authentic Aboriginal culture with pre-contact temporal dimensions that we have dismissed or ignored Native stories that do not meet our criteria for historical purity. We might proceed, blindly oblivious to what we are missing by applying such ethnocentric, historically deterministic models, were it not that Aboriginal people themselves flatly reject both our model and our criteria. In failing to listen we not only close a door on another way of knowing, we potentially insult the people who share the stories and thereby reduce the likelihood of their generosity continuing.

Like Western scholars, Salish people distinguish between at least two genres of historical narratives, but authenticity is not a criterion used in making that distinction.[29] Stories set in the distant past describing both the work of the Transformers or Coyote as they set about 'making the world right' by transforming it into its present stable and recognizable form and their efforts to introduce special technical or ritual power to heroic ancestors are referred to in Bertha Peters' Stó:lõ Salish language as sxwõxwiyám, and in Harry Robinson's Okanagan Salish language as shmee-ma-ee. In the world of both Bertha Peterses, the other form of historical discourse is called sqwélqwel, whereas for Harry Robinson this category of story was known as teek-whl. Stories of the second type tend to describe more recent happenings associated with events in the lives of living people or people from recent generations, such as those relating to the prophet St'a'saluk. Both sxwõxwiyám/shee-ma-ee and sqwélqwel/teek-whl are considered equally true and real.[30] Whatever differences and similarities exist between the two narrative forms – sometimes the lines between the two blur, making categorization difficult – neither reality (in the Western meaning of the term) nor authenticity is part of the indigenous criteria for assessing them. There are no authentic or inauthentic *swoxwiyam*, only better remembered/conveyed or less well remembered/conveyed *swoxwiyam*. There are no authentic or inauthentic *sqwélqwel*, only more or less reliable sources of historical information.

Historical accuracy in the Salish world is a matter of great concern – no less so than among Western academics. What is different is the way accuracy is assessed. Among literate Westerners, historical accuracy is measured in relation to verifiable evidence. Footnotes provide the reading audience with a means of assessing the relationship between evidence and interpretation. If a scholarly historical interpretation can be shown to run counter to historical evidence it is regarded as poor history: poor scholarship. The conveyors of poor history in the Western model place themselves in a dangerous situation. If exposed they will be branded either as sloppy academics, or worse, as dishonest ones. Such designations have serious consequences in the sense that they will affect historians' ability to have their work published, and their reputation within academia will suffer. They will be marginalized and ostracized within their profession.

Within the Salish world, by way of contrast, historical accuracy is largely assessed in relation to people's memories of previous renditions or versions of a narrative and in relation to the teller's status and reputation as an authority. In cases of conflicting narratives, discrepancies are as often as not dismissed according to familial alliances and associations, or what Wayne Suttles has informally described as the process of asserting 'My family's history is better than your family's history because it is *my* family's history.'[31] However, what Wendy Wickwire has described as oral footnotes – the verbal citing of one's sources and authorities – provides the Salish audience with the principal means of assessing a storyteller's legitimacy, and by extension, the legitimacy of the narrative when such matters are being adjudicated among families. That is to say, if the conveyor of a historical narrative is considered to have failed to establish such credentials, the narrative is likely to be regarded as poor history by third party listeners not allied with the teller's family. The Salish conveyors of poor history, like their Western counterparts, face various sanctions for sloppiness and transgression. It is unlikely, for example, that they will be called in the future to share their stories in a public forum, and moreover they will acquire reputations as poor historians: their status will diminish.

Given the common concern over the accuracy of historical narratives, it is not surprising that people in both the Salish and Western worlds also expressed concern over the consequences of sharing inaccurate or wrong history. In each society, for example, it is understood that poorly conveyed or inaccurate historical narratives pose dangers, not only to the reputation of the speaker but to the listening (or reading) audience. Among Western scholars, this recognition is a relatively recent epiphany, and one related to the recognition of the power that interpretations of the past have to shape the present. This is most apparent among histories written about relatively recent occurrences, and in particular those that discuss violence or exploitation. Nazi history that depicted the German people as not only a betrayed people but a superior race created the context and justification for the brutal conquest of Slavic lands, the occupation of western Europe, and the sadistic execution of six million Jews. In a not dissimilar way, Brian Dippie has shown how a false understanding of Native history allowed American policy makers to embrace a teleological and self-serving notion of the future that in turn justified the physical, social, and economic marginalization of Aboriginal people. Indians were deemed to be a 'vanishing race,' Dippie explains, because history ostensibly revealed their pre-contact civilizations to be inferior and incapable of advancement. Once they had been classified as a historically vanishing people, policies were enacted that actually promoted their political, economic, and cultural disappearance. Unfortunately, it is not only ideologues and self-serving politicians who create dangerous histories. Jeffery Gould has argued that scholars contributed to a perception of Nicaraguan history in which indigenous people were portrayed as having been replaced through the miscegenational process of 'mestizaje' wherein people of mixed European and indigenous ancestry eclipsed Nicaraguan Aboriginal people. With 'real Indians' deemed to have been a casualty of history, contemporary political leaders absolved themselves of responsibility for indigenous people – with tragic consequences.[32]

If Western historians are increasingly aware of the dangers of inaccurate or ideologically driven history, Salish historians have long been sensitive to the need to 'get the story right' – even if the consequences of bad history are conceived differently. For the Salish historian, bad history is considered to have potentially tragic consequences for both the teller and the listening audience. Stories about the distant past, and indeed any story that involves deceased people, is regarded as of interest to ancestors in the spirit world. To retell a story is to convene the spirits of the historical actors described. Ancestral spirits, it is believed, are extremely concerned with honour, integrity, and accuracy – so concerned, in fact, that they can cause 'bad things' to happen when their story is altered or abused. So sensitive are the spirits that many Salish people today are careful not to mention the names of deceased people at night (when spirits are especially active) for fear that either a malevolent, or even an excessively kind, spirit might carry away their soul.

Indicative of the obligation that Salish historians have to maintain the integrity of sacred historical narratives are the protocols and sanctions anthropologist Sally Snyder observed in 1963 among even her supposedly 'acculturated' informants – people she described as being 'compulsive about telling stories "right."' As she discovered, 'If a story was imperfectly recalled it was wrong for [Salish historians] to "guess" meaning, to pad, improvise, paraphrase or omit. It was better not to tell it at all for it was dangerous to omit scenes and to shorten myths. Nubile women in the audience might give birth to deformed children, incomplete or malformed like the abbreviated or truncated story. And shortening myths would shorten the lives of all listeners.'[33]

Regarded in this light it is difficult to imagine a context in which a Salish person could, or would, intentionally modify a historical narrative pertaining to the ancient transformations, and even more difficult to imagine a context in which the community would allow such an individual to get away with it even if they tried. More to the point, in placing the history of literacy within the context of a sacred narrative – one that from a Salish perspective cannot be easily challenged by either indigenous people or non-Native newcomers and their competing chronologies and interpretations – it becomes sacrosanct. To raise the question of 'authenticity' is to challenge not only the narrative but also the 'truth' behind Salish ways of knowing. This is not to suggest that outsiders should not ask about authenticity, just that they should be alert to the significance and implications of their questions to Aboriginal people.

Context for Situating Salish Orality and Literacy

Culture binds Salish stories together and provides them with an internal coherence that is not always apparent to outsiders. Salish prophecy narratives, for example, have been examined from a number of perspectives, most notably with an eye to determining whether they were of genuinely indigenous origin or a borrowed reaction to colonial pressures (that is, whether they were 'authentic'), or, most recently, in relation to what they say about indigenous beliefs and practices in the face of catastrophic challenges to society such as those posed by smallpox epidemics.[34] No one has yet attempted to place the historical actors within a Salish historiography or historical consciousness. Such an approach offers a means of escaping the quagmire of assessing authenticity, while simultaneously elevating the analysis beyond an evaluation of semiotics.

For example, studies of Salish prophecy have avoided the question of the historical reality of the actions and words attributed to prophets. An underlying assumption of these studies is that the prophets were not really prophets; that they could not have known what they claimed to have known in the way they claim to have known it. That is to say, post-Enlightenment Western epistemology does not account for prophetic knowledge, and therefore either the prophets are considered to have acquired their knowledge of Europeans and European ways (including 'mock literacy') from other sources, or the more recent twentieth-century stories about nineteenth-century prophets are not genuinely historical but instead historical fiction designed to serve contemporary purposes. Thus conceived, Mrs Peters' great-great-great-great-grandfather St'a'saluk could not have had a paper with written text because such things could not have been known to Salish people prior to either direct or indirect contact with Europeans.

But what if the Salish understanding of the historical St'a'saluk departs from the Western understandings an individual? Mrs Peters tells us that the name St'a'saluk was also the name of her grandfather and father, and we know that in Salish society when names are passed on so are essential components of the spirit or soul of the person or persons who previously 'carried' the name. Moreover, as mentioned, Mrs Peters tells us that the prophetic paper was passed from son to son. Thus, it is possible that the prophecies actually emanated from what outsiders might consider to have been a series of people over many years. That is to say, there may not have been one St'a'saluk who uttered one set of prophecies, but a series of St'a'saluks who uttered many cumulative prophecies. I am not suggesting that this was necessarily the case, simply that it might have been, and that questions of authenticity, should we feel the need to continue asking them, might need to be recast to account for different measures of historical accuracy and different definitions of what constitutes an historical actor.

Given such context, perhaps the more interesting question is what these stories collectively or individually say about Aboriginal perceptions of literacy. For if the above synoptic accounts of 'beginning of time' literacy tell us that literacy is part of a broader genre of transformation stories, they only indirectly reveal how Salish people understand the process or act of transformation in relation to literacy itself.

For Salish people, transformation stories are as much, if not more, about creating permanency or stability as they are about documenting the change from one state to another. In the two Bertha Peterses' language, the verb that has been translated into English to describe the work of the Transformers is xá:ytem. This term first entered the popular English lexicon in 1995, when the elders of the Stó:lō Shxweli (Spirit) Language Revival Programme were asked to select a name for the new interpretive centre that was being established at the recently protected site of the transformer rock referred to in Bertha's literacy narrative. The elders balked at the request, however, explaining that they 'could not make up a name' for something that had been made by Xá:ls. Instead they suggested that the site simply be referred to as Xá:ytem, which meant 'suddenly and miraculously transformed by Xá:ls.'

Both the name of the Transformers and the verb describing the act of transforming are derived from the same proto-Salish root xá:l. Interestingly, however, as at least one insightful scholar of Salish hermeneutics has observed, perhaps a better way of thinking of the meaning behind xá:l is not to emphasize the act of transformation but the process of 'marking.' The Transformers leave their mark on the world through transformations that in turn are then understood and known through the stories describing that act. Considered in this light, the 'root word Xá:l refers to inscription in the widest sense.'[35]

In terms of helping us understand the meanings embedded in the narratives of both Bertha Peterses, one important context can be derived from the indigenous term Stó:lō people use to refer to literacy itself. During the course of interviews, Stó:lō elders explained to me that the verb to write in their language was xélá:ls. This is significant for two reasons. First, it reveals that the Stó:lō did not choose to borrow the English or French word for literacy as they did for certain other concepts about which they had no prior knowledge. The Stó:lō word for cow, for example is músmes, which is derived from the mooing sound cattle make. Similarly, the word for pig, kweshú, comes from the French cochon, and miyúl from the English mule. It is relatively easy, of course, to imagine a world in which knowledge of certain concrete objects does not exist and for which people therefore borrow the word to correspond with the introduced object. It is more taxing to imagine people not having knowledge of abstract concepts, and so the response to such introductions becomes more creative. While the adoption of an English word should not necessarily be taken as evidence that a given concept did not exist in pre-contact times, the use of an Aboriginal word for an activity or thing that is generally associated with post-contact developments should cause us to reflect on why that word was selected. It should, in other words, provide hints about what pre-existing ideas were used to interpret the introduced phenomenon or idea.[36]

The choice of the word _xélá:ls_ to describe writing is also significant for another reason, for it is derived from the same proto-Salish root for 'marking' as _xá:ls_ and _xá:ytem_. To write, in other words, is to engage in an activity of marking that Stó:lõ people associate with the actions of the Transformer. Thus the central 'Great Spirit' or Xá:ls character in Bertha Peters' narrative was presumably not only punishing the three chiefs for failing to share the knowledge of literacy but was engaged in the act of writing himself. The very act of transforming them to stone was an act of literacy.

A Salish Orality about Literacy

If someone were to create a timeline of literacy for the Salish people living along the lower Fraser River watershed based solely on evidence gleaned from archival records, chances are it would contain very different information, names, and dates from the Salish literacy narratives discussed above. It would probably begin with the establishment of St Mary's residential school in 1862, for it was there, under the watchful eye of Oblate Catholic priests, that Salish students first attended classes to learn their ABCs. By the time Canadian government officials started keeping systematic files on Aboriginal literacy in the region in the 1870s, Indian Agent James Lenihan was able to report that of the 32 girls and 22 boys attending St Mary's, all had 'passed a very credible examination in reading writing [and] grammar.'[37] Two years after St Mary's was built a young alumna of that school established, in the village of Cheam in the central Fraser Valley, what is possibly the first Aboriginal-run Western-style school in Canada's Pacific province. There she taught other Salish youths and adults the rudiments of English literacy. Throughout the late nineteenth century the number of literate Aboriginal graduates was augmented by the work of Protestant teachers at the Methodist and Anglican Indian schools built in Chilliwack, Lytton, and Yale and the Catholic school at Kamloops.

Yet against this mid-to-late-nineteenth-century colonial backdrop Stó:lō prophets, possibly including a namesake descendant of Mrs Peters' original St'a'saluk, continued to use a separate, esoteric literature to preach about the future in relation to the past. According to ethnographer James Teit, as late as 1880 a Salish prophet was travelling among Coast and Interior Salish villages preaching from a divinely inspired manuscript that only he could read. This text, an accountant's ledger book containing a series of pencil drawings and repetitive symbols, is now a part of the ethnographic collection of the Canadian Museum of Civilization in Ottawa and has been catalogued under the title 'Dream Book of a Stalo Prophet.'[38] It does not reflect literacy in a sense immediately recognizable to non-Native outsiders, but a child who glimpsed some of the pages might be forgiven for interpreting the images and symbols as the 'fanciest capital letters.' Moreover, the prophet's literacy was as real and meaningful to his Salish audience as either Bertha Peters' story about the three chiefs was to her or Harry Robinson's account of Coyote's misadventures was to him.

For many, orality is considered the defining characteristic of indigeneity, but these Salish narratives remind us that such a definition perhaps says more about the fact that literacy has for even longer been regarded by elite Europeans as the defining characteristic of Western civilization. All other popular definitions of what it means to be indigenous (to be non-industrial, to have a deep and meaningful relationship with one's local environs, to value collective decision-making processes over hierarchal social and political structures, to be intensely spiritual, and so forth) are products of the same assumption that informed Walter Ong's interpretation of the role of literacy in Western society. Salish oral histories about literacy reveal that to be indigenous is not necessarily to think of oneself and one's history as non-literate.

It was a long-standing assumption of Westerners that to be without literacy was to be without history. The stories told by the two Bertha Peterses and Harry Robinson inject literacy (and therefore history) into the Aboriginal past in a way that they probably believed non-Native listeners would understand. But more important, their stories reveal that literacy was not always interpreted by oral indigenous people in the same way. Their ways of understanding the works of the legendary 'beginning of time' Transformers and influential contact-era prophets indicates that literacy was regarded within the context of earlier understanding of what it meant to inscribe, make permanent, preserve, transform, and reveal.

Salish orality about literacy therefore offers glimpses into Salish historical consciousness. Reflecting on 'the history of active oppression imposed on Native languages and cultural practices,' as well as on the manner in which legal and even ethnographic documents were used to restrict and diminish Native rights, Crisca Bierwert recently observed that 'it would not be a surprise to find "writing" understood as a signifier of domination in a Native American oral tradition.' She notes that among contemporary Salish people on Canada's Pacific Coast, textual and literary representations are largely regarded in terms Walter Ong would have recognized – that is, as 'a weapon capable of inflicting damage.' And indeed, as is revealed through the stories of 'beginning of time' literacy and prophetic literacy, text was regarded as a powerful tool that could be used to undermine, steal, and in other ways diminish not only the sacredness of oration but also the rights of Aboriginal people and their relationship with land and resources. The desire Bierwert observed among many contemporary Salish people to 'keep writing out' of sacred and ritualized ceremonies should indeed be regarded as an 'act of integrity,'[39] but so too should the desire to repatriate literacy (as reflected in the Peterses and Robinson narratives) be appreciated as reflecting a countervailing act of historical integrity.

The task now before us is to better understand the tensions between these two positions within Salish society. That is to say, we must begin shifting our focus away from a binary study of Native–newcomer relations (which inevitably assumes that non-Natives are the most important thing in Aboriginal people's lives and history) to one that recognizes the plurality of indigenous voices within Aboriginal communities and the historical consciousness that informs those voices and beliefs.

NOTES

I am grateful to Bertha Peters, Harry Robinson, and Mrs Bertha Peters for seeing fit to share their knowledge with outsiders. I am indebted to Wendy Wickwire for providing me with an audiocassette copy of her unpublished and untranscribed interviews with Harry Robinson. This paper has benefited from comments from the participants at the University of Saskatchewan's symposium 'Writing about Talking: Orality and Literacy in Contemporary Scholarship' (15 October 2004), as well as from students in my 'Orality, Literacy, Memory, Tradition, and History' seminar (Winter 2006). M.T. Carlson, Jon Clapperton, Mark Ebert, Sonny McHalsie, John

Lutz, and Jim Miller provided helpful and encouraging comments on an earlier draft.

1 For example, Marshall McLuhan, *The Gutenberg Galaxy: The Making of Typographic Man* (Toronto: University of Toronto Press, 1962); Eric A. Havelock, *Preface to Plato* (Cambridge, MA: Belknap Press of Harvard University Press, 1963); Claude Lévi-Strauss, *The Savage Mind* (Chicago: University of Chicago Press, 1966); Jack Goody and Ian Watt, 'The Consequence of Literacy,' in *Literacy in Traditional Societies,* ed. Jack Goody (Cambridge, University of Cambridge Press, 1968); Aleksandr Romanovich Luria, ed., *Cognitive Development: Its Cultural and Social Foundations,* Michael Cole, trans., Martin Lopez-Morillas and Lynn Solotaroff (Cambridge, MA: Harvard University Press, 1976); Jack R. Goody, *The Domestication of the Savage Mind* (Cambridge: University of Cambridge Press, 1977); Walter J. Ong, *Orality and Literacy: The Technologizing of the World* (London and New York: Methuen, 1982); Eric A. Havelock, *The Muse Learns to Write: Reflections on Orality and Literacy from Antiquity to the Present* (New Haven, CT: Yale University Press, 1986).

2 Crisca Bierwert, *Brushed by Cedar, Living by the River: Coast Salish Figures of Power* (Tucson: University of Arizona Press, 1999), 112.

3 See David Murray, *Forked Tongues: Speech, Writing, and Representation in North American Indian Texts* (Bloomington: Indiana University Press, 1991); also Marie Battiste, 'Micmac Literacy and Cognitive Assimilation,' in *Indian Education in Canada,* vol. 1, *The Legacy,* ed. Jean Barman, Yvonne Hebert, and Don McCaskill (Vancouver: UBC Press, 1986), 23–44.

4 Bierwert, *Brushed by Cedar,* 112–13.

5 Even the scholarship emphasizing Salish opposition to literary depictions and representations of their culture contain powerful countervailing stories in which 'literary' options become rationalized as if they are not the only solution, but the best solution, to various orality/literacy tensions. See Bierwert, *Brushed by Cedar,* 112–35.

6 Peter Wogan, 'Perceptions of European Literacy in Early Contact Situations,' *Ethnohistory* 41, no. 3 (1994): 422.

7 Internationally, the best example of enquiry along this path is Adam Fox's *Oral and Literate Culture in England, 1500–1700* (Oxford: Clarendon Press, 2000). In the North American Aboriginal context see J.W. Berry and J.A. Bennett, *Cree Syllabic Literacy: Cultural Context and Psychological Consequences* (Tilburg, Netherlands: Tilburg University Press, 1991); David L. Schmidt and Murdena Marshall, eds., *Mi'kmaq Hieroglyphic Prayers: Readings in North America's First Indigenous Script* (Halifax, NS: Nimbus Press, 1995); Jarold Ramsey, *Reading the Fire: The Traditional Indian Literatures of America,* rev. ed.

(Seattle: University of Washington Press, 1999); Germaine Warkentin. 'In Search of "the Word of the Other": Aboriginal Sign Systems and the History of the Book in Canada,' *Book History* 2, no. 1 (1999): 1–27; Bruce Greenfield, 'The Mi'kmaq Hieroglyphic Prayer Book: Writing and Christianity in Maritime Canada, 1675–1921,' in *The Language Encounter in the Americas, 1492–1800*, ed. Edward G. Gray and Norman Fiering (New York: Berghahn Books, 2000), 189–211; Hilary E. Wyss, *Writing Indians: Literacy, Christianity, and Native Community in Early America* (Boston: University of Massachusetts Press, 2000); Margaret Bender, *Signs of Cherokee Culture: Sequoyah's Syllabary in Eastern Cherokee Life* (Chapel Hill: University of North Carolina Press, 2002). For a New Zealand perspective consult D.F. McKenzie, 'The Sociology of a Text: Orality, Literacy, and Print in Early New Zealand' [1984] in, *The Book History Reader*, ed. David Finkelstein and Alistair McCleery (London: Routledge, 2002), 189–215.

8   Ruth Finnegan, *Oral Poetry* (Cambridge: Cambridge University Press, 1977); Ruth Finnegan, *Literacy and Orality: Studies on the Technology of Communication* (Oxford: Oxford University Press, 1988); R.W. Niezen, 'Hot Literacy in Cold Societies: A Comparative Study of the Sacred Value of Writing,' *Comparative Studies in Society and History* 33, no. 2 (1991): 225–45; Kenneth George, 'Felling a Story with a New Ax: Writing and Reshaping of Ritual Song Performance in Upland Sulawesi,' *Journal of American Folklore* 103, 407 (1990): 3–24; Brian Street, *Cross-Cultural Approaches to Literacy* (Cambridge: Cambridge University Press, 1993).

9   Fox, *Oral and Literate Culture in England*.

10 For example, Billy Sepass, one of the most prominent lower Fraser River Stó:lō leaders of the late nineteenth and early twentieth century, traced his ancestry through his father back two generations to the Colville region of the Columbia plateau.

11 These journeys and transformations are summarized and contextualized in Sonny McHalsie, David Schaepe, and Keith Carlson, 'Making the World Right through Transformation,' in Keith Thor Carlson with David Shaege, Albert McHalsie, David Smith, Leanna Rhodes, and Collin Duffield, eds., *A Stó:lō-Coast Salish Historical Atlas* (Vancouver, Seattle, Chilliwack: Douglas and McIntyre Press, University of Washington Press, and The Stó:lō Heritage Trust, 2001), 1–2. See also discussions of transformer movements as recorded by Franz Boas in *Indianische Sagen von der nordpacifischen Kuste Americas* (1985), recently translated into English and edited by Randy Bouchard and Dorothy Kennedy, in *Indian Myths and Legends from the North Pacific Coast of America* (Vancouver: Talonbooks, 2002). See also the narratives translated by Charles Hill-Tout in the collection edited by Ralph Maud as *Mainland Halkomelem* (Vancouver: Talonbooks, 1977).

12 See McHalsie et al., 'Making the World Right through Transformation.'

13 Sonny McHalsie, personal communication, May 1999. See also James Teit, *Traditions of the Thompson River Indians of BC*, Memoir no. 6 (Boston and New York: American Folk-Lore Society, 1900).

14 Harry Robinson, *Write It on Your Heart: The Epic World of an Okanagan Storyteller*, comp. and ed. Wendy Wickwire (Vancouver: Talonbooks/Theytus, 1989), 43–6.

15 Bertha Peters in conversation with the author, 20 September 1995.

16 Harry Robinson, *Living by Stories: A Journey of Landscape and Memory*, comp. and ed. Wendy Wickwire (Vancouver: Talonbooks, 2005). All of the following quotations come from a chapter titled 'Coyote Makes a Deal with the King of England,' 64–85.

17 The first documented killing of Okanagan Interior Salish by non-Native newcomers occurred in the early months of the 1858 gold rush, although tensions between Okanagan and HBC employees at Fort Kamloops and Fort Shushwap had periodically grown violent in the years preceding the influx of miners.

18 Harry Robinson in conversation with Wendy Wickwire, audio interview, 20 June 1980, copy in author's possession. Edward Brett is described as humble: 'Not a chief, not a councillor; just a band member,' who quietly made the sojourn to Victoria, and ultimately paid more than $250 of his own money to acquire a copy of the 'Black and White.'

19 Jack R. Goody, *Domestication of the Savage Mind* (Cambridge: Cambridge University Press, 1977); Jack R. Goody, *Interface between the Written and the Oral*, (Cambridge: Cambridge University Press, 1987); Jack R. Goody, *The Power of the Written Tradition* (Washington, DC: Smithsonian Institution Press, 2000).

20 Michael Harbsmeier, 'Early Travels to Europe: Some Remarks on the Magic of Writing,' in *Europe and Its Other: Proceedings of the Essex Conference on the Sociology of Literature*, ed. Francis Barker, Peter Hulme, Margaret Iversen, and Diana Loxley (Colchester: University of Essex, 1985), 72.

21 Patricia Seed, '"Failing to Marvel": Atahualpa's Encounter with the Word,' *Latin American Research Review* 26, no. 1 (1991): 19.

22 Until 2004 Marian Smith's fieldnotes were housed in the archival division of the Royal Anthropological Institute in London, MS 268, unpaginated.

23 Wilson Duff, *The Upper Stalo Indians of the Fraser Valley, British Columbia*. (Victoria: British Columbia Provincial Museum, 1952); Wayne Suttles, 'The Plateau Prophet Dance among the Coast Salish,' *Coast Salish Essays* (Vancouver: Talonbooks, 1987), 152–98.

24 Marian Smith, field notes, box 3:4, no. 2, Royal Anthropological Institute, London.

25 Elizabeth Vibert, '"The Natives Were Strong to Live": Reinterpreting Early-Nineteenth-Century Prophetic Movements in the Columbia Plateau,' *Ethnohistory* 42, no. 2 (1995): 197–229.

26 Stó:lō elder Robert Joe, recorded in Duff, *Upper Stalo*, 122. Also, personal communication with Welsey Sam (Robert Joe's grandson), aged seventy-four in 1993.

27 The anthropologist Wayne Suttles describes Salish myths or legends as being set in 'an age when the world was different, its people were like both humans and animals of the present age, and it was full of dangerous monsters ... [This] age ended when xé'ls [Xá:ls] the Transformer came through the world, transforming monsters and other myth-age beings into rocks and animals, and setting things in order for the people of the present age.' Suttles explains that these stories 'usually told how [a community's] founder [came to find his] winter village or summer camp, where the Transformer gave him technical or ritual knowledge, and where he established special relations with local resources.' Wayne Suttles, 'Central Coast Salish,' *Handbook of the North American Indians*, vol. 7, *The Northwest Coast*, ed. Wayne Suttles (Washington, DC: Smithsonian Institute, 1990), 466.

28 By generally I mean historically. A string of recent scholarly studies of Native legends have afforded them due credit as historical sources, even as they recognize the inherent problems of trying to use indigenous histories the way we use Western historical evidence. See, for example, Jonathan Hill, ed., *Rethinking History and Myth: Indigenous South American Perspectives on the Past* (Urbana: University of Illinois Press, 1988); Wendy Wickwire, 'To See Ourselves as the Other's Other: Nlaka'pamux Contact Narratives,' *Canadian Historical Review* 75, no. 1 (1994): 1–20.

29 In my most recent discussions with fluent Halkomelem speakers, a third category of historical narrative has been discussed called *xelth'it*. This too is translated as 'true history.' The context in which this expression is used suggests that it is probably the word applied to a version of historical narrative that has proven more true than another after a council of historical experts has assessed the merits of two or more competing historical discourses.

30 Wayne Suttles, 'On the Cultural Track of the Sasquatch,' *Coast Salish Essays*, 73–99. Also Wayne Suttles, 'Sasquatch: The Testimony of Tradition,' in *Manlike Monsters on Trial: Early Records and Modern Evidence of Bigfoot, Abominable, Snowman, Sasquatch, and Grendel*, ed. Marjorie M. Halpin and Michael M. Ames, (Vancouver: UBC Press, 1980), 245–54.

31 Personal communication with Wayne Suttles, May 2004.

32 Brian Dippie, *The Vanishing American: White Attitudes & U.S. Indian Policy* (Lawrence: University of Kansas Press. 1982); Jeffery Gould, *To Die in This*

Way: Nicaraguan Indian Communities and the Myth of Mestizaje, 1880–1965 (Durham, NC: Duke University Press, 1998). I am grateful to Jonathan Clapperton for our conversations about the consequences of historical inaccuracies, and for drawing my attention to Jeffery Gould's scholarship.

33 Sally Snyder, 'Skagit Society and Its Existential Basis: An Ethnofolkloristic Reconstruction' (PhD diss., University of Washington, 1964), 21–2.

34 Leslie Spier, *The Prophet Dance of the Northwest and Its Derivatives: The Source of the Ghost Dance, Menasha* (Menasha, WI: George Banta Publishing, 1935); Christopher Miller, *Prophetic Worlds: Indians and Whites on the Columbia Plateau* (Seattle: University of Washington Press, 1985); Vibert, 'The Natives Were Strong to Live.'

35 Bierwert, *Brushed by Cedar*, 74.

36 Elsewhere I have developed this thesis more thoroughly with regard to Stó:lō verbs associated with various expressions of trade and exchange and their relationship to indigenous concepts of spatial distance. Keith Thor Carlson, 'Stó:lō Exchange Dynamics,' *Native Studies Review* 11 (1997): 30–5.

37 James Lenihan to the Hon. Superintendent of Indian Affairs, 7 November 1875, DIA Annual Reports, Sessional papers 1876, Library and Archives Canada.

38 James A. Teit, 'Dream Book of a Stalo Prophet,' Canadian Museum of Civilization, MS VII-G-19M, c. 1882.

39 Crisca Bierwert, *Brushed by Cedar*, 112–13.

PART TWO

Writing It Down

Chapter 3

The Philosopher's Art: Ring Composition and Classification in Plato's *Sophist* and *Hipparchus*

TWYLA GIBSON

With Plato, argued media theorist Marshall McLuhan, the Greeks 'flipped out of the old Homeric world of the bards into this new, rational ... civilized world.'[1] McLuhan and other scholars associated with the foundations of media studies cite Plato's writings as evidence for dating the shift from primary orality to literacy in ancient Greek culture. Further research has demonstrated that the 'great divide' of orality versus literacy is untenable; traditional oral modes of communication persist alongside and into written texts.

This study re-examines Plato's dialogues in light of recent research concerning ring composition, an oral formulaic technique found in Homer. Comparative analysis of two exemplary dialogues – Plato's *Sophist* and *Hipparchus* – shows that these works manifest the ring pattern associated with oral traditional modes of communication. This comparative evidence suggests that the dialogues are transitional compositions, and that Plato's writings represented not a break with the oral tradition but rather its transposition to written texts. I explain the implications of these findings for the interpretation of the history and philosophy communicated in Plato's dialogues, in other ancient oral-derived works, and for the study of oral histories and traditions today.

Dialogue, Oral History, and Tradition

Plato 'straddled the written and oral traditions,' explained McLuhan. A 'representative of the new literate culture of ancient Greece,' he nonetheless 'lived in a double world,' and from this frontier 'translated the tribal encyclopedia of the preceding culture into the written, classified form.'[2] McLuhan's deep interest in the technologies employed by the ancient Greek oral culture to record and classify information inspired his famous adage, 'the medium is the message,' by which he meant that the medium of communication conveys information over and above what appears in the content.[3] His research in ancient communication media had its impetus in the work of scholars associated with the foundations of orality and literacy studies, namely Milman Parry, Albert Lord, Eric Havelock, and Walter J. Ong. These scholars inaugurated an approach to media that still stands in a number of disciplines as the dominant paradigm for understanding the rift between oral and written cultures in the Literate Revolution, and the model upon which the Gutenberg and Electronic Revolutions were built.

McLuhan, Havelock, and Ong compared the formulaic style of Homer's epic poetry with Plato's philosophical prose and found no evidence of formulaic patterning in the dialogues. Since Socrates banishes Homer and 'all the other poets,'[4] and attacks the *rhapsodes* and sophists who were heirs to the Homeric tradition (*Gorgias, Protagoras, Critias, Sophist*), early theorists assumed Plato was rejecting the oral tradition and arguing in favour of literacy. The seeming absence of formulaic modes of communication in Plato's dialogues, along with the attack on poetry and sophistic, led them to the conclusion that 'the relationship between Homeric Greece and philosophy after Plato was not continuous, but disruptive and antagonistic.'[5] The notion of a discontinuity in the tradition was linked to a vision of communication and cognition as forming an evolutionary ladder of progress, with Plato delineating the point at which humanity adopted literacy and ascended to a higher, more 'civilized' rung.[6]

In the years since these pioneering studies in orality and literacy were first published, significant developments in the study of orality, oral history, and tradition have contributed to an understanding of oral traditions as complex information technologies for storing and transmitting history, philosophy, and other cultural information. Evidence from a variety of oral cultures that live today has accumulated, and research from ancient, medieval, and contemporary traditions has demonstrated that the notion of a 'great divide' of orality versus literacy cannot be upheld. In contrast to the assumption of a break between oral and written communication styles, scholars now describe a continuum of expressive forms, from ongoing oral traditions to oral traditions that endure together and in interaction with literate forms, to highly textual compositions that still manifest traces of their roots in orality.

Increased subtlety in our understanding of the various forms of oral and oral-derived literature has led to the development of specialized 'poetics': that is, methods of interpretation 'uniquely tailored to works that emerge from oral tradition.' 'Traditional poetics' identify the rules governing oral traditional techniques for organizing information and uncover the meanings they communicate.[7] In the case of Homer, for example, traditional poetics are employed in addition to more conventional literary approaches to exegesis. Of course, there are many points of overlap between text-based and oral traditional approaches. However, as John Miles Foley has explained, without a dedicated poetics to analyse and interpret the artistic principles underlying oral traditional patterns of communication, the meanings they encode remain 'invisible or inaudible, and the experience of [t]his art is diminished.'[8]

Notwithstanding refinements in our knowledge of oral traditions and the communication styles associated with them, few studies have revisited the Greek philosophical works to test hypotheses concerning Plato in light of more recent evidence concerning oral traditions and traditional poetics.[9] In the main, scholars have continued to interpret Plato exclusively through historical and critical methods of interpretation grounded in concepts of individual authorship and literacy. Looking back at the hypotheses concerning Plato presented by McLuhan, Havelock, and Ong in light of the evidence from subsequent research makes apparent an inconsistency between the theory that Plato 'straddled' the oral and literate traditions and the arguments that he was 'a representative of the new literate culture' marking a 'break' and a 'discontinuity' with Homer's style. Some suppositions about a great division between oral and literate media at the foundation of the field have continued as entrenched assumptions. However, if Plato was a bridge between the written and oral traditions, and 'translated' oral classifications into written form, then we should expect to find in the dialogues evidence of what McLuhan described as 'an interplay between styles.'[10]

This study draws on the recent work of Mary Douglas and others concerning ring composition: the oral formulaic technique governing the overall story pattern of Homer's *Iliad*. Ring composition is a convention that places meaning at the centre of the work, framed on either side by parallel sequences of classifications. Douglas pointed out that ring composition is only now being discovered in ancient texts that have been read for centuries without recognizing their circular structure. If rings are not recognized, the meanings that inhere in them are completely overlooked. She argued that works patterned on ring composition have been misread in the history of interpretation, and she calls for a reassessment of significant antique texts from around the world.[11]

In the decades since the foundations of orality and literacy theory were first laid, several studies in the philosophical literature have confirmed the presence of ring composition in some of Plato's dialogues, including the *Sophist*.[12] However, these studies have not acknowledged the communication significance of these traditional forms by recognizing that they convey certain conventionalized meanings.

McLuhan's axiom 'The medium is the message' suggests that meaning is not communicated by the 'content' of the medium but rather by the interplay of form and content – the 'total configuration.'[13] I look at Plato's medium and message in terms of the following questions: (1) If Plato's dialogues manifest ring composition, the formulaic pattern of organization found in Homer's epic poetry and identified with the ancient Greek oral tradition, what is the significance of this compositional form? (2) Why is the presence of ring composition in the dialogues important for understanding how traditional modes of communication interacted with writing? (3) How does recognition of traditional poetics affect the interpretation of the history and philosophy in these ancient Greek works? (4) Why is the identification in Plato of oral-derived patterns of communication central to an understanding of ancient oral-derived literatures, as well as oral histories, traditions, and even contemporary media that were based on the Greek paradigm?

I argue that Plato's writings are a hybrid medium, combining oral traditional modes of communication with an accomplished literate prose style. I show that reading Plato's writings in light of the poetic conventions practised by the ancient Greek oral poets makes it possible to establish the continuity between the oral style and writing. I explain how oral-derived techniques 'inform' the messages communicated in these works and how reading by way of traditional poetics helps make sense of ambiguities and inconsistencies that cannot be explained by way of more conventional literary and philosophical approaches to interpretation. I argue that concentrating on the content of the dialogues and ignoring the overall form into which that content is contoured has led to a misreading and misunderstanding of the messages communicated by these ancient philosophical works, and explain why our understanding of the history and tradition concerning these texts must be reassessed.

I begin by looking at problems in interpreting the history and philosophy set forth in Plato's dialogues more generally, as well as issues of interpretation that have resisted resolution by way of literary critical and philosophical methods of exegesis. I explain the issues surrounding Aristotle's report of Platonic 'unwritten doctrines' that have led scholars to conclude that Plato had an 'oral teaching' that he expounded to his contemporaries but did not document in the dialogues. These interpretive challenges and issues will then be examined through the case study of the historical information contained in the *Hipparchus*, a dialogue that provides significant information concerning the early history of literacy in ancient Greece. Next, I review the theory about the communicative significance of formulaic patterns in Homer's epic poetry through a history of contributions to the field of orality and literacy studies. The purpose of this discussion is to set forth the poetic principles governing the organization of works with roots in oral tradition and to develop hypotheses about how formulaic techniques would have been affected by alphabetization. A related aim is to explain how expectations of a work are changed by reading the content in light of a ring structure. I then focus on the poetic principles governing ring composition in Plato's dialogues through a case study of the rules and procedures for composing rings presented by explicit statements in Plato's *Sophist*. The *Sophist* is important, I argue, because it provides step-by-step instructions in the principles, procedures, and classifications of the ring structure for the definition of the art or technique (*technē*) of imitation (*mimēsis*), a concept that was central to the analyses of Plato presented by McLuhan, Havelock, and Ong.[14]

In other words, I maintain that the *Sophist* describes and explains the poetic principles that give shape to philosophical prose compositions in the Platonic style. I then use the ring pattern from the *Sophist* as a template for examining a parallel structure in the *Hipparchus*. After that, I explain how attending to oral traditional poetics alters the interpretation of the historical information in the *Hipparchus*, and then generalize these findings to the dialogues as a whole. The assumption of an essential difference between Homer's formulaic style and Plato's philosophical prose was a key component in the development of media studies, the basis for the distinction between orality and literacy itself, and the justification for viewing oral traditions and cultures as less 'rational' and less 'civilized' relative to literate cultures. I end with a discussion of the significance of my findings for the interpretation of the history and philosophy communicated in Plato's dialogues, in other ancient oral-derived works, and for the study of oral histories and traditions today.

I would like to begin, then, by outlining the difficulties involved in interpreting the history and philosophy set forth in Plato's dialogues, difficulties that cannot be resolved by conventional methods of analysis but that may be explained by way of a specialized oral traditional poetics.

Ancient History: Facts, Reliability, and 'Truth'

Historical events significantly shaped the philosophy in Plato (427–347 BCE). The dialogues have been dated to a time of great technological, social, and political change in ancient Greek culture. Plato's writings describe events that can be verified by material remains or by references in other ancient writers, and a number of characters are named after historical figures. Hence, it has often been argued that the dialogues record 'facts' that may be used to reconstruct the history of ancient Greece during this important time. Still, a number of difficulties prevent us from accepting at face value either the history or the philosophy presented in the dialogues; accounts presented in one dialogue often contradict reports of the same individuals and incidents presented in other Platonic books. Moreover, Plato's dialogues are not our only source of information about people, episodes, and ideas that shaped Greek history. Alternative renderings of the same information in works credited to other ancient authors call into question the veracity of some of Plato's accounts.

Significantly, during the time when the dialogues were set down in writing, the Greeks were moving from sole reliance on oral traditional modes of communication to literate methods of preservation and transmission. Thus, Plato's teacher, Socrates (469–399 BCE), did not write. He rejected the written word as a vehicle for conveying the most profound philosophical truths and conducted his philosophy solely through oral conversations.[15] After Socrates was put to death for teaching his views, Plato wrote down the conversations of his teacher as well as the history and traditions he inherited from Socrates and other early predecessors. For these reasons, it has often been assumed that Plato's dialogues are more or less accurate transcripts of real-life oral conversations that took place between Socrates and his contemporaries. When the characters in the dialogues discuss the events surrounding the dictatorship of the Pisistratid regime (560/61–510 BCE), the Peloponnesian War between Athens and Sparta (431–404 BCE), the immediate postwar era, and Socrates' trial and execution, the information in these accounts has been interpreted 'literally.' For example, Mark Munn has argued that these 'unique and significant conditions ... both did away with Socrates and gave rise to a profound desire to express the truth, a desire that shines brightest in the pages of Plato.'[16] However, getting at the 'truth' or the 'facts' concerning the individuals and events discussed in the dialogues is more difficult than Munn allows.

The historical and philosophical information that has come down to us from Plato is embedded in an oral performance medium. In other words, Plato's dialogues are 'plays': dramatized oral conversations between a central character (such as Socrates or a Stranger) and one or more supporting characters. Plato – the author – never presents himself as either a character or a narrator in the dialogues. The debates in Plato's plays typically centre on a search for the correct way to classify the topics and ideas in the 'definitions,' and historical references typically come up during the course of these conversations in order to illustrate particular philosophical ideas. Unfortunately, the texts contain few explicit explanations of the principles of the forms and ideas that serve as the foundation of Plato's philosophy. Instead, at key junctures in the conversations, the characters caution that crucial information has been 'omitted,' 'passed over,' or will not be revealed.[17] Since Plato has no voice in the dialogues, scholars have had difficulty determining what his own views of history and philosophy really were, as distinct from the opinions put forward by the actors in his plays.[18] Moreover, the frequent warnings that important information has been left out raises questions about whether the history and philosophy presented by the characters in the dialogues provides a true and comprehensive picture of Plato's own philosophical teaching.[19]

Since Aristotle was a pupil in the Platonic Academy for more than twenty years and wrote detailed critiques of Plato, scholars have frequently consulted his work for information about Plato's views. However, turning to Aristotle as a way of confirming facts about Plato's genuine teaching only complicates matters. For Aristotle (in the *Metaphysics* and other works) attributes theories to Plato that commentators have been unable to locate in the dialogues.[20] Since Aristotle notes a discrepancy between the doctrines in Plato's written dialogues and in his 'unwritten doctrines,' scholars have concluded that Plato had an 'oral teaching' that he shared with members of the Academy but did not record in his writings.[21] At the very least, the consensus is that the philosophy Plato expounded orally in his lectures was either different from the teaching recorded in the dialogues or contained 'something more' than the history and philosophy documented in his plays.[22]

The Historical Excursus in Plato's *Hipparchus*

Plato's *Hipparchus* provides a case study of the kinds of problems encountered when relying solely on interpretive strategies designed for texts when attempting to use the dialogues to discern Plato's genuine views or information about early Greek history and philosophy more generally. Let us consider some of these problems in more detail.

The *Hipparchus* bears the name of one of the sons of Pisistratus, tyrant of Athens in the sixth-century BCE. Not only is the dialogue a key source of information concerning the tyranny and the various players on the historical scene during this time, but it is also one of the major textual sources for our knowledge concerning the period in Greek history when the technologies of the oral tradition and the phonetic alphabet came together and interacted.

The *Hipparchus* begins with Socrates and a friend embarking on a search for a definition – ostensibly, of greed. The major action in the dialogue involves an attempt to organize and classify a range of ideas concerned with distinguishing the virtuous from those who only imitate virtue. In the midst of the discussion, Socrates introduces his testimony about Hipparchus, the 'eldest and wisest of Pisistratus's sons.'[23] This historical digression is set off from the philosophical debate and framed at both ends by Socrates' declaration that he would never deceive a friend. It is connected to the previous discussion by way of a wise saying that Hipparchus copied and presented as his own.

The historical account takes as its starting point proofs of the wisdom of Hipparchus: he introduced the Homeric poems into Greece and put them in order; he was always accompanied by the poet Simonides, whom he plied with 'plenteous fees and gifts.'[24] All that Hipparchus did, states Socrates, stemmed 'from a wish to educate the citizens because he was noble and good.'[25] He set up figures of Hermes along the roads of the city, and inscribed upon two sides of them pithy sayings that he learned from others, so that the citizens would stop admiring the Delphic aphorisms and consider those of Hipparchus as offering the greater wisdom. Socrates refers to one herm in particular. On the stone that stood on the Steiria road was inscribed, 'Do not deceive a friend.'[26] Socrates then describes how Hipparchus captured the attention of a youth who had been the former lover of Harmodius and a student of Harmodius' friend Aristogeiton. When the ruler, Hipparchus, turned the youth against the two friends, they were so wounded by this dishonour that they murdered Hipparchus. At the end of the excursus, Socrates reassures his companion once again, 'I therefore should never dare, I am sure, to deceive you, who are my friend, or disobey the great Hipparchus.'[27] In response to Socrates' assertion that he is speaking the truth to friends even as he obeys the injunction the tyrant inscribed on the herm, his companion replies, 'You cannot persuade me that you are not deceiving me in your speech – though I cannot tell how you do.'[28] The friend's remark echoes the concern of scholars.

The problems with accepting Socrates' assertions of truth and honesty at face value are many and complex. First, the statements in the *Hipparchus* are at odds with descriptions of the same events and individuals in Plato's *Symposium*.[29] The brief statements in the latter dialogue do not mention Hipparchus or the Pisistratids by name. Even so, the reference to 'those who seized power here in Athens' whose 'reign was brought to an end' by the love and friendship of Harmodius and Aristogeiton leaves little doubt about the identity of the rulers under discussion. In the version of the story in the *Symposium*, the reign of Hipparchus is equated with the rule of 'despots' and 'oppressive' tyrants in other lands. This description stands in marked contrast to the portrayal of the 'noble and good' ruler in the *Hipparchus*. Whereas the ruler in the *Hipparchus* sought to educate Athenian citizens out of a desire to have excellent subjects, the *Symposium* states that it did 'not suit the rulers for their subjects to indulge in high thinking or in staunch friendship.' As a consequence, the 'subjects pursued neither philosophy, love, nor sport' due to their 'servility.'[30] Thus, the historical account in the *Hipparchus* cannot be squared with the descriptions of people and events in the *Symposium*.

Second, the views articulated in the *Hipparchus* differ from positions on the same matters expressed in other dialogues in the Platonic collection. For example, the evidence that Socrates offers in the *Hipparchus* as proofs of the leader's wisdom – the introduction of Homer's poems, the companionship with Simonides, the wise sayings – all appear suspicious. It seems strange that the preservation of Homer's epics would be assigned a positive value, or that the poet Simonides would be deemed a worthy companion. In other dialogues, Socrates leads a sustained and merciless attack against poets, their compositions, and their style, with Homer and Simonides the targets most frequently mentioned by name.[31] The tyrant rewards Simonides with fees and gifts but in other dialogues, those who accept financial remuneration for their teaching are always criticized and classified as Sophists. Hipparchus copied wise sayings from others and presented them as his own, which appears to merit praise in *Hipparchus*, whereas in other dialogues, imitation without knowledge is a form of intellectual pretence that is invariably contrasted with original creation based on knowledge of the forms and their patterns. In the *Republic*, for example, Socrates denounces and then banishes from the ideal state Homer and 'all the other poets [who] effect their narration through imitation,'[32] produce deceptive images that do not conform to 'prescribed patterns,'[33] and entertain their audiences while failing to provide any educational benefit.[34] The friendship with Simonides, too, is suspect. Simonides achieved his reputation through his invention of an 'art of memory' based on creating vivid mental images of the information to be remembered and placing those images in different locations in an imagined background. In Plato's *Greater Hippias* and *Lesser Hippias* (perhaps named for the younger brother of Hipparchus), Socrates pokes fun at the educational use of the memory art, and contrasts it with the superior education offered by 'dialectic.'[35] These discrepancies with descriptions in other dialogues make it hard not to question the historical value of the report in the *Hipparchus*.

Third, versions of the story have come down to us via other ancient authors. These alternative testimonies also contribute to the sense that there is something amiss in the *Hipparchus* account. Reports of the murder of Hipparchus by Harmodius and Aristogeiton occur in Thucydides and in Herodotus.[36] These two renditions are aligned with the version presented in the *Symposium*. Hipparchus and his brother are depicted as despots, and his assassins, Harmodius and Aristogeiton, are celebrated as heroes. Further, Aristophanes noted that Simonides was the first to demand and receive payment for poetry, adding that this practice was new to Greece and caused a great public scandal.[37] Again, these alternative versions of the same story challenge the positive portrayal in the *Hipparchus* of both the ruler and Simonides.

At the same time, interpreters run into problems if they assume that the account of characters and events in the *Hipparchus* is inaccurate, for there are a number of points about which all versions agree. Cicero relates that Homer's *Iliad* and *Odyssey* existed in a scattered, confused state for several centuries until they were 'put in order' by Hipparchus.[38] In the centre of the story about Hipparchus in Herodotus is an account of the arrival of the Phoenician alphabet into Greece.[39] Flavius Josephus confirmed that Homer 'did not leave his poems in writing ... They were clearly remembered and put together later from his songs.'[40] Thus, other records attest that the Homeric epics existed as oral stories before the time of Hipparchus; these accounts associate the tyrant with the introduction, ordering, and preservation of the epics, as well as the early use of the alphabet. In addition, Simonides' association with mnemonics is attested by, among others, Quintilian and Cicero.[41] These other documents substantiate much of the evidence presented in the *Hipparchus*, information that is vital to the reconstruction of the history of Greek literacy.

Perhaps most compelling is that the documentary evidence is supported by material remains. One of the herms set up by Hipparchus still exists.[42] The association of Simonides with mnemonics is documented by an inscription on a marble tablet that has been dated to about 264 BCE.[43] Recently discovered fragments from the fifth and fourth centuries BCE prove that the Sophists were heirs to the tradition started by Simonides.[44] Harmodius and Aristogeiton were historical persons who assassinated Hipparchus, for the Parian Chronicle records that statues were erected in their honour in Athens and also that they had ties to Simonides.[45] So much of the history in Plato's *Hipparchus* is corroborated by material artifacts. However, since so many aspects of the account do not tally with alternative renditions of the story in Plato or in other writers, the problems involved in piecing together an accurate historical picture to establish facts with a degree of certainty are nearly insurmountable.

The report in the *Hipparchus* offers a case study of challenges that plague interpretation of information presented in Plato's dialogues more generally. One solution has been to locate the crux of the problem in the difference between ancient and contemporary understandings of history, reliability, and truth. Historical writing in the ancient world cannot be measured against contemporary criteria. Contemporary historiographers have emphasized that in gauging the reliability of ancient sources, understanding the style is crucial. Historical accounts such as the one in Plato's *Hipparchus* were governed by compositional rules that defined both the ideal practitioner and the ideal audience. As David S. Potter has emphasized, ancient history 'is a form of explanation based upon generally agreed principles for validating the statements used to sustain the argument that it presents even if general agreement about the principles of validation changes through time.'[46] Thus, interpretation of ancient history is contingent on knowledge of the artistic principles governing the style in which the historical information is represented.

The second approach is to view descriptions such as the one in the *Hipparchus* as 'classic' cases of irony, where words are used to express something other than, and especially the opposite of, the literal meaning, so it is left up to hearers and readers to solve 'a kind of riddle' in order to ascertain the genuine message.[47] Since the account in the *Hipparchus* is more or less opposite to other evidence, it could be taken as an example of Socrates' irony. However, the problem with assuming irony in this or any other instance lies in determining with certainty whether Socrates' statements should be taken seriously or whether he is making a joke.[48] Again, knowledge of stylistic principles is imperative.

The third suggestion that has been offered through the centuries is that Plato 'concealed' some of his genuine views so that he would not suffer the same fate as Socrates.[49] According to this reading, Plato would have avoided using the character of Socrates to state his actual thoughts about Hipparchus under the threat of persecution. The problem is that no one who has offered this proposal has been able to explain how to uncover the true teaching. Again, if information presented in a composition is concealed, then knowledge of the stylistic rules used to organization information a prerequisite to any attempt to uncover hidden meanings.

My own position is aligned with all three of these suggestions. I propose that there are links among 'oral' and 'written' technologies in Plato's writings; the political situation in Athens that silenced Socrates and made free speech dangerous, if not lethal; Aristotle's comments concerning Plato's 'unwritten' teaching; and the way in which information is organized and classified in the dialogues. If the hypothesis that Plato was a bridge between the oral and literate worlds is correct – and he was a 'translator' who converted the oral encyclopedia into written classifications, the student of a man put to death for openly expounding his views, and the professor of a private 'oral' teaching that was either more comprehensive, or not the same as, the material recorded in the dialogues – then there may be more going on in the *Hipparchus* than meets the eyes of modern readers who view the dialogues solely through the lens of text-based interpretive strategies.

Traditional Poetics

To explain the hypothesis I am urging, let me now consider the poetic principles governing the organization of information in Homer, focusing especially on ring composition. Identifying the rules underlying ring composition will make it possible to formulate hypotheses about how this oral technique would have interacted with the technology of writing to create a hybrid medium.

In the late 1920s, American classicist Milman Parry pointed to the intricate organizational patterns in Homer's epics and argued that they were aids used by poets living in the ages before the introduction of the phonetic alphabet to remember the epics and recreate them in performance.[50] He reasoned that the epics were too long to memorize verbatim without writing. Instead, oral poets 'sewed together' – *rhapsode* means 'sewer of songs' – 'formulas' (phrases that fit into a given length of verse and dovetailed with those that went before and after) into various combinations to create the overall fabric of the verse. Parry argued that it was difficult for the Homeric poets to make up a new formula that would fit into a section of the verse. To express a new idea, poets had to select an existing formula and model the new one after it, so that the 'storehouse' of formulas was built up by imitation of previous expressions.[51]

Parry's assistant, Albert Bates Lord, expanded the definition of the formula to encompass 'themes,' which he defined as 'groups of *ideas* regularly used in telling a tale in the formulaic style.'[52] Lord highlighted repetitions of series of events, acts, or objects that proceeded from the beginning to the end of the sequence, treating each stage in a nearly identical order. Since the theme is a larger-scale ordering principle, it is 'not restricted, as is the formula, by metrical considerations' so it does not rely on 'exact word-for-word repetition' of expressions.[53] Hence, Lord showed that Homeric themes involved the reiteration of identical sequences of *ideas*.

In the late 1950s, Cedric M. Whitman demonstrated that thematic sequences in Homer's *Iliad* connect into a precise series of episodes (A-B-C-B*-A*, the asterisk marking a repeated element) in the formulaic technique known as ring composition.[54] After the middle of the sequence, the previous order of topics is reiterated in reverse, beginning with the penultimate or final episode of the earlier series, and returning to the topic that served as the starting point (A-B-C-B*-A* or A-B-C-C*-B*-A*).[55] According to Whitman, scenes and larger episodes all have a formal and ideational resemblance through the imitation of a few basic patterns. Variation is achieved through expansion, compression, shading, or modification of the original themes and motifs. Whitman postulated that symmetrical arrangement in serial progression on either side of a midpoint was both an artistic principle 'of the most amazing virtuosity' and a technical device that helped poets remember the order of the events under the stress of performance.

By 500 BCE, the Greeks had developed mnemonic techniques that grew out of the formulaic system of the poetic tradition.[56] One branch of the tradition, argued Frances A. Yates, practised the 'art of memory,' said to have been invented by the poet Simonides and identified with later generations of Sophists. A second branch of the memory tradition, associated with the philosophers, rejected the use of images as useless for memorizing abstract concepts. The philosopher's method, called 'dialectic,' concentrated on dividing the material to be remembered and ordering it into sequences of classifications. This technique is described by Quintilian, who mentions that the connections in the sequence were so well known to those who were 'initiates' of dialectic that nothing could be added to the scheme or omitted without it being obvious to them.[57]

This research on the techniques utilized by the preliterate Greek poets served as the springboard for research on orality and literacy contributed by McLuhan, Havelock, and Ong. Finding no evidence of formulaic patterning in Plato's dialogues, and citing Plato's banishment of the poets and critique of the Sophists, they assumed that Plato was rejecting the formulaic style and the oral mentality.[58] After Plato, they argued, the balance of the tension between the oral and literate mindsets swung in favour of writing.[59]

More recently, John Miles Foley has demonstrated that oral traditional techniques such as ring composition were ancient technologies of representation that acted as file folders to index meanings that signified more than the literal sense of the words in the content of a composition.[60] According to Foley, ring composition functioned as a 'code' referring 'institutionally toward a traditional network of associations' that educated people in the oral culture comprehended but that would go unrecognized by people unfamiliar with the tradition and style. Over the course of two and a half millennia, he argued, both the technologies of the oral traditional style and the meanings they communicated were forgotten as the oral tradition was replaced by writing.

Douglas' recent research relied on Lord's arguments concerning oral memory and Whitman's examination of ring composition in Homer's epics.[61] Observing that the ring convention was probably an oral convention, she noted that 'whatever its pre-literate origins, ring composition has of course been transformed by the advent of writing.' She observed that 'a reader who reads a ring as if it were a straight linear composition will miss the meaning,' and the text will be seriously misconstrued.[62] She described seven rules for identifying a ring:

1 A prologue introduces the theme, the characters, the problem, and anticipates the turning point and the ending.

2 The composition is separated into parallel halves, one moving
   forward (A-B-C) and the other backward, in reverse order (C*-B*-A*).
3 The two halves are separated by a centre, or fulcrum (A-B-C-B*-A*
   or A-B-C-C*-B*-A*).
4 Every classification in the first half is matched to a parallel classification in the second half as mirrored pairs on opposite sides of the
   middle, often indicated by key words or phrases that provide clues
   to analogies.
5 There is 'central loading' at the midpoint, with key words that
   accord with the prologue and ending.
6 The overall ring is internally patterned into smaller rings.
7 A closing signals arrival at the ending by linking it to the starting
   point.[63]

Douglas described how ring composition 'controls meaning, it restricts
what is said, and in doing so it expands meaning along channels it has
dug. Though it never completely escapes ambiguity, writing in a ring
ties meaning into a recognizable, restricting context.'[64]

Having set forth the poetic principles underlying ring composition in
Homer by way of a brief history of contributions to the field of orality
and literacy studies, I turn now to the research that suggests how the
advent of writing and literacy affected this technique.

Toward a Transitional Medium

Just as studies in oral tradition have indicated that the transition from
orality to literacy should be conceived as a continuum rather than as a
great divide, so, too, we should anticipate that transitional compositions – those set down during the modulation from utterance to record
– fall along a spectrum of expressive forms, reflecting 'a complex series
of graduations and transitions existing between the two.'[65] Studies have
shown that oral traditional modes of communication are not simply
abandoned when writing appears on the scene. Expressive language
and poetics endure into texts. Especially in the early stages of the new
medium, meanings continue to be cued by the same techniques that
were used to store and retrieve information orally, even though the performance is no longer live.[66]

When ancient oral compositions were first written down, the tendency
was to record information in the same shape it had taken when it was
preserved by way of oral technologies, so that formulaic structures of

organization were simply documented in writing. Oral compositions did not 'flatten out well on a printed page'; they tended to reveal their roots by displaying inconsistencies and illogicalities where formulas were sewn together, or where information from more than one source was patched into a work.[67] In the Homeric poems, for example, poetic rhythms remain intact and the verse contains a number of inconsistencies. These facts suggest that the epics as they have come down to us preserve in written form what might be called a 'pure formulaic' style (because it would have been difficult to alter the linked phrasing of the verse without doing damage to the poetic rhythm).

As writing became more widespread, the process of composition was liberated from the pressures of extemporized performance. Writing made it possible to read over what had been written, to manipulate traditional forms and subject matter, and to smooth over rough spots where traditional elements were imperfectly stitched together. Over time, there was a shift from the strict economy of expression necessitated by the improvisational style of oral presentation to the more lengthy, prepared, and deliberate style associated with written texts. When an orally shaped composition was edited and revised, the tendency was to elaborate on the original by adding words to make the composition more intricate and sophisticated in structure.[68]

Elaborations led to the development of prose, thought to be a purely written use of language. As details and embellishments were gradually inserted into a traditional composition, formulaic patterns were 'expanded and split by other words.'[69] Additional words and phrases were interspersed among formulaic structures, so that eventually, accretions began to envelop the patterns. The traditional patterns became 'buried in layers of prose' as the basic themes and motifs were expanded, separated, and covered over by later elaborations. Even so, as Havelock had noted, research indicates that in the initial stages of the transition to texts, 'prose at first conformed to the previous rules for the poetic.'[70] Traditional structures remained, embedded as an oral stratum within the prose. In other words, it may be hypothesized that the poetic principles of variation by 'expansion, compression and modification of motifs' described by Whitman continued as the precepts governing the elaborations that went into compositions in the transitional phase, so that the sequential order of topics, themes, and episodes remained the same. To expand the composition, variations and elaborations were inserted *between* the formulas. To compress it, excess verbiage removed so that formulas were pared to the minimum. To vary the work, words were mixed in with the pure formulas or juxtaposed with them. The result would have been a hybrid form that was both oral traditional and literate, but not quite either.

This research indicates that in the early stages of literacy, traditional patterning became *more complex* with the ability to reread, study, refine, insert additions, remove inconsistencies, manipulate material, and perfect traditional forms and subject matter. This is the sort of style we should expect to find in Plato's writings. If Plato translated the tradition into texts, then we should anticipate that the dialogues represent the culmination of the oral style of philosophy, in which traditional patterns became more intricate and exacting through techniques of writing. We should also expect that traditional patterns are embedded in Plato's prose.

Case Studies: Plato's *Sophist* and *Hipparchus*

If the Platonic dialogues are transitional compositions wherein patterns have become 'buried in layers of prose,' then traditional structures will be even more difficult to identify than in works such as Homer's, where formulaic patterns remain undiluted. Even so, if the dialogues are constrained by the same stylistic principles governing ring composition, then it should be possible to compare different works to see if there are consistencies of form, even if the content varies.

Noburu Notomi pointed out that the overall structure of questions in the *Sophist* 'may be regarded as a kind of "ring composition," which is a traditional structural device in Greek literature, or as a "pedimental" composition with the brief argument on dialectic at its top.'[71] Notomi identified ring composition as the principle governing the overall plot in this dialogue. I propose that there are smaller rings within this ring, and that circular patterning governs the organization of information at the thematic level of the dialogue as well. But more importantly, I show that the Socratic definitions are grafted onto the rings so that the sequence of topics in the definition conforms to a circular pattern.

The central character in the *Sophist* is the Stranger, who guides the supporting actors through a number of sequences that make up the different classifications of the definition of art or technique (*technē*). At the end of the dialogue, he presents the branch of the definition designated to imitation or representation (*mimēsis*). He specifies with precision the divisions in this series, and he gives precise directions for allocating ideas to different classes. Moreover, he classifies the art of poets, orators, dramatic actors, writers, Sophists, and other speechmakers within this mimetic sequence. He also deals directly with honesty and deception in discourse.[72] As he marks off the divisions, he acknowledges that he is using the method of 'dialectic' to search for the 'real cleavages among the forms.'[73] He establishes that thinking and discourses are among the most important 'kinds of forms.'[74] Let me underscore then, that these are direct statements indicating that 'Plato's forms' are the underlying principles governing the shape of the discourse in this dialogue. I hypothesize as well that the forms are present as underlying matrixes to the historical and philosophical content in other Platonic works.

I argue that ring composition serves as the framework for ordering the classifications of the definitions in the dialogues. I also contend that the definitions in the philosopher's system of dialectic provide the key ideas (rather than key words, as described by Douglas) that function as cues to the way a discourse corresponds to a definition, and also to the analogies between matched pairs on opposite sides of the middle of a ring. In addition, I posit that the historical and philosophical content is mapped on to this sequential and circular definitional framework. Unlike Homer, whose epics are inextricably linked to the ancient Greek language by formulaic phraseology, Plato is famous for his theory of *ideas*. Ideas are independent of the particular words and phrases used to express them, and so the patterns are obvious even in translation. Indeed, as Lord demonstrated, even in Homer, thematic progressions rely on identical sequences of ideas. Though it appeared to modern readers that Plato never provided a comprehensive discussion of the principles that grounded his system, this example from the *Sophist* shows that the dialogues are exemplars of the forms. Plato presents the rules governing the arrangement of information in this style, both by express statements in the content and implicitly through the underlying forms that give shape to the contours of the content.

I have selected as the template the passages from the *Sophist* that present instructions for the definition of the art of imitation. Comparing the sequential order of the information concerning imitation in the *Sophist* with the serial order of ideas in the passages dealing with the same theme in the *Hipparchus* will make it possible to identify consistencies, and to get a sense of some of the implications communicated by the transitional medium.

In the demonstration that follows, I highlight in Figure 1 the topics and ideas in the ring that underpins the definition of imitation spelled out in the *Sophist*. Though there are some inaccuracies due to translation from

Figure 1: Ring Composition of the Definition of the Art (*Technē*) of Imitation (*Mimēsis*) in Plato's *Sophist* 218b-d; 265a-268c

A **art:** We began by dividing **art** (*technēn*) into acquisitive (which includes education) and productive and ... (218b-d; 265a-b)

B **acquisition:** ... under the **acquisitive** (*ktētikēn*) we had hunting, contention, trafficking, and other kinds ... (265a)

C **production:** ... and two kinds of **production** (*poiētikēn*), divine and human. For **imitation** is a kind of **production** of images ... (265b-c)

D **divine:** Mortal animals, plants, seeds and roots, lifeless bodies beneath earth, elements of nature, these are **divine** (*theion*) art (265b-266c).

E **human:** ... and the things made out of them by **man** are works of **human** (*anthrōpinon*) art (265e-266c).

F **original:** We are **original** (*autopoiētikon*) offspring of divine work, human art in building makes an actual house (266b-c)

G **image-making:** these are attended by **images** (*eidōlourgikēs*), one likenesses, the other semblances. Dreams or ... (266b-c)

H **likeness-making:** reflections (reversed [*enantian*] images) are divine **likenesses** (*eikastikon*), painting is a manmade dream ... (266b-c)

I **semblance-making:** **semblances** (*phantastikon*) called shadows are divine. Images have kind of falseness (266b-c).

J **tools:** And there is the semblance produced by **tools** (*organōn*) and another sort where the ... (267a)

K **mimicry:** ... producer takes his own person as an instrument to **mimic** (*mimētikon*) traits or speech. Mimicry is of two sorts (267a-b)

L **knows:** ... Some **know** (*gignōskōntos*) the thing they impersonate and many ... (267b)

M **does not know:** have **no knowledge** (*agnoounta*) but mimic it in words and actions; they have opinions that mimic virtue (267c).

N **simple:** And the **simple-minded** (*euēthēs*) sort who imagines what he believes is knowledge and the opposite type ... (267c-268a)

O **ignorant, ironic** (*eirōnikon*): ... who pretends to know but is ignorant (*agnoei*). Or is it the opposite? (267c-268a)

P **public:** One dissembles **publicly** (*dēmosia*) in long **speeches** (*logois*) before a large assembly and the other ... (268a-b)

Q **private:** ... uses short **speeches** (*logois*) in **private** (*idia*), forcing others to **contradict** (*enantiologein*) themselves (268b)

R **statesman:** Shall we identify the long-winded with the **statesman** (*politikon*) or demagogue? (268b)

S **demagogue:** The **demagogue** (*dēmologikon*). Shall we call the other ... (268b).

T **wise man:** ... **wise** man (*sophon*) or **sophist** (*sophistikon*)? Not **wise** (*sophon*) but as ... (268b-c)

U **sophist:** ... **a mimic of the wise** (*sophou*) he is the **true sophist** (*sophistēn*) (268b-c).

V Shall we collect all the elements of this description from the end to the beginning? (268c)

U* **sophist:** [ ]

T* **wise man:** [ ]

S* **demagogue:** [ ]

R* **statesman:** [ ]

Q* **private:** The kind that says the opposite (*enantiopoiologikēs*) of what is and makes contradictions ... (268c)

P* **public:** [ ]

O* **ignorant, ironic** ... of the **ironic** (*eirōnikou*) part ... (268c-d)

N* **simple:** [ ]

M* **does not know:** ... of the art of opinion (*doxastikēs*) ... (268c-d)

L* **knows:** [ ]

K* **mimicry:** ... of mimicry (*mimētikon*) ... (268c-d)

J* **tools:** [ ]

I* **semblance-making:** ... of the **semblance**-making (*phantastikou*) breed ... (268c-d)

H* **likeness-making:** [ ]

G* **image-making:** ... derived from **image**-making (*eidōlopoiikēs*), distinguished as a portion ... (268d)

F* **original:** [ ]

E* **human:** ... of **human** (*anthrōpinon*) ... (268d)

D* **divine:** ... not **divine** (*theion*), and of the **conjuring** part ... (268d)

C* **production** (*poiēseōs*): ... that presents a shadow play of words—such is the lineage of the true Sophist (*sophistēn*) (268d)

B* **acquisition:** [ ]

A* **art:** [ ]

Figure 2: Ring Composition of the Definition of the Art (*Technē*) of imitation (*Mimēsis*) in Plato's *Hipparchus* 228a–229e

U **sophist:** you are *attempting to deceive me*, deliberately saying the *opposite* (*enantia*) of what was just agreed (228a).

T   **wise man:** No, by Zeus, Socrates! Quite the opposite ... (228a).

S   **demagogue:** ... it is you who are *deceiving me* ... (228a).

R   **statesman:** ... by *moving upward and downward* ... (228a)

Q   **public:** ... in your speech (*logois*) and I do not know by which way you are twisting them together! (228a).

P   **private:** *Hush!* It would not be right of me to not obey a good and wise (*sophō*) man. Who is that? (228b)

O   **ignorant:** *Hipparchus*, an example of his wisdom (*sophias*): he brought the works of *Homer* to this land (228b)

N   **simple:** He always kept *Simonides* of Ceos around him by supplying him with large fees and gifts (228c).

M   **does not know:** He did these things *with a view to educating the citizens* (228c).

L   **knows:** When people *in the city had been educated* ... he proceeded with those from the country as well (228d).

K   **mimicry:** After *selecting his own wise* (*sophias*) *lore, both learned from others and found out for himself* ... (228d)

J   **tools:** ... what he thought were the wisest (*sophōtata*), he put these into elegiac verse and *inscribed them* ... (228d)

I   **semblance:** ... on the *Herms* ... (228d)

H   **likeness:** ... *as verses of his own* ... (228d)

G   **image:** ... and as examples of *his wisdom* ... (*sophias*) (228d)

F   **original:** ... so that in the *first place* ... (228e)

E   **human:** ... *his people would not admire* ... (228e)

D   **divine:** ... those wise (*sopha*) Delphic inscriptions, 'Know Thyself,' and 'Nothing in Excess' ... (228e)

C   **production:** ... but would instead regard as wise (*sophias*) the *words of Hipparchus* (228e)

B   **acquisition:** and second, *acquire a taste for his wisdom* (*sophias*), and *complete their education* (228e)

A   **art:** There are two sides to the *inscriptions*: on the left side of each Herm ... (229a)

B*   **acquisition:** [   ]

C*   **production:** ... it is inscribed that ... (229a)

D*   **divine:** ... the *god* says that the Herm stands in the middle of the city or the deme ... (229a)

E*   **human:** ... while on the right side it says: This is a monument of *Hipparchus* ... (229a)

F*   **original:** [   ]

G*   **image:** [   ]

H*   **likeness:** [   ]

I*   **semblance:** ... 'walk with justice in mind' ... (229a)

J*   **tools:** There are other fine *inscriptions* ... (229a)

K*   **mimicry:** ... of *his poetry on other figures* of Hermes. One says: 'Do not deceive a friend' (229b).

L*   **knows:** So since I am your friend, *I would not dare to deceive you* ... (229b)

M*   **does not know:** and disobey the great man ... (229b)

N*   **simple:** ... after his death, the *Athenians* were ruled ... (229b)

O*   **ignorant:** ... under the tyranny of his brother *Hippias* for three years ... (229b)

P*   **public:** ... and *you might have heard* that it was only in these three years that there was tyranny in Athens ... (229b)

Q*   **private:** In fact, *the subtler sort of people* say that Hipparchus's death came about ... (229b)

R*   **statesman:** ... because *Harmodius* had become the favorite of *Aristogeiton* and had been educated by him (229c)

S*   **demagogue:** ... and they killed *Hipparchus* (229d).

T*   **wise man:** Well then Socrates, it seems likely that either you do not regard me as your friend, or if you do ... (229d)

U*   **sophist:** ... that you do not obey *Hipparchus* (229e).

the Greek, the ring and the classifications are still observable. Figure 1 will then serve as a template for comparison with Figure 2, which shows how the sequence of classifications in the *Sophist* provides a latent contour to the historical excursus dealing with imitation in the *Hipparchus*. In both Figure 1 and 2, I label each classification (A-B-C-C*-B*-A*) and emphasize in bold the main idea for each topic in the series. Separated from the main idea by a colon is an edited quotation that establishes the divisions that separate the classifications, as well as some of the ideas stored in each place in the sequence.[75] When there are no explicit statements in the discourse that deal with the topics in a place in the series, I indicate these silences by way of square brackets [ ]. Again, Figure 1 is the template of the series of classifications in the ring composition in the *Sophist*, and Figure 2 shows how the classifications in the ring are manifest in a shortened, abstract version of the full discourse in the *Hipparchus*. These two figures can then be compared with Table 1, which sets forth the full text of this passage in the *Hipparchus*, showing how two strands of the *same sequence* (i.e., the sequence for the definition of *mimēsis*, or imitation) are 'twisted' together (as the dialogue describes) to create the chain of the discourse. In Table 1, I use three columns to represent how the two series are interwoven in the full text of the discourse in the *Hipparchus* passage. The left column uses bold for the sequence that moves in forward progression (A-B-C); the right column uses italics for the second, inverted sequence (C-B-A*-B*-C*). In the centre column, which sets forth the entire passage, bold and italic are used to indicate key words or phrases in the discourse that match the sequences in the classifications for *mimēsis*. Bold italics indicate the links when two strands overlap and connect at certain points.

The occurrence in the *Hipparchus* of the ideas from the series of classifications for imitation described by explicit statements in the *Sophist* – with so many parts in the same order (straightforward in the bold type ring, A-B-C, and in inverted order in the second, italicized ring, C-B-A*-B*-C*) – is unlikely to be random or accidental. The organization of information in both dialogues tallies with the rules governing ring composition described by Whitman and Douglas:

1 Both dialogues contain a prologue, the first of Douglas' seven criteria. The *Hipparchus,* for example, introduces the characters, announces the themes of greed versus virtuous action, and sets forth the problem of truth and deception in speech and in writing.
2 Both compositions are divided into parallel halves, one moving 'downward' from the starting point A-B-C and the other moving

Table 1

Occurrence in Plato's *Hipparchus* of Two Interwoven Sequences of the Definition of the Art (*Technē*) of Imitation (*Mimēsis*) Established in Plato's *Sophist*.

Definition of Imitation Moving in Downward Progression (A-B-C)	Plato's *Hipparchus* 228a–9e	Definition of Imitation in Upward and Downward Progression (C-B-A*-B*-C*)
	Socrates. Look, you are *attempting to deceive* me deliberately, saying the *opposite* of what was just agreed (228a)	sophist (mimics the wise)
	Friend. No, by Zeus, *Socrates*, but it is you who are *deceiving me* by moving *upward and downward* in your *speech (logois)*, and I do not know by which way you are twisting them together!	wise man demagogue, statesman public
	Soc. *Hush*! It would not be right of me to not obey a good and wise (*sophō*) man.	private
	Fr. Who is that? What are you talking about? (228b)	
	Soc. I mean my and your fellow-citizen, Pisistratus's son *Hipparchus* of Philaïdae, who was the eldest and wisest (*sophōtatos*) of **Pisistratus's children**. In addition to the many fine deeds which serve as examples of his wisdom (*sophias*), it was he who first brought the *works of Homer* to this land, and compelled the *rhapsodes* at the Panathenaea to recite them in relay, one man following on another, as they still do now (228c). He also sent a fifty-oared ship for Anacreon of Teos, and brought him to the city. He always kept *Simonides of Ceos* around by him by supplying him with large fees and gifts. He did these things with a view *to educating the citizens*, in order that he might have subjects of the highest excellence; for he thought it was not right to begrudge wisdom (*sophias*) to anyone, so noble and good was he (228c). And *when*	ignorant
		simple-minded
		does not know

art, acquisition
production, divine
human, original
image
likeness

semblance

tools
mimicry

knows

does not know

simple

ignorant

public

his people in the city had been educated and were admiring him for his wisdom (*sophia*), he proceeded with the **design** of **educating** the **people** from the country as well. He set up **figures of Hermes** along the roads in the middle of the city and each deme; and then, after **selecting from** *his own wise (sophias) lore*, both *learned from others* and **found out for himself, what he thought were the wisest (*sophōtata*), he put into elegiac verse** and *inscribed them on the Herms as verses of his own* and as *examples of his wisdom (sophias)* (228e) so that in the *first* place, his *people* would not admire those wise (*sopha*) *Delphic inscriptions, '***Know Thyself*' and '*Nothing in Excess*,' and the other sayings of this sort, but would instead regard as *wise (sophias)* the *words of Hipparchus*; and second, he did this so that when passing upward and downward, they would *read his words* and **acquire a taste for his** *wisdom (sophias),* **and would come from the country to complete their education** (229a). There are two sides to the *inscriptions*: on the left side of each *Herm*, it is inscribed that *the god* says that the *Herm* stands in the middle of the city or the deme, while on the right side it says: 'This is a monument of *Hipparchus*: walk with justice in mind.' There are many other fine *inscriptions* of his *poetry* on other *figures of Hermes*. One in particular, on the Steiria road, says: 'This is a monument of Hipparchus: *do not deceive* a friend' (229b). *So, since I am your friend, I would not dare to deceive you and* **disobey the great man**. After his death, the *Athenians* were ruled under tyranny by his brother, *Hippias*, for three years, and **you might have**

knows

mimicry

tools, semblance
likeness
image
original
human
divine

production

acquisition

art, [acquisition]
production, divine

human, [original]
[image], [likeness]
semblance, tools
mimicry

knows

does not know
simple-minded
ignorant

private	*heard from all of those of earlier times*, that it was only in these three years that there was tyranny in Athens, and that at all other times the	*public*
statesman	Athenians lived as when **Cronos was**	
	King. And *the subtler sort of people*	*private*
demagogue	say that **Hipparchus's** death did not come about in *the way that the common people think* – that it was because his sister was dishonoured in carrying the basket, for that is silly	
	– but because **Harmodius** had	*statesman*
	become the favorite of **Aristogeiton** and was educated by him. *Aristo-geiton* also prided himself on educating this fellow, and he regarded **Hipparchus** as an antagonist. At that time, Harmodius happened to be a lover of one of the handsome and noble men of that time; they do say his name, but I cannot remember it (229d). Well, for a while this youth admired both Harmodius and Aristogeiton as *wise (sophous) men*, but after associating with *Hipparchus*, he	
	despised them, and they were so hurt by this dishonour that they killed *Hipparchus* (229e)	*demagogue*
wise man	Well then **Socrates**, it seems likely that either you do not regard me as your friend, or if you do, that you do	*wise man*
sophist (mimics the wise)	not obey **Hipparchus**. You cannot persuade me that you are not deceiving me in your speech – though I cannot tell how you do it.	*sophist (mimics the wise)*

'upward' and then 'downward' in inverted order C-B-A-A*-B*-C*, satisfying the second criterion. Whereas the thematic sequence in the *Sophist* follows the pattern A-B-C*B*-A*, the *Hipparchus* 'twists' the sequence in the opposite direction, C-B-A-A*-B*-C* (represented in italics in the right hand column), and contains within it a second series A-B-C (represented in bold).

3 In both dialogues, the two halves are separated by a centrepiece, the third criterion. The *Sophist* announces the turning point at the 'collection' at V; the *Hipparchus* turns at U.

4 The rings in the two dialogues are ordered so that the classes in the initial sequence offer clues to like meanings in corresponding places in the reverse order series, meeting the fourth criterion. Thus Hipparchus (the so-called 'great man') is classed as **ignorant** in the initial series just like his brother, Hippias, in the parallel class on the opposite side of the ring. Socrates is a 'wise man' at both B and B*. Simonides is slotted into the **simple-minded** class in the first half of the inverted sequence (perhaps for inventing a silly 'memory art,' a mere imitation of dialectic, which 'he believes is knowledge'), just as the *Athenians* in the second half are classed as **simple-minded** (perhaps childlike, naïve, or uneducated). Notice the classification for **mimicry,** described in the *Sophist* as the 'producer who takes his own person as an instrument to mimic traits or speech,' and in the reverse sequence simply as **'mimicry,'** has a parallel in the same place, both in the downward progression and in the first half of the inverted *Hipparchus* ring as 'selecting his own wise lore, both learned from others and found out for himself'; and in the second half of the inverted ring as 'he put into elegiac verse and inscribed them on the Herms as verses of his own.' The implication is that no matter how you cut it, Hipparchus is an **imitator** of a just man and a hypocrite of the worst sort. Further, both the *Sophist* and the *Hipparchus* have formal and ideational resemblances through the imitation of the basic pattern for imitation. Variations expand, compress, shade, or alter the same motifs. Thus, the **private** class in the *Sophist*, described as using 'short arguments in **private,** forcing others to **contradict** themselves,' provides clues to that class on both sides of the ring in the *Hipparchus*. It seems that Socrates shapes his short *private* talk so that if his friend is one of 'the subtler sorts of people,' he will know that Hipparchus' death was not caused by the reasons most frequently offered. The ruler showed no respect for friendship when he deceived the youth into turning against his friend and former lover. Socrates exposes this contradiction between Hipparchus' actions and the wisdom and sincerity he presents to the **public.** The ruler, classed as a **demagogue,** was justly executed by Harmodius and Aristogeiton, who are indexed as **statesmen.**

5 To continue, there is 'central loading' at the pivot, the fifth criterion. This principle is easy to see in the full text of the *Hipparchus* above, where the centre presents a very condensed kernel of the story.

6 Further, in the *Hipparchus*, the inverted ring (in italics) contains within it a second, half ring (in bold), meeting the sixth criterion. If

there are doubts about the interpretation of the first ring, the second ring confirms and locks in the message via an alternative route even as it adds further dimensions of meaning. Thus, Cronus is a **statesman** ruler, contrasted to Hipparchus the **demagogue.**

7 Finally, the endings in both dialogues return full circle to the classification that served as the starting point, the seventh criterion. The *Sophist* ends and begins with the notion of **art.** The *Hipparchus* ends by classifying Hipparchus as a **sophist** and corresponds with the denial of deception in the prologue. Thus, the compositional structure in the *Hipparchus* satisfies all seven criteria established by Douglas. The *Sophist* in my presentation conforms to six of the seven rules, as I have diagrammed only the central ring in that work.

The definition from the ring composition in the *Sophist* informs the historical content in the *Hipparchus*. Superimposing the template of the definition from the *Sophist* over top of the excursus in the *Hipparchus* makes it easier to see how the classifications for imitation are present as an 'invisible and inaudible' background. In describing the sons of Pisistratus, Socrates has relied on the ring and the meanings connoted by the definition to 'twist' the implicit meaning into the *opposite* of what he says by way of explicit statements. Receptive listeners and readers, 'the subtler sort of people,' get the message that **Hipparchus** is an **ignorant,** insincere, **sophist** who **deceives** the **simple-minded** citizens with his 'air of knowledge' and virtue. The dialogue plays on opposites and mirror images, using the many variants of wisdom and **wise** man to emphasize the difference between the man who is genuinely **wise** (Socrates) and the opposite sort, the pseudo-**wise** man (Hipparchus). The 'wise lore' of Hipparchus is 'learned from others,' and he passes off these imitations as **original** wisdom of his own. **Hipparchus** is not a **wise man.** He is an **imitation** of a **wise man.**

By contrast, Socrates truly *is* a **wise** and virtuous man. His **knowledge** of the forms is genuine and not simply an 'air of **knowledge.'** He does not 'effect his narration through imitation' of others or use **images** to deceive the **simple-minded** into thinking that he **knows** the forms. His discourses are **original** representations pure and **simple** that conform to the 'prescribed pattern' for the traditional form of the definition of **imitation.** He uses the method of dialectic to deceive only those who **do not know** these patterns but pretend that they do. It is precisely because he **knows** the forms that he is able to prevaricate. He does not express his genuine views explicitly in the content of his statements.

However, the outline of the content remains true to form. By casting his words in the mould of the traditional pattern, he is able to tell the truth to friends who **know** the forms and can decode his message. His command of the dialectical art makes it possible for him to 'walk with justice in mind' and to avoid deceiving his friend, even as he takes care not to leave himself open to the reprisals of an oppressive political regime. Socrates entertains the audience and at the same time provides an educational benefit, both through the example of his own person and by the 'amazing virtuosity' he displays in the way he shapes his speech. His friend's statement that 'you cannot persuade me that you are not deceiving me – though I cannot tell how you do it' is a cue to those familiar with the traditional medium that Socrates *has* contrived to tell the truth in his talk (though the friend 'cannot tell us how').

Plato's Dialogues, Ring Composition, History, and Oral Tradition

Four questions served as the focus of this investigation. Having examined how the classifications for imitation in the ring composition inform the historical and philosophical content in two exemplary dialogues, we are now in a position to offer answers to them.

To the first question – What is the significance of ring composition in Plato? – the answer is that the sequences of divisions called 'definitions' and explained by overt statements in Plato's *Sophist* are thematic progressions that map onto rings, the compositional pattern found in Homer's poetry and identified with the oral tradition. The passages in the *Sophist* and *Hipparchus* are both organized in circles, and moreover, the sequence of ideas in the *Hipparchus* corresponds point by point to the series of ideas in the classifications in the *Sophist's* definition. Thus the ideas in the classifications in the definition for imitation *informs* the content in both dialogues and provides the crucial framework for analysis.

In addition, diagramming the ring in the *Sophist* shows how certain links in the chain are passed over or omitted in the reverse order series, represented above as [ ]. Quintilian asserted that the connections in the system of dialectic were so obvious to those who were initiates of this art that nothing could be added or left out without it being evident to them. Thus, the unwritten parts of the structure can be figured out by initiates (friends familiar with the subtle rules of dialectic) as a kind of riddle, based on the parts of the structure that are mentioned explicitly, in tandem with a knowledge of oral traditional techniques of composition. In other words the unwritten Platonic teaching must be produced by those who know the sequence well enough to identify the silences in the framework and then use the poetics of dialectic to reason out the missing pieces. Similarly, when Socrates in the *Hipparchus* passes over in silence all the classifications pertaining to **human production** of **original images** and **likenesses** and moves directly to **semblances**, readers and listeners educated in dialectic would have detected these absences, based on their understanding of the 'total configuration' and the 'interplay' between the form and the content in his composition.

In terms of the second question – Why is the presence of ring composition in the dialogues important for understanding how traditional modes of communication interacted with writing? – the two case studies show Plato's dialogues as having characteristics that scholars have identified with transitional compositions. Readers are invited to set the *Sophist* ring alongside the full text in any standard translation of Plato. The complete historical excursus from the *Hipparchus* was presented in the preceding section, along with the structure of the rings. Comparison of the rings with the complete texts in both examples should make it clear how the words in the ring are a kind of pared-down essence of the definition and the argument, and how this essence is embedded within the more lengthy and elaborate full text of the prose. Whereas the full text is more detailed and qualified, the composition mapped on to the ring shows a strict economy of expression. Notice as well how intermediary statements in the full text have been inserted between the divisions of the classifications through techniques of 'expansion, compression, and modification of motifs.' The order of the classes and the ring composition that binds them remain stable, even though details have been added into the categories in the full text. In other words, the classifications have been 'expanded and split by other words,' so that the full text is more complex and wordy. This research suggests that traditional patterning in the early stages of literacy became *more complex* with the ability to document, change material, make corrections, and refine traditional forms and subject matter. These two case studies support these findings, and suggest that Plato's dialogues represent the culmination and perfection of the traditional style of philosophy made possible by writing.

To the third question – How does recognition of traditional poetics affect the interpretation of history and philosophy in these ancient Greek works? – the *Sophist* and *Hipparchus* provide graphic illustration of the serious misunderstanding that results from attempting to read the historical and philosophical information in works composed in a traditional style 'as if they were straight linear compositions,' as Douglas observes, and by way of exegetical strategies designed for texts. Ancient ways of understanding history, reliability, and truth were not the same as current standards for authenticating information. Determining the veracity of the information communicated in these ancient texts involves recognizing the stylistic rules the ancients used to validate statements and arguments. Knowledge of the principles of the style makes it possible to cut through ambiguous and ironic statements. Even when information has been hidden or is not presented by express statements, it may inhere in a composition, protected by what Douglas calls 'rules of silence.'[76] Knowledge of those stylistic rules is crucial to uncovering hidden meanings. In a civilization in transition from an oral to a literate culture especially, there is often a lingering suspicion of written words not supported by voice, body language, and physical context. Douglas wonders whether techniques that require a great deal from readers, such as ring composition, might have been utilized to make up for the absence of these physical cues for authenticating meanings in order to protect taboos and secrets, 'control the young, and keep foreigners out.'[77] In all cases, understanding the medium is a precondition to understanding the message.

Recognizing the exegetical function of ring composition makes it possible to align the information in the historical excursus in the *Hipparchus* with the accounts of the same events and people in the other dialogues. The history can now be reconciled with the *Symposium*.[78] Hipparchus was a **demagogue**, 'despot,' and a mere **semblance** of the **wise** man in both instances, and the Athenian citizens were poorly educated. The introduction of Homer's poems was classed under **ignorance**, the friendship with Simonides under **simple-minded**, the 'wise sayings' under **mimicry**. Reading in light of the *Sophist* template makes it apparent that the proofs of the ruler's **wisdom** were really proofs of his **ignorance**, the 'wise' lore' on his inscriptions were not **art** but pseudo-art, the **productions** of a **demagogue** 'who had **no knowledge** of virtue but only **mimicked** it in words and actions.' The definition makes it clear that Hipparchus and those in power who came after him had no knowledge of the forms and their patterns; otherwise, they would have understood what Socrates was really saying. Socrates *is* 'playing a joke' and speaking in 'riddles,' and the joke is on all those who have pretensions to knowledge of dialectic.

Moreover, reading the excursus in light of the master pattern for imitation from the *Sophist* makes the history in the *Hipparchus* tally with information presented in the *Republic,* in which Socrates decries all imitators who 'produce deceptive images that do not conform to prescribed patterns.' Similarly, Simonides' **simple-minded** invention of the 'art of memory' comes into accord with the statements in Plato's *Greater Hippias* and *Lesser Hippias,* in which Socrates scoffed at the use of the memory art for educational purposes and contrasted it with the superior education offered by 'dialectic.'

What is more, the classifications of the definition for imitation help to verify the historical information in the *Hipparchus* by bringing it into line with descriptions of these peoples and events in other ancient authors. The *Hipparchus* account can now be rationalized with the reports of the slaying of the ruler by Harmodius and Aristogeiton presented in Thucydides and Herodotus. According to the definition, Hipparchus and his brother were classed as a pair of **ignorant** 'despotic rulers,' and Harmodius and Aristogeiton were celebrated as **statesmen** and heroes. The fees and gifts Hipparchus gives Simonides now fit in with the account of the poet's scandalous demands for payment in Aristophanes. Reading the *Hipparchus* in light of the template of the ring from the *Sophist* virtually eliminates the discrepancies with information in other dialogues and ancient works, thereby clearly establishing its historical value. Additionally, recognizing traditional patterning in Plato sheds new light on Aristotle's comments concerning Plato's 'unwritten teaching,' and holds out the potential for resolving issues that have puzzled scholars for centuries.

The significance of this traditional style for understanding the history and philosophy communicated in ancient compositions, as these case studies have shown, is that recognition of traditional poetics makes it possible to clarify a number of challenging issues of interpretation. Listeners and readers need to look beyond the literal meaning on the surface to the traditional forms that serve as the stable background. Critical strategies that focus exclusively on the historical and philosophical content while ignoring the overall form will be incomplete, if not misguided.

McLuhan, Havelock, and Ong took the banishment of the poets and attack on the Sophists as evidence that Plato was dismissing the oral tradition, its communication technologies, and its modes of cognition. It is now clear that this evidence was susceptible to other readings. Yates identified two different strands of the Greek tradition. The strand that utilized the 'art of memory' was identified with Simonides and other poets and, later, with the Sophists. The strand that employed dialectic was associated with the philosophers, who declined to use the trivial images of the memory art. When Socrates banished the poets for not ordering their stories in correct patterns, he was probably not rejecting the oral mindset so much as he was criticizing the poets for imitating and regurgitating formulas and patterns of composition without any genuine knowledge of the forms and ideas. When he made fun of the Sophists for their use of images, he was probably objecting to the way these ostensible teachers of wisdom used as memory aids mental pictures that cluttered the mind with images bearing little relation to the actual items to be remembered and were useless for abstract ideas. In this reading, Plato's Socrates was denouncing the poets and Sophists in favour of *a different branch of the tradition,* not because he was advocating writing and literacy.

In contrast to either the formulaic phraseology used by the poets or the art of memory employed by the Sophists, the philosopher's art must have been a more accurate and efficient system for storing and retrieving information, and especially for the creation of new ideas. Parry has argued that in Homeric verse, creating a new formula was a challenge due to the restrictions of rhythm and verse. The poet had to choose an existing phrase as the pattern for a new one, so that adding new ideas to the storehouse of stock phrases was accomplished by *imitation of original* expressions. That inconsistencies and poetic rhythms still exist in Homer is evidence of how hard it was to make changes and additions without damaging the verse. The art of memory entailed creating mental images for the material to be remembered, but these images would have been inaccurate representations. The case studies of the *Sophist* and *Hipparchus* suggest that the philosopher's art was based on fixed taxonomies of classifications ordered into rings that served as frames of reference for distinguishing and organizing ideas. Ideas were deposited in different places in between the divisions among the classifications in a definition. So a new idea could be added to the collection of notions gathered together in any given category in a definition. To create a discourse using Plato's forms, philosophers would improvise as they went along by drawing the most appropriate idea from among the different notions assembled under each class, and moving from one classification to the next in the sequence, they would shape new conceptions as they went along during the course of a philosophical performance. Thus, in comparison with formulas and the art of memory, the philosopher's art would have provided a much more flexible and versatile system for giving expression to new and different thoughts.

In terms of the fourth question – What is the significance of these conventionalized patterns for understanding ancient literatures, as well as oral histories, traditions, and even contemporary media? – the identification in Plato of the oral formulaic techniques that convey inherent meanings has implications for a number of disciplines that have been influenced by media studies – and for orality and literacy studies in particular. The postulation of an essential difference between Homer's verse and the style of Plato's prose was central to the development of media studies, the basis of the distinction between 'orality and literacy,' and the evidence for hypothesizing the Gutenberg and Electronic Revolutions as analogues to the Literate Revolution.

Viewing Plato as marking a decisive move 'out of' the mentality associated with the Greek oral tradition to a new, more 'rational,' and 'civilized,' indeed superior, stage of communication is a major component in the intellectual scaffolding that has and continues to justify the wholesale destruction of the languages and traditions of oral societies around the world.[79] So long as Plato's dialogues are seen as delineating a progression to a more advanced stage in communication and culture – rather than as a translation *from one kind of medium into another* – our interpretations of ancient history and philosophy will inevitably view the language and traditions of oral cultures as relatively backward and inferior in an evolutionary scheme of value. Observers have pointed to numerous examples of how literate societies have used the written word to dominate and control oral cultures. J. Edward Chamberlin, for example, described how Canadian Aboriginal people were denied property rights and status as a culture and a people because they possessed no form of written language. Douglas underscored that 'once literacy begins to be wide-spread, it changes the whole basis for social life by redistributing power in favor of the literate.'[80]

The Platonic texts have had a profound influence on the history of ideas and played a key role in the formation of current media theory. As Alfred North Whitehead famously stated, the history of the Western tradition 'consists of a series of footnotes to Plato.'[81] If Plato's dialogues are hybrids of oral and written styles, constructed by way of rules and conventions encoding messages that have not been accurately decoded before, then a reassessment will bring new information to our understanding of ancient history and philosophy. Such a re-evaluation of Plato's role in the Literate Revolution has the potential to bring positive change to the way we understand and value oral cultures and traditions, both ancient and contemporary.

NOTES

1 Marshall McLuhan, *Understanding Me: Lectures and Interviews*, ed. Stephanie McLuhan and David Staines (Toronto: McClelland and Stewart, 2003), 227.
2 Ibid., 125.
3 Marshall McLuhan, *Understanding Media: The Extensions of Man* (New York: McGraw-Hill, 1964), 26; McLuhan, *Understanding Me*, 116–17.
4 Plato, *Republic* 379a, 393c, 398b, 608.
5 According to Walter Ong, 'Plato's relationship to orality was thoroughly ambiguous. On the one hand, in the *Phaedrus* and the *Seventh Letter* he denigrated writing in favor of oral speech. On the other hand, when in his *Republic*, he banished the poets, he did so, as Havelock shows, because they stood for the old oral, mnemonic world. Paradoxically, Plato could clearly and effectively formulate his preference for orality over writing only because he could write. See Walter J. Ong, *Orality and Literacy: The Technologizing of the Word* (1982; reprint London and New York: Routledge, 1991), 167–8.
6 Twyla Gibson, 'Orality,' *Encyclopedia of Religion, Communication, and Media*, ed. Daniel Stout (New York: Routledge, 2006), 301–4.
7 According to John Miles Foley, research priorities should shift from the 'oral' to the 'traditional' nature of oral traditional poetics. This shift in emphasis does not diminish the significance of the oral origins of works that have reached us as textual records. Rather, 'traditional poetics' highlights both the *genesis* and the *persistence* of traditional styles involving rules and conventions that encode meanings in addition to what appears in 'writing.' These meanings would have been obvious to those fluent in a traditional style, and they demand a dedicated poetics to uncover them. See Foley, *Homer's Traditional Art* (University Park: Pennsylvania State University Press, 1999), xiv.
8 Ibid.
9 A review of the literature reveals a dearth of studies applying the research on oral traditions to Plato's dialogues. Exceptions are the recent work of Naoko Yamagata, 'Plato, Memory, and Performance,' *Oral Tradition* 20, no. 1 (2005): 111–29; and Harold Tarrant, 'Orality and Plato's Narrative Dialogues,' *Word into Text: Orality and Literacy in Ancient Greece*, ed. Ian Worthington (Leiden: E.J. Brill, 1996), 129–48. In the latter study, Tarrant could not find an 'obvious debt to oral narrative in Plato's narrative dialogues. Such a search fails.' For examples that emphasize 'literary approaches' to interpretation, see Gerald A. Press, 'The State of the

Question in the Study of Plato,' *The Southern Journal of Philosophy* 34 (1996): 507–32; Gerald A. Press, 'Introduction,' in *Plato's Dialogues: New Studies and Interpretations*, ed. Gerald A. Press (Lanham, MD: Rowman and Littlefield, 1993), 1–13; Richard A. Kraut's 'Introduction to the Study of Plato,' in *Cambridge Companion to Plato*, ed. Richard A. Kraut (Cambridge: Cambridge University Press, 1992), 1–51; E.N. Tigerstedt, *Interpreting Plato* (Uppsala, Sweden: Almquist and Wiksell, 1977).

10 Marshall McLuhan, interview with Eric Norden, "The Playboy Interview: Marshall McLuhan – A Candid Conversation with the High Priest of Popcult and Metaphysician of Media," *Playboy* (March 1969), in *Essential McLuhan*, ed. Eric McLuhan and Frank Zingrone (New York: Basic Books, 1995), 92.

11 Douglas offers a concise summary of current research. See Mary Douglas, *Thinking in Circles: An Essay on Ring Composition* (New Haven, CT: Yale University Press), 2006.

12 Robert S. Brumbaugh, *Platonic Studies of Greek Philosophy: Form, Arts, Gadgets and Hemlock* (Albany, NY: State University of New York Press, 1989), 17–22; Noburu Notomi, *The Unity of Plato's 'Sophist': Between the 'Sophist' and the 'Philosopher'* (Cambridge: Cambridge University Press, 1999), 39–42; Kurt Pritzl, O.P., 'The Significance of Some Structural Features of Plato's *Crito*,' in *Plato and Platonism: Studies in Philosophy and the History of Philosophy*, vol. 33, ed. Johannes M. Van Ophuijsen (Washington, DC: Catholic University of America Press, 1999), 60–83; Holger Thesleff, *Studies in Plato's Two-Level Model* (Helsinki: Societas Scientarum Fennica, 1999), 143; Holger Thesleff, 'Looking for Clues: An Interpretation of Some Literary Aspects of Plato's Two-Level Model,' in *Plato's Dialogues*, ed. Press, 107–28.

13 McLuhan, *Understanding Media*, 7.

14 See, for example, Havelock's *Preface to Plato* (Cambridge and London: Belknap Press of Harvard University Press, 1963).

15 Plato, *Phaedrus* 274b–278b; Plato, *Protagoras* 328e–329b; Plato, *Letters* II.312–314c and VII.341b–e, 344c.

16 Mark Munn, *The School of Athens in the Age of Socrates* (Berkeley: University of California Press, 2000), 249.

17 Plato, *Republic*, 509c; Plato, *Timaeus* 48c-e; Plato, *Meno* 76e–77a; Plato, *Phaedrus* 107b.OK

18 Ludwig Edelstein, 'Platonic Anonymity,' *American Journal of Philology* 83 (1962): 1–22; L.A. Kosman, 'Silence and Imitation in the Platonic Dialogues,' in *Methods of Interpreting Plato and His Dialogues*, ed. James Klagge and Nicholas Smith, *Oxford Studies in Ancient Philosophy* supplement (Oxford: Oxford University Press, 1992), 73–92.

19 A.A. Krentz, 'Dramatic Form and Philosophical Content in Plato's Dialogues,' *Philosophy and Literature* 7 (1983): 32–47; see also James A. Arieti, *Interpreting Plato: The Dialogues as Drama* (Lanham, MD: Rowman and Littlefield, 1991).

20 Aristotle, *Metaphysics* I.IV.985b–VI.988a; John Dillon, *The Middle Platonists: 80 B.C. to A.D. 220* (Ithaca, NY: Cornell University Press, 1977), 3; Luc Brisson, 'Premises, Consequences, and Legacy of an Esotericist Interpretation of Plato,' *Ancient Philosophy* 15 (1995): 124; Harold Cherniss, *The Riddle of the Early Academy* (Berkeley: University of California Press, 1945), 7; Kenneth Sayre, *Plato's Late Ontology: A Riddle Resolved* (Princeton, NJ: Princeton University Press, 1983), 78, 11.

21 Aristotle, *Physics* 209a30–210a1

22 Gregory Vlastos, 'On Plato's Oral Doctrine: Review of H.J. Krämer,' *Platonic Studies* (Princeton: Princeton University Press, 1973.), 399–403. See also Luc Brisson, 'Premises, Consequences, and Legacy of an Esotericist Interpretation of Plato,' *Ancient Philosophy* 15 (1995): 124.

23 Plato, *Hipparchus* 227b.

24 Ibid., 228b.

25 Ibid., 228c.

26 Ibid., 229b.

27 Ibid., 229b

28 Ibid., 229e.

29 Plato, *Symposium* 182b–d.

30 Ibid., 182c.

31 Plato, *Republic* 331d–335e; Plato, *Protagoras* 316d, 339a–347a; Plato, *Hipparchus* 228c; Plato, *Letters* II.311a.

32 Plato, *Republic* 393c.

33 Ibid., 379a, 398b.

34 Ibid., 608.

35 Plato, *Greater Hippias* 285b–286a; Plato, *Lesser Hippias* 368c–369a.

36 Thucydides, 1.18–20, 6.54–59; Herodotus, 5.55–62, 6.123.

37 Aristophanes *Peace* 695.

38 Cicero, *De Oratore III* xxxiv.137.

39 Herodotus, 5.55–62, 6.123.

40 Flavius Josephus, *Against Apion* 1.2.12.

41 Quintilian, *Institutio Oratoria* XI.ii; Cicero, *De Oratore II* lxxxvi.352–5.

42 L.H. Jeffery, *The Local Scripts of Anchaic Greece* (Oxford: Oxford University Press, 1961), 78.

43 The tablet, known as the Parian Chronicle, records dates for significant discoveries (for example, the publication of the poetry of Orpheus, the invention of the flute, the introduction of corn) with a particular focus on

the prizes awarded at festivals. We know from other sources that Simonides was awarded the chorus prize in his old age. The inscription reads, 'From the time when the Ceian Simonides, son of Leoprepes, the inventor of the system of memory-aids, won the chorus prize at Athens, and the statues were set up to Harmodius and Aristogeiton, 213 years' (i.e., 477 BCE). Cited as translated in the collection of references to Simonides in ancient literature gathered together in *Lyra Graeca,* ed. and trans., J.M. Edmonds, Loeb Classical Library series vol. 2, no. 476 (Cambridge, MA: Harvard University Press, 1924), 249.

44 R. Pfeiffer noted that a recently published Simonidean fragment indicates we must accept Simonides as the 'proto-Sophist' and forebear of the early sophists. See R. Pfeiffer, *History of Classical Scholarship: From the Beginning to the End of the Hellenistic Age* (Oxford: Clarendon Press, 1998), 16, 55.

45 Brumbaugh, *Platonic Studies,* 17–22; Notomi, *Unity of Plato's Sophist,* 39–42; Pritzl, 'Significance of Some Structural Features,' 60–83; Thesleff, *Studies in Plato's Two-Level Model,* 143; Thesleff, 'Looking for Clues.'

46 David S. Potter, *Literary Texts and the Roman Historian* (New York: Routledge, 1999), 7, 151.

47 Gregory Vlastos, 'Socratic Irony,' *Classical Quarterly* 37 (1987): 79–96.

48 Rosemary Desjardins, *The Rational Enterprise: Logos in Plato's Theaetetus* (New York: State University of New York Press, 1990), 251.

49 Numenius frag. 41, as quoted in Numenius of Apamea, *The Father of Neo-Platonism: Works, Biography, Message, Sources and Influence,* ed. Kenneth Sylvan Guthrie (London: George Bell and Sons, 1917), 42; Leo Strauss, *Persecution and the Art of Writing* (Chicago and London: University of Chicago Press, 1952), ch. 2; Leo Strauss, 'Exoteric Teaching,' in *The Rebirth of Classical Political Rationalism: Essays and Lectures by Leo Strauss,* ed. Thomas L. Pangle (Chicago: University of Chicago Press, 1989), ch. 4; Leo Strauss, 'On a Forgotten Kind of Writing,' *What Is Political Philosophy? and Other Studies* (Glencoe, IL: The Free Press, 1959), ch. 9.

50 M. Parry, *The Making of Homeric Verse: The Collected Papers of Milman Parry,* ed. and trans. Adam Parry (Oxford: Clarendon Press, 1971).

51 Ibid., 8.

52 Albert B. Lord, *The Singer of Tales* (Cambridge, MA: Harvard University Press, 1964), 68.

53 Albert B. Lord, 'Composition by Theme in Homer and Southslavic Epos,' *Transactions of the American Philological Association* 82 (1951): 73.

54 Cedric M. Whitman, *Homer and the Heroic Tradition* (Cambridge, MA: Harvard University Press, 1958), 249–84.

55 If the sequence has no central core (e.g., A-B-C-C*-B*-A*), it is known as *hysteron proteron* (meaning 'the latter before'). See Steve Reece, 'The Three

Circuits of the Suitors: Ring Composition in *Odyssey* 17–22,' *Oral Tradition* 10 (1995): 207–29.
56 Frances A. Yates, *The Art of Memory* (Harmondsworth, UK: Penguin Books, 1966), 11, 230.
57 Quintilian, *Institutio Oratoria* XI.ii.24–6, 38-9.
58 Eric A. Havelock, *Preface to Plato* (London: Belknap Press of Harvard University Press, 1963), 46.
59 Ibid., vii.
60 Foley, *Homer's Traditional Art*, 3.
61 Douglas, *Thinking in Circles*, 12, 104–8, 124.
62 Ibid., x.
63 Ibid., 36–7.
64 Ibid., 13.
65 Foley, *Homer's Traditional Art*, xiii. See also Robert L. Kellog, 'Oral Narrative, Written Books,' *Genre* 10 (1977): 655–65.
66 Foley, *Homer's Traditional Art*, 17–18, 45.
67 Berkley Peabody, *The Winged Word: A Study in the Technique of Oral Composition as Seen Principally through Hesiod's Works and Days* (Albany: State University of New York Press, 1975), 1–2, 70.
68 Ian Worthington, 'Greek Oratory and the Oral/Literate Division,' in *Voice into Text: Orality and Literacy in Ancient Greece*, ed. Ian Worthington (Leiden: E.J. Brill, 1996), 165.
69 Paul Kiparsky, 'Oral Poetry: Some Linguistic and Typological Considerations,' *Oral Literature and the Formula*, ed. Benjamin A. Stolz and Richard S. Shannon (Ann Arbor: University of Michigan Publications, 1976), 82.
70 Havelock, *Preface to Plato*, 39.
71 Notomi, *Unity of Plato's Sophist*, 40.
72 Plato, *Sophist* 267a–b.
73 Ibid., 266d.
74 Ibid., 254b–255e, 263d–e.
75 Plato, *Sophist* 265a–268c.
76 Douglas, *Thinking in Circles*, 18.
77 Ibid.
78 Plato, *Symposium* 182b–d.
79 J. Edward Chamberlain, 'Hunting, Tracking, and Reading,' in *Literacy, Narrative and Culture*, ed. Jens Brockmeier, Min Wang, and David R. Olson (London: Curzon, 2002), 72.
80 Douglas, *Thinking in Circles*, 12–13.
81 A.N. Whitehead, *Process and Reality: An Essay in Cosmology*, ed. D.R. Griffin and D.W. Sherburne (New York: Free Press, 1978), 39.

Chapter 4

The Social Lives of Sedna and Sky Woman: Print Textualization from Inuit and Mohawk Oral Traditions

SUSAN GINGELL

To write about the social lives of Sedna and Sky Woman is not to pass on hot gossip about how two powerful women get around but to consider how their stories do, tracing their movement from multiple iterations in oral tradition to various print versions. The short stories 'Summit with Sedna, the Mother of Sea Beasts,'[1] by Inuit artist and writer Alootook Ipellie, and 'This Is History'[2] by Mohawk/Kanien'kehaka author Beth Brant/Degonwadonti are prime examples of the extension of the social life of stories from oral tradition into literature. The specifics of the stories' relationship to the oral and their political point, however, are both made clearer by comparison with other print textualizings of the same stories.[3]

The model for this investigation is based in significant part on two studies by anthropologist Julie Cruikshank, *The Social Life of Stories: Narrative and Knowledge in the Yukon Territory* and 'The Social Life of Texts: Editing on the Page and in Performance.' In the book Cruikshank observes that the transcribed stories of Yukon elders continued to be referred to when members of the community in which the stories had been told orally wanted to convey socially important concerns either within or outside those communities. She writes, 'Meanings of oral narratives are not fixed: they have to be understood in terms of how they are used.'[4] Cruikshank's essay shows that elders like Angela Sydney, Kitty Smith, and Annie Ned edited their own tellings of traditional stories in a number of ways, including in performance, on the page, and in sculpture.

The Yukon elders' stories assumed different meaning and form depending on the circumstances in which they were told. So, for example, on one occasion, Sydney told the narrative of K̲aax̱'achgóok to welcome home her son, Peter, who had been serving overseas in the Canadian army during the Second World War. The story tells of a hunter who set out to sea, was blown off course, and after a long time on an island, returned to his people using the sun as his guide. Upon his return, he found his senior wife mourning for him on the shore, but the younger one had already been given to a new husband. Kaax'achgóok had difficulty reintegrating into his society because of the changes that had taken place in his absence, and Sydney must have wisely anticipated that the horrors her son had known while overseas, and the changes the years had wrought at home would vex his return.[5] Clearly, however, she also identified with the senior wife because she told Cruikshank during a 6 July 1985 retelling of the story, when her son was already seventy, how hard his long and dangerous time abroad had been for her: 'Five years he's gone – just like that Kaax'achgóok story I told you.'[6] At another time, Sydney used the same story to mark the opening of the new Yukon College, and this time another detail of the story, the way that Kaax'achgóok used the sun to guide him back to his people, became the most salient feature. In this telling, Sydney interpreted education as the sun that would guide students home now that they no longer had to leave the territory for their advanced schooling and now that Yukon Aboriginal peoples had more control over curriculum and pedagogy. Depending on what personal or community issues needed to be addressed, different features of the story were foregrounded. In this way, then, storytellers 'invoke the past in order to talk about the present and the present to talk about the past.'[7] Furthermore, both past and present can be related to the future through story.[8] So it is that stories acquire a social life.

Cruikshank's insight provides a context for understanding how Ipellie, in 'Summit with Sedna,' and Brant, in 'This Is History,' extend the lives of traditional stories into contemporary contexts in order to build better futures, and in the process perpetuate oral traditional practices. The presence of oral markers of style, evident in some ethnographic textualizings but far more prevalent in Brant's story than in Ipellie's, also shows that writing can be used to extend, rather than replace, the characteristic style of oral traditions.

Of course any writers, Indigenous or otherwise, who retell old stories in new contexts are in a sense extending the social lives of stories.[9] Indeed, all cultures, as J. Edward Chamberlin has demonstrated in *If This Is Your Land, Where Are Your Stories?* create narratives that sustain the social lives of the people who tell them, working as ceremonies of belief that invite a believe-it-*and*-not response.[10] What may be different about the written retelling of many Aboriginal narratives is the way in which at least a number of writers conceptualize the relationship of their telling to earlier oral ones. In the print textualized talk 'Keep the Drum Playing,' Brant articulates her view of how writing and its various related technologies perpetuate oral traditional practice, or, to put matters another way, are integrated into the circles of oral tradition. Writing, she remarks,

> is an active and new way to tell the stories we have always told. Native writing is only about one hundred years old. Previously, we told the lessons, told the history, told the ancestors' biographies. At this time, we write, but we also tell. I can't think of any Native writer who does not like to read his or her work aloud. This is what makes the writing harmonious and circular. We write, we speak, we write. It all belongs together, for our oral ways are not lost or forgotten. Some of us write longhand, some use typewriters, some use computers; none of *this* is important, because the idea of story has not changed.[11]

While many non-Aboriginal writers enjoy reading their work aloud, rarely do they perceive themselves to be extending oral traditions so that their narratives will continue to be passed on orally. Poet Lorna Crozier, for instance, certainly seems to want to celebrate the imaginative vigour she perceived in her prairie Euro-Canadian people's stories when in 'Spring Storm, 1916' she retells their tall tales about a cyclone, but she provides no indication that she sees herself as enabling further oral circulation of the stories.[12] And prose writer Warren Cariou is blunt about his literate's distrust of oral transmission.[13] Although he and his siblings orally recounted among themselves as children the wonderful tales their brilliantly inventive father told them, Cariou comments, 'These performances, too, disappeared as soon as the words were spoken, and I worried. I didn't have Dad's instinctive trust in the resilience of the story as it passes from mouth to memory and on to other people like a benevolent bacterium, always alive and giving life.'[14]

Brant's statement about writing as an extension of oral tradition is striking for two reasons: how very different her understanding of the relation between the oral and the written is from the one usually found in Western scholarly writing on the subject; and how she communicates a sense of the possibility of this 'benevolent bacterium' thriving in oral as well as written form. The dominant academic view of the relationship between the oral and the scribal, in more or less subtle versions, has been, at least until recently, that the written supplants the oral in a linear development from the primitive to the more sophisticated.[15] Though she makes no claims about sophistication, Natalia Khanenko-Friesen in this volume talks first about how textualization produces the death of a storytelling tradition before explaining that the textualized oral narrative gives the story a 'second life.'[16] In Brant's account of the relation between the oral and the scribal, writing is part of a regenerative cycle in which death has no part.

Confirmed literates, who, as Cariou suggests, will probably be sceptical of a story 'pass[ing] from mouth to memory and on to other people,' will seem even more likely to doubt that a story can move back into oral form once it has been written down. However, the play script is one genre of writing specifically designed to effect such movement, though the transmission of plays in literate societies depends at least as much on written scripts as on oral performances. Those peoples a lot closer to a primary oral culture, such as late-twentieth-century Kenyans, offer evidence of the movement from the written back to the oral.[17] Socialist novelist and playwright Ngũgĩ wa Thiong'o published first in English but realized he was thus excluding the majority of the Kenyan population from his audience because they were illiterate and spoke little or no English. Increasingly critical in his work of the neo-colonialism in which the Kenyan elite were intricately and self-servingly involved, he began to write in his native Gĩkũyũ and produced, with Ngũgĩ wa Mirii and Kamiriĩthu villagers, what proved to be an incendiary play, *Ngaahika Ndeenda* (later translated as *I Will Marry When I Want*). The power of the oral transmission of what had once been written caused the government, long annoyed by Ngũgĩ's criticisms, to shut down the performances of the play and imprison him because they knew that the combination of the vernacular language and oral transmission represented a real threat to them.[18] Released a year later, Ngũgĩ published a Gĩkũyũ novel, *Caitaani-Mũtharaba-Inĩ* (*Devil on the Cross*), which was read aloud in bars and markets, and on lunch breaks outside factories, as well as in other gathering places, by literate members of the community to those who were not.[19] Next he scripted *Maitu Njugira* (*Mother, Sing for Me*), a polylingual historical play based on Kenyan oral traditions of different ethnicities, a play that showed how Kenyans, despite political independence from Britain, were not free because of oppression by their own countrymen.[20] Denied a licence to perform the play and locked out of the Kenyan National Theatre, where the play was to have been staged, the Kamiriĩthu group moved 'rehearsals' to the University of Nairobi. As word of the play and its suppression spread, people from many parts of Kenya bussed in to the capital and along with locals jammed every available space in and around the university's theatre to see or even hear what they could of the performances. Before the Kenyan government ordered the university not to allow the group further use of the campus theatre, an estimated 12,000 to 15,000 people had seen the play in its week-long run. The government followed up by razing the home base of the performing company, the Kamiriĩthu Community Education and Cultural Centre, thus pushing into exile Ngũgĩ wa Thiong'o, Ngũgĩ wa Mirii, and Kimani Gecau, the director of *Maitu Njugira*.[21] This remarkable history can be explained only by the political power of oral verbal art moving from mouth to hand (and hence page) to mouth and memory again – a vital bacterium indeed!

Cruikshank herself also provides evidence of the movement from mouth to page to memory and mouth again when she testifies, 'I continue to marvel at the social lives transcribed texts gain in the communities where they originate and continue to be told ... Written texts become points of reference narrators can allude to when they want to make socially significant statements to family members, to other members of their community, or to the larger world.'[22]

Despite such evidence of still vibrant oral traditions, to claim that no Indigenous peoples anywhere have any worries about the survival of the oral traditions that inform their subjectivity would of course be ridiculous. Angela Sydney was clearly concerned that her stories continue to live because the stories were so central to her sense of self and that of her people. She not only asserted that she had tried to live her life 'just like a story'[23] but also used traditional stories to help structure her oral life history and claimed that her stories were the only wealth she had to leave her grandchildren.[24] However, she knew that her grandchildren did not speak Tagish and Tlingit, the two Indigenous languages she spoke, and that they would get much of their knowledge from English-language books rather than in the old way. Thus she faced a new problem in passing on stories to them. Of one great-grandchild she said to Cruikshank, 'Well, she's six years old now. She's going to start school now. Pretty soon paper's going to talk to her!'[25] Sydney's solution was to collaborate with the anthropologist to produce anglophone booklets the children could read. Cruikshank's interpretation of this situation is worth quoting, too, for its understanding of the way the oral tradition's reproduction of the life cycle is perpetuated in writing: 'Schools teach things totally outside the experience of elders; stories, on the other hand, recreate the life cycle. Women see their books of stories as a connection between the world of tradition and the schools' "paper world" and feel that, thus legitimized, the stories should be part of the school curriculum.'[26] In Sydney's and Cruikshank's statements we have evidence that textualizing stories in print is seen as a means of extending the *oral* tradition because writing is conceived of not as what supersedes the dying oral world but as a means of enabling paper to talk and thus transmit the oral stories. Writing the stories down thus provided a bridge between the oral traditional world and its life cycles on the one hand and the unknown territories of the Western literate tradition and the lives lived within it on the other. Furthermore, if Cruikshank is right in her perception that stories are understood as recreations of the life cycle, then we have a further connection to the regenerative cycle of which Brant speaks.

If, however, the textualization of oral stories is approached as if it were a wholly positive activity, the resulting account would be one sided. What is needed is an awareness of both positive possibilities and perils entailed in venturing into the contact zone of Indigenous oral traditions and Western-style writing in English, an awareness such as Stl'atl'imx poet and scholar Peter Cole articulates in *Raven and Coyote Go Canoeing*. The book exemplifies the creative regeneration of some dimensions of Indigenous oral traditions, and in a passage that refers to more than, but surely includes, oral traditions and their transformation into textualized orature, he remarks,

we are growing   toward refiguring   regenerating our traditions
                                                    [traditionalizing
modernity   (re)dressing the old ways in new clothes   building solidarity
                                                    [within our
communities as well as with neighbours   including newcomers.[27]   .

On the other hand, he is unequivocal about the fundamental changes wrought by print textualization and uneasy about the political effects of translation:

orality is not about 'writing down' anything   it is about discourse
                                                    [speaking together
not concatenating events cursively   uncially   on paper   but living them
when *ucwalmicwts* words and ideas are 'translated' into english
do they remain *ucwalmicwts* words ...
                            for me they remain *ucwalmicwts* words
only the 'sense' is translated   but 'whose' sense.[28]

Non-Indigenous scholars and students are usually quick to see the benefits of bringing oral traditional stories into print and seldom inclined to dwell on the drawbacks. Reasons are not far to seek: print textualized stories are easier to study than oral ones because the latter go out of existence even as they are being told,[29] and the Western academy trains far more scholars to analyse literature than it does analysts of orature. Scholars may believe that literary training equips them to analyse orature when it is textualized in print, but they know such training rarely prepares them to work with oral verbal art. Textualized orature offers readers from outside the culture from which an oral story comes access to important dimensions of other cultures' ways of looking at the world; moreover, the losses sustained in textualization are primarily to Indigenous cultures. Besides, if the process was once initiated by people of European ancestry, Indigenous writers, who are all too familiar with the distortions that can occur when non-Indigenous people textualize the stories, are now clearly seeing the benefits of doing it themselves. Their principal purposes for doing so may well be different from those of outsider textualizers, however, especially given that most if not all Indigenous writers are acutely concerned with providing benefits to their own people.

For Anishinaabe scholar Gerald Vizenor, stories both oral and written provide a salient mode of ensuring Indigenous survivance, their right of succession and/or the reversion of their former estate in the face of colonial and neocolonial misappropriations: 'Survivance is an active sense of presence, the continuance of native stories ... [which] are renunciations of dominance, tragedy, and victimry' and 'cues of modernity.'[30] That active sense of presence inherently counters the 'manifest manners' that are part of Euro-North American dominance, 'the racialist notions and misnomers sustained in archives and lexicons as "authentic" representations of *indian* cultures.'[31] Thus, when we consider stories like Alootook Ipellie's 'Summit with Sedna' and Beth Brant's 'This Is History,' which respectively bring an Inuit and a Mohawk oral traditional story to the page, we need to be mindful of both positives and negatives involved in the textualization process, and of the problem of scholars trained in literary analysis working on stories that are based on oral ones and make use of oral storytelling methods.

When orature is technologically mediated by transcription or other modes of recording, it is abstracted from its full performative.context, and much of its illocutionary force (i.e., the meaning created by such effects as cadence, pitch, stress, and volume, and such paralinguistic signals as facial expressions, gestures, and other forms of body language) can be lost along with the community-building effects of face-to-face storytelling.[32] Moreover, to textualize orature is often to remove it from the community of commitment in which the values and worldview encoded in the performance are lived out,[33] so that new ethical issues arise as the text is more widely disseminated than would be possible in its oral form. Concerned about the loss of wordplay in the Indigenous language as well as the effects of disembodying words, Peter Cole asks specifically about the erosion of community:

> what becomes of ambiguity   playful misdirection trickster discourse
> gesture   eye contact   being in good relation with
> audience participation   breathing the same air
> walking the same earth together   be/com/ing in the same weather
> sharing context   consensuality commensality   a meal
> celebrating together   grieving   being hungry wet warm cold together[34]

Donald Fixico suggests that embodied narration promotes embodied response when he insists that 'oral tradition is imperative for holding communities together ... listening to stories allows people to "feel" and become a part of the past and sharing [sic] a sense of time and place with the people.'[35]

Cole also asks us to consider that print publication depends on ecocide and he represents book making as putting language into bondage as it is

> pressed onto clearcut forests   arranged in reams   seams   spines
> bindings in the translation or transcription of spoken sounds   rhythms[36]

Though he argues that saving an Indigenous language like *ucwalmicwts* 'on paper is preferable to clearcutting [it] altogether,'[37] his verbs describing textualization and at least some forms of academic study of Indigenous languages and stories arraign these activities as criminal, commodifying and contributing to the demise of Indigenous languages and oral traditions rather than preserving them:

> when our stories are stolen   brokered   borrowed if you will   held
>   [hostage in academia
> trans/fixed onto alien media   stripped of their original context
> placed into archives   subjected to analysis   by *imperialismus albinorum*
> english words   intervene   take up spaces   our languages used to inhabit[38]

Even when an English-language text code-switches to an Indigenous language, Cole argues that English is an 'acid atmosphere' for the words of that Indigenous language because of the discursive contexts into which the untranslated terms are introduced:

> our words never get into english except as descriptions of 'other'ness es
> alteric spectacle *mirabilis* oracle always trans lated foreign ground[39]

Cole's formulations clearly represent the translating, textualizing, and interpreting as most transgressive when done by and for those outside the Indigenous culture, but his reservations are more generalized perhaps because of the ideological constructions of the oral and the written that have pervaded Western scholarship. As noted above, among the prejudicial constructions is the idea that literature develops naturally out of oral tradition.[40] In this paradigm, the textualization of Indigenous orature is part of the alleged progress from the oral to the written, a conception of the relationship between the two that situates oral storytelling in the past. Cole's wordplay 'trans lated' takes apart the idea of oral tradition being rendered anachronistic, or belated, in a literary context and challenges 'the *a priori* presumption ... that the written word is of paramount worth.'[41]

Thomas King's memorable formulation in *The Truth about Stories* of the Western ideological construction of the relation of the oral to the written, namely that 'as we move from the cave to the condo, we slough off the oral' like a reptilian skin, similarly ironizes the Western presumptions that Cole attacks, adding to his targets the related idea of written literature having 'an inherent sophistication that oral literature lacks.'[42] King insists rather on the contemporaneity of the oral and the written, emphasizing that 'the advent of Native written literature did not, in any way, mark the passing of Native oral literature. In fact, they occupy the same space, the same time. And, if you know where to stand, you can hear the two of them talking to each other.'[43] At the same time, King is aware that writing in a colloquial way can create problems, at least with sacred materials. He acknowledges that by telling the Sky Woman story in a conversational style suitable for a general audience, then following that creation story with the Genesis story rendered in a rhetorically distant style cognizant of the decorum appropriate for a learned audience, he produces an unwanted result because of the discursive context into which the colloquially toned story enters: 'In the Native story, the conversational voice tends to highlight the exuberance of the story but diminishes its authority, while the sober voice in the Christian story makes for a formal recitation but creates a sense of veracity.'[44] King cites Basil Johnson to cement his point: 'It is precisely because our tribal stories are comical and evoke laughter that they have never been taken seriously outside the tribe.'[45] Nonetheless, King is also like Cole in devising multifaceted strategies for textualizing the oral in both creative and critical writing, finding ways to extend the social life of Indigenous stories and oral storytelling in the medium of print.

King uses the story of Sky Woman in *The Truth about Stories* to illustrate oral variations of a story produced by different occasions and locations, remarking in particular on the capacity of creation stories to diminish the sense of alien-ness between people of different cultures. Recalling for the audience of his first Massey lecture a childhood desire to get as far out of his hometown as interplanetary travel could take him, King reported that he chose as his intended destination the tiny, cold, and lonely (then) planet, Pluto.[46] The adult King, who has taken more than a few flights of fancy, announced that should he ever get to Pluto, he would like to begin a relationship with the Plutonians by exchanging stories, and the kind he'd most like to hear would be a creation story because, he explains, 'contained within creation stories are relationships that help to define the nature of the universe and how cultures understand the world in which they exist.'[47] His favourite, he tells both the audience of the lecture and the readers of the printed version of it, is the story of Sky Woman, so not surprisingly, he proceeds to tell it. People who have heard or read the creation narrative of the Cree/Nehiyawak, Ojibway/Anishinaabe, and Iroquois/Haudenosaunee, to name just three First Nations whose oral traditions include this story, will recognize King's story as 'the same' one they have encountered before; but they'd also tell you King's is different from the other versions. The difference arises because King makes the story his own by using a contemporary North American colloquial English and by including certain details: his Sky Woman, for example, holds a conversation with her toes to find out whether having fewer or more than five is preferable, thereby illustrating the point that she is an extremely curious woman:

Hey, she said, how come there are only five of you?
You're being curious again, said her Toes.[48]

Animated toes that talk back to the curious Sky Woman are, to the best of my knowledge, unique to King's telling.

One of the first points King makes in his inaugural Massey lecture is that though he has heard many times the story about the woman who falls out of the sky onto the back of a turtle, no two tellings are alike: 'Sometimes the change is simply in the voice of the storyteller. Sometimes the change is in the details. Sometimes in the order of events. Other times it's the dialogue or the response of the audience.'[49] But if the story is transcribed word for word, is the telling of this story in written form just one more change of the type to which King refers, or is it of a different order from those King articulates? In what ways can a writer simulate the speaker–audience interactions? Does the lecture or the story on the page have a different function from the lecture or story presented to a live audience? Beginning to answer such questions is among the contributions that literary scholars can make to the study of oral traditions.

The activities of literary scholars can be seen as a critical complement to the labours of the social scientists who do field work in oral traditions. As King remarks, ethnographers who 'went west to collect and translate Native stories, thereby "preserving" Native oral literature before it was lost' produced as a result 'an impressive body of oral stories ... now stored in periodicals and books that one can find at any good research library. Not that anyone reads them. But they are safe and sound. As it were.'[50] If literary scholars and teachers are prepared to do the work of learning about orature, they can help the stories to re-sound by reading, writing about, and teaching textualized orature, thus maximizing the potential of the print medium for preserving endangered oral traditions. Through the study of ethically textualized orature, they can contribute to enhanced cross-cultural understanding, and in this way offset at least some of the undeniably negative effects of the textualization process.

Literary analysis of textualized orature needs to be informed by a well-developed sense of the pragmatics, aesthetics, and protocols of specific oral performances, and part of the analytic task involves developing a strong grasp of what kind of changes occur when orature is textualized, or to put the matter another way, what the differences are between orature and textualized orature. As we have already seen argued, the embodied community-building dimension of oral storytelling is lost when orature is textualized, as is the immediacy of the audience's interactive effect on storytelling; moreover, a specific performance is gone once complete, whereas a written version, especially when printed and produced in multiple copies, remains to be consulted. That oral traditions are fluid and that writing fixes them is a commonplace of comparisons of the oral and written, though an oral story continues to circulate in a community beyond any one telling, and anyone who has ever spent five minutes looking at the variants in a critical edition of a literary text will know that the oral = fluid/written = fixed binary opposition needs a more nuanced formulation. Furthermore, poststructuralist theory has taught us to see the fundamental instability of text, and reader-response theory has made literary scholars aware that meaning is constructed anew by each reader in each set of circumstances.

The fluidity of orature is often similarly overgeneralized. Certainly there are good reasons why many Indigenous people share the view of the unidentified Inuk whom Robin Gedalof quotes in the introduction to her anthology *Paper Stays Put*. Asked why he wanted to see funding go preferentially to community newspapers over other media, he reportedly replied, 'By ear we forget, but paper stays put.'[51] There are some genres of orature whose force depends upon exact recitation. The learning of both oral genealogies and some forms of oral ritual requires the student to master the exact words of the oral tradition being handed down; yet recent Western scholarship continues to affirm the overgeneralized idea that *verbatim* reproduction in predominantly oral cultures is understood differently from in cultures where literacy is widespread.[52]

While remaining aware of differences between the oral and the written, we also need to understand the continuities between oral and written storytelling. Studying various versions of the Sedna and Sky Woman stories allows us to see that writers who come from societies with strong oral traditions can textualize oral narratives for literate audiences so that these narratives continue to serve at least some of the critical functions they served in primary oral contexts. At the same time, these textualizations allow those from beyond the community in which the story originally circulated to begin to grasp how people from that community understand their world and their place in the cosmos. Thus, textualized orature can benefit not only the people among whom it was first told, but as Inuit writer Rachel A. Qitsualik, suggests, it can also work the 'ultimate magic' of permitting readers unfamiliar with that people 'to live ... for a while' among those they wish to understand.[53]

Alootook Ipellie's 'Summit with Sedna, the Mother of Sea Beasts' not only works this magic, but can also be understood as regenerative within the Inuit context. The social life of the oral traditional story is extended into an attempt to heal Inuit society of ills that have resulted from sexual abuse. Sedna is known across the coastal Arctic by a variety of names that suggest both benevolent and malevolent aspects, including Arnâluk Takánâluk (The Woman Down There), Takánakapsâluk (The Bad One or The Terrible One Down There), Nuliajuk (She Down There), Nerrivik (The Food Dish), and The Ghastly Woman or Infernal Goddess.[54] However, she is now most widely known in non-Inuit contexts at least, as Sedna, her name in the Oqomiut and Akudnirmiut narrative that the influential ethnographer Franz Boas published in 1888 in *The Central Eskimo*.[55] All these versions point to the belief that Sedna controls the abundance or paucity of the sea mammals on which the Inuit depend for so much, including food, clothing, and fuel for their lamps. Ipellie's story also communicates the traditional belief that famine is caused by the breaking of one or more taboos, and it represents the spirit journey of the shaman to Sedna's realm beneath the sea in order to intercede on behalf of the starving people. This intercession typically entails the shaman combing out Sedna's dirty, tangled hair, though the reason for her unkempt state is variously explained as indicating breaches of taboo and other human misdeeds,[56] the transference to Sedna of the appearance of women properly observing their states of taboo,[57] abortions infesting her hair,[58] and the combined effect of sea creatures living in her hair and her being unable to comb it because she lacks fingers.[59] Whatever the cause for her dirty and dishevelled state, the attention paid in these accounts to Sedna's hair is important because hair is charged with sexual connotations.

Before Ipellie's short story was written, Sedna's social life had already been extended many times in verbal, sculptural, and other visual art forms, and in written explanations of the visual art when it was exhibited or reproduced in books and gallery catalogues. Birgitte Sonne's 'The Acculturative Role of Sea Woman' traces changes in textualized versions of the myth to changes in the meat-sharing, trade, and social relations of Inuit among themselves and the later development of such relations with the newly arrived white whalers and missionaries. Sonne argues that all variants of the story are at their core about relationships of exchange but that these relationships varied over time and location.[60] In South Greenland, Sea Woman was early on associated with sites of assembly and trade connected to the Inuit whale hunt and valuable soapstone deposits (these latter figure in some versions of her story as the soapstone lamp in her house beneath the sea), but Sonne maintains that in other locations Sea Woman became associated with the ancestress of whites through the melding of two previous stories, one about a young girl with a fulmar, or stormy petrel, as husband, and another about a dog husband, probably after the Hudson's Bay Company established Fort Churchill in 1717.[61] Moreover, Sonne observes that previous scholars such as J.G. Oosten and Rémi Savard had felt the need to explain the changing life story of Sea Woman by recourse to prehistoric environmental changes and the cognitive process of rationalization developing in Inuit cultures.[62] The conclusion Sonne reaches is precisely that stories have a social life, though she does not use this term: 'Social and ideative changes lead to a rethinking of myth, or religion, or political ideas. Combinations of stories and rearrangements of elements and motifs have the purpose to make explicit a new meaning, a new "truth," which better corresponds to the contemporary state of affairs.'[63]

If anthropological studies such as those of Sonne, Oosten, and Savard indicate that Sedna had had a lively social life before Ipellie took up with her, sculpture, prints, tapestries, and other forms of material culture such as Inuit packing dolls offer still further evidence of her past and recent social engagements. Michael P.J. Kennedy's 'The Sea Goddess Sedna' offers a valuable catalogue of Sedna's appearances in a variety of artistic forms.[64]

Of course, only verbal renderings of the story can preserve the oral qualities of the traditional narrative. Anthropologist Franz Boas brought the Sedna story to the page in his 1888 book *The Central Eskimo* in a way that at times seems to be trying to preserve something of its orality; he dramatically renders Sedna's lament at being tricked into marrying a fulmar and then being mistreated by him and his relatives, and his additive syntax and parallel phrase structures heighten the oral effect. Boas even begins and ends his textualization of the song with the traditional Inuit ideophone *aja*, though he renders the lament in prose form, albeit with some spacing to suggest pacing: 'Aja.   O father, if you knew how wretched I am you would come to me and we would hurry away in your boat over the waters. The birds look unkindly upon me the stranger; cold winds roar about my bed; they give me but miserable food. O come and take me back home.   Aja.'[65] The oral effect is diminished, however, when Boas' textualization interjects the Latin scientific terms that precisely identify for those he understands to be his primary audience, Western academics, the sea mammals mentioned in the tale. In this way he destroys the effect of oral storytelling among the Inuit, storytelling that readers might earlier have had the sense they were getting to overhear. Describing the rescuing father's desperate cutting loose of his daughter's grip on the boat when the birds raise a storm after discovering his murder of her husband and Sedna's flight, Boas' text recounts, 'The cruel father then took a knife and cut off the first joints of her fingers. Falling into the sea they were transformed into whales, the nails turning into whalebone. Sedna holding on to the boat more tightly, the second finger joints fell under the sharp knife and swam away as seals (*Pagomys foetidus*); when the father cut off the stumps of the fingers they became ground seals (*Phoca barbata*).'[66]

Boas follows this version of the story by referring to several others, before observing that sometimes 'The myth of Sedna is confused with another which treats of the origin of the Europeans and of the Adlet,' the latter being, according to Sonne, 'either some spirit race of the inland or, in areas where Indians are encountered, they become Indians.'[67] One such version Boas prints later in *The Central Eskimo* under the heading 'Tales and Traditions,'[68] and in it Sedna is called Niviarsiang and lives alone with an old man, her father, refusing all suitors but a dog. When the father drowns Niviarsiang's husband, she sends her children to avenge his death by having them gnaw off their grandfather's hands and feet, for which he in turn flings her overboard when he has her in his boat, and cuts off her fingers when she grasps the gunwale. From these severed fingers all sea mammals come.

This version of the story is very like the one that Knud Rasmussen heard from the Iglulirmiut shaman Orulo and published in *The Intellectual Culture of the Iglulik Eskimos* under the title 'The Sea Spirit Takánâluk Arnâluk: The Mother of Sea Beasts.' However, Orulo localizes the narrative by asserting that the island to which Takánâluk Arnâluk's father rows her and her children when he gets tired of providing meat for them 'was Qiqertârjuk,' and Orulo remarks on the difference in the names of the father in the Iglulirmiut version ('We call him Takánâlûp angutialua, the father of the sea spirit') and the Netsilingmiut version, in which he is called Isarraitaitsoq.[69] As Orulo comments, 'perhaps [this] was his name in the days when he lived among men.'[70] This story begins,

There once was a little girl who would not have a husband. No one was good enough. At last her father grew angry and said:
  'Then she may have my dog!'
  And then one evening, when they were going to rest, a strange man came in. No one knew who he was. He had the fangs of a dog hanging down on either side of his chest as an amulet. This man lay down beside the girl and took her to wife. It was the father's dog in human form, and thus the threat was carried out.[71]

Could this sexual bestiality perhaps be explained by Boas' account in another context of the meaning of a dog vomiting? While discussing the courting male fulmars' habit of regurgitating a 'peculiar oil' to 'feed to their chosen females,'[72] Sonne cites Boas' decoding of vomiting in *The Eskimo of Baffin Land and Hudson Bay*: 'The "dog" of a copulating father *in-spe* vomits "dog food". It means semen, which is thought to feed the embryo.'[73] Whether or not Orulo understood the father's dog in this way, the story makes clear that the girl eventually gives birth 'to a whole litter, some as dogs and some in right human form.'[74]

As a non-Inuit, when I read for the first time this and Boas' textualizing of the story 'Origin of the Adlet and the Qadlunait [Whites],' discussed below, I had no notion that they might be centrally about sexual coercion or even incest, or that the mongrel offspring might thus be a way of describing the results of a woman being tricked or forced into an unnatural or even incestuous relationship. The way I had been introduced to the story meant that I read it as simply about the origin of the sea mammals and differing peoples. Thus I am reminded of what Basil Johnston says in 'Is That All There Is? Tribal Literature' about a 'shoddy translation' of the Anishinaabe story 'The Weeping Pine'; the translation, he says, was 'presented as an explanation for the origin of pine trees' rather than as a narrative that raises profound questions 'about love and marriage and the span of either.'[75]

Thus the question arises whether the way Rasmussen and Boas present the Sedna story tends to keep readers from seeing layers of meaning that Ipellie's version of the story reveals and/or whether some versions of the story in Inuktitut ignore or put into the background issues of sexual misconduct. It is noteworthy that the potential for incest is inherent in the first version Boas records, for it begins with the details that 'there lived on a solitary shore an Inung with his daughter Sedna. His wife had been dead for sometime and the two led a quiet life.'[76] The story later records that because of the violence the father commits against Sedna in severing her fingers (an action symbolic of her being rendered impotent in the meat preparation that was the female role in Inuit meat-sharing relations[77] and would thus render her unmarriageable), Sedna conceives 'a deadly hatred against him.'[78] Boas' 'Origin of the Adlet and of the Qadlunait' is less explicit about the dead wife, but also indicates the isolation of Sedna and her father: 'Savirqong, an old man, lived alone with his daughter. Her name was Niviarsiang (i.e., the girl), but as she would not take a husband she was also called Uinigumissuitung (she who would not take a husband).'[79]

Kristina Fagan's '"Private Stories" in Aboriginal Literature' (this volume) makes clear that Indigenous peoples who traditionally lived in small isolated groups in harsh environments depended for their survival on a high degree of group cohesion, so that they, and their descendants, are characteristically reticent about direct confrontation of damaging behaviours. Moreover, Shelagh D. Grant's 'Imagination and Spirituality: Written Narratives and the Oral Tradition' points to *ilira*, the long-standing Greenland and North Labrador 'tradition of dealing with any uneasiness about people or situations,' that entails responding by 'withdrawing from the situation or showing "love" in order to appease the one who had instilled the fear.'[80] Such traditions could perhaps account for the backgrounding of such elements as incest or violence against women in early versions of the Sedna story, elements that Christopher Trott, an anthropologist specializing in Inuit culture, advised me recur frequently in Inuit narratives.[81]

This prevalence suggests that violence against woman may in fact be a pervasive problem in Inuit society.[82] Contemporary Inuit storyteller Mary Carpenter certainly understands Sedna's story in such a way, as she introduces her tellings of the Skeleton Woman and Woman of the Sea stories with the comment, 'I refuse to normalize the abnormal that's happening in Inuit country ... [T]his applies to all the battering of physical, emotional, creative, spiritual, and instinctive natures.'[83] Of course a reticence to speak about such matters as incest and sexual violence to outsiders such as Rasmussen, Boas, and others is a further potential factor in the sanitizing of the narrative, and the influence of the Moravian and other missionaries on storytelling practices should also be considered. Moreover, Western ethnographic and literary translators and scholars have, according to Craig Womack, exhibited a penchant for depoliticizing oral traditions, and he objects to 'the pablum out there in terms of coffee table books of myths and legends and complicated narratives turned into kiddie stories. "Indian stories" are popular stuff, as long as the creation, hero, trickster, and coyote stories fail to explicate the tribally specific cultural meanings, especially the political ones.'[84] While Womack is specifically concerned with the politics of national sovereignty, might the political concerns of oral traditions not also have included women's self-determination understood within the context of the need for group solidarity? Now that group cohesion is no longer quite as crucial for survival as it once was, perhaps storytellers like Carpenter and Ipellie can afford to be more direct in their confronting of critical problems for women in their society.

The plot and language of 'Summit with Sedna' are carefully tailored to fit Ipellie's political purposes. The story is narrated in the voice of a shaman whose people are experiencing a great famine, so he makes a spirit journey to neighbouring shamans to see if others in the region are similarly afflicted. Not only does he find that they are but he also learns of a major decline in shamanic powers. He questions his fellow shamans about their recent encounters with the sea goddess, when they went to plead with her for the release of the sea beasts, and he reports a staggering discovery: 'Unbelievably, what I found out from my peers could well go down in history as a **sexual misconduct** that had the potential to wipe out the Inuit nation from the face of the earth.'[85] Apparently since the onset of winter, Sedna had been making sexual advances to the visiting shamans because she had never been able to achieve orgasm and hence was in a state of high frustration. As a result she either could not, or would not, release from her realm the sea beasts so crucial to Inuit survival.[86] As one of the Arctic's most powerful shamans, the narrator is chosen to 'prepare a summit with Sedna.'[87]

Though Ipellie's syntax shows the high degree of subordination associated with literacy and both parallelism and repetition are rare in his narrative, he sometimes integrates into the flow of his prose phrasings that seem formulaic. One example is the slightly odd phrase 'a **sexual misconduct**' in which the words *sexual misconduct* are in bold. The phrase 'go down in history' and the awkward conjunction of two phrases 'wipe out the Inuit nation from the face of the earth' are other examples, though to those tutored in a literary aesthetic, they may seem merely clichéd. Shelagh Grant's comment about Inuktitut, that it is 'a language of phrases and ideas, rather than of words and structural sentences'[88] may offer an explanation for Ipellie's formulaic style, but she cites no authority for her comment. In *Orality and Literacy,* Ong explains the persistence of formulaic phrases in contemporary discourses in the following manner:

> The clichés in political denunciations in many low-technology, developing cultures – enemy of the people, capitalist war-mongers – that strike high literates as mindless are residual formulary essentials of oral thought processes. One of the many indications of a high, if subsiding, oral residue in the culture of the Soviet Union is (or was a few years ago, when I encountered it) the insistence on speaking there always of 'the Glorious Revolution of October 26' – the epithetic formula here is obligatory stabilization, as were Homeric epithetic formulas 'wise Nestor' or 'clever Odysseus', or as 'the

glorious Fourth of July' used to be in the pockets of oral residue common even in the early twentieth-century United States.[89]

Despite evidence in Ipellie's prose of what may be residual formulas, his diction sometimes has fresh force, as, for example, his choice of the term *summit*. Though part of Western political discourse, where it is used to name a high-level meeting of powers, it is also appropriate for describing an encounter designed to help Sedna achieve her sexual peak.

The political force of Ipellie's narrative becomes more apparent as the story unfolds. After a week's concentrated study, the shaman devises a plan for a collective solution to the problem, a plan that involves the joint creation of a giant, malevolent Inuit Frankenstein, bestowed with the power of a hundred spirit souls to accompany the shamans on their spirit journey.[90] The narrator's comment on his plan is suggestive in relation to a people who have encountered only frustration in the many times they have sought solutions to problems with a power that governs their welfare but is outside their world and seems indifferent to their fate: 'We had never before gone out of our way to try to make [Sedna] submit to our demands. Our foolproof method was always to plead with her to release the animals. So it was with some apprehension that we proceeded to try our luck.'[91] Though reading this new course of action as suggestive of the Inuit's banding together to push Ottawa into recognizing Northerners' needs, I am not arguing here for a well-developed symbolic equation between Sedna and the Canadian government because I think there is a far more likely and more important link between Sedna and Inuit women who have been subjected to incest and other forms of sexual abuse. This latter link becomes clear when the shamanic protagonist discovers that while Sedna was still in the natural world, 'Her father had sexually abused her many times' in assaults lasting 'for hours on end' and as a result 'she became emotionally, mentally, and physically doomed to sexual impotency.'[92] I do wonder, however, whether the violence of Ipellie's shamans' approach is a carryover from the harpooning of Sea Woman during Sedna festivals, and/or if the change in approach to Sedna to which Ipellie's shaman attests is a result of colonizing influences.[93]

Sedna's problem is ultimately solved not by the narrator-shaman acceding to her unnatural request to have sex with him, since that would only be another form of unhealthy relationship, but by having the Frankenstein monster confront her and put her in a trance that allows her to have a dream in which her proper counterpart, a sea-god named Andes, brings her to orgasm. The explosion of her orgasmic juices also produces the desired release of the sea beasts, who immediately travel to 'the hungry Arctic world.'[94] The foremost anthropologist of Inuit culture, Bernard Saladin d'Anglure, argues that the much-vaunted Inuit sexual communism was controlled mainly by shamans 'in a context of sexual markings imposed upon women and communal violence inflicted on young people, particularly young couples. These have to undergo the sharing of their production, of their offspring and of their sexuality, for the benefit of older people, mature men and especially shamans.'[95] Thus that Ipellie does not resolve Sedna's problem by having his powerful shaman sexually satisfy her is a most meaningful plot decision.[96]

The implications of Ipellie's story are multiple. The health of the Inuit nation has been imperilled by the breaking of a taboo and a shamanic spirit journey to Sedna must be made in order to discover which taboo has been broken so that the transgression can be brought out into the open and reparations made. Incest has taken a terrible toll on the community, and, given the attenuated powers of the shamans and the magnitude of the problem, only forceful collective action can solve it.[97] That the first-person narrator of all the stories in *Arctic Dreams and Nightmares* is a shaman and seems to be in part autobiographical suggests that Ipellie may see writers, or more generally, artists, as the new shamans of the North.[98] This idea is rendered more credible when we know that Ipellie gave the name Shakespeare to a shaman in another story, 'The Five Shy Wives of the Shaman.'[99] The plot development of 'Summit with Sedna' also implies that community leaders, and especially spiritual leaders, must resist the powerful temptations that might seduce them into abusing their power, especially when, in the case of shamans, the culture had previously tolerated if not altogether accepted the idea of their having rights of sexual access to the women they desired. The outcome of the summit with Sedna further suggests that when the abuses stop and past abuses are brought into the open, then health and bountiful life will return to the Inuit nation.

Health in this story is very like health as Beth Brant envisions it in her essay 'Physical Prayers,' when she describes a story she was told about the open, communal love making that followed feast days in traditional Mohawk culture: 'Sexuality, and the magic ability of our bodies to produce orgasm was another way to please Creator and ensure all was well and in balance in our world,' she writes, before going on to assert emphatically, 'I will not make distinctions between sexuality and spirituality.'[100] Ipellie's story also seems to me to refuse this distinction, as he reanimates the traditional story of a goddess to talk about the very contemporary problem of abuses of power, especially sexual abuses. Moreover, because the goddess figure has an explicitly sexual problem, healing, when it comes, has both spiritual and sexual force.

Not surprisingly, the same refusal to binarize the spiritual and the sexual exhibited in Ipellie's 'Summit with Sedna' is evident in Brant's retelling of the Mohawk creation story in her narrative 'This Is History.'[101] Like Ipellie and the Yukon women with whom Cruikshank collaborated, Brant extends the social life of a traditional narrative, reaffirming traditional values in the process, even as she inflects the story in order to address contemporary problems in her community. As a lesbian, Brant is particularly concerned with what in the essay 'Recovery and Transformation' she refers to as 'the disease of homophobia' that has infected her society as a result of colonial contact: 'This disease has devastated my Indian family as surely as smallpox, alcohol, glue-sniffing and tuberculosis have devastated our Nations,' she writes.[102] Thus, when she retells the story of Sky Woman falling out of the heavens onto the back of Turtle and then animals getting mud from the depths in order to create the land on which she, plants, and animals can live, the details of the story reflect Brant's concern to find healing for the malady of homophobia as well as her desire to counter the depreciation of Mohawk spirituality and its divorce from sexuality. The story also offers traditional Mohawk alternatives to the 'ecocidal' and sexist attitudes authorized by the biblical story of the creation and fall, a story that gives man dominion over the natural world and woman.

Unlike the woman from the sky in the versions that Mohawk storyteller Seth Newhouse related to ethnographer J.N.B. Hewitt and that museum curator Rona Rustige brings to the page in *Tyendinaga Tales*,[103] Brant's Sky Woman is not pushed out of the Sky World by an ailing husband who believes he can thus restore his health; Brant establishes in the second paragraph that her protagonist is so curious about the world that in leaning over an opening she has created in the clouds, she intentionally falls through. She is not much lamented by those who do try to grab her as she falls, however, because 'The others were tired of her peculiar trait [curiosity] and called her an aberration, a queer woman who asked questions, a woman who wasn't satisfied with what she had.'[104] Brant uses the adjective *queer* again in the next paragraph, emphasizing that the Sky People saw her as a nuisance – 'a queer woman who was not like them – content to walk the clouds undisturbed' – exploiting the dual meanings of the word *queer* so that readers will understand from the outset that her protagonist is lesbian.

From the start of her time on Turtle Island, Sky Woman is instructed by the animals about how to live in a good way, but Turtle's admonition is exemplary. It is also written in an additive, rather than subordinative, style, with several instances of parallelism, both features that Walter J. Ong has identified as characteristic of the oral: 'You will live here *and* make this a new place. You will be kind, *and* you will call me Mother. I will make all manner of creatures and growing things to guide you on this new place. You will watch them carefully, *and* from them you will learn how to live. You will take care to be respectful and honorable to me.'[105]

Whether Brant intended it or not, the passage, with its strongly oral style, can be read as a speaking back in writing to the literary Christian account of the creation and fall. She does not have the first human woman made from a man's rib by a male creator as in the Genesis account, nor does she have that male creator exchange one rib of the first human female and male as did the earlier, more egalitarian Mohawk acculturations of the Genesis story into their own Indigenous tradition.[106] Nor does she present a male creator who grants the man the sole right to name aspects of the Lord's creation, as the Judeo-Christian God does. Instead Brant writes the mystery of female origins as a function of a female Turtle's creative power and Sky Woman's fecund body, and she grants joint naming rights to the two women. Turtle tells Sky Woman, 'Inside you is growing a being who is like you and not like you. This being will be your companion. Together you will give names to the creatures and growing things. You will be kind to these things. This companion growing inside you will be called First Woman.'[107] In fact, it is the act of jointly bestowing names that cements the bond between the maturing First Woman and Sky Woman. The narrator reports, 'They named together and in naming, the women became closer and truer companions.'[108] The companionship turns into sexual intimacy that is represented as a form of medicine, and thus accords with the union of the spiritual and sexual that Brant wrote about in 'Physical Prayers': 'They touched each other and in the touching made a new word: love. They touched each other and made a language of touching: passion. They made medicine together. They made magic together.'[109] Not just the parallelism but also the repetition in this passage is a marker of the oral according to Ong, and together they offer evidence that Brant is writing her version of a story from Mohawk tradition in a way that extends its oral style as well as its substance.[110]

In her counter-Christian discourse, Brant may well have been imagining her way back to the Mohawk story before contact, a task made necessary by the repression of traditional narratives on her own reserve and the hybridization of the stories from other reserves where the oral traditions had survived, but in altered form.[111] In introducing Onondaga, Seneca, and Mohawk versions of the creation story, J.N.B. Hewitt wrote, 'Regarding the subject-matter of these texts, it may be said that it is in the main of aboriginal origin. The most marked post-Columbian modification is found in the portion relating to the formation of the physical bodies of man and of the animals and plants, in that relating to the idea of a hell, and in the adaptation of the rib story from the ancient Hebrew mythology in connection with the creation of woman.'[112]

Brant may even have been responding specifically to an earlier version of the creation story textualized in *Tales of the Mohawks* by another Mohawk woman, Alma Greene/Gah-wonh-nos-doh (Forbidden Voice). In marked contrast to Brant's lesbian-centred version affirming traditional Mohawk spirituality and sexuality and written in an orally influenced style, Greene's decidedly literary version shows a heavy Christian influence not only in its title, 'The Beginning of Sin,' but also in its phraseology and in the characterization of the female figure equivalent to Brant's Sky Woman in terms suggestive of the Virgin Mary and of the biblical voice that announces an upcoming birth: 'In the beginning there was no land. One day the creatures who dwelt in the water heard a voice saying that a young maiden who was to become a mother was going to be sent down to live with them.'[113] The turtle in this story is male, but neither he nor the maiden are accorded creative powers and neither is recognized as sacred in the conventional grapholectal way: 'Various things gathered around the turtle, and gradually a large piece of land with trees and shrubs was formed. Thus the maiden had a comfortable place where she could live.'[114] Greene or those from whom she heard the story appear to have truncated its creative dimensions in order not to compete with the theology of the Genesis account, and to have tailored all aspects of the story in order to bring it into as close an alignment with Christian narrative as possible.

Though no other version of the story that I have found makes explicit the sexual dimension of the relationship between Sky Woman and First Woman or their equivalents the way Brant's does, the Anishinaabe re-creation story that Basil Johnston tells in *Ojibway Heritage* makes the sex of Sky Woman's procreative partner ambiguous, indicating that there was nothing in at least some oral accounts to bar interpretation of the relationship between the women as a lesbian one:

> High in the heavens there lived alone a woman, a spirit. Without a companion she grew despondent. In her solitude she asked Kitche Manitou for some means to dispel her loneliness. Taking compassion on the sky-woman, Kitche Manitou sent a spirit to become her consort.
>
> Sky-woman and her companion were happy together. In time the spirit woman conceived. Before she gave birth her consort left. Alone she bore two children, one pure spirit, and the other pure physical being.[115]

Johnston encodes his respect for the Great Spirit, Manitou, through his capitalization practice, but despite identifying the sky woman as a spirit, he, unlike Brant, does not use the capitalization convention of the grapholect to recognize her status as sacred. As an ethnologist rather than a literary author, he also makes no clear attempt to replicate aspects of oral style, though he keeps his sentence structures simple.

Johnston's actual recounting of the creation of Turtle Island is similar in broad outline to that in Brant's story, but his narration of the creation is shown to be part of a much larger cycle of stories, and in this respect is more like the story cycle of the creation that curator Rona Rustige collected on Brant's home reserve and textualized in *Tyendinaga Tales*. Described by Rustige as a collection of folk tales, the book is illustrated and printed in a large font, both of which qualities suggest a young target audience, an audience well suited to stories typically about two pages in length. This textualization is, like Greene's and Johnson's, popular rather than scholarly, in that Rustige, while stating that she 'transcribed the tales verbatim and edited only enough to make them readable,' provides no information about where she altered the texts of the stories, just as she provides the names of her 'informants' but does not indicate which story was collected from which storyteller.[116]

One important index of Brant's and Rustige's differing attitudes to the material is the capitalization practices of the two. Whereas Brant capitalizes the names Sky World, Sky People, Sky Woman, Turtle, and First Woman in accordance with the English grapholect's practice of capitalizing the names of sacred beings, Rustige does not treat them as proper nouns, perhaps because she does not see the 'tales' as sacred stories.

Brian Maracle, who textualizes the Sky Woman creation story as 'The First Words,' is like Brant in emphatically registering the spiritual importance of the story. However, he is aware that the creation narrative of his people, the onkwehón:we of the Six Nations Iroquois Confederacy/Rotinonhsyón:ni, will be received by most in the way that Rustige apparently took the version or versions she heard on the Tyendinaga reserve, as just an entertaining tale: 'To most people, the story ... is just that – a story. Quaint and colourful, yes, but just a story. But it is far more than that to the people who have been telling it since Shonkwaya'tíson [the Creator of people] told it to the first human beings.'[117] Rather than signalling the sacred through capitalization as Brant does, however, Maracle encodes the holiness of the story by codeswitching, integrating into the mainly English text words from the language that Shonkwaya'tíson gave to the Rotinonhsyón:ni at 'the moment of Creation ... *the* defining moment in our history ... when our character as a people was determined ... when we were given the gift of speech and, with it, a unique way of looking at and understanding the world. That was when we were given the sacred responsibilities that shape our lives.'[118] Maracle's point about the uniqueness of the Mohawk worldview as encoded in language is important for our understanding of the losses entailed in translation, as is clear from his example in the commentary at the end of 'The First Words.' He explains that the language the Creator gave the onkwehón:we

> made it clumsy for us to express things that involve negative concepts. For example, we don't have a word in our language for 'zero,' 'empty,' or 'failure' ... We have many more ways of describing exactly who is doing what than English has. For example, although there is only one word for 'we' in English, there are four in our language, depending on the number of people involved in the 'we' and whether 'we' includes the person being spoken to.'[119]

Part of Maracle's larger political and cultural project is to restore the Mohawk language to its nation-defining status among the onkwehón:we, the people 'who [speak] the language of the Creator,'[120] so his version of the story accords a place to that language that Brant, being, on the evidence of 'This Is History,' more concerned with homophobia and environmental degradation, does not. Maracle's extension of the social life of his people's creation story also serves his politics in another way, however, because he remarks that the story 'specifically tells us that the onkwehón:we did not arrive here on what we now call Turtle Island by walking over some land bridge from Asia.'[121] Thus his textualized storytelling works to subvert the way the stories of white science can be used to undermine onkwehón:we land claims that are based on that people's connection to the territory given to them by the Creator. Yet because Maracle retells the creation story to participate in the Dominion Institute's foundational project of broadening Canadian understanding of the country's history – particularly in the volume *Our Story*, which prompts us 'to step out of preconceived notions of not only what constitutes our history but how our history is constituted' – his version, like Brant's, argues that the Mohawk creation story is history.[122]

Brant's version is similarly like and unlike the versions in Thomas King's postmodern novel *Green Grass, Running Water*.[123] In four recountings of the Algonkian creation story, King mirrors Brant's honorific capitalization practice, and in one he explicitly presents this origin story as predating the Christian story, thus contributing to the ways in which the novel operates as counter-colonial discourse.[124] King's characters, while similar in some respects to Brant's, undergo various metamorphoses. For example, Brant's Turtle becomes grandmother Turtle, and her Sky Woman initially becomes King's First Woman, who creates a garden where she lives with Ah-Damn in a parody of the Judeo-Christian origin myth. She later reappears as Changing Woman, who falls not onto Turtle's back but into the poop of patriarchy in a big white canoe full of Noah's animals. She resists the patriarch's attempts to dominate her psychologically and sexually and so is abandoned on an island, where she is eventually found by Herman Melville's equally patriarchal Ahab. The captain is in search of 'the great male white whale' but when his crewmen report the sighting of a 'Blackwhaleblackwhaleblackwhalesbianblackwhalesbianblackwhale,' Ahab insists that the creature is 'Moby-Dick, the great male white whale.'[125] This punning displacement of negatively racialized (black) by positively racialized (white) and of the lesbian gynocentric by the signifier of the heterosexual androcentric represents a racist blindness and the occlusion of some Aboriginal female-centred story by the Judaeo-Christian West's male-centred narrative. King's story thus participates in the same critique of a racist colonialism, patriarchy, and heterosexism that Brant's story offers, and his ushering of a pair of lesbians into the line of black whales may be a form of extending recognition to Brant's own introduction of lesbian characters into her version of the Sky Woman narrative.

Before Brant concludes her retelling of the traditional Mohawk story of origins, she inflects her narrative in other gynocentric ways. She reappropriates from Western constructions of the menstruating woman as unclean the idea that it is a 'wondrous' thing First Woman's body could do.[126] Moreover, she writes a version of First Woman's two sons as good and evil specifically in their relations to women and the Turtle Mother, Earth:

> Inside you are growing two beings. They are not like us. They are called Twin Sons. One of these is good and will honor us and our Mother. One of these is not good and will bring things that we have no names for. Teach these beings what we have learned together. Teach them that if the sons do not honor the women who made them, that will be the end of this earth.[127]

By contrast, in Rustige's version, as in most of the textualized versions, the sons account for the generalized good and evil in the world, the strongest formulation of their contrary natures that I found in textualized versions being those in Marius Barbeau's *Huron and Wyandot Mythology* and Brian Maracle's 'The First Words.' In Barbeau's textualization, the good brother 'made everything in such a way that – if left undisturbed – hunger, work, and pain would have been unknown to the people. His brother, ... however, would always disturb and upset what [the good brother] had done.'[128] Maracle's version says of the first twin that he 'was right-handed and had a good mind' while the other was 'left-handed and had an evil mind.'[129] The latter is so self-centred that he ignores his brother's urgings to follow him in a vaginal birth, instead tearing his way into life through the mother's side, thus killing her. Moreover, Maracle details the way in which the evil-minded twin tries to spoil each of his brother's positive creations so that the story becomes as much about them as it is about Sky Woman and her consort. In Johnston's version the first of two sets of twins is presented as binary opposites unrelated to gender, while the second is presented as complementary in their male and femaleness; and in Greene's, one of the first pair of two sets of twins is characterized as generally 'restless and quarrelsome,' and in his haste to be born forces his birth and kills his mother, while the remaining infants are not represented in gendered terms.[130] That the evil son causes his mother's death in childbirth by tearing – usually through her armpit (see Hewitt's Onondaga and Mohawk versions, for instance) but sometimes through her navel (as in Hewitt's Seneca version) – shows how Brant's even more strongly gynocentric representation of the twins is grounded in earlier renderings of the story.

Setting versions of the Sedna and Sky Woman stories alongside one another and considering their oral and written contexts clearly shows that the extension of the social life of stories through print entails both costs and benefits. When the translation is from one language to another as well as one medium to another, important aspects of a people's way of relating to one another and the world can be lost, as is shown by Brian Maracle's point about the onkwehón:we's language having no easy way to express negative concepts and having multiple words to designate the possible configurations of inclusion and exclusion that English effaces in its single word *we*. Even code-switching to signal an originally Indigenous language medium for the story is no panacea for the translation problem, as Peter Cole suggests in remarking on the 'alteric spectacle' that using Indigenous words in predominantly English-language texts makes of those words.

Because textualization of any kind can carry stories outside the community of shared values in which they originated, the attendant risks of textualization include the de-sacralizing of narratives as colourful but quaint tales, a mode of reception on which Maracle remarks, and the trivialization of making often complex narratives into simplified children's stories, of which Womack complains. The de-sacralizing and trivializing of these oral stories provide evidence that maintaining Aboriginal communities' protocols surrounding who could tell what stories to whom and in what circumstances was not simply an arbitrary exercise in power. And when textualization involves an attempt to carry across colloquial and humorous aspects of oral storytelling, the power of sacred stories can be further diminished, as Thomas King shows in *The Truth about Stories*. Commentators like Maracle, Cole, and King offer persuasive arguments that the apparent ability of textualization to supersede the limits of space and time that constrain the reach of orally transmitted stories is of a piece with the ideologically freighted privileging of the written over the oral on the basis of the allegedly always fleeting and relatively unsophisticated nature of the oral and the permanent and more sophisticated nature of the written. Clearly literates don't share the strong faith in oral memory that those who rely solely on the oral for verbal communication do, as both Cariou and the unnamed Inuk quoted in the introduction to *Paper Stays Put* attest. However, simply bringing stories to the page does not ensure that they will be read, and this fact, combined with other limitations of textualized orature, means that although Sky Woman and Sedna may live on through the medium of print, sometimes their meanings can be so changed or their force so attenuated that their extra time is a kind of half-life at best.

Despite some writers' demonstrated awareness of the many problems involved with textualizing the oral, Aboriginal authors such as
Ipellie, Brant, Cole, King, and Maracle continue to bring oral stories to
the page and to use oral storytelling styles in doing so. Their practice
suggests that on balance they see the benefits as outweighing the costs,
perhaps judging that the majority of the benefits as well as the costs ac-
crues to their people. Moreover, to those accustomed to thinking of the
relationship between the oral and the written as chronological, Brant,
Ipellie, and other textualizers of oral traditional stories may seem to be
abandoning or subverting the oral tradition by entering the realm of
print; but the testimony of both Yukon elders participating in textualization projects and fiction writers like Brant and King shows that they
conceive of themselves as extending the oral tradition. Seen in this
light, the idea that these writers also carry across some aspects of an
oral style – Brant's additive syntax, parallel structures, and repetitions
and Ipellie's use of phrases in a way that would seem natural to someone raised with an aesthetic and perhaps even a language conditioned
by the oral formulaic, as Shelagh Grant suggests – seems more fitting
than it might otherwise appear.

The extension of the social life of the Sedna and Sky Woman stories
through print textualization facilitates comparison of versions of their
telling that allows us to see how the meaning of the stories changes
depending on what the textualizers understand to be the needs of their
respective communities at the time. Comparing Ipellie's principal concerns in 'Summit with Sedna' with those in other written versions of the
Sea Goddess' story heightens our sense that the Inuit writer is speaking
to particular problems – most notably incest and leaders' abuse of
power – that contemporaneously threaten the health of his people.
When Beth Brant's 'This Is History' is similarly set against other versions of the Algonkian creation story, her focus on the effects of sexism,
homophobia, and the degradation of the environment experienced by
her people becomes even clearer than it is if her story is read on its own.

Julie Cruickshank has made apparent that people for whom the oral
transmission of stories has been a defining part of their culture characteristically adapt their stories to contemporary needs and concerns in
their societies, but such adaptation is now a matter of mode as well. The
extension of the cultural life of stories through print, and increasingly
through other technological media, not only recognizes the changes in
how most people today are used to receiving culturally significant information and narrative entertainment but also capitalizes on the special

abilities of print and these other media. A material archive of oral traditional stories allows people to do a number of things to address their
anxiety that the wisdom, knowledge, and pleasure-giving abilities carried by oral tradition will be lost: look stories up if and when people
don't have access to oral storytellers' iterations, and compare versions to
learn about the concerns particular storytellers had at particular times in
their people's history.

Both Ipellie and Brant, like their Indigenous peers, write in a context
in which textualized forms of storytelling are fast becoming more familiar to an increasing number of people than oral traditional storytelling
is. In this sense, then, we can see the textualization of oral stories as the
traditionalizing of modernity of which Cole speaks. By telling their
stories in print, Ipellie and Brant also extend the reach of their narratives, so that they can speak to social, political, and spiritual problems
that undermine well-being in the non-Aboriginal world as well, offering tellings of sacred stories as medicine for what ails us all.[131]

NOTES

1 Alootook Ipellie, 'Summit with Sedna, the Mother of Sea Beasts,' in *Arctic
   Dreams and Nightmares* (Penticton, BC: Theytus, 1993). For economy's sake,
   I will most often refer to the story by the abbreviated title 'Summit with
   Sedna.'
2 Beth Brant, 'This Is History,' in *Food and Spirits* (Vancouver: Press Gang,
   1991), 19–26.
3 The qualifier in the term 'print textualizings' is necessary because an oral
   performance can be textualized not only in print but also on audiotape,
   film, video, and in digital or other media.
4 Julie Cruikshank, in collaboration with Angela Sydney, Kitty Smith, and
   Annie Ned, *Life Lived Like a Story: Life Stories of Three Yukon Native Elders*
   (Lincoln: University of Nebraska Press, 1990), 135.
5 Julie Cruikshank, 'The Social Life of Texts: Editing on the Page and in
   Performance,' in *Talking on the Page: Editing Aboriginal Oral Texts*, ed. Laura
   J. Murray and Keren Rice (Toronto: University of Toronto Press, 1999),
   97–119 reports this detail: 'Despite his successful return, he faced the
   difficult business of acknowledging how much life had changed during
   his absence' (106). She then refers readers to her longer discussion of
   Mrs Sydney's use of the story (Julie Cruikshank and Angela Sydney,
   '"Pete's Song": Establishing Meaning through Story and Song,' in *When*

Our Words Return: Writing, Hearing, and Remembering Oral Traditions of Alaska and the Yukon, ed. Phyllis Morrow and William Schneider [Logan: Utah State University Press, 1995], 53–75). In this version and those in *Life Lived Like a Story* and *The Social Life of Stories: Narrative and Knowledge in the Yukon Territory* (Lincoln: University of Nebraska Press), his difficulties in reintegrating are implicit in details such as that his younger wife had been given to another husband: 'Pete's Song,' 63; *Life Lived Like a Story*, 144; *Social Life of Stories*, 34.

6 Cruikshank, *Social Life of Stories*, 37.

7 Ibid., 2–3.

8 Cruikshank observes that the Yukon College telling of the story 'commemorated an event with significance for the future' (*Social Life of Stories*, 42).

9 Cruikshank replicates the process of telling the story in different contexts by printing either full or synoptic accounts in chapter 16 of *Life Lived Like a Story*; 'Pete's Song'; 'The Social Life of Texts'; and chapter 2 of *The Social Life of Stories*. Moreover, the complete transcriptions of the 1945 telling in 'Pete's Song,' *Life Lived Like a Story*, and *Social Life of Stories* show how the story continues to change as it is reprinted in different contexts. Many of the differences, such as the italicizing or not of Aboriginal names, the comma or lack thereof after *too* when that word comes at the end of a line, and variant spellings of 'Waa, waa' versus 'Wah, wah' and 'till' versus ''til' can be explained by the differing house styles of the publishers, but variants such as 'Wake up, you boys' versus 'Wake up you boys' and 'Sun down' or 'Sundown' affect a reader's sense of the cadence and rhythm, and changes in stanza breaks alter the length of pauses and therefore affect a reader's sense of what Mrs Sydney emphasized. Such changes constitute variations in meaning, however slight.

10 J. Edward Chamberlin, *If This Is Your Land, Where are Your Stories? Finding Common Ground* (Toronto: Knopf, 2003), 34.

11 Beth Brant, 'Keep the Drum Playing,' in *Writing as Witness: Essay and Talk* (Toronto: Women's Press, 1994), 40.

12 Lorna Crozier, 'Spring Storm, 1916,' in *The Garden Going on without Us* (Toronto: McClelland and Stewart, 1985), 84–7.

13 Warren Cariou, *Lake of the Prairies: A Story of Belonging* (N.p.: Doubleday Canada, 2002), 220. Only as an adult did Cariou find out about his paternal grandmother's protectively suppressing knowledge of her being Métis in order to ease the way for her children following the Riel-led resistance because Métis people were considered traitors to Canada in that political climate. The surprised young man had trouble integrating this knowledge, as his reaction at the time makes clear: '*I* was white, after all, and so were

my parents. Everyone in Meadow Lake would have said so.' Without denying this heritage, Cariou remained reluctant to claim that he is Métis, especially since there is a certain amount of very contemporary cachet in being Aboriginal, at least in some academic circles. Though he is clearly trying to learn more about this dimension of his heritage, his compelling contrast of his life course to that of his schoolmate Clayton Matchee, who despite having a white mother, was raised Cree on the Flying Dust Reserve just outside of Meadow Lake, makes clear that Cariou acknowledges he is culturally white and middle class, and the recipient of all the unearned advantage that perceived identity entails. Thus I treat him as a non-Aboriginal writer, though I concede the possibility that his father's storytelling skills may have been influenced by Warren's paternal grandmother, who, Cariou reports, 'had the most vivid and entertaining dreams of anyone I've ever known, and ... was always willing to recount them' (234). It is clear, moreover, that his grandmother's French- and Cree-inflected variety of English was one of the stimulants to Cariou's own consciousness of variant oralities. See the chapter 'Marie Clemence,' 228–43.

14 Cariou, *Lake of the Prairies*, 11.

15 See further discussion of this point on pp. 118–19, below.

16 Khanenko-Friesen, this volume. For a challenge to the presumed chronology of the written replacing the oral, see Carlson's argument, this volume, that literacy among the Salish is something their narratives suggest was taken away by colonization rather than provided by it, and note especially his discussion of the ethnocentric assumptions about evolutionary progress and development.

17 Walter J. Ong defines primary oral cultures as 'those untouched by writing in any form' (*Orality and Literacy: The Technologizing of the Word* [London: Routledge, 1982], 9).

18 For an account of the politics of the oral and the written in the Ngũgĩ case, see Ingrid Björkman, *Mother, Sing for Me: People's Theatre in Kenya* (London: Zed Books, 1989). For other examples of oralizing and re-oralizing, see John Miles Foley's *How to Read an Oral Poem* (Urbana, IL: University of Chicago Press, 2002). He cites a number of examples that show that the 'imagined one-way street leading from oral poetry to literary texts ... [is in fact] a broader thoroughfare that permits and even fosters two-way traffic' (42). His examples include the Anglo-American folk ballad, Pushkin's *Eugene Onegin*, and the oral dramatic poetry developed from it, and interrelated Balinese oral and literary poetry. For evidence that the two-way traffic can take place even across centuries, see Carl Lindahl, 'The Re-Oralized Legends of Robert Mannyng's *Handlyng Synne*,' *Contemporary*

Legend: The Journal of the International Society for Contemporary Legend Research 2 (1999): 34–62.

19 Cited in Björkman, *Mother, Sing for Me,* 3.

20 Cited in ibid., 8–9.

21 Ibid., 60.

22 Cruikshank, *The Social Life of Stories,* xiii-xiv. See also Cruikshank's discussion of the elders' deliberations at a 1994 southern Yukon festival about whether their words should be recorded verbatim, or whether they should be rendered into 'standard' English. Cruikshank reports that the elders 'were less troubled about whether recording oral narrative may inappropriately disembody, decontextualize, and crystallize it than about how the printed page allows readers to "hear" the words of those who are no longer living' (15). This account again suggests that the elders see the written versions of stories as extensions of the oral tradition into a different medium.

23 Cruikshank, *Life Lived Like a Story,* 20. This idea of living life like a story is not foreign to Western tradition either, as J. Edward Chamberlin shows by both invoking both Psalm 90's assertion, 'We live our life as a tale that is told' and citing that brilliant talker, Oscar Wilde, admonishing us, 'We should live our life as a form of fiction. To be a fact is to be a failure' (*If This Is Your Land,* 124).

24 Cruikshank, *Life Lived Like a Story,* 36.

25 Ibid., 16.

26 Ibid.

27 Peter Cole, *Coyote and Raven Go Canoeing: Coming Home to the Village* (Montreal and Kingston: McGill-Queen's University Press, 2006), 17.

28 Ibid., 48.

29 Ong, *Orality and Literacy,* 32.

30 Gerald Vizenor, *Manifest Manners: Narratives on Postindian Survivance* (Lincoln: University of Nebraska Press, 1999), vii, viii.

31 Ibid., vii.

32 For a discussion of illocutionary force and its management in text, see David R. Olson, *The World on Paper: The Conceptual and Cognitive Implications of Writing and Reading* (Cambridge: University of Cambridge Press, 1994), 92–5.

33 Dr Barbara Belyea argued this point in a postcolonial research group seminar on oral literature at the University of Calgary, 9 December 2004. Cruikshank makes the related point that 'effective performance of oral tradition ... demands an expressive community sharing similar expectations' (*Social Life of Stories,* 43).

34 Cole, *Coyote and Raven,* 48–9.

35 Donald Fixico, *The American Indian Mind in a Linear World: American Indian Studies and Traditional Knowledge* (New York: Routledge, 2003), 29.
36 Cole, *Coyote and Raven*, 48.
37 Ibid., 49.
38 Ibid.
39 Ibid.
40 Vizenor, *Manifest Manners*, 72.
41 Cole, *Coyote and Raven*, 21.
42 Thomas King, *The Truth about Stories: A Native Narrative*, CBC Massey Lectures (Toronto: House of Anansi Press, 2003), 100.
43 Ibid., 101–2.
44 Ibid., 22–3.
45 Cited in ibid., 23.
46 Ibid., 2.
47 Ibid., 10.
48 Ibid., 11.
49 Ibid., 1.
50 Ibid., 100–1.
51 Robin Gedalof, *Paper Stays Put: A Collection of Inuit Writing*. (Edmonton: Hurtig, 1988), 7.
52 See for example, Ong, *Orality and Literacy*, 57; Olson, *World on Paper*, 86–7; 106–7; but cf Olson's citation of Vansina, *Oral Tradition: A Study in Historical Methodology*, trans. H.M. Wright (London: Routledge and Kegan Paul, 1961), 99.
53 Rachel A. Qitsualik, Contributor's note to Tantoo Cardinal, Tomson Highway, Basil Johnston, Thomas King, Brian Maracle, Lee Maracle, Jouette Marchessault, Rachel A. Qitsualik, and Drew Hayden Taylor, *Our Story: Aboriginal Voices on Canada's Past* (Toronto: Doubleday Canada, 2004), 36.
54 Knud Rasmussen, *The Intellectual Culture of the Iglulik Eskimos*, trans. W. Worcester, *The Report of the Fifth Thule Expedition*, vol. 7.1 (New York: AMS Press, 1976), 62; Michael Kennedy, 'The Sea Goddess Sedna: An Enduring Pan Arctic Legend from Traditional Orature to the New Narratives of the Late Twentieth Century,' in *Echoing Silence: Essays on Arctic Narrative*, ed. John Moss, Reappraisals: Canadian Writers series (Ottawa: University of Ottawa Press, 1997), 211, provides a more comprehensive list of Sedna's alternative namings.
55 The first textualizing of the Inuit Sea Goddess' story was, however, that taken down by the missionary Paul Egede from South Greenlanders in 1737, according to Birgitte Sonne, 'The Acculturative Role of Sea-Woman: Early Contact Relations between Inuit and Whites as Revealed in the

Origin Myth of Sea Woman,' *Meddelelser om Grønland, Man and Society* 13 (1990): 8, and in that version she was known by the name Nivigkâ.

56 Rasmussen, *Intellectual Culture*, 127, explains: 'Her hair hangs down loose all over one side of her face, a tangled, untidy mass hiding her eyes, so that she cannot see. It is the misdeeds and offences committed by men which gather in dirt and impurity over her body.'

57 Sonne comments that 'Even in details her poor look is modelled on the appearance of the earthly women during periods of tabu: Her hair hangs loose; filth accumulates in her hair and on her body; deprived of her fingers she is barred from doing any work whatsoever' ('The Acculturative Role,' 7).

58 Franz Boas reports, 'The abortions (agdlerutit) infest the hair of the deity of the sea-mammals and induce her to withhold the food-supply' (*The Eskimo of Baffin Land and Hudson Bay: From Notes Collected by Capt. George Comer, Capt. James S. Mutch and Rev. E.J. Peck*, article 1, *Bulletin of the American Museum of Natural History* 15 [New York: American Museum of Natural History, 1901–7], 358).

59 Mary Carpenter, who calls the Sea Goddess Nuriviq, relates:
Her chopped off fingers came back to her as fish, seals, walruses, and whales, all making their homes in her hair. But she couldn't comb this hair as she'd been able to do before. She didn't have any hands. All she could do was sit there at sea bottom, legs drawn up to her chest, and watch her hair grow more and more filthy with each passing day. Thus it is that shamans must swim down to the depths of the sea and comb Nuriviq's hair for her. And in her gratitude, she offers humankind all the creatures of the sea. The bounty in her long, spreading hair is endless ('Stories: "Skeleton Woman," "Woman of the Sea,"' in *Echoing Silence*, ed. Moss, 229–30).

60 Sonne, 'The Acculturative Role,' 7.

61 Ibid., 17, 20.

62 J.G. Oosten, *The Theoretical Structure of the Religion of the Netsilik and Iglulik* (N.p.: Meppel, 1976); Rémi Savard, 'La Déese Sous-Marine des Eskimo,' in *Échanges et Communications: Mélanges Offerts à Claude Lévi Strauss à l'Occasion de Son 60ème Anniversaire*, vol. 2, ed. Jean Pouillon and Pierre Maranda (The Hague and Paris: Mouton, 1970, 1,331–55; Sonne, 'The Acculturative Role,' 31.

63 Sonne, 'The Acculturative Role,' 32.

64 Michael P.J. Kennedy, 'The Sea Goddess Sedna: An Enduring Pan Arctic Legend from Traditional Orature to the New Narratives of the Late Twentieth Century,' in *Echoing Silence*, ed. Moss, 211–24. Alootook Ipellie,

being a visual artist as well as a writer, has also contributed to the enriching of Sedna's social life in his illustration of his own 'Summit with Sedna' (in *Arctic Dreams*) and of a story by Taivitialuk Alaasuaq, which Robin Gedalof introduces as a Sedna story that tries 'to reconcile the old beliefs with the technology brought north by the white traders' (Alaasuaq, 'The Half-Fish' in *Paper Stays Put: A Collection of Inuit Writing,* ed. Robin Gedalof, drawings by Alootook Ipellie [Edmonton: Hurtig, 1980], 94.)

65 Franz Boas, *The Central Eskimo.* Sixth Annual Report of the Bureau of Ethnology (1888; reprinted, Lincoln: University of Nebraska Press, 1964), 176.

66 Ibid. J. Edward Chamberlin comments that scientists properly belong to the company of namers, and he provides the reminder that 'naming things is one of the oldest forms of storytelling,' backing up his assertion with eloquent examples: 'inscriptions on ancient tombs like King Tutankhamun's ... monuments like the Vietnam War Memorial ... the names of wildflowers in the mountains of the Northwest where I grew up – Tweedy's snowlover, Tiling's monkeyflower, pussypaws or wooly pussytoes – [and] wonderfully named places like Froze-to-Death Lake and Hell-Roaring Plateau and Sundance Pass and Bumpy Meadows' (*If This Is Your Land,* 127). However, Boas' introduction of Latin scientific names into the Inuit narrative ruptures the sense of an Inuit voice speaking to us in traditional style.

67 Boas, *The Central Eskimo,* 179; Sonne, 'The Acculturative Role,' 20.

68 Boas, *The Central Eskimo,* 229.

69 Rasmussen, *Intellectual Culture,* 63, 66.

70 Ibid., 66

71 Ibid., 63.

72 Sonne, 'The Acculturative Role,' 11.

73 Boas, *Eskimo of Baffin Land,* article 2, 403, quoted in Sonne, 'The Acculturative Role,' 11.

74 Rasmussen, *Intellectual Culture,* 63.

75 Basil Johnston, 'Is That All There Is? Tribal Literature,' in *An Anthology of Canadian Native Literature in English,* 3rd ed., ed. Daniel Moses and Terry Goldie (Toronto: Oxford University Press, 2005), 103.

76 Boas, *The Central Eskimo,* 175.

77 Sonne, 'The Acculturative Role,' 9–10.

78 Boas, *The Central Eskimo,* 176.

79 Ibid., 229.

80 Shelagh D. Grant, 'Imagination and Spirituality: Written Narratives and the Oral Tradition,' in *Echoing Silence,* ed Moss., 199.

81 Christopher Trott, e-mail to the author, 27 October 2004.

82 Trott, who works in the University of Manitoba Native Studies Department, gave me this information in response to an earlier version of this paper that I gave at a conference entitled 'For the Love of Words: Aboriginal Writers of Canada' in Winnipeg, 30 September–2 October 2004. He also advised me to consider the relationship of the Sedna narrative (a spring or summer story) to the complementary origin story of the sun and the moon (a winter story), in which the girl who becomes the sun is not only required to expose her genitals to beings with long claws who violently scratch her exposed vulva but is also subjected to incest by her brother, who becomes the moon. For an exhaustive accounting of the complementarity of the two stories, see Savard, 'La Déese Sous-Marine des Eskimo.' Some of the features of east and southeast Greenland versions of the Sun and Moon story make the connection to the Sedna narrative even more interesting, in that the moon is represented as a 'fertilizing spirit-dog' (Sonne, 'The Acculturative Role,' 29). The bear-dog-moon equation of these variants is also noteworthy because Moon, being a winter spirit, is seen as the source of snow, which he produces from his belly by blowing it out a tube attached to his mouth. Sonne comments, 'His production of snow is thus likened to "vomiting," that is to ejaculation. Thus the snow he emits would, most likely, be his semen' (15). I am also grateful to Trott for the many bibliographical leads he gave me to the anthropological literature on the Sedna story.

83 Carpenter, 'Stories,' 225–6.

84 Craig Womack, *Red on Red: Native American Literary Separatism* (Minneapolis and London: University of Minnesota Press, 1999), 62.

85 Ipellie, 'Summit with Sedna,' 36. I have chosen to quote from the version of the story that appears in *Arctic Dreams and Nightmares* even though most students who know the story will probably have read it in *Anthology of Canadian Native Literature in English*, 3rd ed., ed. Moses and Goldie, 315–17. The latter replaces the bolding of certain words and phrases in the *Arctic Dreams and Nightmares* version (phrases such as 'sexual misconduct' in the passage quoted here) with quotation marks around the phrase. The attention called to this latter phrase may relate to its being appropriated from anglophone legal or psychological discourse, and quotation marks would then be the more textually conventional way of signalling that a formulaic phrase is being cited. The other bolded words in this story in the *Arctic Dreams* text are 'Frankenstein' and 'Andes,' both of which are names imported into Inuit discourse. Trott advised me that he has never encountered the name Andes in any other Inuit stories and that it cannot even be transliterated into Inuktitut. However, a number of other instances of

bolding in *Arctic Dreams* signal emphatic performance – 'It felt so wonderful to finally be a **free spirit**! (15), '**Serious** business' (72), and 'I **am** Rudolph Nureyev' (120), for example – make it difficult to determine whether the bolding of a phrase like 'sexual misconduct' is meant to signal a discursive import or emphasis, and for that reason, I follow the text over which Ipellie would have had some control.

86 First Ipellie says that Sedna can't release the sea beasts – 'She had begun to solicit for sexual favours before she *could* release the sea beasts to the Inuit living in the natural world' ('Summit with Sedna,' 36, emphasis added) – and then he reports a deliberate holding back: 'Sedna ... had decided to withhold all the sea beasts until a shaman, any old shaman, succeeded in releasing her sexual tensions' (37).

87 Ibid., 37.

88 Grant, 'Imagination and Spirituality,' 199.

89 Ong, *Orality and Literacy*, 38–9.

90 Like many who learn orally of Frankenstein rather than from Mary Shelley's novel, Ipellie refers to Frankenstein's monster as Frankenstein.

91 Ipellie, 'Summit with Sedna,' 38. The notion of shamans coercing the release of the sea mammals was reportedly evident in some ritual practices associated with Sedna. In 'The Eskimo of Baffin Island and Hudson Bay,' Boas observes that during the Sedna festival, shamans would invite Sedna to visit the people, but when she approached, a shaman would harpoon her, causing her to return to her undersea dwelling, whereupon she would release the mammals under her control. To hasten her descent, Boas remarks, Inuit men exchanged wives, a process in which, according to J.W. Bilby, the shaman exercised the right to pick first (*Among Unknown Eskimo: An Account of Twelve Years Intimate Relations with the Primitive Eskimo of Ice-Bound Baffin Land* [London: Seely Service, 1923], 210), followed by the most rhetorically or economically powerful men, and so on down to the youngest and relatively powerless adult male. The women had no choice in the matter, so that Sedna's violent coercion can be seen as a metonymy for the coercion Inuit women in general could suffer.

92 Ipellie, 'Summit with Sedna,' 39.

93 See n. 92, above.

94 Ipellie, 'Summit with Sedna,' 41.

95 Bernard Saladin d'Anglure, 'The Shaman's Share, or Inuit Sexual Communism in the Canadian Central Arctic,' *Anthropologica* 35 (1993): 60.

96 In the story that immediately precedes 'Summit with Sedna' – 'Public Execution of the Hermaphrodite Shaman,' in *Arctic Dreams and Nightmares*,

6–32 – another shaman who *does* trade on his powers for sexual benefit meets a terrible end. For making a journey to Sedna, he accepts payment of a night with a 'beautiful, virginal daughter ... faithful to her father' (28). The father barters the night in exchange for the shaman's help in overcoming his lack of success in hunting, but the night of bliss exposes the shaman's somatic sexual ambiguity, and as a result he is publicly executed.

97   I am grateful to anthropologist Chris Trott for pointing out to me that the story of the origin of the sun and moon suggests that incest has been a long-standing issue among the Inuit, not just a product of colonialism. Rasmussen heard this story from the Iglulik shaman Ivaluardjuk (Knud Rasmussen, *Across Arctic America: Narrative of the Fifth Thule Expedition* [New York: Greenwood Press, 1969], 124–5) and Boas provides another version in *The Central Eskimo*, 189–90. Savard, 'La Déese Sous-Marine,' 1335, produces a table showing that the moon god was in fact the dominant divinity among the Bering, Alaska, and east Greenland Inuit, thus suggesting how widespread his story was.

98   The shaman narrator of 'Ascension of My Soul in Death,' (in *Arctic Dreams and Nightmares*, 10–15) reports that his 'dear father, Joanassee' (12) was experiencing a spiritual resurrection simultaneous with his own, and the book *Arctic Dreams* is dedicated in part 'to the memory of my parents, Napatchie and Joanassie' (iii). Moreover the drawing on the front cover is titled 'Self-Portrait: The Inverse 10 Commandments' and shows a demonic shaman, his hair spread out like that of Ipellie in the photograph on the back cover. In the story for which this drawing was created, the narrator recognizes that the devilish face of this shaman is 'an incarnation of myself' (5).

99   Alootook Ipellie, 'The Five Shy Wives of the Shaman,' in *Arctic Dreams and Nightmares*, 58–66.

100   Beth Brant, 'Physical Prayers,' in *Writing as Witness*, 55.

101   The Mohawk story of the creation of Turtle Island is part of a shared heritage with other peoples from the Algonkian language family. In his preface to *Ojibway Heritage* (Toronto: McClelland and Stewart, 1976), which book includes a retelling of the creation of Turtle Island along with many other oral traditional narratives, Basil Johnston explains, 'Many, if not most, of the stories related in this book will be found to be similar to the stories of the Cree, Abenaki, Blackfoot, Micmac, Menominee, and other Algonkian speaking peoples. That this is so ought not to be astonishing. The similarities that exist simply suggest a common view of life' (8).

102   Beth Brant, 'Recovery and Transformation,' in *Writing as Witness*, 44.

103 Rona Rustige, collector, *Tyendinaga Tales* (Montreal and Kingston: McGill-Queen's University Press, 1988).

104 Brant, 'This Is History,' 19.

105 Ong, *Orality and Literacy*, 37–8; Brant, 'This Is History,' 21, emphasis added.

106 See, for example, the Mohawk version of the creation story in J.N.B. Hewitt's 'Iroquoian Cosmology,' in *Twenty-First Annual Report of the Bureau of American Ethnology*, by J.W. Powell (Washington, DC: Government Printing Office, 1908), 322. Brian Maracle's 'The First Words' (in Cardinal et al., *Our Story*, 11–32) has the Creator 'scoop[ing] up a handful of clay from the riverbank, and shap[ing] it into the doll-like form of a man,' before 'gently [blowing] into its mouth' (16) in order to show the first woman how she was made. He thus reverses the priority of male and female creation in the Genesis account, as Brant does, but he then makes his story more androcentric than hers by suggesting that the male person was more like the Creator in bodily form: 'He had the same muscles and form as the glowing figure' (16).

107 Brant, 'This Is History,' 21.

108 Ibid., 23.

109 Ibid., 24.

110 Ong, *Orality and Literacy*, 40. Though Brant had earlier added to the Coyote stories of her people's oral tradition in 'Coyote Learns a New Trick' (in *Mohawk Trail* [Toronto: Women's Press, 1985], 31–5), and had.in that story shown a positive attitude to two-spirited people by making both her main characters, Coyote and Fox, lesbians, her first extension of the oral tradition into writing made no apparent attempt to bring that tradition's oral style to the page.

111 In her 1988 introduction to *Tyendinaga Tales*, Rustige reports that 'the folklore of the Mohawks at Tyendinaga ... is almost non-existent' (ix).

112 Hewitt, 'Iroquoian Cosmology,' 137.

113 Alma Greene/Gah-wonh-nos-doh (Forbidden Voice), 'The Beginning of Sin,' in *Tales of the Mohawks* (Canada: J.M. Dent, 1975), 4.

114 Ibid.

115 Johnston, *Ojibway Heritage*, 13.

116 Rustige, *Tyendinaga Tales*, xiv–xv.

117 Maracle, 'The First Words,' 27.

118 Brian Maracle, Contributor's note to Cardinal et al., *Our Story*, 14.

119 Maracle 'The First Words,' 28.

120 Ibid.

121 Ibid.

122 Rudyard Griffiths, Preface to Cardinal et al., *Our Story*, 2.

123 Thomas King, *Green Grass, Running Water* (Toronto: HarperCollins, 1993).

124 In King's retelling of the narrative in *The Truth about Stories*, he does not use capitalization when he refers to the woman who fell from the sky until he suggests to the audience that 'we call her Charm' (12) but he does refer to the animals in his story as Birds, Moose, Rabbit, Fish, Badger, Ducks, and so on, to indicate that they are characters. When King's character the Lone Ranger begins to tell the Genesis creation story, Ishmael admonishes him, 'That's the wrong story ... That story comes later' (10).

125 Ibid., 164.

126 Brant, 'This Is History,' 24. The reference to menstruation in Brant's story is not an extraneous element that she alone introduces into the creation narrative. A Seneca version that Hewitt collected from John Armstrong and Andrew John explains menstruation by having one of the grandsons of the female man-being who fell from the sky throw blood clots at her in anger (Hewitt, 'Iroquoian Cosmology,' 252–3).

127 Brant, 'This Is History,' 26.

128 C.M. Barbeau, *Huron and Wyandot Mythology: With an Appendix Containing Earlier Published Records*, Department of Mines Geological Survey Memoir 80, Anthropological series no. 11 (Ottawa: Government Printing Bureau, 1915), 45.

129 Maracle, 'The First Words,' 20.

130 Greene, 'The Beginning of Sin,' 4.

PART THREE

Going Public

Chapter 5

'Private Stories' in Aboriginal Literature

KRISTINA FAGAN

In 2004 Cherokee writer Thomas King delivered the prestigious Massey Lectures and they were subsequently published as a book under the title *The Truth about Stories: A Native Narrative*. This published version, however, contains a final chapter, entitled 'Private Stories,' that was not part of the lectures. In this chapter King tells the story of his friends John and Amy Cardinal and their struggles with their adopted daughter, who has fetal alcohol spectrum disorder. As I read this chapter I was troubled by King's use of his friends' names and his public exposure of the family's problems.[1] Apparently he, too, was disturbed by his telling of the story. He writes, 'The story about John and Amy Cardinal is not a story I want to tell. It is, quite probably, a story that I should not tell. It is certainly not a story that I would want anyone to hear.'[2]

So he did not *tell* it in this lectures and no one *heard* it. But by writing and publishing it, he still exposed his friends to the public. Why did King view speaking and writing this story as substantially different acts? He goes on to offer a justification that is grounded in the different ways in which we experience the written and spoken word. He argues that because this story is on the page, it is a 'private story,' while oral stories, such as those spoken in a lecture theatre, are 'public stories.'[3] He cannot speak this story aloud to a listening audience, he writes, because he would 'end up weeping' over his own failure to help his friends.[4] Ashamed of this failure and uncomfortable with his emotional response to it, King did not want to share this story with a room full of strangers. But sitting alone at his desk, he was able to write the story of John and Amy Cardinal without feeling as though he was telling anyone and without having to face his audience's response. In writing, it felt like a 'private story' – though this was of course an illusion, since the story was to be published and thus made public.

Thomas King's struggle with whether and how to tell his friends' story exemplifies the different privacy protocols in oral and written forms of communication. The literary and the oral create different kinds of relationships between the teller/writer and the audience. Furthermore, as theorists of orality and literacy have argued, these different kinds of relationships have in turn had an effect on oral and literate cultures. In this essay I argue that with the arrival of literacy, Aboriginal people have had to grapple with a mode of communication in which teller and audience are separated in time and space. Aboriginal writers have sought to use the advantages of this mode while still respecting the traditional guidelines of their cultures over appropriate speech, guidelines that are grounded in face-to-face interactions. Examining a sampling of Aboriginal writing from its inception to the present in the region now known as Canada reveals an ongoing and conscious engagement with the questions of why, whether, and how to communicate 'private stories.'

The private is socially constructed, and its definition varies greatly between and within social groups and across time.[5] In general terms, however, the private is seen as belonging to an individual or a group and as inappropriate to share with the wider public. Because to expose the private is believed to cause harm, the maintenance of privacy is formally and informally policed; at the same time, however, the line between the private and the public is continually challenged. As an example, consider the ongoing debate over what constitutes appropriate clothing for girls and women in the Western world. Which body parts are too private to be exposed and in which situations? In this example, the private is a matter of public concern and discussion.[6] Similarly, this chapter is about the public negotiation – in Aboriginal literature – of privacy.

The line between the private and the public, I argue, has been drawn differently within Aboriginal and Euro-Canadian societies. Of course, in trying to discuss such a broad cultural difference, one is confronted with enormous cultural and individual diversity and with endless exceptions. Nevertheless, for the purposes of this essay, I would like to explore how this broadly defined difference sheds light on the development of Aboriginal literature. This difference is profoundly linked to the differences between orality and literacy, and more specifically, to the difference between thinking of communication as an *act* and as a *text* respectively.

To conceive of communication as an act is not a new idea. However, philosopher John Austin made this way of thinking explicit when he introduced speech act theory to the academy in 1955.[7] He pointed out that a sentence does not only (or even necessarily) make a statement *about* the world; it can itself be an action in the world. Language does more than provide information; it can also be used to promise, curse, command, abuse, threaten, testify, marry, and so forth, all of which we see as important and real acts. Speech acts occur in all cultures and in both writing and speech, but we often view them as more powerful in oral form, which is why we cannot get married by mail and why we insist that court testimony be given in person.[8] J.E. Chamberlin gives a striking example of the difference between act and text in his discussion of comedian Lenny Bruce, who was charged for a second time with obscenity for reading aloud the transcript of the court case in which he had been tried for obscenity. How, Chamberlin asks, can it be illegal to read aloud a legal document: 'What *is* there about the power of the spoken word and of performance? Wherein lies its exceptional power to offend?'[9] The answer, I believe, lies in the fact that we see the transcript as a text and reading it as an act. The immediacy of speech, its embodiedness, its unquestionable attachment to its speaker, and the physical proximity of its audience all lead us to see it as an act, an act for which we have a strong social responsibility (lest, like Bruce, we offend, or worse).

None of this is news to Aboriginal people. The assumption that speech is an act, that it can create (and not just reflect) reality, and that one must therefore be careful with it, is widely shared in Aboriginal societies. Arguably, that Aboriginal people were, until relatively recently, exclusively oral, has made this assumption particularly strong. Folklorist Barre Toelken confronted this belief in his work on Navajo Coyote tales. He saw himself as working on oral texts, albeit texts with great cultural value. But eventually he was warned by his informants that he was placing himself and his family in danger by dealing with stories that had the possibility, if used in the wrong way, of causing physical harm. He was in danger, he was told, of becoming a witch, and so he gave up further work on the tales. He realized that the Coyote stories were acts. Explaining the belief underlying this incident, Toelken writes, 'The Navajos believe that language does not merely describe reality, it creates it.'[10]

Thomas King's discussion of storytelling in *The Truth about Stories* echoes this idea that public speech is an act for which one is responsible. He writes that Aboriginal traditional oral stories are 'public stories,' told in a social context with social consequences. Storytellers must consider circumstances and relationships in order to avoid telling stories that are inappropriate. In Aboriginal North America, these social responsibilities have led to a sense of caution about speech. Thus, in traditional Aboriginal societies, the creation of stories is governed by protocols about what kinds of stories can be told and under what circumstances. As King explains, 'For Native storytellers, there is generally a proper time and place to tell a story ... Some are told only in the winter when the snow is on the ground or during certain ceremonies or at specific moments in a season. Others can be told only by certain individuals or families.'[11] To ignore these protocols is to risk very concrete consequences, from ostracism to, I have heard in Cree country, snakes and lizards in your bed.

So what does all this have to do with privacy? In a world where speech is seen as an act with social consequences, Aboriginal people have learned to be careful about what they say, observing the personal and cultural privacy of oneself and others, not exposing things that might be socially harmful.[12] Pueblo scholar Paula Gunn Allen explains that she was raised with these kinds of restraints around communication: 'Among the Pueblos, a person is expected to know no more than is necessary, sufficient and congruent with their spiritual and social place. One does not tell or inquire about matters that do not directly concern one. I was raised to understand that "street smart" around Laguna meant respecting privacy and modesty, and that to step beyond the bounds of the respected propriety was to put myself and others at risk.'[13]

Privacy protocols can protect not only individuals but also a society's social structures. Wayne Suttles describes, for instance, how in traditional Salish societies, the upper class maintained their status in part by maintaining a 'private or guarded knowledge' that they would not share with the lower class.[14] In such cultural contexts, where speaking is seen as risky, not speaking can become the preferred response to an uncomfortable situation, a response that may be responsible for the stereotype of the stoic and silent Indian. Pomo-Miwok writer Greg Sarris says that this is 'the Indian's best weapon': 'Be an Indian, cut yourself off with silence any way you can. Don't talk.'[15] Of course, such silence can be easily misinterpreted, as Rupert Ross learned when working as a Crown attorney in Northern communities. Ross recounts how he regularly confronted silence among Aboriginal witnesses, many of whom were unwilling to testify in court, even against people who had done them wrong. The accused also often refused to speak of the crime, and their psychiatric assessments, Ross recalls, almost invariably read something like, 'in denial, unresponsive, undemonstrative, uncooperative.'[16] These assessments, Ross came to realize, revealed more about cultural differences in communicative practices than they did about the accused individual. Both the accuser and the accused were part of a culture that discouraged the revealing of private and painful events, while the culture of the court and the psychologist's office valued disclosure.[17] And just as oral privacy protocols transferred to the court, they also, as I will show, transferred into Aboriginal literature.

By contrast Western culture often values personal disclosure, whether in courts, in therapy, on talk shows, or in literature, and many have argued that this value is connected to the Western world's long immersion in literacy.[18] People usually write and read alone, creating the *feeling* that these are private acts, cut off from social consequences. With literacy, knowledge is passed on 'not in a noisy community of other persons but in the silence of the library and isolated consciousness.'[19] Alberto Manguel writes that reading can be the ultimate retreat from the world: 'a self-centred act, immobile, free from ordinary social conventions, invisible to the world.'[20] It is perhaps because of this sense that reading and writing are removed from social norms and consequences that people will sometimes write a letter or an email to say something that they cannot bear to say face to face. And the mass reproduction of the printed word through the printing press and, more recently, through electronic media, creates an even greater separation between writer and reader. Unlike a storyteller, the published writer will often never meet his or her readers or know their response. This sense of privacy, sometimes even anonymity, allows for a level of personal disclosure in print (and over the internet) that one rarely finds in oral communication. As a result, within contemporary Western literary tradition a person's most intimate thoughts and experiences are very often at the centre of a text, and this sense of entering into the private life of a writer or character is seen as one of the most enjoyable aspects of reading. Jean Ronstand gives an apt definition of literature: 'Literature: proclaiming in front of everyone what one is careful to conceal from one's immediate circle.'[21]

This distancing of the written word from social consequences and responsibilities could be described as the emergence of the text. The term *text* is sometimes used simply to refer to the words that make up a composition or to any literary work; it also has a particular meaning within postmodern and deconstructionist theory. However, I use it here to emphasize the idea of the verbal work as an *object* rather than an action. In my usage a text is something that we may read, listen to, or watch, study, analyse, and evaluate, but it is not seen as having a direct and concrete consequences. This view of the text is why, when reading aloud from a literary work in my university classes, I will read any swear words, though I would never say those words to my students in my own voice. We are distanced from the words because they belong to the world of the text (though based on my students' occasional giggles, they may not all buy this distinction). This view of communication as text is particularly dominant in the world of literature and literary studies. In this world there is a widespread assumption that the written word is distanced from its author. Roland Barthes famously declared the author dead, and 'New Criticism' influentially insisted that neither the writer's intention nor the reader's response is relevant; our object of focus should be the text itself. And, while New Criticism has to some extent fallen from grace, literary critics are still primarily focused on what a text *means* rather than what it *does*. Those who insist that we take responsibility for a text's social function (such as those arguing for the censorship of particular books) are generally shouted down by those arguing for freedom of expression.[22] This discourse of freedom is radically different from the assumption of responsibility that is associated with speech acts. Of course, these issues are not settled in Western society. The debates over hate literature and erotic/pornographic writing, for instance, reveal a society not entirely certain of the line between text and act. Nevertheless, the assumption that literature is a text, detached from social responsibilities, seems to be linked to a culture of disclosure in the Western world.

Such disclosure of the private has not, however, always been part of Western communicative traditions. Its cultural emergence can be linked to the development of literacy and the printing press. Even the most cursory look at ancient oral-based poems, such as *The Iliad* and *Beowulf*, reveals them to be fundamentally different from what we now think of as poetry. They are not about the poet's individual and intimate feelings and experiences; rather, they tell stories that were part of their cultures' public domain. As Eric Havelock points out, the preliterate lyric was, in style and substance, 'other-oriented, not in any abstract sense, but in the sense that the other is an audience ... a listener.'[23] This other-orientation, he goes on to claim, is characteristic of societies based on oral communication.[24] Scholars have located the birth of modern Western conceptions of privacy and individuality at various points in history, but many argue that these concepts emerged in seventeenth-century Europe when the mass-produced book enabled a newly distanced relationship between writer and reader.[25] Havelock draws a sharp contrast between the pre-literate lyric and mass-printed poetry. Since the invention of the printing press, he says, the writer of poetry has become increasingly separated from the reader, increasingly introspective and personal, creating poetry as an 'exercise of the private imagination.'[26] Private reading in the seventeenth century also led to the development of the novel, which is widely argued to be the most individualistic and private of literary forms.

A similar process has occurred more recently in Aboriginal North America with the arrival of literacy and, with it, a literary tradition of the private writer and of personal disclosure. This tradition encountered an Aboriginal storytelling tradition that emphasized the public nature of speech and encouraged privacy and restraint. These two traditions suggest very different approaches to communication, as Métis writer Maria Campbell notes in the introduction to her collection of traditional stories, *Achimoona*: 'Now came the big job, to take those oral stories and put them on paper. It was hard, we had to change from telling a story to a group of people to being alone and telling the story to the paper.'[27] As Campbell's comment reveals, however, Aboriginal writers were not, as some communication theorists have suggested, unwitting victims of 'technological determinism,' that is, of automatic psychological and cultural changes that occur with the introduction of literacy.[28] Ong, for example, claims that 'it takes only a moderate degree of literacy to make a tremendous difference in thought processes,' suggesting that even a touch of literacy changes an individual's world view, and Havelock argues that these changes are largely unconscious.[29] However, more recent ethnographic studies have asserted that Native people were conscious of the impact of literacy and made calculated use of literary forms.[30] And indeed, a look at Aboriginal literature confirms that many writers made a decision to use writing for their own purposes but that they were also aware of the potential conflicts between oral and written protocols. They have tried to strike the balance that writer Ray Young Bear describes: 'I tried to make it a point to learn the English language, write it, and think in it, while at the same time trying to present some aspects of Mesquakie culture – without dealing with sensitive material.'[31]

The move to the written word is not, of course, simply a switch to another form (as it can sometimes seem in binarized descriptions of the oral and literate). The written word offers a wide range of communicative techniques. Seymour Chatman, in his study of narrative, has identified a range of possible positions for the teller of a story: the real author, the implied author, or the narrator. Similarly, the audience can be constructed within the narrative as a real audience, an implied audience, or a narratee.[32] This continuum can, I think, be associated with the continuum between orality and literacy. Oral narratives clearly have a real author (or, more accurately, speaker) and a real audience. The written fictional narrative, such as a novel or short story, with an imagined narrator and an implied or imagined audience who live entirely within the world of the text, relatively detached from social responsibility, is at the opposite end of the spectrum. In the remainder of this essay, I explore how Aboriginal writers have, over the centuries, moved along this continuum from the oral to the literary, from act to text, with a consequent increasing exposure of the private. I do not see this movement as a progression from less to more sophisticated, but rather as a gradual and conscious exploration of the potential of literacy as a tool, similar in many ways to the development of literacy in Europe.

Faced with significant differences between oral and written communicative protocols, Aboriginal people who first took up writing very often chose a form that, like oral speech, is based in relationships and involves direct social consequences – the letter. To use Chatman's terms, a letter is constructed to speak from a real author to a real audience. Seventeenth-century Jesuits recounted that the Huron were impressed by the ability of a letter to create a long-distance connection between people: 'They said that little paper had spoken to my brother and had told him all the words I had uttered to them here, and that we were greater than all mankind.'[33] The Huron were far less enthusiastic, however, about the private practice of reading books by writers who were personally unknown to the reader, a practice that would not have fit within their existing values about communication: 'They are astonished by the value we place upon books.' Farther north, letter writing was so enthusiastically adopted by the Inuit – who used it to send messages to family members across vast distances – that it actually spread ahead of European contact. And letters were also quickly seen as a powerful tool in dealing with white society.[34] Abraham Ulrikab, an Inuit man who was exhibited in European zoos in the 1870s, recounts that, when a member of his group was beaten by the zookeeper with a dog whip, he threatened to write a letter to England, publicly exposing this mistreatment, and his threat was effective.[35] Other early Aboriginal writers, such as Joseph Brant, Catherine Sutton, and Shinguaconce, also used letter writing in an effort to give Western legitimacy to their political causes.[36] It is not surprising then that the earliest extant pieces of writing that we have by Aboriginal writers are letters.[37] These letters are generally highly formal, working within both oral and written conventions of politeness and showing the heavy influence of oratorical traditions, and they make almost no references to personal feelings or relationships, focusing instead on events and on political and religious matters. Brant's letters, for instance rarely use 'I,' speaking instead for the collective 'we' and addressing issues of community concern. Early letter writing in England followed a similar pattern: 'Before 1640, letters were overwhelmingly political, religious and anonymous ... One rarely has the sense of individual voices; rather, the letters seem to be mouthpieces for ideas.'[38]

Literacy theorists have argued that in Europe, letter writing began the movement toward the figure of the private author[39] and indeed many of the first novels in English were epistolary in form: 'In an era in which oral literature was being replaced by the printed page, the absent correspondent was a symbol of the unknown and distant author, whose thoughts were transmitted, not in person, but via the ink marks on the page.'[40] A similar process appears to have taken place in North America; letter writing among Aboriginal people introduced the notion of the 'distant author,' and many of the earliest published works by Aboriginal writers clearly show the influence of letter writing, addressing the reader directly. As in earlier letters, these direct addresses were often a strategic effort to create a specific outcome. Lydia Campbell, for instance, an Inuit woman who published her autobiography in 1895, pleads directly with her readers: 'If I have interested any of you a little, my dear readers, pitty me and so send me a few yards of something for a skirt to keep my poor old tattered clothes from tearing in the woods and pulling me down with my snow shoes in deep snow.'[41]

At times the autobiography seems to be addressed to the minister who gave her the paper on which to write, but at other times she recognizes that her audience is distant and anonymous and calls them 'whoever you are'[42] moving from the 'real audience' of the minister to the 'implied audience' of a larger public. She also ends her autobiography in letter form: 'Goodbye, – God bless you. Your faithful friend, Lydia Campbell.'[43] Similarly, Henry Pennier, whose autobiography *Chiefly Indian* was published in 1972 when he was sixty-eight, begins with a friendly direct address: 'My name is Henry George Pennier and if you want to be a friend of mine please you will call me Hank'[44] and ends with the expectation that the book will create social relationships: 'Y'rs truly / Hank Pennier / P.S. write me a letter some time.'[45] Both these works are autobiography, a popular form for early Aboriginal writers, which allowed them to speak in their own voice as the 'real author.' Yet early Aboriginal autobiographies differ significantly from the typical Western autobiography, which is based in the revealing of the author's private life and thoughts. For example, despite the personal tone of Campbell's and Pennier's work, they are notably careful about what they share with their readers. Lydia Campbell, for instance, scarcely mentions her relationships with her two husbands or the deaths of many of her children, topics that would form the core of the typical Western autobiography; she focuses instead on community history, traditional stories, and the daily details of her work. Pennier similarly does not mention the details of his personal life. His wedding, for example, is wryly summed up: 'When I was twenty, I signed the lifelong contract for better or for worse. Which meant I really had to work for the rest of my life.'[46] Pennier is aware of the social consequences of writing too much: 'So I guess that's my story up to now or as much as I can remember of it and if I wanted to tell you the truth, as much as I want my wife to know about me. A man has to have some secrets.'[47] Unlike the Western autobiographical tradition, which emphasizes personal introspection and development, the works of Campbell and Pennier can instead be seen as part of a tradition that emphasizes the shared and social aspects of communication.

Maria Campbell's groundbreaking 1973 autobiography *Halfbreed*, while sharing some characteristics of Lydia Campbell's and Pennier's works, moved closer to the model of the private writer. She has said that her work emerged out of letter writing. However, unlike Campbell and Pennier, Maria Campbell wrote during a time of life when she was isolated, cut off from family and community, and so her book is a 'letter to nobody': 'I started writing a letter because I had to have somebody to talk to, and there was nobody to talk to. And that was how I wrote *Halfbreed*.'[48] Hence, although the narrative occasionally addresses the audience – 'I write this for all of you, to tell you what it is like to be a Halfbreed woman in our country'[49] – that audience is not depicted as a real entity who might send cloth or write a letter. It is perhaps because of the privacy out of which *Halfbreed* emerged that it was the most personally revealing work published by an Aboriginal writer in Canada to that point. Unlike previous Aboriginal works, which had been largely oriented toward describing events in the world, *Halfbreed* turned inward: 'Like me the land had changed, the people were gone, and if I was to know peace I would have to search within myself.'[50] As part of this personal search, Campbell describes her years as a prostitute and drug addict, her time in a mental institution, and even criticizes several Aboriginal leaders by name. As such, her work fits more clearly into the Western literary tradition of disclosure, which may be part of the reason that it rose instantly to the top of the bestseller list. As Campbell says, 'Canada wanted to know about Aboriginal people' and for the first time a book had appeared that revealed personal details of an Aboriginal person's life.[51] *Halfbreed*, however, still contains areas that seem to be too private to be disclosed. For example, Campbell's children, whom she repeatedly put into the care of others, are almost unmentioned.

Years after the publication of *Halfbreed*, Campbell began to work with director Paul Thompson and actor Linda Griffiths, both non-Native, to turn the material from *Halfbreed* into a play. This process, which turned out to be painful and confrontational, is documented in *The Book of Jessica*. Most critics have discussed this book in terms of race relations. However, the trouble arguably arose out of the movement from the written book to the oral form of the theatre. Like King, Campbell soon found that it was easier to write something than to have it said out loud. Griffiths recalls that she couldn't see the Maria whom she met as the person who had written the revealing *Halfbreed*: 'The person speaking to me was so reserved. Quiet, dignified, removed.'[52] Indeed, Campbell was raised to be very careful about what she said aloud: 'I could hear my grandmother telling me, "Think carefully before you say or think things. Be responsible, because the energy you put out can hurt others, and will come back to you."'[53] Not surprisingly then, it was difficult for Campbell to hear what she had written in *Halfbreed* said aloud by Griffiths before a 'real audience.' She explained to the actress: 'Do you realize how appalled I was at myself when I heard you *say* those things? ... I'd think, "How could I *say* something like that?" [emphasis added].'[54] Griffiths, meanwhile, was a believer in art as a way to break through social norms: 'I know now, there wasn't a sacred feather I didn't ruffle, a profound image I didn't tromp on, a gentle subtlety I didn't scream out to the skies.'[55] Despite the theatre's oral form, Griffiths saw the play as a text, as living in the world of the 'theatre gods' rather than the gods of everyday life.[56] Maria responded with increasing discomfort at the way that Griffiths was revealing her story to the world – 'I don't understand why you have to be so explicit'[57] – and she resisted the idea of art as disclosure: 'Today, most art is ugly ... It takes your stuff and hangs it up on the wall and it says, "Look what I've done. Isn't that wonderful. I'm an artist."'[58] The open struggle over the appropriate way to tell Maria Campbell's story in *Jessica* reveals the profound differences between privacy protocols in oral and written modes. And the publishing of *The Book of Jessica* is an example of how these differences are explicitly addressed within Aboriginal literature.

After the success of *Jessica* many Aboriginal writers turned to theatre, perhaps because drama's public and communal communication is similar to oral storytelling. Playwrights such as Tomson Highway, Daniel David Moses, and Drew Hayden Taylor were prolific and successful, and for many years Aboriginal literature in Canada was dominated by drama. In contrast, Aboriginal writers in Canada have been slow to take up novel writing (compared to their use of drama, poetry, autobiography, and political writing), despite the fact that novels are generally the most publicly acclaimed and financially rewarding form of literature.[59] When they have taken it up, their efforts have not always been widely understood or appreciated. This lack of Aboriginal novels is not surprising, however, when we consider that the traditional novel is in many ways diametrically opposed to the public and communal nature of orality.[60] With its solitary and imaginary narrator, its introspective and psychological voice, and, because of its length, its virtual requirement of private reading, the traditional novel is profoundly different from the oral story. Early European development of the novel and the genre's eventual dominance of Western literature have been linked to the increasing value placed on privacy in Western society.[61] As Ian Watt influentially argues in *The Rise of the Novel*, 'The development of the novel's concentration on private experience and personal relationships is associated with a series of paradoxes. It is paradoxical that the most powerful vicarious identification of readers with the feelings of fictional characters that literature had seen should have been produced by exploiting the qualities of print, the most impersonal, objective, and public of the media of communication.'[62] Aboriginal novels in Canada have grappled with this paradox. Rather than accepting the conventions of the traditional novel, Aboriginal writers have found ways to include traditional oral stories and oral conventions around privacy in this written genre.[63]

The first novel written by an Aboriginal person in Canada was Edward Ahenakew's *Old Keyam*, which he wrote in 1922 but which was not published until 1995 as Part Two of *Voices of the Plains Cree*. *Old Keyam*, however, is not a conventional novel but the oral, public voice transferred into written form. In each chapter an old storyteller, Keyam, speaks at length to a group of Aboriginal friends who have gathered to listen to him (here we have the emergence of Chatman's 'imagined audience'). He speaks on political matters, tells traditional stories, and recounts tribal history. Keyam is the main character but we know almost nothing of his personal life. In one chapter, for instance, he makes a lengthy but very general speech about the virtues of Aboriginal women.[64] At the end of the chapter, we are briefly told that that spring Keyam began to visit the camp of a woman named Cochena.[65] We are told no details of their relationship and so are as shocked as the rest of the community when the missionary announces Keyam's and Cochena's wedding a few lines later: 'Keyam went fishing up at one of the other lakes. I lent him my horse and rig. He and Cochena left right after their wedding ... I supposed that everyone knew. There was nothing hidden or secret about it.'[66] Here, of course, the missionary is wrong. The wedding was hidden, at least within the novel. Where a typical Western novel would make such a romance the focus of the reader's attention, Ahenakew has subordinated this private matter to the more public issues on which the novel is focused. It is not surprising that Ahenakew's novel was rejected by a number of publishers in his lifetime; it was surely not seen as fitting within the novel form as it is usually conceived.[67]

More recent Aboriginal novelists have had some similar difficulties with readers. Jeannette Armstrong's 1985 novel *Slash* has been criticized for containing the 'meetingest bunch of Indians I've ever come across.'[68] Helen Hoy says that when studying the novel, her students complained that 'they were "infuriated by the elision of the good parts" [that would have revealed] how the protagonist felt ... that characters were undifferentiated mouthpieces for position papers.'[69] Both of these comments emphasize the ways that *Slash* avoids the private and internal aspects of characters, favouring instead 'public speech.'[70] Similarly, Richard Wagamese's 1994 novel, *Keeper'n Me*, much like Ahenakew's novel, relies heavily on lengthy speeches from an Aboriginal elder who is teaching the younger generation about life and culture.[71] Reviewers complained that Wagamese's novel does not have fully developed characters, that it 'sacrifice[s] fiction to polemic,' and that it becomes a 'political tract,' again showing discomfort with the novel's preference for public voice over private reflection.[72] Ruby Slipperjack's 1987 novel *Honour the Sun* is a portrait of her Northern Ojibway community.[73] Slipperjack remembers felling ashamed when her book came out, feeling that she had violated privacy protocols: 'I used to burn everything I wrote because I would be so embarrassed that somebody would see these things.'[74] She also noted, 'All the years of burning stories – I never wanted anyone to see them, and here they were, out there for everyone to see. I remember a panic feeling!'[75] Despite these feelings of embarrassment, however, this is hardly a revealing novel; rather, it is marked by a striking 'discursive reticence,' and access to the Ojibway community's world is, according to Thomas King, 'remarkably limited.'[76] In her thoughtful essay on the novel, Helen Hoy tries to push beyond the kind of resistance other reviewers have shown to novels that refuse to expose the private. She examines many possible reasons for the silences in the novel; the silences, she writes, may be 'not only a withholding before an appropriating white gaze ... but also the enactment of an alternative metaphysics.'[77] I agree, and would add that this 'alternative metaphysics' may be deeply connected to the Ojibway people's long immersion in orality.

Aboriginal writers seem to be becoming more comfortable with putting 'private' material into their novels. Tomson Highway's *Kiss of the Fur Queen* and Eden Robinson's *Monkey Beach* both combine traditional oral stories with portraits of characters' private lives.[78] Although both works are distinctively Aboriginal in approach, drawing heavily on Aboriginal traditions in terms of structure and imagery, they also come closer to the 'private' novel than any previous Aboriginal novels in this country. They have an imagined narrator, do not rely heavily on public speeches, are written in a complex and imagistic style, and reveal intimate details of their characters' lives. And, perhaps not coincidentally, both have been critically acclaimed and nominated for numerous awards. However, neither novel moves unquestioningly into the realm of the private; rather, they contain complex explorations of the concept of privacy.

Eden Robinson has explained that she was filled with concerns about what she could appropriately write in *Monkey Beach*: 'I can't write about certain things or someone will go fatwa on me.'[79] However, Robinson revels in the privacy and anonymity of writing: 'I'm a very selfish writer. The best stuff comes when I'm not thinking about an audience, when I don't think about who's going to read this, what market it's going to.'[80] Perhaps because of this sense of privacy, Robinson's novel has crossed some cultural lines: 'I wrote about a feast, and I found out later you're not supposed to write about feasts in Haisla culture.'[81] These worries over appropriate balancing of the private and the public are also preoccupations within the novel itself. The narrator, Lisa Marie, is part of a Haisla community that has experienced a great deal of trauma – from epidemics, residential school abuses, and the like – and that deals with this history largely by keeping quiet about it. Lisa Marie has a special ability to receive messages from the land of the dead, an ability that allows her access to much of her community's painful past. But whenever she tries to talk about this, she is told that she is behaving inappropriately. For instance, she tries to ask her grandmother about the things that she sees and hears, but the traditional woman warns her away from potentially harmful knowledge: 'When someone dies, you have to be careful ... Best not to deal with it at all if you don't know what you're doing.'[82]

As the novel goes on, we see Lisa Marie gradually internalizing the caution about speaking the private. She even begins drinking and taking drugs as a way of blocking out the voices she hears. The novel itself replicates the kind of silencing that Lisa has learned; the section that deals with this period in her life is nearly completely elided, with two years covered in a few sentences: 'A catalogue of the parties I remember, the amount I drank, the drugs I did would be pointless. It's a blur. A smudge. Two years erased, down the toilet.'[83] Lisa Marie also becomes part of the silencing of other members of her community. For instance, when her friend Pooch commits suicide, probably because he was sexually abused, Lisa participates in the covering up of this underlying cause. Her friend Frank says that Pooch's ghost appeared to him, perhaps to tell him about the abuse, but Lisa responds by quieting him:

> 'That's a death sending,' I said, 'It's nothing to worry about. He probably just wanted to say goodbye.'
> 'Mm-hmm,' Frank said, obviously only half-listening, distressed. 'I saw that. He said ... he ... '
> 'Hey, hey, hey,' I said when he started to hyperventilate. 'You don't even have to tell me, okay?'[84]

This novel raises many questions about what constitutes appropriate speech. Can traditional ideas about privacy and caution become repressive or damaging? Are there circumstances in which speaking out about 'private' matters is necessary for individual and community health? The novel ends with conflicting messages about communication. In Lisa's final vision, her brother Jimmy's spirit orders her to 'Tell her,' that is, to tell his girlfriend a secret that he himself had covered up in life. But other ghosts refute this message, telling Lisa to just go home and have babies.[85] We never do find out whether Lisa does indeed tell the secret, and the novel leaves unresolved its questions about privacy.

Tomson Highway's *Kiss of the Fur Queen* also reflects on how one can tell about painful personal events while remaining part of a traditionally reticent culture. The fictionalized autobiography tells of Jeremiah and Gabriel Okimasis, of the abuse the Cree brothers suffered in residential school, and of the ongoing effects of that abuse on their adult lives. This novel is Highway's first time writing, albeit through the filter of fiction, about the sexual abuse that he himself suffered in school, abuse of which, for many years, he was unable to speak. In a 1990 interview he said about his residential school experience, 'A lot of kids got some really severe physical punishment, and there were a lot of darker occurrences which to this very, very day are next to impossible to talk about.'[86] In order to finally find a way to tell his own story, Highway turned away from the public world of the theatre, where he had previously worked, and to the private world of the novel.

Kiss of the Fur Queen is filled with scenes of explicit and abusive sexuality, and with revelations about the main characters' struggles with exploitive and self-destructive behaviour. Yet the novel also deals with the difficulty in saying these things aloud, and particularly in exposing them to the Cree community. Like Lisa Marie's Haisla community, the Cree community in Highway's novel is unwilling to speak about residential school abuse and other historical traumas. When the brothers see a ghost fire on an island where a shaman had once been captured by the Catholic church, their mother's only response is 'Don't look at it.'[87] So it is not surprising that the boys do not feel they can talk to their parents about what is happening to them at school. Even as an adult, Gabriel is unable to tell his mother that he has AIDS – 'How do you say AIDS in Cree, huh?'[88] The problem for Gabriel is not the Cree language itself but the tradition of personal restraint that comes with it. It is only as he moves into the more private world of writing that Jeremiah can begin to express his traumatic past. But he finds that he cannot do so directly, so he instead uses the metaphors of his culture, particularly the Weetigo, an insatiable cannibalistic monster. In his play he shows 'the cannibal spirit shedding his costume at death, revealing a priest's cassock.'[89] However, the play's reviewers do not understand this metaphorical message about the residential school priests, describing it as an 'image that comes from nowhere. And goes nowhere.'[90] Jeremiah's story, his brother tells him, was simply too indirect, too restrained: 'You didn't say it loud enough, Jeremiah.'[91]

Kiss of the Fur Queen is Tomson Highway's effort to 'say it loud enough,' though, like Jeremiah, he often prefers to speak through Cree metaphors.

For example, Highway describes Gabriel being molested by a priest: 'A dark, hulking figure hovered over him, like a crow. Visible only in silhouette, for all Jeremiah knew it might have been a bear devouring a honeycomb, or the Weetigo feasting on human flesh.'[92] Some critics have suggested that this metaphorical and aestheticized language serves to 'soften' the reality of abuse. Is it 'loud enough'? In both its form and content this novel works with questions about how to appropriately express personal experiences that are painful and potentially disruptive.

The deep cultural conflicts around these questions became clearer to me when I taught *Kiss of the Fur Queen* in an Aboriginal literature course with many Cree students. In class, I raised the topic of sexual abuse in the novel and read some of the passages describing the abuse aloud, inviting the students' responses. The usually talkative Cree students in the class were silent. Then, after class, an older Aboriginal woman approached me. She explained that she had worked with sexual abuse victims for many years and felt that Highway was responding to his own history of abuse in an unhealthy way. She said that she encouraged the people she worked with to write about their abuse and then to burn the piece of writing, symbolizing the process of letting their painful history go. Highway, she insisted, should never have published his book; he should have burned it. It was not good for him to speak about these private things.

In the next class, I decided to raise this issue. Is it appropriate to write about abuse like this, I asked. Suddenly, the Aboriginal students came to life. Virtually unanimously they expressed negative feelings about the novel. While acknowledging that it could play an important role in opening non-Native eyes to the reality of residential schools, they said that would do nothing but harm within Native communities. While their comments varied, there were several common threads. The students generally disliked the explicit abuse scenes and felt uncomfortable hearing them read out loud. These scenes, the students argued, just kept old wounds open. For others Highway's mistake was revealing not only his own but his late brother's private life. (Highway's brother Rene died of AIDS.) Meanwhile several non-Aboriginal students spoke forcefully in defence of the book, arguing that telling the explicit truth about residential schools was both personally healthy and politically necessary. This debate brought home to me that issues of privacy protocols are still very much alive in Aboriginal communities and that the cultural conflicts around privacy continue. I also began to understand what a difficult decision it must have been for Highway to bring this story into the public eye.

Both Robinson and Highway raise the question of the extent to which privacy protocols rooted in an oral world are still useful today. Traditionally, within small Aboriginal groups, difficult issues could often be dealt with without open discussion or disruption. However, Aboriginal people now live in an increasingly globalized world, where they are affected by people, cultures, and events far outside their own communities. For many Aboriginal writers, one way to try to make things better has been to open up their lives and their communities' lives to the larger public through writing and publishing. However, this writing often breaks through many of the traditional protocols about privacy, and the struggle with how much to tell is apparent in the works.

In returning to Thomas King's 'Private Stories,' it becomes clear that his explicit ethical dilemma about the story of John and Amy Cardinal is part of a long tradition of Aboriginal writers dealing with just such dilemmas. I have framed this predicament in terms of oral versus written traditions and their corresponding protocols around privacy. But at its core the issue is one of different sorts of responsibility. In King's case, for instance, he is torn between his responsibility to his friends and his responsibility to try to improve the world. His argument in this chapter is that we should face our responsibilities and not duck out on them when things get too hard, as he did when his friends were having problems. Like many of the writers I have discussed, he can see the good that can be served by disclosing personal pain. In the end he decides to tell this particular story, but remains throughout the book noticeably silent on the topic of his own wife and his adopted children. Some stories remain truly private.

King's active engagement with the question of his responsibilities as a storyteller and a writer is an important reminder that many Aboriginal writers, like him, have consciously and responsibly engaged with the differences between orality and literacy. Too often, literacy has been described as either an assimilative force in Aboriginal culture – a colonial form that is destroying oral storytelling – or, alternatively, as a potential salvation for disappearing oral traditions. Both of these stances depict Aboriginal people as objects to be changed, destroyed, or saved by powerful cultural forces rather than as active subjects.

Alternatively, we can consider the findings of Sylvia Scribner and Michael Cole, who, through extensive experimentation, studied the impact of literacy on the Vai people of Africa. Their findings were 'in direct conflict with persistent claims that 'deep psychological differences' divide literate and non-literate populations.'[93] Scribner and Cole instead concluded that the Vai were able, as individuals, to work with various cultural influences: 'We have seen that Vai culture is *in* Vai literary practices ... But literary activities are carried out by individuals, and our research has shown that psychological skills are also *in* Vai literary practices.'[94] Much like Scribner and Cole, I want to emphasize that Aboriginal people are capable of holding orality and literacy, act and text, private and public in tension, of seeing the usefulness and dangers of each. Furthermore, by being aware of this active engagement in Aboriginal literature, we can see the marked silences, the areas of privacy in so much of the literature, not as literary failings but as deliberate choices about what should and should not be told.

NOTES

1 King does not mention whether or not he changed the names for publication.
2 Thomas King, *The Truth about Stories: A Native Narrative* (Toronto: House of Anansi, 2003), 166.
3 Ibid., 154.
4 Ibid., 166.
5 Mark Le, 'Privacy: An Intercultural Perspective,' *Broadening the Horizon of Linguistic Politeness*, ed. Robin Lakoff and Sachiko Ide (Amsterdam: John Benjamins, 2005), 275–82.
6 There are, of course, private moments that will never be more widely shared, but such 'true' privacy is not my concern here.
7 John L. Austin, *How to Do Things with Words*, William James Lectures, 1955 (Cambridge, MA: Harvard University Press, 1962).
8 There are exceptions of course. A written contract, for instance, is seen as more legally powerful than a spoken promise. Though, for many, 'giving one's word' is more morally binding than giving one's signature.
9 J.E. Chamberlin, 'Doing Things with Words: Putting Performance on the Page,' *Talking on the Page: Editing Aboriginal Oral Texts*, ed. Laura Murray and Karen Rice (Toronto: University of Toronto Press, 1999), 69–70.
10 Barre Toelken, 'Life and Death in the Navajo Coyote Tales,' *Recovering the Word: Essays on Native American Literature*, ed. Brian Swann and Arnold Krupat (Berkeley: University of California Press, 1987), 390.
11 King, *The Truth about Stories*, 153; For a useful discussion of Aboriginal concepts of privacy, particularly in the context of sacred cultural material, see David Moore, 'Rough Knowledge and Radical Understanding: Sacred Silence in American Indian Literatures,' *American Indian Quarterly* 21, no. 4 (1997): 633–62.

12 See accounts of this concern with privacy in Roger Spielmann, *'You're So Fat!': Exploring Ojibwe Discourse* (Toronto: University of Toronto Press, 1998); Ronald Scollon and Suzanne B.K. Scollon, *Linguistic Convergence: An Ethnography of Speaking at Fort Chipewyan, Alberta* (New York: Academic Press, 1979); Paula Gunn Allen, 'Special Problems in Teaching Leslie Marmon Silko's *Ceremony*,' *American Indian Quarterly* 14, no. 4 (1990): 379–80; Rupert Ross, *Dancing with a Ghost: Exploring Indian Reality* (Markham, ON: Octopus, 1992); Clare C. Brant, 'Native Ethics and Rules of Behaviour,' *Canadian Journal of Psychiatry* 35 (1990): 534–9; Mary Black-Rogers, 'Ojibwa Power Interactions: Creating Contexts for "Respectful Thought,"' in *Native North-American Interaction Patterns*, ed. Regna Darnell and Michael K. Foster, Proceedings of the conference on Native North American Interaction Patterns, Edmonton, 1982 (Hull, QC: Canadian Museum of Civilization, 1988), 44–68.

13 Allen, 'Special Problems in Teaching,' 379–80.

14 Wayne Suttles, 'Private Knowledge, Morality, and Social Classes among the Coast Salish,' *American Anthropologist* 60 (1958): 501.

15 Greg Sarris, *Keeping Slug Woman Alive: A Holistic Approach to American Indian Texts: A Holistic Approach to American Indian Texts* (Berkeley: University of California Press, 1993), 81.

16 Ross, *Dancing with a Ghost,* 33.

17 As I discuss later in this chapter, such reticence has also been misunderstood in a literary context.

18 Of course, the widespread disclosure of 'private matters' in Western cultures may also be related to other causes, such as the feminist movement or the sexual revolution, but for the purposes of this chapter, I focus on the links between privacy and literacy. Also it is true that Western cultures deeply value some forms of privacy, such as the privacy of the doctor's office or the confessional, but I am primarily concerned with how the value placed on disclosure has affected literature.

19 Alvin Kernan, *Samuel Johnson and the Impact of Print* (Princeton, NJ: Princeton University Press, 1989), 220–1.

20 Alberto Manguel, *A History of Reading* (New York: Viking, 1996), 153.

21 Jean Ronstand, quoted in Ralph Keyes, *The Courage to Write: How Writers Transcend Fear* (New York: Henry Holt, 1995), 38.

22 The debate in Canada in the 1980s and '90s over literary appropriation of the Aboriginal voice is an example of the tension between valuing a work's social function and valuing its free expression, a tension that played itself out largely along Aboriginal/non-Aboriginal lines.

23 Eric Havelock, *The Muse Learns to Write: Reflections on Orality and Literacy from Antiquity to the Present* (New Haven, CT: Yale University Press, 1986),

20. Homer scholar Ruth Scodel has recently confirmed this insight in her study of the Homeric audience, *Listening to Homer: Tradition, Narrative, and Audience* (Ann Arbor: University of Michigan Press, 2002).

24 Havelock, *The Muse,* 20.

25 Cecile M. Jagodzinski, *Privacy and Print: Reading and Writing in Seventeenth-Century England* (Charlottesville: University Press of Virginia, 1999), 1.

26 Havelock, *The Muse,* 20.

27 Maria Campbell, *Achimoona* (Saskatoon: Fifth House, 1985), x.

28 Peter Wogan 'Perceptions of European Literacy in Early Contact Situations,' *Ethnohistory* 41, no. 3 (1994): 408.

29 Walter J. Ong, *Orality and Literacy: The Technologizing of the Word* (London: Routledge, 1982), 50; Havelock, *The Muse,* 29.

30 Wogan, 'Perceptions of European Literacy,' 408.

31 Ray Young Bear, quoted in Moore, 'Rough Knowledge,' 647.

32 Seymour Chatman, *Story and Discourse: Narrative Structure in Fiction and Film* (Ithaca, NY: Cornell University Press, 1978), 28.

33 Seventeenth-century Jesuits, quoted in Wogan, 'Perceptions of European Literacy,' 412. Wogan rightly points out that we should be suspicious of Jesuit accounts of how the Hurons saw them as godlike, a claim that could clearly be self-serving. Nevertheless, this description of the response to letter writing seems valid (if perhaps exaggerated).

34 Penny Petrone, *Native Literature in Canada: From the Oral Tradition to the Present* (Toronto: Oxford University Press, 1990), 60–70.

35 Abraham Ulrikab, *The Diary of Abraham Ulrikab: Text and Context*, ed. Hartmut Lutz (Ottawa: University of Ottawa Press, 2005), 29.

36 For an overview of many of the extant letters by early Aboriginal writers, see Penny Petrone, *Native Literature in Canada.*

37 Ibid., 70.

38 Jagodzinski, *Privacy and Print,* 77–8.

39 M.M. Bakhtin, *The Dialogic Imagination: Four Essays,* ed. Michael Holquist (Austin: University of Texas Press, 1981), 143.

40 Jagodzinski, *Privacy and Print,* 124.

41 Lydia Campbell, 'Sketches of a Labrador Life by a Labrador Woman,' typescript, Labrador, 1895, p. 14.

42 Ibid.

43 Ibid., 45.

44 Henry Pennier, *Chiefly Indian: The Warm and Witty Story of a British Columbia Half Breed Logger,* ed. Herbert L. McDonald (West Vancouver, BC: Graydonald Graphics, 1972), 11.

45 Ibid., 30.

46 Ibid., 50.

47 Ibid., 129.

48 Maria Campbell, Interview with Hartmut Lutz, in *Contemporary Challenges: Conversations with Canadian Native Authors*, ed. Hartmut Lutz (Saskatoon: Fifth House, 1991), 53.

49 Maria Campbell, *Halfbreed* (Toronto: McClelland and Stewart, 1973), 2.

50 Ibid.

51 Maria Campbell, quoted in Ned Powers, 'Friends Revisited: Therapy through Writing – Campbell's Bestseller Began as Letters to Self,' *StarPhoenix* (Saskatoon), 1 November 2005, C1.

52 Maria Campbell and Linda Griffiths, *The Book of Jessica: A Theatrical Transformation* (Toronto: Coach House, 1991), 33.

53 Ibid., 61.

54 Ibid., 31.

55 Ibid., 32.

56 Ibid., 41.

57 Ibid., 69.

58 Ibid., 84.

59 The history of the Aboriginal novel differs substantially in Canada and the United States. In the United States, the most prominent Native writers (Leslie Marmon Silko, N. Scott Momaday, James Welch, Louise Erdrich, and so forth) were university educated and often employed by universities. These writers, presumably deeply familiar with the novel, turned quickly to this form. In Canada, the most prominent Aboriginal writers generally emerged from the 'grassroots' of activism, community arts programs, and so on, and were arguably more deeply versed in orality than in literary traditions. One of the most prominent Aboriginal novelists in Canada, Thomas King, comes from the United States and from an academic background. The reasons for this difference are complex and beyond the scope of this essay.

60 Of course, the relative lack of Aboriginal novelists in Canada is also surely connected to practical matters. For instance, until recently, few Aboriginal people could afford the luxury of full-time writing and therefore perhaps did not have the long stretches of time needed for novel writing.

61 Walter Benjamin, 'The Storyteller,' in *Illuminations: Essays and Reflections* (New York: Harcourt Brace Jovanovich, 1968), 87; George Steiner, 'Literature and Post-History,' *Language and Silence: Essays on language, Literature, and the Inhuman* (New York: Atheneum, 1970), 389.

62 Ian Watt, *The Rise of the Novel: Studies in Defoe, Richardson, and Fielding.* (Berkeley: University of California Press, 1957), 206.

63 Many critics have explored the ways in which Aboriginal novels in Canada challenge the conventional novel form by including oral stories, traditional cultural elements, community concerns and voices, political priorities, and so forth. However, none have examined the treatment of privacy in the novels.

64 Edward Ahenakew, *Old Keyam*, in *Voices of the Plains Cree* (Regina: Canadian Plains Research Center, 1995), 76–8.

65 Ibid., 79.

66 Ibid.

67 Stan Cuthand, 'Introduction to the 1995 Edition,' *Voices of the Plains Cree*, xiii.

68 Keeshig-Tobias, quoted in Helen Hoy, *How Should I Read These?: Native Women Writers in Canada* (Toronto: University of Toronto Press, 2000), 39.

69 Ibid., 35.

70 Jeanette Armstrong, *Slash* (Penticton, BC: Theytus, 1990).

71 Richard Wagamese, *Keeper'n Me* (Toronto: Doubleday, 1994).

72 Joseph Kertes, 'An Outsider Goes Home to His Indian Roots,' review of *Keeper'n Me*, by Richard Wagamese, *Toronto Star*, 13 August 1994, F2; Review of *Keeper'n Me*, by Richard Wagamese, *Quill and Quire* 60, no. 5 (1994): 24; Paula Simons, 'First novel shows a real promise,' review of *Keeper'n Me*, by Richard Wagamese, *Edmonton Journal*, 21 August 1994, C2.

73 Ruby Slipperjack, *Honour the Sun* (Winnipeg: Pemmican, 1987).

74 Ruby Slipperjack, quoted in Kathleen Keena, 'Writer's Secret Thankfully Exposed,' *Toronto Star*, 15 October 1993, B13.

75 Ruby Slipperjack, quoted in Jennifer David, *Story Keepers: Conversations with Aboriginal Writers* (Owen Sound, ON: Ningwakwe Learning, 2004), 27.

76 Hoy, *How Should I Read These?* 64, 65.

77 Ibid., 80.

78 Tomson Highway, *Kiss of the Fur Queen* (Toronto: Doubleday Canada, 1998): Eden Robinson, *Monkey Beach* (Toronto: Knopf Canada, 2000).

79 Eden Robinson, quoted in Suzanne Methot, 'Spirits in the Material World: Haisla Culture Takes Strange Shape in Eden Robinson's Monkey Beach,' *Quill and Quire* 66, no. 1 (2000): 12.

80 Ibid.

81 Ibid.

82 Robinson, *Monkey Beach*, 152–4.

83 Ibid., 296.

84 Ibid., 313.

85 Ibid., 374.

86 Tomson Highway, Interview with Adrienne Clarkson in *Tomson Highway: Native Voice*, Adrienne Clarkson Presents series (Toronto: CBC Educational Video Sales, 1990).

87 Highway, *Kiss of the Fur Queen*, 90.
88 Ibid., 296.
89 Ibid., 285.
90 Ibid.
91 Ibid.
92 Ibid., 79.
93 Sylvia Scriber and Michael Cole, *The Psychology of Literacy* (Cambridge, MA: Harvard University Press, 1981), 251.
94 Ibid., 259.

Chapter 6

From Family Lore to a People's History: Ukrainian Claims to the Canadian Prairies

NATALIA KHANENKO-FRIESEN

When in 1932, Ivan Pylypiw recounted his coming to Canada to Professor Ivan Bobersky,[1] neither of them could have predicted that Pylypiw's story would acquire a life of its own, serving, in more than one way, not only the Pylypiw descendants but also the history of Ukrainian Canadians at large.[2] It was early spring when the Winnipeg-based professor set out to visit Pylypiw on his rural Alberta farm. The train took him the majority of the distance, but Bobersky still had to travel by sleigh for the last three-quarters of an hour after leaving the town of Lamont. For Bobersky, the locale and the rural western Canadian frontier's ambiance were as memorable as the stories he was about to record:

> The snow was melting so the sleigh had to cross puddles of water and mud ... The farm house was a two-storey building. I found the lady of the house in a well-heated room. She felt very weak and did not want to talk. Her face was pale from illness and her hands had no strength ... The rooms were spacious but untidy. The almanac *Kanadiisky farmer* lay on the table. The yard was big. So was the barn and the stable, even though in Canada farmers get by without them ... The whole area was covered in deep snow. A wide road, which ran parallel to the farm in both directions, led to the railway station. Telephone poles ran alongside the road and a line from one of them carried electricity to the house. This distant farm in the midst of a snow-covered expanse was connected to the world.[3]

Only at dusk did the professor make it back to town, just in time to take a train to the community of Chipman, where the next day he interviewed another early Ukrainian settler, Wasyl Eleniak, who, as the academic noted, 'told his story calmly and sincerely, choosing his words carefully.'[4]

The two men Bobersky sought out on that spring, Eleniak and Pylypiw, had long ago been pronounced the 'trailblazers of the Ukrainian immigration to Canada' by some Ukrainian-Canadian writers.'[5] One can assume that this encounter – forty-one years after their arrival in Canada – was not the first time the two Ukrainian farmers had spoken to others of their move to the new country. In talking to a professor from Ukraine, Eleniak was solemnly reconstructing his life story. So was Pylypiw. As Bobersky wrote, 'a friend of Ivan Pillipiw's, a farmer from Star, listened to our conversation and helped him remember different things.'[6]

It may also be expected that by 1932 not only had the words already been assigned their positions in the men's respective stories but also the ideas – the social and folkloric commentary they used in their stories – had long been sequenced in a particular narrative order. Together they presented the listener, in that case a professor from Ukraine, with an already structured account of a particular moment in their past. It happened that Bobersky published only Pylypiw's story, choosing it over Eleniak's. Although Eleniak's recollections were also eventually publicized, it is Pylypiw's story that travelled further into the world of Ukrainian-Canadian history.[7]

In this chapter I explore the Ukrainian-Canadian mechanics of myth-making and the narrativization of history by analysing the life and organization of Ivan Pylypiw's story of coming to Canada. I place Pylypiw's account within the context of other similar oral and written stories recounted on the prairies throughout the twentieth century, with the idea to demonstrate that the narrative principles of orality played an important role in creating and maintaining Ukrainian-Canadian society's cultural memory, history, and identity.

My approach to this question is informed by the disciplines of folklore and anthropology. Both, especially as practised in North America, have been shaping my understanding of the world for more than a decade. As a folklorist I cannot bypass the oral principles behind the organization of life story narratives such as Pylypiw's. As an anthropologist I must explore the relationship between these principles and the mechanisms of further narrativization – and mythologization – of the beginnings of Ukrainian-Canadian culture on the Canadian prairies.

Let me return to the story and to Mr Pylypiw himself. First I will briefly discuss the historical contexts into which both the man and his story were born. Then I will look at the organization of the story in order to underpin its oral and vernacular nature and to look at its further mediation and post-oral life. Since Pylypiw's experience of coming to Canada was similar to the experiences of many others, my analysis will be made against the background of the vast numbers of other accounts of Ukrainian immigration and settlement that were voiced, documented, reproduced, and gradually storied in various forms throughout the twentieth century as Ukrainian Canadians progressively tried to shape their family and public histories. The two different levels of analysis, one of a story itself and the other of a collectively storied memory of 'the Move,' shall be employed jointly to facilitate an understanding of the self-maintenance mechanisms of an ethnic culture; mechanisms that continue to rely on oral and vernacular modes of communication even in times of late modernity.

The Man and His Time

A farmer in western Ukraine, Ivan Pylypiw was born in 1859, a time when Europe was experiencing mass emigration to what was called the New World. Until the last third of the nineteenth century, Pylypiw's home village of Nebyliw, as well as the rest of his province of Galicia, then a part in the Austro-Hungarian Empire, was on the fringe of the major migration thoroughfares. Starting in the 1860s the situation changed, with thousands of Ukrainian peasants taking off for the Americas lured by promises of free farmland. In the 1890s the Canadian government decided to recruit prospective immigrants from eastern Europe to set up farms in western Canada. Galicia was hit hard by the aggressive Canadian campaigning, particularly because it promoted the idea of free land to the short-of-land Ukrainian peasants. After learning about the free lands on the prairies from German acquaintances who had emigrated there earlier, Pylypiw did not miss an opportunity to explore Canada for himself.

Pylypiw was endowed with a profound sense of agency, which he successfully utilized throughout his life to better his lot. This occasion was no exception. In this case, however, his and his family's relocation to a new world coincided with, if not contributed to (as community speakers would often have it), yet another profound turn in the course of Ukrainian history.

Having been among the very first officially registered immigrants from Ukraine to settle and farm the 'lands beyond the ocean,' Pylypiw and Eleniak were inevitably linked by future researchers to the starting point of Ukrainian-Canadian culture. Being the first served them well;

as trailblazers both took high positions in the symbolic pantheon of Ukrainian-Canadian history makers. Being entrepreneurial and successful farmers, who never abandoned their community, most certainly helped them to achieve such high placement. Had their stories been ones of immigration failure or community desertion, their lives would not have been celebrated in such a hagiographic fashion, as Ukrainian-Canadian grassroots annalists have done for over a hundred years.

As an outcome of such self-positioning in history, Ukrainian Canadians are routinely informed that it is due to the actions of Pylypiw and Eleniak that the Ukrainian exodus to Canada ultimately swelled to 170,000 immigrants between 1891 and 1914. Such an interpretation of history has also found its way into the Canadian cultural mainstream:

> Ukrainian immigration commenced in 1891 when Ivan Pylypow of Nebyliv, Kalush district, Galicia, learned about the 'free lands' available on the Prairies ... After investigating settlement possibilities in Manitoba and Alberta with Wasyl Eleniak, a fellow villager, Pylypow returned to Galicia to bring back both men's families and as many friends and relatives as could be persuaded to accompany them. Although he was arrested and tried for sedition by the Austrian authorities, and prevented from making his way back to Canada until 1893, the publicity generated by his trial advertised Canada more effectively than he himself could have done. By 1894 a Ukrainian settlement had emerged in the vicinity of Star, Alberta.[8]

Let me return to the Pylypiw's story itself. By the time of Bobersky's interview, Pylypiw was seventy-three years old and had been in Canada for forty-one years. He was a successful farmer with many ambitions. His family had added several generations to the one that arrived on the North American continent, and his story of coming over had been retold repeatedly in various circles of family members, neighbours, and friends. On the larger scale of things, the Ukrainian-Canadian community had accumulated by now the additional shared experiences. During the First World War they were interned by the Canadian government and, between 1924 and 1932, derided as 'bohunks' by Anglo-Protestant Canadians. Pylypiw and others of his generation who had weathered these challenges lent support to the 40,000 second-wave Ukrainian immigrants who arrived on the Canadian prairies during that time. In addition to advice and assistance, Pylypiw and others of his generation offered up their own personal immigration and settlement stories. Over time these narratives assumed ever greater public weight and in the process they were transformed from personal narratives into normatized and shared cultural commodities. And in the process, they began to be written down.

The form and the aesthetic 'packaging' of Pylypiw's story attest to both his skills as a storyteller and to the narrative principles of oral culture of which he was a bearer. When relating his experiences to a professor from afar, in order to impress a visiting historian, Pylypiw appears to have made a special effort to present his story in a coherent, normative manner that would be appreciated and understood by the outsider. As a Ukrainian Pylypiw possessed a culturally specific way of organizing, and speaking about, his experiences. He was, in short, a product of his culture, and ordered his recollections according to the narrative forms and folkloric principles with which he had been inculcated throughout his life.

Almost eighty years later, we are denied the opportunity of participating in the Pylypiw/Bobersky storytelling event. What is left to us, the twenty-first century curious, is only the written text of Bobersky's interview. It is a record of Pylypiw's own reminiscences that throughout the remaining years of the twentieth century migrated from one publication to another, from one language to another (Ukrainian to English), and eventually seeped back to the old country, Ukraine, as Ukrainians in the early 1990s began celebrating the hundredth anniversary of their – that is Pylypiw's – settlement in Canada.

Although Bobersky did not have a tape recorder with him, he carefully transcribed the detailed notes he took during his conversation with Pylypiw, thus preserving most of the original wording and cadence of Pylypiw's speech. Throughout its life as captured oral literature, the story has been abridged many times to suit the needs of subsequent Ukrainian-Canadian publications. Still, in its fullest versions, from 1937 and 1978, the text attests to the vitality of oral tradition as well as oral principles of composition, narrative organization, and plot development in the face of rising literacy and emerging modernity. In what follows I discuss the genre and the content of the story and look at the oral principles behind its narrative organization.

The Story

Had folklore scholars analysed Pylypiw's account, they would have labelled it either a *memorat*,[9] a *true experience* story,[10] a *family saga*,[11] or an *immigrant tale*. All would have agreed, though, that the account is held together by many folkloric threads common to Ukrainian oral tradition. On one level this loose application of established principles of orally composed narratives, according to Robert Klymasz, is the defining feature of a *memorat*, in our case a story of an immigrant's move from one world to another.[12] On another level it is an indication of orality's vitality and adaptability to dynamic modern contexts.[13] Such stories follow a particular line of content development. The account starts in the 'old country,' as the narrator provides a historical rationale for his emigration. The structuring depends on threefold repetition, dramatized dialogues, and endings signalled by a sudden and explosive climax. Yet no matter how loose the structure and how flexible the framework of these stories, they do follow certain organizational principles.

The first-person accounts, and the dialogues inserted in them, are often conveyed through direct speech and the present tense. Other narrative devices these stories rely upon on include hyperbole – 'Even if it rained [as far as away] in Winnipeg, everything would already be floating in the house' – and the constant juxtaposition of 'then' and 'now,' the 'old' and the 'new,' the 'good old days' and the evils of 'today.'[14]

Inserted within the interview with Bobersky, Pylypiw's tale unfolds in a similar fashion. As an immigration tale it clearly stands out from the rest of the interview material. It starts with the fairy-tale-like beginning of a 'once upon a time' kind:

> *One day* I asked one of the Germans, 'Do you have the address of your relatives?'
> 'I have.'
> 'Write it down for me.'
> '*Very well.*'
> Harvey wrote the address of his son and daughter, and I wrote them a letter. They answered, 'Leave *the hills and the valleys* behind and move here.'[15]

The tale progresses, observing many formal principles of orally composed narratives at the level of both *composition*, where particular 'laws' of oral narrativity typical of the Anglo-European vernacular epic are observed, and *morphology*, where scene and character development follow rules characteristic of folk tales observed in Slavic contexts.[16] The vernacular and oral nature of his narrative is readily apparent at the composition level. Pylypiw-the-storyteller followed the established ways of telling a story, relying on traditional speech patterning (stock phrases, epithets, and so forth) and repetition. Throughout the whole story, the tale utilizes common stock phrases, expressions like 'the hills and the valleys' and 'simple folk,' characteristic of the Ukrainian vernacular storytelling, although nowadays seen as clichéd expressions. The story also relies on repetition of words and phrases. 'Very well,' for example, is often repeated, as are whole expressions as reflected in the following excerpt:

> People asked me all kinds of questions: where I had been and what I had seen. [Pylypiw recalls his encounters with his co-villagers after returning from Canada to Nebyliw to get his wife]. I told them many stories about Canada and urged them, *'Flee, flee this place, for here you have nothing, and there you will have free land and be your own boss.'*
> The curious ones would stay around me. I would tell them all they wanted to know. I would say, *'Flee, flee, for here you have no land, and there you will have plenty of land. Here you are drudges; there you will be masters.'*[17]

Combinations of three – as in number of people, objects, actions, and repeated phrases – is another principle demonstrated:

> But my wife did not want to go. She had a fear of the oceans and foreign countries. Every day she would repeat to me, 'I will not go, I will not go, I will not go.'
> 'Very well, then stay here.'
> ... Three of us set out: Wasyl Eleniak, Yurko Panischak, and myself.[18]

One of the key folkloric principles of story development is repetitive enlisting of peoples and geographic names. Every time he describes his travel to and from Canada, for example, Pylypiw enlists the names of all cities and towns in the order in which he travelled through them. In a similar fashion he names all his co-travellers on each of those journeys – a method of repetitive enlisting that also helps to extend the content of the narrative.

In addition, Pylypiw's story tends to present (and preserve) events that took place in real time in the past in the 'once upon a time' indefinite historical setting of a folk tale, even though the storyteller was routinely prompted during the interview to recount the facts about the real past, its details, and exact dates. His past, as it emerges in the tale apart from the other interview material, has the tendency to remain indefinite and is marked by such time markers as 'one day,' 'one morning,' the 'third day after Easter,' and so on.[19]

Within his narrative, these principles of formal story organization served Pylypiw as mnemonic devices. Thus they ensured the storyteller's skills at remembering and reintegrating the elements of his past into the elements of the story he was telling. They also served as internal laws of oral storytelling, called 'epic laws' by Axel Olrik.[20] In print they remain important elements of Pylypiw's accounts of coming to Canada, reminding us of the forty years' distance between the real events and the storytelling event.

Apart from folkloric conventions discussed above, the Pylypiw story is also disciplined by principles that hold the tale together at its morphological level. Vladimir Propp, analysing the extensive body of European, and especially Slavic, traditional fairy tales, compares the morphological organization of these fairy tales to that of language. The rules of grammar regulate and limit the combination of various elements of speech used in the text, producing specific meanings from these combinations. Just as grammatical rules govern the rendition of sentences, morphological rules govern the composition of fairy tales. As in the case of a fairy tale, the meaning (the message and the moral lesson) of Pylypiw's story, and of course the future understanding and interpretations of it, is generated and encoded not just through the application of principles of oral narrativity but at its morphological level, remaining true to the emergent genre of the immigrant tale in the Ukrainian-Canadian tradition. These meanings are created in the expected actions of characters, the juxtaposition of their initial and final positions in the story, their expected moves within the story and between the settings, and their expected interactions with other characters, with forces external to them, and with the environment.

Narratives are never, of course, simply the creation of their narrators. Historical and cultural context both constrain and breathe life into any story that finds resonance with an audience. The fixed narrative order of its formal and internal elements has the propensity to provide a more fixed meaning at a given historical moment. Thus the sequencing of the hero's actions as well as the description of his encounters with others and of his systematic overcoming of numerous obstacles on the way to his goal speak not of narrative representation of a real experience but, more important, of a particular kind of narrativization of immigration experience. I will return to this point after a discussion of the morphological organization of Pylypiw's story.

Propp has long been credited with discovering the structural foundations of the vitality of the fairy tale as a genre. When Propp looked at the organization of fairy tales, he was interested not in their formal qualities but in the actions and interactions of their characters, their initial and resulting positions, and the changes in their status in between. These he calls functions of the fairy tale, claiming that there is a limited number (thirty-one) of them.[21]

For example, according to Propp, each tale begins with the statement of an initial situation: 'In the remote village, once there was a young lad.' Such an introduction points out the status of the hero, describes his family situation, thus, outlining his initial position before the hero ventures out into the outside world in search of his goal (the princess, the lost sister, or, in Pylypiw's case, the free land in Canada). Not all tales fulfil all thirty-one functions, but the same basic line of plot development, Propp claims, is followed in all cases.

Given Propp's scenario, in any given fairy tale, the hero takes off in pursuit of some noble and hard-to-achieve goal. The path toward the goal is never straight and easy, and it takes the hero away from the comfort and safety of the home environment and into the dangerous and unknown outside world. In pursuit of his goal, the hero is presented with numerous tests, which he has to pass in order to proceed further on his journey. These tests are often set up by the villains who oppose the hero. Often, while trying to overcome an obstacle, the hero is helped unexpectedly (to him) by a stranger (if not one, then three, seven, or thirty-three helpers). Typically, the hero's path winds through the wild forests, 'no man's land,' or across immense waters, the latter being a common folk motif representing the fine line between life and death. In most cases the hero cannot reach his goal in one set of trials or in a single effort. He is made to repeat the journey again (usually three times). Each time he might be helped by helpers, or donors might endow him with some magical objects or useful advice.

Often, if the hero is accompanied from the very beginning by two other companions, he ends up being the only one to make it to the world of beyond. At the end of all these ordeals and trials, the hero is rewarded with the realization of his goal, and the tale ends with reference to a 'life to be lived happily ever after,' in which the hero enjoys what he sought from the beginning. Propp argues that this is the basic line of the plot development for all fairy tales; it becomes more complex not by the invention of new functions but by embedding and utilizing the same functions over and over again.

Similar to this outline of fairy tale actions and happenings, the actions and experiences of Pylypiw-the-hero depict comparable challenges. Thus, at the beginning, he sets off from Nebyliw along with two other villagers. Quickly, the one with the least money is left behind as a result of the first test:

> We arrived to Stryj, and then went to Peremyshl, and from there to Oswienci [Auschwitz]. Here our papers were checked.
> 'Show me your money,' one official demanded.
> I had 600 rynsky, Eleniak had 190 rynsky, and Panischak had 120 rynsky. The officials ordered Panischak to go back home to his village ... Only two of us reached Hamburg.[22]

The two continued the journey through lands and cities foreign to them, by the big waters, and through the wild forests:

> There, an agent put us on a big ship which took us across the ocean. We traveled for twenty two days, it was pretty fair voyage. The ship crossed the ocean and sailed up a river to a big city. It was Montreal. We disembarked in the morning, and in the afternoon we boarded a train and were on our way across Canada. The trip was quite long, time dragged for two and a half days as we traversed rocks, lakes, and open spaces where *no one lived*. It was quite clear that we were traversing a wilderness.[23]

Throughout the story, many 'helpers' and 'donors' come to the foreground to help the two in their search for the good land. In a classical fairy tale, the helpers assist the hero to get to the destination faster, sooner, before others, and so on, and the donors provide him with magical objects or with the wise words that bring him closer to his goal. In Pylypiw's story, as in a fairy tale, the helpers remained unnamed: 'an agent came to us,' 'we stayed at the farmer's place for a whole week,' 'a German who spoke Ukrainian told us,' and so forth. As well, 'One German fellow, a shoemaker from Winnipeg, who also came from Kalush, said to me, 'In Alberta, it is warmer; go there and see for yourself.''[24]

Accepting the advice from this donor, Pylypiw-the-hero takes off for Alberta in search of his goal, good farming land. After a search there, he returns to Winnipeg to receive another piece of advice from another donor: 'Here we met some Jews from Russia. They said to us: "Go to Gretna in Manitoba, not far from here. There you will find good land."'[25] This was the third place where the hero and his companion went in search of their goal, and the last one. Eleniak stayed there while Pylypiw set off to the old country to get their wives and children and, they hoped, some other families.

Upon his return to his village, no one believed, at first, that he had been in Canada. As he himself recollects – and this is where the story breaks away from the fairy tale format and introduces the element of reflection – people did not know how to treat his return or the news he brought. His news of the world 'out there' – real and inhabited by people like the villagers themselves – matched neither the locals' traditional folk interpretations of the world beyond theirs as unreachable and uninhabitable nor their understanding of economic freedom. They were not ready to believe the news:

> The peasants did not understand that across the ocean free lands were available, without landlords, which could actually be acquired for little or no money. They listened to my stories and wondered.
>
> The news spread around that a man had arrived from God only knew where and wanted to lead the people out to some sort of place called America.[26]

In any fairy tale the hero undergoes a number of trials (usually three). Often the hero is summoned to meet the high powers (such as the king of the kingdom where the action takes place) and is requested to solve three riddles (or fight three dragons, and so forth). Pylypiw's story tells us that such a trial took place. Notably, three testers question him, and Pylypiw bravely withstands the tests:

> One day the magistrate of the village, the priest, the clerk, and a trustee of the church paid me a call. They spread a map on the table and told me to stand aside.
>
> The clerk asked me, 'Where were you?'
>
> I answered, 'In America.'
>
> Very few knew where this country was, and even today it is difficult to tell someone who has no knowledge about the world.
>
> 'Which way did you go?' the magistrate asked.
>
> I answered, 'I went to Cracow, from there to Berlin, then to Hamburg. Then I traveled across the ocean to Montreal and from there by train to Winnipeg. I went by rail and by ship.'
>
> I stood aloof, talking, while they were searching the map.
>
> 'Where exactly have you been?' asked the priest.

I answered, 'The country is called Canada. I was in Winnipeg, in Calgary, in Gretna. Wasyl Eleniak stayed behind in Gretna, at a farmer's place.'[27]

He is let go, but soon faces another, non-metaphorical, trial. Arrested on the grounds of enticing villagers to leave their villages and to go to Canada, he appears in court:

> The judge asked me: 'What do you need land for? Don't you have enough here?
>
> I replied, 'We have too little land.'
>
> The judge said, 'You are enticing people to leave.'
>
> I answered, 'No, they want to go themselves.'
>
> The judge lashed out at me, 'Why don't you hold your tongue? You should have gone alone without dragging others along with you. You sold out the people to the agent. Our most illustrious emperor once helped to bring our people back from Argentina, thirty families at his own expense; do you expect him to come to the rescue again should anything go wrong?'
>
> The trial lasted about *three* hours. We were sentenced to one month in jail.[28]

According to Pylypiw's story, the judge speaks only three times, and the trial lasts three hours. The hero's high and moral qualities are tested again, and the hero withstands this test successfully. To the listener it is clear from the very beginning that the hero and the hero's morals will persevere and he will be rewarded for his search.

After his imprisonment was over Pylypiw prepared his family for the long journey across the ocean, and they departed in the spring of 1893: 'On the *third* day of Easter, I set out. With me were my wife and four children. The youngest, Anna, was six months old.'[29]

In the remaining part of his story, Pylypiw describes his second journey across the ocean, listing all geographic points he passed on his way to Canada and naming all his fellow villagers who travelled with him, repeatedly omitting the names of his and other men's wives. In a fairy-tale-like fashion Pylypiw gives his version of a 'life happy ever after,' providing a concise and detailed outline of how the good land he was searching for rewarded him throughout the years. The story ends with his pontificating on the subject of how good, or bad, the two worlds – the old country and the new one – have been for the Ukrainian people.

All in all, when analysed from the perspective of Propp's functions of fairy tales, Pylypiw's story conforms closely to most of the rules of morphological organization of a fairy tale.

From Story to History

Pylypiw's story intrigued the folklorist in me not for its uniqueness but for its universality. The story can be easily compared to the myriad other personal accounts of immigration, scattered by now throughout numerous publications by Ukrainian Canadians. In each of these accounts the narrative proceeds in one way: from the old country to the new, from oppression to freedom, and from poverty to prosperity. A traditional fairy tale is made up of a particular number of 'functions,' the building blocks of the story. These blocks are selected, in order, from a long chain of all possible actions, interactions, and moves for the hero to make. Thus, a tale emerges consisting of some but lacking other functions. In a similar way, Pylypiw's account presents us with an example of what a Ukrainian immigrant tale from early-twentieth-century western Canada can be like. Other, similar Ukrainian-Canadian stories of immigration and settlement consist of their own limited number of story elements but maintain the same progressive sequence in which their contents are presented. Although Pylypiw's story – elaborate and rich in folkloric detail – is similar to many others, it stands out for its complexity and its proximity to the traditional folk narrative. Therefore, I see it as a representative example of its genre.

As outlined above, the fixed ordering of events and actions, with its propensity to create a fixed meaning and message for the narrative, speaks of a particular kind of narrativization of the immigration experience as it happened throughout the twentieth century in the Ukrainian-Canadian context. Overall, in the first half of the twentieth century, immigrant tales of exodus to Canada were a highly productive genre of the Ukrainian-Canadian vernacular oral culture, competing only with pioneer settlement stories.[30] Both were often combined in personal narratives. Unfortunately, little systematic scholarly attention has been paid to the collection and analysis of these immigration tales, though occasional Ukrainian-Canadian folklore anthologies have included examples of or excerpts from such stories.[31] During the first three or so decades of the twentieth century, if these stories appeared in print, as Pylypiw's did in the 1930s, they were published in the Ukrainian language in various Ukrainian-Canadian community almanacs, calendars, and newspapers.

Some time after the Second World War, and especially in the sixties, new interest in these stories arose in the communities in which they had earlier circulated as oral lore. At that time many communities in Canada found themselves in a commemorative mood, producing local history books, first in conjunction with Canada's centennial in 1967 and then for the seventy-fifth anniversaries of Alberta and Saskatchewan in 1980. These were times for these communities to formulate and tell their own stories of origin. Personal sagas of immigration and settlement, once mere folklore, came in handy, gaining a new public profile. Another resurgence of these stories in local discourses can be linked to the 1991 centennial celebration of Ukrainian-Canadian culture. Since that time, many of the oldest Ukrainian-Canadian clans have officially marked the hundredth year of their own residence in Canada, publishing in family history books their once personal stories of coming to Canada. In 2000 in the community of Mundare, for example, the local Ukrainian museum even set up a special exhibition of Ukrainian-Canadian centennial family history books.[32]

Eventually, as family history books were compiled and local histories written, family immigrant tales entered a new stage of their life as written texts. With their firm incorporation into various family and local histories, the typical characteristics of orally composed tales are less observable in most cases, since their presentation began to be governed by literary modes of content 'storing.' Ironically, although it can be seen as a death of a storytelling tradition, this shift in discursive practices allowed the stories to take on a second life. This new life has been marked by a great degree of defolklorization of the *formal* properties of once oral stories. Nowadays family historians usually make an effort to restore an air of historicity to the accounts of their predecessors, in order to lay out their family claims to 'History.' Thus the original time markers of the 'once upon a time' kind tend to be replaced by specific dates (of arriving in Canada, acquiring a farm, building a new house, buying a first car, bearing a first child, and so forth).

The ongoing reproduction of numerous accounts of 'the Move' in various public discursive spaces of Ukrainian Canadians has been an important step toward their further formalization. Often, their abbreviated versions, stripped of details and local specifics, appear in community museum displays, newsletters, school textbooks used in bilingual Ukrainian-Canadian schools, and more recently, on Ukrainian-Canadian websites. Of course, the family gatherings for dinner on the prairies may still involve listening to the family elders' reminiscences, including their stories of family beginnings at the turn of the twentieth century, but these occasions involve the original settlers less and less.

The two different lives of an immigration tale speak of two distinct modes of reflexivity, one privileging orality and the other literacy, as primary modes of communication.[33] For some time now, Ukrainian Canadians have been fully involved in modern ways of reflecting upon their past, ways that rely to a great extent on written narratives, new technologies such as printing, faxing, home computing, photography, photocopying, audio, video, and the internet.

From a historical perspective the invention of new means of communicating and preserving knowledge has affected modes of human thought as profoundly as the did the technologies of writing and printing.[34] In times of late modernity, especially in the Western world, the mass availability of new technologies has been responsible for the further reorganization of people's ways of reflecting upon themselves and the world around them. Ukrainians in Canada have been certainly more privileged than have villagers in Ukraine in their access to modern technologies for preserving their memories: producing family photo albums, computerized genealogies, and local, community, and family histories; and establishing museums. The availability of these modern sites of documented memories has also affected the ways in which people remember their personal and communal pasts. In my own ethnographic work, many of my informants resorted to their own copies of local history books or family histories to relate to me, the ethnographer, their personal histories.

Still, modern vernacular reflexivity continues to favour oral principles of narrative composition. When dealing with their family history most family historians resort to the same principles as those on which Pylypiw's narrative rests. In speaking of what once happened, the authors continue to employ the narrative and impose order on reality by sequencing the heroes' actions, discussing heroes' encounters with others, and outlining the obstacles on their way to their goals.

Since narratives always convey certain moral or ideological stances of their times, they speak not only of narrative representation of a real experience but also of a particular kind of ideological narrativization of an experience, in our case, the way in which Ukrainian-Canadian history portrays its own beginnings. One can say that despite the invention of modern technologies, oral culture continues to have a strong hold over the vernacular narrativization of Ukrainian-Canadian history. First, the texts of many local family histories, and to a great degree the displays of many Ukrainian-Canadian museums, all sequence the past into a well-defined beginning, a main part of a story, and an end. Such sequencing is the most characteristic aspect of the formal qualities of a narrative. Second, the texts usually do not reveal the identity of the narrator, and therefore, as in a traditional historical narrative, the facts presented in the stories seem to speak for themselves.[35] Third, the narrative dictates a particular order in which the events are mentioned, thus suggesting, if not imposing, particular meanings and interpretations of the past. Another main hero, apart from the family ancestor(s) profiled in the story, emerges in such texts, construed as 'our people,' or 'Ukrainian people.'[36]

Through these numerous stories dealing with immigration and settlement in Canada, the grand story of the Ukrainian Canadians' beginnings emerges. The master narrative emerges in the reader's mind through repeated exposure to the same motifs of Ukrainian immigration at the turn of the twentieth century. The sequence of motifs – departing from the known world into the unknown, enduring the journey, overcoming obstacles, and finally conquering 'no man's land' and making it 'the lived' world – echoes the underlying organizational principles and motifs of many traditional narratives, especially those of fairy tales. Speaking of the morphology of the fairy tale, Propp maintained that despite the vast number of plots, characters, and settings, the narrative progresses, albeit with some variations, along the same sequence.[37] Various kinds of representation – family history books, museum displays, and community histories – follow the same morphological principles in their narratives of Ukrainian-Canadian history on the prairies. Their local worlds, both Ukrainian Canadian and western Canadian, worlds are defined in terms of beginning at a well-defined point in history and of mutual territorial and genealogical continuity. Thus, an archetypal story of all stories emerges in these writings, clearly speaking of the beginning of a new mythology of Ukrainian Canadians.

Such narrative representations have another important property in common: they were created selectively. The materials included in history books and museum displays were meant to produce one particular picture of history. Events and facts that did not contribute to the overall grand picture of Ukrainian success in Canada were exiled from the pages of such history books. Neither the family history books, the local histories, nor the Ukrainian-Canadian museums refer to the alcoholism, family abuse, racial prejudices, or denominational disagreements that were present in the earlier days of Ukrainian settlement in Canada.[38]

This non-representation is not surprising, since the narrative serves to communicate collective histories, memories, and destinies, forging group identities of those who believed and shared those histories. Anthony Smith points out that narratives are capable of accomplishing such identity projects because of the presence within those groups of 'potent ethnic myths, memories, and symbols.'[39] These myths – of origin, return, and descent, to name a few of the central motifs – were as responsible for mobilizing ancient populations into 'nationalisms' (Smith's word) as contemporary local narratives of emigration, settling in the new country, and so on are responsible for the creation, maintenance, and assertion of ethnic identities in the new world.[40]

For contemporary cultural groups that are still in the process of historical formation, such myths may not yet be fully developed. In such cases the experiences of individual members of the group must underpin the formation of the archetypal story, or mythology, for the group to pursue its sense of territorial association, common ancestry, shared history, and solidarity. This is accomplished first through their ongoing narration or storytelling (in which the accounts are in a continuous process of development) and then through their narrativization (in which the accounts come to be somewhat fixed and structured according to narrative principles).[41]

Thus, Pylypiw's account of coming to Canada and its post-oral life speak of a culturally unique intersection of ethnic history and folklore in times of modernity. The story closely observes the formal and morphological rules of a folk narrative and serves as an example of a particular narrativization of the Ukrainian-Canadian experience on the prairies. In the recreation, retelling, and rewriting of this originally personal and then public story, we can see the strong hold of orality and folklore on Ukrainian-Canadian culture and identity throughout the twentieth century. The post-oral life of this story also invites us to consider how many other published contributions to Ukrainian-Canadian history – personal memoirs and community and family histories – attest to the vitality of these modes of cultural knowledge transfer in times of late-modern reflexivity.

NOTES

1 Ivan Bobersky (Iwan Boberskyj), born in Dobrohostiv, western Ukraine, graduated from Lviv University, where he became a professor

of German language and gymnastics. In 1920, he was sent to Canada by the Western Ukrainian People's Republic in exile, to act as its plenipotentiary. When that government ceased to exist, he remained in Canada until 1932. There he actively participated in various Ukrainian organizations.

2 As is evident from the titles of publications that follow, Ivan Pylypiw's name has been spelled in various ways by various writers. Like some of them, I follow the most common transliteration of his name.

3 As cited in Vasyl A. Czumer, *Recollections about the Life of the First Ukrainian Settlers in Canada* (Edmonton: Canadian Institute of Studies, 1981), 18.

4 Ibid.

5 Marshall A. Nay, *Trailblazers of Ukrainian Emigration to Canada: Wasyl Eleniak and Ivan Pylypow* (Edmonton: Brightest Pebble, 1997); Mitch Sago, 'They Were Trail Blazers (Ivan Pylypiw and Wasyl Eleniak),' *Generations* 7, no. 4 (1982): 3–8.

6 Czumer, *Recollections*, 18.

7 Detailed information on Ivan Pylypiw (1850–1936), as well as on commemorative Ukrainian-Canadian projects related to these two men, can be found in Nay's thoroughly researched *Trailblazers of Ukrainian Emigration*. According to Nay, both Pylypiw and Eleniak were interviewed numerous times throughout their lives. References to those interviews and their coverage in the media can also be found in Nay's notes and bibliography (163–203).

8 Cited from Library and Archives Canada, *Canada's Digital Collections*, Alberta Past to Present, 'Alberta: Home, Home on the Plains,' Settlement, Ukrainian settlers, http://epe.lac-bac.gc.ca.

9 Robert B. Klymasz, *Folk Narrative among Ukrainian-Canadians in Western Canada*, National Museum of Man paper no. 4 (Ottawa: Canadian Centre for Folk Culture Studies, 1973).

10 Linda Degh, *Folktales and Society: Story-Telling in a Hungarian Peasant Community* (Bloomington: Indiana University Press, 1989).

11 Mody Coggin Boatright, *The Family Saga and Other Phases of American Folklore* (Bloomington: University of Illinois Press, 1958).

12 Klymasz, *Folk Narrative*, 12.

13 Folklore theorists such as André Jolles, Albert Wesselski, Mark Azadovskii, Linda Degh, and Richard Dorson long ago pointed out the continuing creation of new folk narratives in everyday experiences.

14 Klymasz, *Folk Narrative*, 12.

15 Harry Piniuta, *Land of Pain, Land of Promise: First Person Accounts by Ukrainian Pioneers, 1891–1914* (Saskatoon: Western Producer Prairie Books, 1978), 27–8, emphasis added.

16 As discussed by Vladimir Propp in his study of Russian folk tales, *Morphology of the Folktale,* trans. Laurence Scott, Publications of the American Folklore Society, Bibliographical and special series 9 (1928; Austin: University of Texas Press, 1968).

17 Piniuta, *Land of Pain,* 31–2, emphasis added.

18 Ibid., 28.

19 Bobersky omitted his numerous questions from his transcript of their conversation. In the account, it is easy to see where the otherwise naturally flowing story was interrupted by the interviewer's questions seeking precision.

20 Axel Olrik, *Principles for Oral Narrative Research,* trans. K. Wolf and J. Jensen (1921; Bloomington: Indiana University Press, 1992), 41–61.

21 Propp worked with Russian fairy tales, but scholars like Alan Dundes and others promoted his ideas in the English-speaking world, suggesting the universal applicability of his theory.

22 Piniuta, *Land of Pain,* 28.

23 Ibid., emphasis added.

24 Ibid., 30.

25 Ibid.

26 Ibid., 31.

27 Ibid., 32.

28 Ibid., 33, emphasis added.

29 Ibid., 33–4, emphasis added.

30 These first began to be collected by the Alberta Pioneer Association, established in 1941.

31 Robert B. Klymasz, *Ukrainian Folklore in Canada* (New York: Arno Press, 1980); Robert B. Klymasz, *Sviéto : Celebrating Ukrainian-Canadian Ritual in East Central Alberta through the Generations* (Edmonton: Alberta Culture and Multiculturalism, Historical Resources Division, 1992); Jaroslav B. Rudnyc'kyj, *Materi ï aly do ukraïns'ko-kanadiis'koï folkl'orystyky i di ï alektolohiï* (Winnipeg: Ukraïns'ka vil'na akademiia nauk, 1956); Jaroslav B. Rudnyc'kyj, *Readings in Canadian Slavic folklore* (Winnipeg: University of Manitoba Press, 1958).

32 Natalia Shostak, 'Local Ukrainianness in Transnational Context: An Ethnographic Study of a Canadian Prairie Community' (PhD diss., University of Alberta, 2001), 80–2.

33 The first kind of reflexivity is more characteristic of rural communities of Ukraine, while I found the latter to be more common in the Ukrainian-Canadian communities throughout the prairies.

34 Goody distinguishes between oral and literate cultures and has also looked at literate cultures in which orality continues to play a significant role. Goody also notes that both literate and oral traditions are necessarily

partial in writing societies. Jack R. Goody, 'Oral Culture,' in *Folklore: Cultural Performances and Popular Entertainment*, ed. Richard Bauman (New York: Oxford University Press, 1992), 13; Jack R. Goody, *The Interface between the Written and the Oral* (Cambridge: Cambridge University Press, 1987); Walter J. Ong, *Orality and Literacy: The Technologizing of the Word* (London: Routledge, 1982).

35 Hayden V. White, *The Content of the Form: Narrative Discourse and Historical Representation* (Baltimore: Johns Hopkins University Press, 1987), 3.

36 Shostak, 'Local Ukrainianness,' 49–51.

37 Propp, *Morphology*, 23.

38 Myrna Kostash, *All of Baba's Children* (Edmonton: Hurtig Publishers, 1977).

39 Anthony Smith, 'Ethnic Myths and Ethnic Revivals,' in *European Journal of Sociology* 25 (1984): 289.

40 Smith addresses the question of ethnic myths, memories, and symbols while dealing with the larger issue of ethnicity and ethnic survival. In his work, ethnicity is treated as 'a named social group with alleged common ancestry and shared history, one or more elements of distinctive culture, a sense of territorial association and an active solidarity' (ibid., 284). Ethnicity can persist through time if it relies on collective myths and symbols of origin, descent, a heroic age, and at times, on myths of migration, communal decline, and finally of rebirth (292).

41 Hayden White discusses narrativization in his work on history writing. White, *The Content of the Form*, 26–57.

PART FOUR

Subverting Authority

Chapter 7

Literacy, Orality, Authority, and Hypocrisy in the *Laozi*

GARY ARBUCKLE

> A word after a word
> after a word is power.
>
> Margaret Atwood, 'Spelling'

Readers will probably remember the scene early in *The Matrix* when Neo, or 'Mr Anderson,' first experiences the powers of the nefarious Agent Smith. He is placed under arrest, and Agent Smith tells him that he is expected to cooperate in the hunt for an international terrorist. 'Mr Anderson' responds by declaring, 'You can't scare me with this Gestapo crap. I know my rights. I want my phone call.' Agent Smith's response is to smile and remark, 'And tell me, Mr Anderson, what good is a phone call if you are *unable to speak*?' At this point, 'Mr Anderson' finds that his mouth has disappeared, the lips melting into a featureless membrane, a development that Agent Smith clearly finds amusing.

In this essay I suggest that the Daoist philosopher Laozi 老子, or perhaps more properly the book that goes under this name, intended to deal with the ordinary people of ancient China in much the same way that Agent Smith dealt with Mr Anderson.[1] True, this characterization fits poorly with the popular image of the harmless wise man preaching harmony with nature and battling against Confucian constraints and Legalist legal severity, characteristics that have long made the *Laozi* the hottest commodity in the whole of ancient Chinese philosophy.[2] I do not intend to quarrel with what artists or religious believers have made of the text, though most of these readings can first be attested only centuries after its appearance.[3] I merely wish to underline that the *political* ideas of the *Laozi* are little more than an exercise in hypocrisy designed to produce a false consciousness of contentment among the ruled, controlling their words in a more subtle but scarcely less effective way than the literal sealing of their mouths. Indeed, one of the chief characteristics of the *Laozi*'s ideal polity is that its victims are never meant to realize that they have lost their ability to speak, and will thus never be able to resist the machinations of rulers who have thereby put themselves beyond the influence of their inferiors.

The sinister aspects of the *Laozi*'s political program, which have made it one of the fountainheads of totalitarian thought in China, appear most clearly when the text is interrogated on questions of literacy and orality. I came to the question from this angle, thinking to write on the Daoist attitude to writing and speech and the relationship between them. This appeared a simple problem, but its simplicity was deceptive.

Some years ago, I presented a paper on the interplay between orality and literacy in the early Confucian school.[4] This described, among other phenomena, a debate that went on throughout the second and first centuries BCE on the comparative trustworthiness of oral and written transmission of canonical texts. Since the values that Confucians found in their canon were seen as immutable, they eventually concluded that the fixed form of writing was superior to the chances and hazards attendant on oral transmission. It was a fortunate outcome for the Confucian school as a whole, since Confucian teaching in the four centuries after the Han was erratic and of poor quality. Nevertheless, since Confucian truth was sufficiently embodied by the texts themselves, this long, arid chasm did not cast doubt on the basic veracity of the canonical texts.

The question is not as simple when we ask some of the same questions of the Daoist school, the main philosophical rivals of the Confucians in ancient China. Zhuangzi 莊子, one of the pair of writers whose works are generally taken to define Daoism in pre-unification China (before 221 BCE), had a commendably clear attitude toward language. He seems to have believed that the Way, the Dao 道, which informed and shaped the universe and its workings, was in constant motion, ever changing and so only describable in a provisional or oblique manner. It was not that Zhuangzi believed language was incapable of reflecting *some* sort of reality. The problem was that reality refused to stand still, so any description in any medium, even the spoken word, had a very short shelf life: 'Saying is not blowing breath, saying says something; the only trouble is that what it says is never fixed. Do we really say something? Or have we never said anything? If you think it different from the twitter of fledglings, is there proof of the distinction? Or isn't there any proof? By what is the Way hidden, that there should be a genuine and a false?'[5]

Moreover, even as momentary expressions, positive statements were inevitably made from a particular viewpoint, and were valid only for that viewpoint: 'There they say "That's it, that's not" from one point of view, here we say "That's it, that's not" from another point of view. Are there really It and Other? Or really no It and Other?'[6] The meaning of words was arbitrary and could be legitimately challenged, mutated, and subverted, since 'the man who sees right through knows how to interchange and deem them one.'[7]

If this is true even of spoken discourse, it will of course be even more true of the written word. Writing, fixed by its very nature, was outrun by the mutability of the Way before the ink was dry. A written text that had been sitting around as long as the sacred canons of Confucianism had was thus nothing but 'the dregs of the men of old.'[8] It could contain nothing that was worth study in the present; it was a waste of time at best, a source of delusion at worst.

Words stand in the way of the Way, except insofar as they can indirectly evoke its immediate apprehension: here is a clear and arguable thesis, even if we disagree with it. But when we take this assertion with us into the study of the second paradigmatic Daoist, Laozi, we immediately run into trouble. He, or his book, was in the teaching business. He purported to offer useful advice; more than that, he hoped to compete with the Confucians at the business of saving the world. Did he too think that words stand in the way of the Way? If he did, how did he propose to overcome this defect?

Laozi: Maybe a Man, Certainly a Book

The legends surrounding 'Laozi' are a scholastic minefield, one where we need not trespass much. It will be sufficient here to say that he is traditionally dated to the sixth century BCE and was supposedly a highly educated man, an archivist. Disgusted with the decline of the Way, he is said to have left China in his old age, pausing briefly to write a short book when the warden of the mountain pass through which he disappeared requested an account of his teachings. This book now goes either by his name, *Laozi*, or by some variant of *The Canon of the Way and Its Power* (in Chinese, *Daodejing* 道德經).[9]

Thus, the legend says that the *Laozi* (as we will refer to it from now on) was written by a single person at a single time. The legend has been shot to ribbons over the centuries, and more questions than answers remain. We do not even know if the writer's name was Lao (the *zi* 子 is a respectful suffix meaning roughly 'master'), or whether it is a pen name, 'the old master.' Nevertheless, the essential unity of the text – its formation under one hand at one time, more or less – is plausible.[10]

I believe the most defensible position to be that the *Laozi* was written by a single person using 'Laozi' as a pen name, perhaps putting on the mantle of an 'elder' for his own rhetorical purposes. It seems to have begun as a treatise on how to reform society and government, and probably began to circulate some time in the first half of the fourth century BCE. There are problems with the text in places – it would be astonishing if there were not, given its age – but no major questions of authenticity. The earliest known fragmentary manuscripts are from circa 300 BCE, and a little more than a century later we have complete texts that have survived to the present, almost identical to the text we have today.

The *Laozi*'s attitude to language is announced in the very first lines of the text and reiterated consistently throughout. This attitude is very similar to that found in Zhuangzi: the position that words have no constant validity, since the Way is in motion and the descriptive power of words is static

道可道非常道
名可名非常名
無名萬物之始
有名萬物之母

The Way can be described, but the description will not be unchanging;
A term can be defined, but the definition will not be invariant.
Undefined is how Heaven and earth began,
Definition is the mother of all things.[11]

To be a 'thing,' broken away from the unitary whole, is to fall away from the primal state and to enter into a secondary and inferior order of being. The reason for this decline is 'definition' or 'naming,' making things discrete by conferring on them names that in turn foster the illusion that they are unchangeable and independent of the movement of the Way.

Defining, moreover, does not merely cut things away from the Way, illegitimately breaking it into parts alienated one from the other by illusion. It also calls into being mirror images, companion illusions, since to define a thing is also to define its opposite by implication:

天下皆知美為美斯惡已
皆知善之善斯不善已
故有無之相生
難易之相成
長短之相形
高下之相傾

When the world all knows the why of beauty, then ugliness appears.
When they all know the why of doing good, then wicked behaviour
appears.
Thus the defined and undefined engender each other;
The difficult and the easy accomplish each other;
The long and the short construct each other,
The high and the low complement each other.[12]

Virtue engenders vice, and vice virtue, in an ever-accelerating flight
from primal unity:

大道廢焉有仁義
智慧出焉有大偽
六親不和有孝慈
國家昏亂有貞臣

When the great Way is ruined, there is humanity and a sense of the right.
When wisdom and perception appear, there is great fraud.
When family and kin clash, there is filial piety and parental love;
When the state and its ruling house is chaotic and rebellious, there are
loyal and pure ministers.[13]

We note that this is not *merely* opposition to the rigidity of textuality. Nothing, explicit or implicit, limits the rigidity to the written word. Any defining speech, any word that pretends to be 'constant,' is susceptible to the same criticism. Words that attempt to dictate reality instead of passively following it and dropping into the shadows the instant they become outdated, create *false* reality. This is the core objection the *Laozi* has to programs of salvation that depend on the deliberate propagation of morality: when a moral rule is put forth, the good that it produces quickly stales, while the evil that it calls up and that mirrors itself on it remains ever fresh and fertile. If language is used to embody anything intended to be timeless, it will run counter to the Way just as soon as the Way changes – and this will be almost instantly.

This is an odd position for a work that hopes to give useful advice on government. Nevertheless, as counterintuitive as it may seem at first glance, the *Laozi* had a very definite program for the aspiring ruler of a state or the world – 'nonactive' actions guaranteed to bring about the golden age. Here is where the interaction of language and power is made clear.

The Devious Daoist: The *Laozi* and Rule

The problem of how to rule in the Daoist tradition is obviously a sticky one. Zhuangzi finesses it entirely by abandoning any idea of social progress and fixing his hopes on the salvation of a few exceptional individuals, attuned to the Way by hereditary talent. The apprehension of the Way was not a truth that could be written or taught, but then it was not a truth that *had* to be written or taught. Those who could learn, would learn; those who could not, such as Confucius, would never have more than a sense of regret about what they were missing.[14]

Leveraging Confucian ideas of the power of rule by example, other early Daoists identified by A.C. Graham as followers of Yang Zhu hoped that if a ruler was absolutely non-interfering, his altruistic and selfless behaviour would have such a powerful influence on his subjects and neighbours that they would spontaneously form a non-state state, with him as the reluctant nexus.[15] This was not only rather charming in itself but also harmonized perfectly with general Daoist assumptions that overt attempts to force others to one's will must inevitably backfire. All the same, as a practical plan of government, one that could be sold to sceptical rulers in a dog-eat-dog world, it had obvious deficiencies.

The ideal ruler of the *Laozi* was to be different from this. He did indeed remain formally committed to 'non-action' – or to be more exact, no unnatural or contrived action, *wuwei*.[16] But what in the end *was* natural? Several passages make it clear that the 'natural' actions that the *Laozi* ideal ruler was allowed to take had become quite – shall we say – *reactionary*:

是以聖人之治也
虛其心實其腹
弱其志彊其骨

常使民無知無欲
使夫知者不敢為

The rule of the sage king empties the people's minds but fills their bellies, weakens their wills but strengthens their bones. He invariably deprives the people of knowledge and desires, and makes sure the wise dare do nothing.[17]

小國寡民
使民有什伯之器而不用也
使民重死而不遠徙
雖有舟輿無所乘之
雖有甲兵無所陳之

Make the state small, make its people few. Make sure the commoners have military equipment, but do not employ them. Keep men close to their homes through fear of death, so that they will not ride on boats and carts even if they have them, they will not fall into ranks even if they have armour and weapons.[18]

Commentators tend to become lost in admiration of the supposed primal simplicity expressed in these passages, but it is worth taking a moment to think of the implications, and of what would *necessarily* be implied by its implementation in practice. For the *Laozi*, the definition of 'natural' action has been broadened to include all actions that bring people back to the 'natural' state that their rulers assume ideal for them. It is a program fit for a residential school; Agent Smith would have been speechless with admiration.[19]

As Margaret Atwood points out in the epigram at the head of this chapter, 'a word after a word after a word is power.' We cannot control that of which we cannot speak. Thus, the dominion that the *Laozi* ruler exercised over his subjects centred on controlling the common people's words to destroy their power and to negate any threat they might pose to the ruler's program. It was a state of absolute subjection.

Literacy is the most obvious target. For people condemned to live in an eternal, unreflective present, free of the 'tyranny' of definition (though not of other forms of tyranny), written records would have been at best a nuisance. Something for bookkeeping was all that was required:

使民復結繩而用之

> Make the people return to knotting cords and using them [instead of writing].[20]

Note particularly the use of 'return to' (復 *fu*) here. The writer is *consciously* reactionary. He is under no illusion that he is merely preserving the purity of a primal oral society. His plan is to *impose* orality (or what he believes to be orality) and *proscribe* literacy.

What was so fearful about literacy? Why should the *Laozi* have been at such pains to ban it? A clue can be found in a quotation from a text usually considered much the harsher, the notorious *Book of Lord Shang* (*Shangjunshu* 商君書), one of the most enthusiastically condemned documents of the 'totalitarian' Legalist school:

> Whenever government officials or people have questions about the laws or mandates to ask of the officers presiding over the law, the latter should, in each case, answer clearly according to the laws and mandates about which it was originally desired to ask questions, and they should, in each case, prepare a tablet of the length of 1 foot 6 inches, on which should be distinctly inscribed the year, month, day, and hour, as well as the items of law about which questions were asked, for the information of the government officials or of the people ... If in their treatment of the people, the government officials do not act according to the law, the people should inquire of the law officer, who should at once inform them of the punishment (for the illegal action in question) fixed by the law. The people should then at once inform the government officials, formally, of the law officer's statement. Thus the government officials, knowing that such is the course of events, dare not treat the people contrary to the law, nor do the people dare infringe the law.[21]

Irony of ironies: in the Legalist tyranny, the people are at least allowed to read the laws under which they live, and to insist that their immediate superiors obey them as well. Under the rule of the *Laozi*, this would have been impossible: the people would not have been able to read anything at all.[22] They would have been imprisoned in a timeless, unreflective present.

Literacy was not alone in coming under the disapproval of the *Laozi*. Orality was a target as well. Induced incuriosity through the enforcement of illiteracy was to be reinforced by deliberately impoverishing the *spoken* language of the people, since words, 'a word after a word after a word,' have powers the author assumes ordinary people cannot be trusted with. The common people of the *Laozi* are thus to be allowed no *spoken* words to blame – or for that matter to praise – the entities that control their entire lives behind the scenes:

太上下知有之 ... 功成事遂百姓皆曰我自然

With the best of all [rulers, his] inferiors know [no more than that] he exists ... When [the sage's] task is accomplished and [his] work done, the people say, 'We happened of ourselves to be thus!'[23]

Thus, the ruler is to act, but the people are to be deceived into believing that the results are 'natural.' If this is not a demand for the deliberate creation of a false consciousness among the common people, so that they attribute to themselves or 'nature' the results of being worked on by others, I do not know what else it might be termed.

One of the universal assumptions of ancient Chinese thought is that inferiors, as far as they find it possible, model the behaviour of their superiors. This means that the *Laozi* ruler must be a hypocrite as well as a deceiver if he is to maintain his inferiors in a state of ignorance. The *Laozi* sage is warned he must present an outward appearance very different from the clear-eyed ambition he would need in practice to carry out his program:

聖人之在天下歙歙焉
為天下渾渾焉
百姓皆注其耳目
聖人皆咳之

A sage's public persona exhibits befuddlement, and when ruling he is impenetrably obscure. The eyes and ears of all the people are occupied, and the sage treats them all like children.[24]

In public (literally, in his 'being in the world'), the sage appears to be other than he is; he makes himself unreadable by others; he sees that the perceptive powers of his commoners are 'occupied.' In other words, he is a conscious and consistent hypocrite. The outward face of rule must be kept suitably witless, so that through modelling themselves on this false face, the commoners become similarly stupid. The aim is simply to make them easier to rule:

古之善為道者非以明民將以愚之
民之難治以其多知也

故以知治國國之賊也
不以知治國國之福也 ...
乃復至於大順

Those of old who were expert in ruling according to the Way did not en-
lighten others thereby, but made them dull of mind. The reason the people
are hard to govern is that there is too much wisdom in them. Using wisdom to rule the state will be a calamity to it; not using wisdom to rule it
will be a blessing ... Then [the people] will revert to a stage of total
submission.[25]

The task of the ruler, in short, is to *deprive* his subjects (once more, note
the use of *fu* 復, 'go back to, revert') of any and every ability to learn of
their true state. They are not to be allowed to observe the true state of the
ruler directly; they are to be deprived of any way of criticizing him orally; and they are to be rendered incapable of keeping or consulting written records. All opportunity of finding out what their superiors are up
to, much less reflecting on, debating, and evaluating the performance of
those superiors, is to be systematically stripped away from them.[26]

What is the desired final state of such a society? We have already
touched on it: one of total passivity on the part of the people, complete
illiteracy, impoverished orality, and a lumpish incuriosity toward their
situation and surroundings. These will fix them safely in place, their
minds vacant of dangerous thoughts and overly exciting impressions:

民各甘其食美其服
安其俗樂其業
鄰國相望雞犬之聲相聞
使民至老死不相與往來

Each and every commoner will find his or her food delicious and clothing
beautiful. He or she will be at peace with his or her customs, and rejoice in
his or her calling in life. Neighbouring states may be within eyeshot of
each other, so that the people of each can hear the chickens and dogs of the
others, but the people will have been brought to the point where they will
never once in their lives go there for a visit.[27]

Those who habitually, and rightly, criticize the Legalist ideal of universal obedience to a harsh law fixed arbitrarily by superiors, and the Confucian dream that everyone should learn to accept his or her place in a

patriarchal, sexist, and hierarchical society, might consider what still harsher terms they should use to describe a Daoist submission obtained through the deliberate diminishing and delusion of eye and tongue.

It may be objected that the above is a far too cynical reading of the *Laozi* to hold water. It does indeed omit citation of some passages where the author of the text expresses concern about the condition and circumstances of the people. Clearly, the author wished the people to be as happy as he thought they could ever realistically hope to be. This is not, however, the key point.

No one would ever try to present the author of the *Laozi* as a deliberate monster, and no ancient Chinese ruler was anything other than authoritarian. All the same, the *Laozi* differs from other works of its time in a way that deserves emphasis. Both Legalists and Confucians would at least have everyone playing by the same set of rules, which were to be public and accessible to all, though hardly egalitarian, much less fair, gender neutral, or democratic. For Confucian and Legalist alike, the deck may be stacked, but all the cards are on the table. In advising that the masses should be *made* illiterate, and arguing at length that ordinary people should be rendered incapable of talking back to, or even thinking about, their superiors, the *Laozi* achieved a much less common compounding of authoritarianism with hypocrisy. It is the most private of private texts, a whisper in the reader's ear by which we are taken behind the scenes and shown things that the Great Unwashed must never read or even speak of. This is how the author of the *Laozi* gets around the awkward dilemma of writing a book that demands a ban on writing, and arguing in matchlessly subtle and poetic prose that speech should be cut back to the bone, impoverished almost to the level of nods and grunts. This too, I suspect, is the guilty secret of the *Laozi* enthusiast, an unacknowledged and indeed all but unspeakable aspect of the book's enduring popularity.[28]

Fantasies of Submission: The Author, the Attitude, and the Presentation

So much for the program; what of the presenter? Orality is implicated here too, in interesting ways.

It is often said that the *Laozi* text either went through an oral stage of transmission or contains oral elements.[29] One of the chief reasons for this assertion is that the phraseology of many passages is reminiscent of proverbs or popular sayings. Some translators and students of the text, such as Michael LaFargue, even try to identify these and speculate about changes that the 'Laoist' author or authors might have made to them.[30]

I believe that there may be another reason for these hints of orality. They may derive not from a true oral background but from the lack of one – from the desire to *sound* like an oral text, with all that might imply. Here we must speculate, but I think that the author's attitude toward textuality and orality is sufficiently suggestive that such speculation is justified.

The key point is that the ideal society of the *Laozi* is not the sort of oral society that is found in real life, but rather a typical example of an oral fantasy world, a sentimentalized, mythologized orality. Its delivery is closer to the *faux* spoken style found in early fiction about indigenous people, as discussed by Wolfgang Hochbruck, who calls it 'fabricated orality':

> It is important to notice that regardless of its connection with traditional culture, the fabrication of forms of 'orality' always serves to spatialize on the page a form of identity that is perceived of as different ... and as constructing a language of proximity ... In this sense, the fabrication of a special and different 'language of proximity' is not even limited to allegedly oral traditions but can (and usually does) extend to the fabrication of a general 'culture of proximity' which is set off against the 'culture of distance.'[31]

As an example, Hochbruck gives the constructed 'Scottishness' of Sir Walter Scott, 'basically a romantic irony.' This suggestion opens up the possibility that the 'oral' touches to the *Laozi* may have been deliberate stage setting, intended to scaffold, or even simply to decorate, the author's desire to whisper in the reader's ear about his imaginary return to a mythical, oral past.

One telltale sign of the artificiality of the 'culture of proximity' in the *Laozi* is its impoverishment. Hochbruck notes that all dynamic oral cultures necessarily contain two complementary impulses in the narratives circulating in their midst: the 'cyclical, reiterative, and reassuring' tales that ensure and embody social security, and the 'excitement of novelty no culture can do without' from the tales brought by 'the wanderer, the traveling merchant, and the migrant tradesperson.' In the take on orality in the *Laozi*, the latter type of orality is not just neglected but systematically excluded from the range of social possibilities as the worst of dangers. Given how literary the 'primitive' lifestyle in the *Laozi* is, this is not surprising. The ideal village in chapter 80 of the *Laozi* is a frozen dream, not a real place, and its imaginary population is little more than a collection of waxworks.

Thus, the crowning irony may have been that the author of the *Laozi*, writing some time before 350 BCE, was a pioneer in ways that he never suspected and probably would not have welcomed. He was first by many centuries in making the same mistake that some early Western students of orality did. Perhaps, if the legend of the author's original occupation as a royal archivist has some truth to it, 'Laozi' came from a highly literate, text-centric background and was soaked in the literary civilization of his time. Reacting against it, he made the typical romantic error of confusing a primary oral society with his own fantasies of what a 'primitive' oral society *should* be and assuming that primary orality means a complete lack of the ability to reason and think critically. His scale of values was different from later imperialist scholars – he intended 'primitive' as a compliment and a goal, rather than a denigration – but his other assumptions about the world-changing role of text and critical thought were startlingly similar.

'Laozi' thus concluded that by getting the ear of a suitable ruler and inducing him to manoeuvre or force the people under his rule back to a state of what he sentimentally imagined was primary orality, he would be able to effect a radical change in their thinking processes. In the process, the urge to discriminate and define that he believed separated them from the Way would be rooted out. It was all for their own good, naturally – but Agent Smith would have said the same thing.

NOTES

1 Daoists are known as 'Taoists' in the older Wade-Giles romanization. Since Chinese is not an alphabetic language, its pronunciation can be represented in more than one way, and unfortunately there are at least two systems still in use. For the same reason, resemblances between 'Zhuangzi' and 'Chuang-tzu,' the *Laozi* and the *Lao-tzu*, and the *Daodejing* and the *Tao-te ching* are not accidental.

2 The three main schools of classical Chinese thought, the Daoists, the Confucians, and the Legalists, are not easy to distinguish clearly and tend to blur into each other at the edges. At least some members of all three schools are included more as a result of the efforts of desperate bibliographers in ancient libraries than of real similarities or differences among the

thinkers concerned. However, some generalities about the two latter schools, which are not our main subject above, may help readers new to the field.

Confucians held that the example set by the sage kings of the past, and the books they were assumed to have authored, were highly relevant to society in all ages. They believed in social control through ritual, education, and moral example, a traditional social order with local centres of power, and they distrusted law as at best a blunt and unsubtle instrument to control human beings. If there was a great deal of crime in the state, the responsibility lay not only with the criminals but also with their superiors, who had failed to set them a good enough example.

Legalists denied the contemporary relevance of the sage kings, since they argued that times had changed, enforcing a change in the way society should operate. People should be educated in the laws of the ruler, which should be the only standard for the state, applicable equally to all below the rank of the ruler. The social hierarchy should be levelled, with the only superiors those who held appointments as the king's servants, removable at the king's pleasure. Law was the way to control people's behaviour, and deterrence was assumed to work perfectly: double the punishment, and you would halve the number of crimes; make the punishment unspeakably severe, and there would be no crime at all. Thus, harsh punishment was defended as the only true mercy.

3 The influence of the *Laozi* on art is explored in most discussions of the text, early or late. Its role in the development of Chinese popular religion is also covered in more recent accounts. The most accessible and up-to-date source for both is Allan Chan, 'Laozi,' *Stanford Encyclopedia of Philosophy* (2007) http://plato.stanford.edu/entries/laozi; See also Ronnie Littlejohn, 'Laozi (Lao-tzu),' *Internet Encyclopedia of Philosophy* (2006), www.iep.utm.edu/l/laozi.htm.

4 Gary Arbuckle, 'Literacy and Orality in Early China,' paper presented at the Calgary Institute for the Humanities, June 1994.

5 *Zhuangzi* 2, *Chuang-tzu: The Inner Chapters*, ed. and trans. A.C. Graham (London: Unwin, 1986), 52.

6 *Zhuangzi* 2, *Chuang-tzu*, 53.

7 Ibid.

8 *Zhuangzi* 13, *Chuang-tzu*, 140.

9 Chan, 'Laozi,' is very useful on these and many other details. For an ingenious theory on the relationship between author and book, see A.C. Graham, *Disputers of the Tao: Philosophical Argumentation in Ancient China* (La Salle: Open Court, 1989), 215–18.

10 The unity of the *Laozi* text has recently come under new attack with the 1998 publication of a partial copy, excavated from a tomb at Guodian in 1993. Robert G. Henricks has produced a book-length translation of these, and I agree with him that the incomplete Guodian text does not prove that the *Laozi* had not yet taken final form by the date of the tomb within which it was found, around 300 BCE. See Robert G. Henricks, *Lao Tzu's Tao Te Ching: A Translation of the Startling New Documents Found at Guodian* (New York: Columbia University Press, 2000), 19–22.

I suspect that one can put too much weight on editions of texts found in tombs, especially if such tombs are not those of the very highest members of society, for whom funeral expenses would not have been an issue. The occupant of the Guodian tomb was apparently a Confucian or heavily interested in things Confucian, a member of 'the lowest rank of the aristocracy,' and possibly the tutor of the heir apparent. Henricks, *Lao Tzu's Tao Te Ching*, 4. We recall what Xunzi had to say about the nature of grave goods:

> The ceremonial offerings include a cap with bands but no strings, earthen water and wine jugs that are empty and never filled, and there are bamboo mats but neither beds nor couches. The carvings on the wooden vessels are left incomplete. Earthenwares are left as unfinished objects. Thin wares are too incomplete to be used. The reed pipes and reed organs are whole but are not tuned. The zithers and lutes are strung but are not adjusted. The carriage is buried, but the horses are returned. All these practices are to indicate that these articles are not intended to be used. The articles of life are taken to the tomb to give the impression that only the abode has changed. A selection from his belongings is made, but the whole of them is not entombed; so the form is there, but no substance. (*Xunzi* 19, 'A Discourse on Ritual Principles,' in John Knoblock, *Xunzi: A Translation and Study of the Complete Works*, vol. 3, books 17–32 [Stanford: Stanford University Press, 1994], 67–8).

Clearly, people could be more extravagant if they chose, in some cases. But this passage also underlines that with Confucians, at least, there is no certain way to assume that texts buried in a tomb are of high quality. The Guodian copies of parts of the *Laozi* seem more casual notes than anything else. It is at least possible they were put into the tomb because no one alive would have much missed them.

11 *Laozi shiyi* 老子釋議 (*The Laozi, Explicated and Interpreted*) (Taipei: Liren shuju, 1980), 1; *Mawangdui Han mu boshu* 馬王堆漢墓帛書 (*The Silk Texts Found in a Han Tomb at Mawangdui*), vol. 1 (Bejing: Xinhua, 1980), 114; Chen Guying 陳鼓應, *Laozi zhuyi ji pingjie* 老子註譯及評介 (Beijing: Zhonghua Shuju, 1984). All translations here are my own, and all are based on the

modern text given in the *Mawangdui Han mu boshu,* consulting the modern Chinese translation and notes in Chen Guying and the notes in the *Laozi shiyi.* The page numbers refer to the comparative table of the two manuscripts discovered at Mawangdui and the received text.

12 *Laozi shiyi,* 2; *Mawangdui Han mu boshu,* 114.

13 *Laozi shiyi,* 18; *Mawangdui Han mu boshu,* 118.

14 *Chuang-tzu,* 17.

15 Graham, *Disputers of the Tao,* 53–64.

16 This is why one finds the term 'non-action' (*wuwei* 無為) used also by Confucians and even by Legalists, the harsh believers in a human order ruthlessly and impartially enforced. The wiggle room provided by changing definitions of what exactly was 'contrived, unnatural, forced' (*wei* 為) helped greatly to harmonize the differing positions of the three schools when philosophical synthesis became popular. It also makes 'non-action' a largely empty term, one that indicates nothing certain concerning the thought or behaviour of the person or thought system it is applied to.

17 *Laozi shiyi,* 3; *Mawangdui Han mu boshu,* 114.

18 *Laozi shiyi,* 80; *Mawangdui Han mu boshu,* 109. Chapter 80 is out of order in the two Mawangdui manuscripts, being inserted after the present Chapter 66. However, I do not think this implies anything about its reliability.

19 Chan is typical in merely noting the sinister possibilities of this advice, but it is clearly out of his own personal 'comfort zone,' and he moves on with alacrity to more agreeable concepts:

> Those who fully realize 'virtue' in the Daoist sense do not act in the way that men and women of conventional morality typically act or are expected to act. Paradoxes of this kind function as a powerful rhetorical device, which forces the reader, so to speak, to move out of his or her 'comfort zone' ... In this context, one can also understand some of the provocative statements in the *Laozi* telling the ruler, for example, to keep the people in a state of 'ignorance' (ch. 65) ... Perhaps the *Laozi* in chapter 65 of the current text did mean to tell the ruler literally to keep the people ignorant or stupid for better control, which as a piece of political advice is not exactly extraordinary ... The concept of *wuwei* does not only initiate a critique of value but also points to a higher mode of knowledge, action, and being. (Chan, 'Laozi').

For my part, I believe that a proposal to turn the vast majority of the state's population into zombies deserves more attention than this, however fascinating and beautiful the other parts of the *Laozi* might seem.

20 *Laozi shiyi,* 80; *Mawangdui Han mu boshu,* 109.

21 J.J.L. Duyvendak, 'The Fixing of Rights and Duties,' in *The Book of Lord Shang,* vol. 26 (London: Probsthain, 1928), 328–31.

22 The Confucians, for their part, expected ordinary people to take the moral initiative and think for themselves at critical junctures. The most discussed was probably the illegal-orders dilemma, when a superior gave a command that clearly violated more general canons of morality. One classic example was a father who on his deathbed demands his concubine be killed and buried with him. The standard Confucian gloss was that on giving such an order, the father instantly and automatically loses the moral standing that would ordinarily compel instant obedience from his children – he is no longer a 'real' father, and no longer commands the 'natural' respect and allegiance that 'real' fatherhood entails. Later Confucians, such as some in the *Gongyang* tradition 公羊傳 of *Annals* 春秋 interpretation, justified a woman killing her husband in the defence of her mother-in-law; indeed, they praised her as comparable to the Zhou dynasty sage kings Wen and Wu. Thus the idea that an inferior should use his or her own intellectual or moral capabilities to debate, deliberate, and act decisively with regard to the performance of a superior was not a novelty in ancient China, though its more extreme manifestations must always have been exceptional in practice. Cf Gary Arbuckle, 'Former Han Legal Philosophy and the *Gongyang zhuan,*' *B.C. Asian Review* 1 (1987): 1–25.

23 *Laozi shiyi,* 17; *Mawangdui Han mu boshu,* 118.

24 *Laozi shiyi,* 49; *Mawangdui Han mu boshu,* 104.

25 *Laozi shiyi,* 65; *Mawangdui Han mu boshu,* 108–9.

26 One recalls Wendy Wickwire's account of Coyote and his journey to visit the king of England to see that the 'Black and White' is enforced, and to appeal to a law that is to last 'until the end of time.' Coyote could have got away with making such an appeal under a Confucian or even a Legalist ruler, though it would not necessarily have been successful. Under a ruler in the *Laozi* mould, the 'Black and White' would have been forever unreadable and forbidden, the King's location would have been a mystery, and society would have been arranged so that Coyote would never be able to develop the skill he needed to persuade, or the curiosity that led him to roam. See Harry Robinson, *Living by Stories: A Journey of Landscape and Memory,* ed. Wendy Wickwire (Vancouver: Talonbooks, 2005).

27 *Laozi shiyi,* 80; *Mawangdui Han mu boshu,* 109.

28 For those who find this suggestion too cynical, I ask that they answer this question: how do you see yourself, in your imagination, while reading and contemplating what you read of the world of the *Laozi*? As the sage or his adviser, literate, expressive, and powerful, or as one of the ignorant,

incurious, and hobbled peasantry? What the *Laozi* preaches for the lower orders is the imposition of a lifestyle that all but a few enthusiasts for the book would regard as death in life. Indeed, there is a formal contradiction here for fans: if such a lifestyle is good, then enthusiasm for *any* book becomes paradoxical.

29 Cf Chan, 'Laozi.'
30 Michael LaFargue, *The Tao of the Tao Te Ching* (Albany: State University of New York Press, 1992).
31 Wolfgang Hochbruck, '"I Have Spoken": Fictional "Orality" in Indigenous Fiction,' *College Literature* 23, no. 2 (1996): 132–42.

Chapter 8

Unstable Texts and Modal Approaches to the Written Word in Medieval European Ritual Magic

FRANK KLAASSEN

In the late 1520s one of the most influential Western authors on magic, Heinrich Cornelius Agrippa von Nettesheim, wrote to a friend concerning his attempt to absorb, understand, and synthesize the diverse written traditions of Jewish, Greek, Latin, and Arabic magic circulating in his time:

> O how many writings are read concerning the invincible power of the magic art, concerning the prodigious images of the astrologers, the marvellous transformation of the alchemists, and that blessed stone which Midas-like immediately turns every base metal it touches to gold or silver. All these writings are found vain, fictitious and false as often as they are practised to the letter. Yet they are propounded and written by great and most grave philosophers and holy men. Who will dare call their teachings false? What is more, it would be impious to believe that they have written falsehoods in those works. Hence the meaning must be other than what the letters yield up.[1]

Agrippa's three-volume magnum opus, *On Occult Philosophy* (*De occulta philosophia*) has often been regarded as a work that is credulous on an encyclopedic scale. Yet this passage reveals a powerful level of doubt about how to extract truth from the magical texts upon which it was based. Elsewhere in his writings this is expressed as a fairly thoroughgoing scepticism toward the written word. His *Concerning the Uncertainty and Vanity of Arts and Sciences* (*De incertitudine et vanitate artium et scienciarum*), published in tandem with *On Occult Philosophy* and commonly regarded as an elucidation of it, rejects as effectively empty all human claims to truth not inspired by the divine. As a humanist scholar, he effectively exploits his extensive learning and sensitivity to texts in his rejection of human arts. No text can in itself convey truth. Even the Bible, which is the only textual access to divine truths available to humans, can be understood only through divine inspiration. This inspiration comes to those with the gift of interpretation, something God gives to only a few. Texts thus pose tremendous interpretive problems. In addition, while a text might bear some relation to the truth, only the divine can close the gap between signifier and signified.[2]

At the same time, Agrippa chooses to communicate his ideas through the written word. The paradox implicit in Jacques Derrida's written works is by no means new, and like Derrida's, Agrippa's written works present difficulties as texts in themselves. Agrippa intentionally wrote *On Occult Philosophy* in obscure language. Although it quickly became a standard source book for practising occultists, Agrippa's intentions and the precise nature of the magical practices he promotes remain in large measure unclear. In part Agrippa does this to protect himself. In part he also seeks to protect the knowledge contained in the work from the ignorant who could (and no doubt did) corrupt it from its original intent. In this latter sense, the work may be characterized as esoteric. His approach to writing compels his readers to enter a hermeneutic spiral in which the text, practical experience, and divine enlightenment all seem play a part.[3] *On Occult Philosophy* ostensibly presents itself as containing some shreds of truth, or at least the means by which truth can be derived. It also makes clear that real truth, manifested by powerful magical operation, may ultimately be reached only through divine inspiration, here figured as 'divine frenzy.' The text thus has a profoundly ambiguous status. Magical books remain an essential part of transmitting the elements of an ancient religious magic but are more like participants in the communication of this information than its container.

That this work was printed in numerous editions and translations certainly meant that more or less the same text was widely available in numerous copies. Yet while it was certainly the most influential work of Renaissance magic, the ritual magic tradition was no more unified afterward than before. And if his readers followed his advice, it could not have been otherwise. Agrippa's powerful struggle with the written word has led some to regard his works as the expression of a larger crisis in Renaissance thought.[4] This may be true, but an examination of the medieval traditions of ritual magic reveal that his concerns and responses were by no means new. Rather, Agrippa is one representative of a centuries-old tradition of ritual magic in which authors confronted the same difficulties with their books and in their own way contributed to them. A closer examination of this tradition yields valuable insight into the nature of textuality and its relationship to orality in the West.

The literature on orality and literacy divides roughly into two groups. One, epitomized by the work of Jack Goody, Walter Ong, and Eric Havelock, focuses on the ways in which inherent features of the written word affect consciousness and the cultures that employ it.[5] Historical analyses that focus on broad social and cultural changes, such as the medieval European shift from memory to written record, have often followed their approach. In particular they have concerned themselves with the effects of technologies that take advantage of the standardizing and stabilizing potential of the written word. A written contract was less subject to the vagaries of memory than an oral one. So too the new written forms of literature and law made them more static than was possible in the old oral and consensual systems. This in turn made objective analysis possible, and truth increasingly came to be identified in an iconic sense with the written word, the book or the legal document.[6] Elizabeth Eisenstein makes similar arguments with reference to printing.[7] Another group of scholars have argued against universalizing claims about the nature of orality and literacy, emphasizing instead the social and cultural context of the written word and the ways in which its usages are culturally mediated.[8]

The present analysis falls firmly into the latter camp by arguing that in order to contribute to a rationalizing process a specific social context for textual technologies was necessary, a context that was by no means a necessary result of literacy. However, it begins by examining some of the inherent features of texts. Through an analysis of medieval ritual magic manuals we may see that many essential features of texts – even printed ones – run counter to a rationalizing or standardizing process. This is particularly the case when, as in the case of ritual magic, the intellectual culture surrounding the production of texts revels in, and self-consciously employs, the ambiguous or unstable features of the written word. Moreover, as an illicit tradition, ritual magic could not depend upon the same kind of institutional and communal support as conventional intellectual communities – with the result that its written tradition was unstable. Authors were aware of this problem and regarded a stable social context for transmission as an important way to counter it. Interestingly, this alternative approach to texts was founded on conventional ideas and promoted by members of what we may broadly consider to be the 'rationalizing class' of the high and late Middle Ages. In this sense we need to be careful to avoid regarding the magical tradition as proposing an 'alterior' or subversive approach to texts. Rather, the approach to the written word evident in these works is better understood as a distinctive modality that did not necessarily preclude the same authors from employing texts in other ways in other circumstances. In summary, medieval European ritual magic provides an example of how, in certain modes of thought, but particularly in the absence of related stable social networks and a desire to standardize, texts and textuality may serve as principles of instability rather than of rationalization.

Before going any further, let me give a brief description of the nature of medieval and Renaissance ritual magic. Those who wrote and transmitted its texts were the learned, those with sufficient training to be able to work more or less comfortably with written texts and the Latin language. This class is commonly associated with the 'rationalization' of Western European institutional structures such as civil and canon law or ecclesiastical and civil administrations. They were not only lawyers, notaries, administrators, doctors, and teachers but also priests and monks, men educated in the universities who made a living in secular and church contexts through the use of texts.[9] Although there existed no precise medieval equivalent for the term 'ritual magic,' modern scholars use it to refer to a set of practices that employ complex elaborations on conventional Christian ritual combined with Arabic, Greek, and Hebraic magical traditions to draw upon the power of demons or angels for a variety of ends. These practices typically demand high levels of personal purity and religious devotion in the form of sexual abstinence, fasting, regular prayer, confession, communication, contemplation, and attendance at religious services. Two principal genres of texts fall under this broader category. In the first are texts that refer to themselves as necromancy (*necromantia*) or nigromancy (*nigromantia*). These tend to focus on more mundane goals and commonly employ a combination of astrological lore and liturgical ritual, particularly exorcisms and prayers. They typically call on both angels and demons, sometimes to perform tasks such as producing a magical horse or other illusions, but most commonly to reveal information in the form of visions or dreams. The information may be quite mundane, such as the location of hidden treasure, or relate to higher truths such as the structure of the cosmos or the powers of demons and angels. The *materia magica* include magical circles, incense, incantation, prayer, blessings, exorcisms, magical swords or sceptres, and a variety of devices such as crystals, flames, or reflecting surfaces in which a 'skryer' (i.e., a medium) or the operator would see visions or converse with spirits.[10] The second group of texts proposes a more purely angelic or divine magic, often referred to as theurgic.[11] In this group the major texts are the *Notory Art* (*Ars notoria*) – a text putatively by Solomon that promises the infusion of spiritual and intellectual gifts by angels – and the *Book of Visions* (*Liber visionum*) by John of Morigny, a more highly Christianized version of this art. The *Sworn Book* (*Liber iuratus*) is another important text of this kind and promised the operator no less than a vision of God in his glory.[12] All ritual magic texts require of the operator a quasi-priestly life of chastity and religious observance. They were written, collected, and redacted by a variety of literate individuals, commonly religious (monks and priests) but also others in the educated elite such as medical doctors, engineers, courtiers, and other members or products of the universities.

The most compelling illustration of the complex circumstances surrounding magical texts, their authors, and their readers is the mythic prologue to the *Sworn Book of Honorius*. It begins with a fictional account of the events that led up to its composition. Fearful of the power of magicians who could control them, the demons convinced the officials of the institutional church that they needed to root out the magical arts.[13] The bishops and prelates accordingly convinced the Pope to begin a misguided persecution of magical practitioners. Having been forewarned by God of the great persecutions to come, the holy Masters of Magic decided that rather than use a host of wicked spirits to destroy their enemies they would simply compile their art into a single book. This measured response is no doubt designed to convince readers of the near saintly character of the magicians:

> Wherefore we called one general council of all the masters in the which council of 811 masters which came out of Naples, Athens, and Toledo we did choose one whose name was Honorius, the son of Euclid, Master of the Thebans, in which city this art was read, that he should work for us in this said art, and he, through the counsel of a certain angel whose name was Hocroel did write seven volumes of art magic, giving unto us the kernel and to others the shells, out of the which books he drew out 93 chapters in the which is briefly contained the 100 sacred names of god and therefore it is called sacred, as you would say, made of holy things, or else because by this book he came to the knowledge of sacred or holy things, or else because it was consecrated of angels, or else because the angel Hocroel did declare and show unto him that it was consecrated of God.[14]

The church authorities are then described as having satisfied them-selves by burning trifles, while this volume survived, the core of a sacred and divinely sanctioned magic. The prologue ends with rules on the transmission of the text, to which any owner of the volume must swear compliance. Only three copies can be made at a time, and they cannot be given to a woman or a minor but only to a godly man, tested for one year. The practitioners must be joined in a loyal community, must not reveal their secrets, even at the risk of their own lives, and must aid each other in the spirit of love and brotherhood. Finally, should the 'master' not be able to pass on the work to a suitable dis-ciple, the work must be buried with him.

This unique and fanciful prologue provides an illustration of the characteristically complicated status of a magical manual as text, its vulnerability, and the necessity of a stable social environment for its preservation. The *Sworn Book* was produced in a complex relationship between the human arts, the chosen wise man, and the divine. Honorius took the entire art of magic and boiled it down into seven books, giving 'shells' to some and 'kernels' to others. Whether some of these seven volumes were deceptive, containing only 'shells,' is unclear. However, there is no question that to deceive the initiated, Honorius either wrote works of false magic or has left behind rejected portions of the editing process. This claim serves to promote the *Sworn Book* as a singular text, the kernel of truth in a sea of empty shells. Yet it suggests that many, if not most, magical texts may be fallacious or even mendacious, even those written by ritual magic's greatest authors. It is a common feature of esoteric writing that the text is written in intentionally obscure lan-guage to protect its secrets from the ignorant or uninitiated; the writer of magical texts both communicates and deceives.[15] The process of redac-tion was also not possible for even the wisest of the wise to accomplish on his own. The angel Hocroel was necessary not only to transfer infor-mation from the divine to the human sphere during the text's original composition but to aid in the proper transmission and interpretation of existing texts to subsequent readers. Unaided human efforts were ap-parently unequal to the task of writing, interpreting, and transmitting truth in texts. Finally, while the rules governing its transmission cer-tainly serve rhetorically to intensify the sense that the work contained great and secret treasures, they also clearly recognize the unstable na-ture of the written word and its vulnerability. The simple act of writing down the text by no means guaranteed its survival. Moreover, unlimited copying was not desirable. One could make only three copies, and the reason is made clear by the subsequent injunctions against allowing the ignorant access. If the text should fall into the hands of the uninitiated or ignorant, or fall victim to unlimited copying, it could become corrupted. As we shall see, such corruptions were potentially very dangerous. Yet the rules of transmission are more complex than even this implies. They say nothing about being sure that the copy is error free but concern themselves principally with the context in which the text is transmitted. This deserves more detailed treatment.

In examinations of medieval literate culture, it has been a habit to focus on either the static text, such as the unchanging legal document, or the solitary monk or scholar reading alone and in silence.[16] As a description of an ideal 'textual community' the prologue to the *Sworn Book* provides a medieval perspective that demonstrates one way in which modern views have been anachronistic. The fraternal community of practitioners is central to the rules for the transmission of the *Sworn Book*, making clear that this process was ideally a matter of collective action. A person competent to interpret it and to use it in the right manner, the 'master,' must accompany the text. Proper transmission of the text must take place in a carefully controlled community of pious, loyal, learned, and committed individuals. The model in the mind of the author was either the university or monastery, although the terms 'scholar,' 'disciple,' and 'master' suggest the former. Whatever the case might be, intellectual communities in both of these contexts (and in fact they frequently overlapped) maintained their intellectual coherence in large measure because of their institutional affiliation and the oral interaction that took place therein. While a school of thought, or 'textual community,' may be associated with individuals, their interpretation of a text, and their written work, the maintenance of that school and its dissemination in the long term depended on collective action in an institutional context. The work of both Daniel Boyarin and Nicholas Howe on early Jewish and Anglo-Saxon notions of reading, respectively, has emphasized how reading was understood as a speech act, including the senses of reading aloud, public performance, giving council, and expounding upon a text.[17] Howe expands on Stock's notion of the textual community in an important way, arguing that 'both readers and listeners belong in a community at once textual and spiritual, written and oral, in which intellectual and spiritual life is created through the communal interchange of reading.'[18] To this I add something implicit but not emphasized in Howe's discussion – and very much part of Stock's – that reading is understood not as passive but as also involving interpretation. It must be emphasized (although it is perhaps implicit in these studies) that textual interpretation is also a form of collective action.[19]

This can be seen most dramatically in the medieval university, where the process of reading and interpreting texts was in significant measure a public matter. Achieving a lasting and more or less stable interpretation was also consensual. When Abelard defeated William of Champeaux in public debate it was more than a personal triumph. It was the occasion for a public shift in interpretation without which Abelard's written works would not have become intellectual standards and subsequently preserved. The institutionalized and ritual forms of oral interaction of the University of Paris (as well as the community of the Dominican order) were essential to the ongoing life of scholastic theology at Paris. For this reason when we speak of the school of Chartres or the school of St Victor, or when we speak of schools of thought in relation to more modern intellectual traditions, we mean more than a group of people who happen to hold a coherent set of similar ideas. Such terms also include the sense of a definable place, some kind of institutional affiliation, teaching and learning, group interaction (not precluding differences of opinion), and persistence through time, perhaps over many generations. While schools might arrange themselves in relation to a set of texts, such schools developed and maintained themselves not by the promulgation of a static and unchanging set of principles but through an amorphous process of mutual consent, much like the consensual and oral processes we commonly associate with non-textual legal systems.[20] It seems likely that the author of the *Sworn Book* recognized these processes (or a somewhat simplified version of them) as an inherent and desirable part of textual transmission. These aspects of learned communities need to be kept in mind as we turn to the examination of other magical works.

The concerns and conditions expressed mythically in the *Sworn Book* are borne out in a variety of ways in other texts of ritual magic. In the *Book of Visions*, an autobiographical prologue to his reworking of the *Notory Art*, John of Morigny, a fourteenth-century monk, provides us with an intimate account of his life and interactions with magical traditions and the world of visionary experiences. After having been introduced to the *Notory Art* by an acquaintance, John says that its operations seemed to work for him, rendering visionary experiences in which he was taught by numinous beings that he believed to be angels. Yet he was increasingly plagued by disturbing visions in which apparently divine forces tried to convince him that this magical art was in fact evil. In one an angel demonstrated that the prayers he had been saying were secretly woven together with demonic incantations. His ignorance was due to the fact that many of the prayers were written in unknown words (*verba ignota*), which the text purports to be transliterated Hebrew, Greek, and Syriac. The result was that he had been summoning demons, not angels, and without angelic guidance in the matter he might never have known the difference. Not only was the text corrupt and false but John regarded concourse with demons as problematic from a religious perspective and whatever information they provided as suspect. As a result, when he developed what he thought was good magic, he had reason to fear committing a text to parchment. Once it left his hands there was no guarantee any subsequent copyist would not alter it accidentally, maliciously, or under demonic influence.

Nonetheless, John ultimately composed his own work of quasi-theurgic operations in which he claimed to be guided by angels and the Blessed Virgin. This new text plundered elements from the original, bad *Notory Art* and created a new one in which the operator employed a variety of prayers and contemplative exercises to achieve spiritual and intellectual gifts. A strongly worded injunction that the text not be altered makes clear that John was very much aware of the potential problems. Interestingly enough, however, he qualified this injunction. If a subsequent operator was instructed by God to do so, he could alter John's revised and good version of the art.

Magical texts were not only literally unstable and changing; they were understood by their users to be unstable in other ways was as well. In the first place, how was one to know if the text was divine or demonic, false or true, or what its hidden meanings might be? Second, while the text itself remained physically stable, there was no guarantee that the divine would continue to approve or endorse it. And finally, it was impossible to know if a subsequent author, mistakenly or intentionally, had altered the text *without* divine permission. In short, without divine guidance one could not confidently confirm the legitimacy of a text. The only stable element in the equation was the standard set by the divine.

Another interesting aspect of Brother John's account (and of the ritual magic tradition in general) is the principle that the magical art was not simply a matter of slavishly following the instructions laid out in a manual. In his description of his initial operations with the *Notory Art* John implies that one had to move beyond the literal sense to *learn* how to make the magic work:

Above all I desired with my whole heart to come to the knowledge of all the sciences and since it was not possible to do this by taking courses [*doctrinam successivam*] on account of my poverty, and in the foresaid book was contained a means by which I might be able to attain my purpose by instant teaching [*doctrinam subitaneam*], setting aside all other studies I undertook to study it more frequently; and I studied in it so much that I figured out what I had to do to make it work.[21]

Although one could, in principle, follow the instructions of the *Notory Art* to the letter on first reading,[22] John here makes plain that something more than the literal reading of the text was necessary to make the operations work. I conjecture that what he learned probably related to the contemplative exercises and some kind of attunement to dreams or other presumed points of contact with the divine. The necessity of learning what a text was about was perhaps particularly poignant for John. Although he speaks of encouraging others to use his techniques and seems to have learned from their experiences, nowhere does he describe being taught by another person. In large measure his learning process appears to have been a solitary confrontation with a text whose meaning had to be discerned in non-textual ways.

To complicate matters more, several features of ritual magic encouraged the production of new and different texts in the same way that John of Morigny had done. Works such as the Solomonic *Notory Art* and *Book of Visions* set out techniques that would in principle result in visions giving the operator some indeterminate knowledge or information about a broadly defined, hidden aspect of the spiritual or natural world. The *Liber Rasielis*, discussed in more detail below, promotes itself not as a repository of wisdom but as a device for getting a wide variety of divine knowledge that might differ depending on the operator.[23] Each user in its transmission through a long lineage from Adam through Noah to Solomon gained something quite different from it. The text thus does not produce a standardized product but one that varied entirely from user to user. Far from a standardizing force its mythological presentation gives the impression of a conduit through which diverse and sometimes entirely unrelated forms of truth may be derived.

Necromantic manuals also employ angelic and demonic rituals to acquire new information about magic to supplement (and potentially supersede) whatever the book provided. In two demon-conjuring procedures

from a fifteenth-century magical manual in the Bodleian Library, the operator is advised to gather certain salient information during visionary
experiences:

> When the spiryt is apperyd: What is thy name? Under what state and
> what dynite [i.e., dignity] hast thow? What is thy powyr and thy offyse?
> Undyr what planet and sygn art thow? Of what parte arte thow of the
> world? Of which element art thow? Whych is thy monyth? What is thy
> day and thyn owyr? What is thyne howre, day or nyght? Whych is thy
> winde? What be they caretes that thow obeyst to? Whych is thy mansion
> and thy day? Which is thy sterre? Which is thy stone? Which is thy erbe?
> What is thyne offyse to do? What is thy metale? What is thyne Aungellys
> name that thow moste obeyst to? And in what lykenes aperyst thow? How
> many commyst thow wythall?[24]

And elsewhere in the same manual, 'And if [the spirit] appears, show
him the pentacle of Solomon and ask him his name and his office and
what his character is and under what governor he is and what his days,
hours, and months are, etc.'[25]

These procedures demonstrate that the magical operations were entirely open ended. The operator, assuming he was able to achieve a visionary experience himself or to employ an effective medium or 'skryer'
to have (or invent) one for him, would record this new information and
use it in subsequent operations. It would almost certainly be useless for
anything else.

That these kinds of processes and the information they provided could
be used to compose new magical texts is attested by numerous examples.
The myth of Honorius and the account of Brother John both involve the
rewriting of texts based on visionary experiences. A mid-sixteenth-century
British manuscript records the visionary experiences of a magical operator and the communications made to him by other-worldly beings
through his skryer.[26] Perhaps the most famous example is the voluminous
set of notes written by the sixteenth-century mathematician, cartographer,
and natural philosopher John Dee to document his conversations with
various angels. Not only did Dee's angels answer questions he had about
the hidden nature of the world but they also dictated new magical material to him to be used in future operations. These, in turn, have found a
place among the texts of magic in the West as source books in their
own right.[27] The result of this situation, which predates Dee by several
centuries, was a particularly unstable tradition in which texts were

regularly and significantly altered. Agrippa's complaint cited at the beginning of this chapter was thus quite justified and understandable.

So in a variety of ways the tradition of ritual magic had a tense relationship with the written word. The texts could be delivered in finished written form by angels, and angels might aid in their composition, but unaided human efforts were not deemed sufficient to the task. In addition, the ability of the reader to distinguish true from false in a magical text was perpetually in doubt. To make matters worse, readers understood that the text they were using might have been unintentionally corrupted by an ignorant scribe and that some texts, even some of those by the wisest of the wise, had been *intentionally* written to deceive the reader. Only divine assistance in the interpretation of a text could assure the safety of the operator. In addition, even when one's interpretation was correct, the immediate sense of the text might not be sufficient for conducting successful operations. Only individual experience could fill in the gaps or inadequacies of the written word. This is not to say the every magical text was an original work. The *Notory Art* is an identifiable and relatively standard text, and some copies of the *Book of Visions* were painstakingly duplicated from their exemplars.[28] Even the necromantic literature contains a library of somewhat unstable but at least roughly identifiable texts. Copying these texts or even writing new ones expressed the desire to stabilize or the belief that the received text was stable. At the same time, powerful impulses in the intellectual culture of ritual magic made the received texts suspect and encouraged their scribes to individual or even vision-inspired readings or reworkings of them.

The relationship of ritual magic to conventional thought also bears on the ways in which its proponents viewed texts. Writers of ritual magic could not draw on the support of a consistent community of interpretation.[29] Although it seems likely that most of the texts were transmitted through personal connections, readers often had to confront these texts independently, relying on their own intellectual resources.[30] John of Morigny confronted corrupt texts and visions of demons and angels largely on his own. Certainly, he was not taught the art by an initiate. The brotherhood of magic in the *Sworn Book* forms the principal feature of how the text was supposed to be transmitted. This suggests an awareness of the value of a stable community for the maintenance of a text but perhaps also expresses the *wish* that such a community could exist. No continuous school of interpretation such as was continually in operation around conventional learning in the universities ever seems to have been associated with ritual magic texts.[31] Most important, they could not depend on support from institutional Christianity, a fact its authors were not always clear about. But as in the case of John of Morigny, whose book was condemned and burned when he naïvely attempted to promote it, they probably found out. In this situation it is understandable why the assurance that a text had been dictated by an angel or composed with divine guidance would be comforting. And in light of this it may be useful to consider some other aspects of these magical manuals.

The *Book of Rasiel* (*Liber Rasielis*) is a work of ritual magic of Jewish origin, which circulated in numerous versions in late medieval Europe. Its operations combine the use of astrological lore with angel magic. Like many other works of ritual magic its author and redactors were concerned to identify it with a distant, holy past. In its two main versions it is associated with Adam and Solomon. In the version that discusses Adam the story begins with the Fall. Adam, ejected from Eden, pleads and prays for some form of redemption. Eventually his miserable prayers are answered. The angel Rasiel appears and is said to 'give him the book.'[32] The text goes on to describe what it looks like and the meaning of its appearance. The crucial moment of transfer is described as follows: 'And Rasiel opened the book and read in Adam's ear. Adam listened solemnly to the words of the book from the mouth of the angel and threw himself face down on the ground with great fear. Raziel said to him, arise, Adam, be comforted and have no fear. Take this book from my hand and turn your attention to it since by it you will know and understand.'[33]

As is common in early Jewish contexts, reading here is regarded as a speech act.[34] This may have additionally been meant to highlight the intimate relationship between Adam and the angel in what is supposed to be a profoundly moving and emotional visionary experience. The angel arrives with a book in hand and physically gives it to Adam, thereby lending the written *Book of Rasiel* a transcendent status akin to the Decalogue or the Bible itself.

The written word is thus mythically connected with the enduring stability of the divine. Yet as I have already shown, this claim creates more problems than it solves for the medieval reader and we need to be careful in how we interpret it. Was the copy in Adam's hands never subsequently changed, and how would one know? By emphasizing a divine source the status of any *earthly* copy is implicitly brought into question. One also hopes that a text of this profundity *would* present some interpretive problems. In turn, the visionary source of the volume tends to push the reader to the numinous to solve these interpretive difficulties. The emphasis on the value of visionary experience also encouraged subsequent writers to seek their own visionary experiences. This is not suggested by this text, but the impulse is amply demonstrated by the other texts examined here. From the examples it is clear that many other authors preferred to have (or invent) visionary experiences of their own rather than simply transmitting existing texts and, as one might expect, the numinous did not decide to give everyone the same book or information. (Would that it could be so easy!) The result is an unstable literature of related but often quite different texts. This leads me to suggest that, where one might be tempted to regard this deifying of the book as the triumph of textuality over orality, or as evidence of a great confidence in the power of the written word, it seems more reasonable to read the claim in exactly the opposite sense, as an attempt to compensate for the inadequacy, tenuousness, and uncontrollability of the text. It would simplify matters too much, however, to suggest that readers and writers of magical texts regarded textual ambiguity only in negative terms.

Other aspects of magical manuals suggest that writers about magic not only struggled with the ambiguities of the written word but actually revelled in them and intentionally sought to enhance or emphasize them.[35] Magic is commonly associated with the bizarre, the surprising, the unknown, or the foreign. Particularly compelling are things that apparently have a meaning, but an unknown meaning. The use of Latin in modern incantations is a good example: it lends an air of power and mystery to the spoken word. In the Middle Ages this impulse expressed itself in the use of Arabic, Hebrew, Greek, and Syriac, referred to by critics as *verba ignota* (unknown words). Similarly, magical images or figures are commonly replete with seemingly significant but indecipherable and bizarre signs, symbols, and words. While some texts use such symbols as a way of implying secret knowledge that was the property of the writer or initiate, this is by no means always the case. The *Notory Art*, for example, explicitly states that the unknown words are included in their original language because they would lose their power if translated.[36] Their efficacy does not extend from knowledge, which can be held exclusively by a small group, but rather inheres in their vocalization, something available to anyone who could read the text or be taught it. The signifying function of the sign or vocalization is part of the attraction, but this signifying function is enhanced (or even supplanted) by its lack of clear meaning for the reader or viewer and the numinous associations this can lend to it. The same applied to mysterious signs, sacrifices, ingredients, and other *materia magica*. Yet these examples apply to the gestural, spoken, or visual elements in the text (although they are of course written down), so let us turn to examples more intimately related to textuality.

Several features of magical manuals specifically seek to push the text beyond its simple signifying function. The simplest example is the use of intentionally archaic hands to suggest age and profundity.[37] A common feature of magical manuals is the insistence that when a new copy is made, the volume must be ritually prepared as a magical artifact in itself. Operators are to use a consecrated pen, to employ ritually prepared ink and parchment, to write the entire volume at one sitting, and to consecrate it when finished. Unless they enhance the written word in this way the text it contains will not be efficacious.[38] A more compelling example is found in the *Notory Art*. Notes (*notae*), the figures that give the art its name, are magical devices meant to enhance the contemplative state of the operator in the attempt to receive spiritual and intellectual gifts from the angels. They are superficially similar to necromantic figures of the kind used in conjuring, but unlike necromantic figures, they usually take the form of a graphic arrangement of a given prayer that the operator is supposed to recite. They are also considerably more complex and required a high level of skill to execute. In one fifteenth-century manuscript, a prayer is written in a thin line of text that spirals outward from the centre of a circle to span a diameter of more than twelve inches. In other cases the prayers are written in complex patterns of connected globes resembling cabalist trees. A considerable amount of time, effort, and attention were required to design the pages and to match the prayers to the size of the various shapes that were to contain them.

All of these lend numinous qualities to the text by revelling in the ambiguities, limitations, and evocative power of written signifiers. Although some of these qualities are associated with other forms of expression, such as speech acts, gestures, and ritual actions, the magical tradition also sought to use texts in this manner. We may wish to regard these as a kind of metatext, an attempt to push the text beyond its inherent limitations while also drawing on its ambiguities. A text or signifier that does not altogether explain itself, and thereby cannot act as a standardizing force, is actually preferable to one whose meaning is clear. While the *notae* may contain a readable and completely understandable text, they also contain elements that seek to push the reader beyond the limited meaning of the text, that seek to complicate or deepen its significance in unclear ways. The intent of these stylized presentations of prayers seems to have been to help the reader to achieve a contemplative state in which the operator literally moved beyond the narrow meaning or significance of the text. Any standardizing of this system would serve only to disenchant it. 'Abracadabra' long ago appeared in magical texts as a powerful magical word, but repeated usage has caused it to become a cliché associated with comical presentations of magic. If magical texts were allowed to have a standardizing function, they would not long remain magical. This impulse drove both the continued renewal and the textual instability of this tradition.

The case of early modern printed works provides a useful coda to this discussion. Despite Agrippa's complaint about the obscurities and inconsistencies of the magical traditions upon which he drew, largely in manuscript, the intentionally esoteric style of his magnum opus, *On Occult Philosophy (De occulta philosophia)*, made his own works just as difficult for subsequent readers, who are by no means in agreement about what he intended.[39] His style was an intentional response to his fear that his ideas would be corrupted by the ignorant, something against which a printed text was no guarantee. Additionally, an author might have control over the first edition, but after that the technology could just as easily drive instability by introducing corruptions on a mass scale. The pseudonymous works printed under Agrippa's name are perhaps the best example.[40]

Printed texts also served as source books for magical manuscripts and spawned new magical traditions that could fundamentally alter the intent of the authors. Perhaps the most telling example of the vulnerability of texts is the case of Reginald Scot's *Discovery of Witchcraft* and its readers.[41] In this work Scot sought to demonstrate that Catholicism was vile, contrary to true religion, and irrational by showing that it was indistinguishable from magic. The text included many examples of magical processes drawn from a wide variety of sources. These Scot were selected for their rhetorical value and not because they were representative of magical traditions. As a result his collection represents a distinctive revision of medieval magic. To complicate matters, almost immediately magical enthusiasts began employing the *Discovery of Witchcraft* as a source book for magic, rewriting or supplementing the text where necessary. In fact, subsequent publishers intentionally supplemented the work with additional magical material to appeal to a readership interested in practising magic, relying on the anti-Catholic and anti-magical program of the text as a cover for their raw opportunism.[42] In short, while one might be tempted to blame instabilities in the transmission and interpretation of ritual magic (not to mention scribal fears about such issues) on the putatively less stable nature of manuscript culture vis-à-vis print culture, these characteristics persisted in the magical tradition in only slightly different form after the birth of printing in 1450. Print could introduce corruptions on a mass scale, and even when the text was uniform in hundreds or thousands of copies, a printed text in itself could provide no more stability in interpretation than a manuscript could.

Thus the ritual magic tradition provides a powerful example of how the written or printed word – particularly when it was not associated entirely with a dominant discourse and accompanying institutional enforcement, an intellectual culture that unqualifiedly sought standardization, or even a stable intellectual community – was anything but a standardizing technology. In part the authors and redactors of this tradition were at the mercy of a technology over which they had little control. Once the text left their hands it was vulnerable to change and alternative interpretation; texts cannot force the authorial intention on the reader.

In part the intellectual culture surrounding these texts worked against any standardizing function the texts might have. Authors and users drew on unstable sources for magical information such as visions or dreams, revelled in the ambiguous features of texts, and intentionally sought to drive the reader beyond the simple and literal meaning of the text. In part this situation (in comparison to which most oral traditions appear very stable and static indeed) was occasioned by the social circumstances surrounding magical texts. Textual communities and their more or less static interpretations, ways of using texts, or schools of thought were made possible by the presence of a text. But they were maintained by non-textual means, in large measure oral and performative. The magical tradition had no comfortable institutional setting but operated at the fringes of orthodoxy. Frequently the intellectual link between the author and the reader was only the text itself rather than direct instruction, a surrounding school of thought, or an instructional program at a university. If the desire for a static text in the magical tradition expressed itself in myths whereby the entire magical text derived from a divine source or was composed with divine intervention, the desire for a stable textual community of interpretation is also clearly mythically expressed in the prologue to the *Sworn Book*.

It might well be argued that the treatment and understanding of texts by authors and scribes of ritual magic can be taken as a symptom of their desire to subvert, of their unconventionality, or even of their irrationality. To put it in extreme terms can anyone so 'flamboyantly transgressive' (to use Richard Kieckhefer's words), strange, or mad be taken as an example of a reasonable human response to the written word?[43] However, such arguments do not hold up under close scrutiny. We cannot regard the tradition of ritual magic unqualifiedly as 'alterior' or 'subversive.' Unlike the Nigerian visionary described by Peter Probst, authors of magical manuscripts were not reacting against the standardizing functions of the text, something controlled by missionaries.[44] As we have seen, many magical texts seek quite conventional intellectual or religious goals, such as knowledge of the arts and sciences or mystical and visionary experiences. They also approach these almost entirely by conventional means (prayer, contemplation, confession, abstinence, and other ritual performances drawn from the liturgy). Except on a few key points the authors work almost entirely within the frame of the conventional intellectual world and commonly seem to regard their work as within the bounds of legitimate Christian practice. In reality this was more or less reasonable. The Christian tradition, from a time prior to its institutionalization, recognized that the correct interpretation of scripture was made possible by the holy spirit and was a spiritual gift.[45] The persistent presence of visionaries considered orthodox by the institutional church, as well as the early medieval explosion of local mythology associated with saints, demonstrates the continued sympathy of the institutional church for non-textual sources of truth and the renewal of the written tradition from non-textual sources. Also, like mysterious signs and words in magical works, religious symbols naturally draw their evocative power from their ambiguous meanings. The notion of the trinity, the incarnation, and the presence of Christ in the Eucharist, for example, are anything but crystal clear ideas. The history of religious dissent and heresy is ample demonstration that only concerted institutional force could maintain any consistency in their interpretation. It is thus not surprising that a tradition with little textual consistency to begin with, which revelled in the ambiguous nature of words and signs and lacked the stabilizing influence of (largely orally based) institutional systems, should regard the written word as fundamentally unstable.

The development of literacy or a culture of literacy commonly accompanies social rationalization or the development of 'complex societies,' and one might easily conclude that written texts, which can certainly contribute to that process, are inherently rationalizing. But this, if I may use the term loosely, is magical thinking. In fact, communal action and oral interaction are central to the process by which a text can become an instrument of standardization. Additional necessary elements appear to be the will to standardize, an intellectual culture that permits standardization, and the social conditions in which a standardized interpretation can be arrived at and maintained. The writers of the ritual magic tradition, like the institutional church, recognized this.

At the same time, from the birth of silent reading, reading was frequently not a communal activity but a solitary one (this is especially the case with ritual magic texts) and our analysis also bears upon this more individual form of interaction with a text. Recent studies of masculinity have emphasized that individuals will vary their public gender identities depending on social context.[46] Similarly, anthropological studies of magic have dispensed with essentialist and evolutionary schema such as religion, science, and magic, preferring the non-essentialist concept of modalities (e.g., Stanley Tambiah's 'participation vs causality') in which all humans share to a greater or lesser degree, regardless of historical or cultural circumstances.[47] In an analogous way, many of the essays in this volume suggest not only that that people relate to oral and textual communication differently depending on the society in which they live, their class, or sex but also that an individual will adopt different approaches in different contexts (e.g., Arbuckle, Chamberlin, and Fagan, this volume). The authors of the magical texts described here certainly used texts in other aspects of their lives in conventional ways. They sought the services of notaries, wrote wills, read and discussed works of scholastic philosophy, and celebrated the mass according to standard written models. They had to. It goes without saying that the cartographic skills of the great sixteenth-century polymath John Dee, which depended on the standardizing capacities of the written word and the printed book, were in no way impeded by his esoteric and magical interests, in which context he read and wrote works in much the way described in this chapter. Thus it may be useful to regard the varieties of approaches to texts, and in fact literacy and orality themselves, as a set of modalities that are not only historically and culturally mediated but between which an individual may shift from moment to moment depending on the text or the circumstance.

NOTES

1 O quanta leguntur scripta de inexpugnabili magicae artis potentia, de prodigiosis astrologorum imaginibus, de monstrifica alchimistarum metamorphosi, deque lapide illo benedicto, quo, Midae instar, contacta aera mox omnia in aurum argentumve is the permutentur: quae omnia comperiuntur vana, ficta et falsa, quoties ad literam practicantur. Atque tamen traduntur ista scribunturque a magnis grauissimisque philosophis et sanctis viris, quorum traditiones quis audebit dicere falsis? Quinimo credere impium esset, illos data opera scripsisse mendacia. Alius est ergo sensus, quam literis traditur (*Epistola* V.14), Henry Cornelius Agrippa, *Opera Omnia* ([1600?]; reprinted Hildesheim: Georg Olms, 1970), 873–4. The letter is dated 1527. Lynn Thorndike, *A History of Magic and Experimental Science*, vol. 5 (New York: Columbia University Press, 1941), 132.

2 The standard intellectual biography of Cornelius Agrippa remains Charles Garfield Nauert, *Agrippa and the Crisis of Renaissance Thought* (Urbana: University of Illinois Press, 1965). The best discussion of recent literature on Agrippa, particularly concerning the subject of magic, can be found in Heinrich Cornelius Agrippa von Nettesheim, *De occulta philosophia libri tres*, trans. and intro., V. Perrone Compagni (Leiden: Brill, 1992).

3 See Christopher Lehrich, *The Language of Demons and Angels* (Leiden: Brill, 2003).

4 Nauert, *Agrippa*.

5 Jack R. Goody, *Domestication of the Savage Mind* (Cambridge: Cambridge University Press, 1977); Walter J. Ong, *Orality and Literacy: The Technologizing of the Word* (London: Routledge, 1982); Eric Havelock, *The Muse Learns to Write: Reflections on Orality and Literacy from Antiquity to the Present* (New Haven, CT: Yale University Press, 1986).

6 M.T. Clanchy, *From Memory to Written Record, England 1066–1307*, 2nd ed. (Cambridge, MA.: Blackwell, 1993), 21; Brian Stock, *The Implications of Literacy* (Princeton, NJ: Princeton University Press, 1983), 12–18 and 87. Although Stock's discussion does follow the lines I have suggested in the passages cited, his engaged study of what he calls 'textual communities' reveals a far more complex set of social and intellectual forces than Clanchy's. Much of what I have suggested in this chapter could, in fact, be regarded as implicit in Stock's work.

7 Elizabeth L. Eisenstein, *The Printing Press as an Agent of Change: Communications and Cultural Transformations in Early Modern Europe* (Cambridge: Cambridge University Press, 1979).

8 Ruth Finnegan, *Literacy and Orality: Studies in the Technology of Communication* (Oxford: Oxford University Press, 1988); Brian Street, *Literacy in Theory and Practice* (Cambridge: Cambridge University Press, 1984); Harvey Graff, *Legacies of Literacy: Continuities and Contradictions in Western Culture and Society* (Bloomington: Indiana University Press, 1987); Kenneth George, 'Felling a Song with a New Ax: Writing and the Reshaping of Ritual Song Performance in Upland Sulawesi,' *Journal of American Folklore* 103 (1990): 3–23; Bambi Schieffelin and Perry Gilmore, eds., *The Acquisition of Literacy: Ethnographic Perspectives* (Norwood, NJ: Ablex, 1986). In the context of medieval studies, Brian Stock's work in some sense begins this trend. Other studies that reflect a more ethnographic approach are discussed below in this chapter. See Daniel Boyarin, 'Placing Reading: Ancient Israel and Medieval Europe,' in *The Ethnography of Reading*, ed. Jonathan Boyarin (Berkeley: University of California Press, 1993), 10–37; and Nicholas Howe, 'The Construction of Reading in Anglo-Saxon England' in *Ethnography of Reading*, ed. Boyarin, 58–79.

9 By rationalization I mean to suggest not only the centralizing tendencies of European institutions that sought to create uniform sets of administrative and legal processes for large geographical territories but also the process in which traditional oral modes of interaction were replaced with more or less uniform and text-based modes of interaction. The success and growth of medieval universities were assured by the growing stream of those seeking employment in jobs associated with texts. The inclusion of church lawyers and administrators in this list is uncontroversial. My inclusion of priests and monks may require some defence. Certainly one of the most powerful effects of texts and textual technologies was the production of pastoral literature, a literature that sought to provide uniform, authoritative, and orthodox aid in the production of sermons and the day-to-day practicalities of pastoral care. Accompanying this literature was an extensive educational system designed specifically for the mendicant orders and their preaching duties. In the sense that these texts and schools were intimately concerned with the systemic, uniform, and organized transmission of Christian orthodoxy, I regard them as also part of the larger 'rationalizing' project of the later Middle Ages. In general see Clanchy, *From Memory to Written Record*. On the *scholar simplex*, the most common student at a medieval university, see Rainer Christoph Schwinges, 'Student Education, Student Lives,' in *History of the University*, vol. 1, ed. Hilde Ridder-Symoens (Cambridge: Cambridge University Press, 1992), 226. See also Ruth Mazo Karras, *From Boys to Men: Formations of Masculinity in Late Medieval Europe* (Philadelphia: University of Pennsylvania

Press, 2003), 67–108. On the association between the development of law and the universities see Harold Joseph Berman, *Law and Revolution: The Formation of the Western Legal Tradition* (Cambridge, MA: Harvard University Press, 1983). On Dominican education see Michelle Mulchahey, '*First the Bow Is Bent in Study ...' Dominican Education before 1350* (Toronto: Pontifical Institute of Mediaeval Studies, 1998). On pastoral literature and clerical education see Richard Rouse and Mary Rouse, '*Statim Invenire*: Schools, Preachers, and New Attitudes to the Page,' in *Renaissance and Renewal in the Twelfth Century*, ed. Robert Louis Benson, Giles Constable, Carol Dana Lanham, and Charles Homer Haskins, (Toronto: University of Toronto Press in association with the Medieval Academy of America, 1991), 201–28. See also H. Leith Spencer, *English Preaching in the Late Middle Ages* (Oxford: Clarendon, 1993), 61–4.

10 Little has been written about this literature. The standard work on the subject is undoubtedly Richard Kieckhefer, *Forbidden Rites: A Necromancer's Manual of the Fifteenth Century* (Stroud: Sutton, 1997); Kieckhefer has argued that many of these texts were produced in a 'clerical underworld.' See his *Magic in the Middle Ages* (Cambridge: Cambridge University Press, 1998), 151–75. For general discussions of the genre see also Frank Klaassen, 'English Manuscripts of Ritual Magic 1300–1500: A Preliminary Survey,' in *Conjuring Spirits: Texts and Traditions of Medieval Ritual Magic*, ed. Claire Fanger (University Park: Penn State University Press, 1998), 3–31; Frank Klaassen, 'Medieval Ritual Magic in the Renaissance,' *Aries* 3, no. 2 (2003): 166–99.

11 The term is somewhat anachronistic, referring more precisely to the practices of the later Platonists in the late antique period. However, it has come to be applied generally to works proposing a gradual spiritual/intellectual ascent by an operator toward the divine, usually employing some form of numinous assistance. See Gregory Shaw, *Theurgy and the Soul: The Neoplatonism of Iamblichus* (University Park: Penn State University Press, 1995), 45–57.

12 On the *Notory Art* and work of John of Morigny, see John of Morigny, *Prologue to Liber visionum* [c. 1304–1318], trans., ed., and intro., Claire Fanger and Nicholas Watson, *Esoterica* 3 (2001): 108–217, www.esoteric.msu.edu. On the *Liber iuratus* see Gösta Hedegård, ed., *Liber iuratus honorii – A Critical Edition of the Latin Version of the Sworn Book of Honorius* (Stockholm: Almovist and Wiksell International, 2002). See also Robert Mathiesen, 'A 13th-Century Ritual to Attain the Beatific Vision from the *Sworn Book* of Honorius of Thebes' in *Conjuring Spirits*, ed. Fanger, 143–62.

13 For a discussion of the prologue see Robert Mathiesen, 'Beatific Vision,' 143–62. Mathiesen uses the term 'beatific vision' to describe the vision to be achieved by the major ritual in this text.

14 Since this volume is addressed to an audience of non-medievalists I have modernized the spellings. For the original text see London, British Library, Royal MS 17.A.XLII, f. 2r–v.

15 On esotericism and the growing field of research in this area see Antoine Faivre, *Theosophy, Imagination, Tradition: Studies in Western Esotericism,* trans. Christine Rhone (Binghamton: State University of New York Press, 2000). See also Wouter Hanegraaf, 'Some Remarks on the History of Western Esotericism' in *Esoterica* 1 (1999): 3–19, www.esoteric.msu.edu.

16 Coleman has rightly criticized the overemphasis on literacy in the interpretation of medieval literary culture at the expense of continuing important oral dimensions. Joyce Coleman, *Public Reading and the Reading Public in Late Medieval England and France* (Cambridge: Cambridge University Press, 1996). On public reading see also Natalie Zemon Davis, 'Printing and the People: Early Modern France,' in *Literacy and Social Development in the West: A Reader,* ed. Harvey J. Graff, Cambridge Studies in Oral and Literate Culture 3 (Cambridge and New York: Cambridge University Press, 1981), 69–95.

17 Although Boyarin is quite right about the development of private reading, he overemphasizes the point at the expense of the fact that the speech-act reading of his early and rabbinical subjects continued in medieval contexts. Daniel Boyarin, 'Placing Reading.'

18 Nicholas Howe, 'The Construction of Reading,' 71. On Anglo-Saxon magic see Felix Grendon, *Anglo-Saxon Charms* (Folcroft, PA: Folcroft Library Editions, 1974); Karen Louise Jolly, *Popular Religion in Late Saxon England: Elf Charms in Context* (Chapel Hill: University of North Carolina Press, 1996); and Audrey L. Meaney, *Anglo-Saxon Amulets and Curing Stones* (Oxford: Bar, 1981). For a specific discussion of the ambiguity of magical signs touching on Anglo-Saxon charms see Claire Fanger, 'Signs of Power and the Power of Signs: Medieval Modes of Address to the Problem of Magical and Miraculous Signifiers' (PhD diss., University of Toronto, 1993).

19 Elizabeth Long's essay on textual interpretation as collective action is particularly useful here although her examples are largely modern. 'Textual Interpretation as Collective Action,' in *The Ethnography of Reading,* ed. Boyarin, 180–211.

20 A dramatic illustration of an oral-based legal system can be found in the

medieval Icelandic work *Njals Saga*. It gives extensive accounts of the 'Althing,' a meeting of clan leaders at which justice was dispensed. Magnus Magnusson and Hermann Palsson, trans. and intro., *Njal's Saga* (Harmondsworth: Penguin Books, 1960), 98–106 (ch. 36–8) and 243–60 (ch. 119–24).

21 *Liber visionum,* 15. I quote from the translation of Claire Fanger and Nicholas Watson.

22 The instructions are relatively straightforward in most of these manuals. For the *Notory Art* see Claire Fanger, 'Plundering the Egyptian Treasure: John the Monk, His Book of Visions, and Its Relation to the Notory Art of Solomon,' in *Conjuring Spirits*, ed. Fanger, 216–49. On the *Sworn Book* see Robert Mathiesen, 'Beatific Vision.'

23 Munich, Bayerische Staatsbibliothek [Bavarian State Library], CLM 51, f. 111v. An interesting parallel to this process is discussed in M. Bloch, 'Astrology and Writing in Madagascar' in *Literacy in Traditional Societies* ed., J.R. Goody (Cambridge: Cambridge University Press, 1968), 278–99. Astrologers in Madagascar employed a wide variety of texts in the interpretation of astrology, rendering diverse and highly individual readings. In short, the astrological and other texts did not provide a coherent standard but multiplied the possible interpretations.

24 Oxford, Bodleian Library, Rawlinson D. 252, f. 65v. In this manual dream visions are commonly employed, but more commonly some form of medium (usually a ten-year-old boy) 'saw' the visions and reported them to the master.

25 'Et si apparet, monstra sibi pentaculum salamonis. Et pete ipsum que [sic] est nomina sua, et que [sic] est officio suo, et que sunt carectera sua, et sub quo gubernator [sic] ipse est, et que sunt dies, hore, et menses eius et cetera' (ibid., f. 102v).

26 London, British Library, Additional MS 36674, ff. 47r–62v.

27 For John Dee see Deborah Harkness, *John Dee's Conversations with Angels* (Cambridge: Cambridge University Press, 1999). A similar circumstance in which occult or esoteric texts were crucial elements in the production of a vision-inspired prophetic/magical text may be seen in the example of a Nigerian visionary, Oshitelu. See Peter Probst, 'The Letter and the Spirit: Literacy and Religious Authority in the History of the Aladura Movement in Western Nigeria' in *Cross-Cultural Approaches to Literacy,* ed. Brian Street (Cambridge: Cambridge University Press, 1993), 198–219.

28 In a paper delivered at the International Congress on Medieval Studies at Leeds in 2004 Claire Fanger described the painstaking copying of the *Book of Visions*. At the same time, the *Book of Visions* is itself a radical rewriting of

the *Notory Art*, which in turn generated progeny that are almost entirely unrelated to the original text. See for example, Paris, Bibliothèque Nationale, lat. 7170A, ff. 7r–9r.

29 Brian Stock has suggested that one of the implications of the development of literacy in the high Middle Ages is the development of 'textual communities,' which he defines as groups of people centred on the interpretation of a text or a common interpreter. Such communities were most dramatically expressed in heretical movements; others were simply schools of thought. If any group were associated with ritual magic texts it would have to have been something like these heretical groups, which is to say, not long lived or socially stable. Although perhaps implicit in Stock's rich examination of medieval literacy, his principal goal was to examine the implications of literacy – to work from the fact of literacy into the society – not the reverse, which would involve the influence of the community on the text itself. See Brian Stock, *The Implications of Literacy*, 88–240.

30 On transmission of ritual magic texts and manuscripts see Frank Klaassen, 'English Manuscripts.'

31 There is evidence of small, scattered groups appearing for periods and then disappearing. However, we cannot speak of a magical equivalent to the school of Chartres or St Victor, much less of a centuries-long community such as the University of Paris, in which successive generations of scholars worked on standard texts, commented on them, shared their commentaries and interpretations in public debate, and formed themselves into competing schools of thought.

32 'Tertio die postquam fecit istam orationem ... venit ad eum Rachiel angelus qui stabat supra riuum in exitu paradisi et disco operint se ei ea hora qua calefaciebat se ad solem qui tenebat in manu sua librum istum quem dedit Ade.' Munich, Bayerische Staatsbibliothek [Bavarian State Library], CLM 51, f. 5r.

33 'Et aperuit Rachiel librum et legit in auribus Ade. Audiuit autem adam verba libri sancte ex ore angeli et eiecit se super faciem suam ad teram cum magno timore. Cui dixit Rachiel Surge adam et confortare et non habeas timorem ... Recipe librum istum de manu mea et respice in eo quia per ipsum scies et intelliges.' Ibid., f. 6r.

34 Boyarin, 'Placing Reading.'

35 For an extended discussion of this issue see Claire Fanger, 'Signs of Power.'

36 'There is so great vertue, power and efficacy in certain names and words of God, that when you read those very words, it shall immediately increase and help your eloquence, so that you shall be made eloquent of speech by them, and at length attain to the effects of the powerful sacred names of

God ... Therefore there are certain notes of the Notory Art, which are manifest to us; the vertue whereof human reason cannot comprehend.' *Ars notoria: The Notary Art of Solomon*, trans. Robert Turner (London: J. Cottrel, 1657), 5–6. 'Neither think, that all words of the preceding oration contain in themselves a greater sense of mystical profundity, of the authority of Solomon; and having reference to his writings, we acknowledge, that these orations cannot be expounded nor understood by humane sense' (ibid., 10–11). Similar ideas can be found in medieval Arabic philosophy. See, for example, Pinella Travaglia, *Magic, Causality, and Intentionality: The Doctrine of Rays in Al-Kindi* (Florence: SISMEL/Edizioini del Galluzzo, 1999), 30–1 and 45–6. For a discussion of the power of foreign words, which is divorced from the speaker's knowledge of their meanings, see James N. Baker, 'The Presence of the Name: Reading Scripture in an Indonesian Village,' in *The Ethnography of Reading*, ed. Boyarin, 89–138.

37 On archaic hands see M.B. Parkes, 'Archaizing Hands in English Manuscripts' in *Books and Collectors 1200–1700: Essays Presented to Andrew Watson*, ed. James P. Carley and Colin G.C. Tite (London: The British Library, 1997), 101–41. On examples in magical texts see Frank Klaassen, 'Religion, Science, and the Transformations of Magic: Manuscripts of Magic 1300–1600' (PhD diss., University of Toronto, 1999), 193–8.

38 On inks see, for example, London, British Library, Additional MS 36674, f. 47r.

39 Debates over Agrippa's intentions have been extensive. For a summary see Agrippa von Nettesheim, *De occulta philosophia*, 1–50.

40 See for example *Henry Cornelius Agrippa, His Fourth Book of Occult Philosophy: Of Geomancy, Magical Elements of 'Peter de Abano,' Astronomical Geomancy, the Nature of Spirits, 'Arbatel' of Magick*, trans., Robert Turner (London: John Harrison, 1655) or *Henrici Cornelii Agrippae liber quartus de occulta philosophia, seu de cerimoniis magicis: Cui accesserunt, elementa magica Petri de Abano, philosophi* (Marburg, [1559?]).

41 Reginald Scot, *Discovery of Witchcraft* (Ann Arbor, MI: University of Michigan Press, Digital Library Production Service, 2001).

42 On the use of this text in the sixteenth century see Frank Klaassen and Chris Phillips, 'The Return of Stolen Goods: Reginald Scot, Religious Controversy, and a Late Sixteenth-Century Manuscript of Magic,' *Magic, Ritual, and Witchcraft* 1, no. 2 (2006): 135–77. For a discussion of the *Discovery of Witchcraft* as a source for magical transmission see Owen Davies, *Cunning-Folk: Popular Magic in English History* (London: Hambledon and London, 2003), 127–59. For the materials added to the seventeenth-century editions, see ibid. 126–7.

43 Kieckhefer, *Forbidden Rites*, 10.

44 Probst, 'The Letter and the Spirit,' 201 and 213.

45 Paul's Epistle to the Corinthians is the most powerful example, in which it is claimed that God 'hath made us able ministers of the new testament; not of the letter, but of the spirit: for the letter killeth, but the spirit giveth life.' 2 Corinthians 3:6.

46 See, for example, Derek Neal, 'Suits Make the Man: Masculinity in Two English Law Courts, c. 1500,' *Canadian Journal of History* 37 (April 2002): 1–22. See also John Klassen, 'The Public and Domestic Faces of Ulrich of Rožmberk,' *Sixteenth Century Journal* 31, no. 3 (2000): 699–718.

47 Stanley Tambiah, *Religion, Science, Magic, and the Scope of Rationality* (Cambridge: Cambridge University Press, 1990), 84–110.

PART FIVE

Uncovering Voices

Chapter 9

A Tagalog Awit of the 'Holy War' against the United States, 1899–1902

REYNALDO C. ILETO

The Philippine–American war commenced in February 1899 when the U.S. Army advanced into territory defended by a Filipino Republican government that had been inaugurated only a few months earlier. The Americans came originally as allies of the Filipino revolutionaries who were fighting against Spain. As U.S. forces trounced the Spanish navy and entered Manila, Filipino nationalists led by Emilio Aguinaldo forced the surrender of Spanish garrisons inland and declared independence on 12 June 1898. The United States refused to recognize Philippine independence, however, and instead 'acquired' the former Spanish colony at the Treaty of Paris in December for some 20 million silver dollars. Thus betrayed, the Filipinos resisted American occupation in a war that dragged on longer than either the Americans or their local allies expected. Even after the official end of the war on 4 July 1902, armed resistance to the new colonial order continued in many parts of the archipelago, although naming the phenomenon 'banditry' or 'fanaticism' helped to deflect attention from its wanton suppression by the constabulary, now made up mostly of Filipinos officered by Americans.[1]

A close examination of the Filipino side of the war against the United States (still misrepresented by many as a minor insurrection within the big event called the Spanish–American war) reveals that guerrilla contingents were continually regrouping and dispersing as commanders emerged and faded away. In the complex process of joining, fighting, waiting, or fleeing, a common soldier would have felt enticed as much as coerced into participation. An examination of language is therefore important. We want to know, for example, what the local commanders said or read to their soldiers. From the very inception of the war, the Republican government and many officers with literary talent produced a stream of speeches, letters, manifestos, and the like, which transposed 'real' events and figures to another key – one in which resistance and the possibility of death made sense.

In reading these texts we should pay attention to how the literate Filipino revolutionists who wrote them were able to link their nationalist goals creatively to popular ideas of community and struggle. In the texts, elements of Spanish and Catholic cultural influences were localized and, along with *ilustrado* (i.e., educated elite) liberal Enlightenment ideas, used as building blocks for a distinctly Filipino idiom of resistance. I demonstrate this process in the sections that follow by focusing on one such text, an *awit* or Tagalog metrical romance that was composed during the war.

Awit of the Holy War

The 'Awit ng Pinagdaanang buhay ng Islas Filipinas' (Awit of the Life Story of the Filipinas) conforms to the traditional awit form of dodecasyllabic quatrains.[2] Dated 15 July 1900, it must have enjoyed wide circulation since its indicated place of publication, Biak na Bato in Bulacan province north of Manila, was a Republican stronghold during the Philippine–American war. Although apparently published, the lack of polish in this awit indicates that it was a piece of oral literature par excellence. In fact, I have not come across any printed version, and the copy I use is in manuscript form, indicating that handwritten copies were made for distribution among Filipino officers and soldiers. It was a practice for manifestos (which were sometimes in verse form) to be copied out and read to groups of soldiers or, more precisely, to be orated or sung in the style appropriate for awit (which literally means 'song').

For the purposes of this chapter, I limit myself to a discussion of *historia* and *nación* – terms deployed in the awit itself. These categories go together: a nation needs a developmental narrative of itself in order to establish its origins in a past state of glory, its decline into a dark age of disunity and ignorance, and its emergence into the age of reason. I address the lingering question of whether the 'masses' understood their participation in the revolution in terms of a rupture in 'their' history, or whether they were blindly following their chiefs. The awit, precisely because it is a history in awit form, slides between perceptions of the past by educated *ilustrados* and by the largely illiterate bulk of the populace. Through its 107 stanzas we can trace various ways in which a sense of belonging to and defending the nation could be rooted in popular consciousness.

We know the awit's author only by his pen name, Dimatigtig (Unswerving). Perhaps he belonged to General Aguinaldo's entourage, for he wrote a shorter awit in 1897 depicting the battles between the Spanish army and the Aguinaldo-led Filipino forces in Cavite. Some of the imagery and language in his two known awit are also found in 'Kantahing Pulube' (Beggar Songs), transcribed from roving bards after the war. The 1900 awit, however, is more learned in tone, borrowing much from religious literature as well as from works in Spanish by educated Filipinos. It should not be regarded solely as Dimatigtig's production for it reflects many strands of the collective mind, the author functioning mainly as an organizing but not originating consciousness.

Dimatigtig was no wandering beggar. His education is evidenced in his use of Spanish words and phrases and his familiarity with the research done by European-educated Filipinos, or *ilustrados*, on the early history of the islands.[3] He also knew the anticlerical literature produced by the Republican revolution in Spain. Yet he was clearly not an *ilustrado* of the sophistication of Jose Rizal or Marcelo del Pilar.[4] Current Philippine scholarship has tended to essentialize the *ilustrado* as a super-elite whose thinking is almost diametrically opposed to the unlettered *tao*, or masses. Yet it can be argued that the warehouseman Andres Bonifacio, credited with fomenting the 'revolt of the masses' in 1896, was himself an *ilustrado* in that he had read Rizal and European writings, even though he wrote exclusively in Tagalog. Judging by his work Dimatigtig seems to have a profile similar to that of Bonifacio, another poet familiar with the traditional awit style.[5] Dimatigtig's awit of 1900, however, evidences a familiarity with biblical history and folk religious beliefs that are absent, or at least unarticulated, in Bonifacio's writing, probably due to his flirtation with masonry.[6]

Based on the level of learning in the awit, Dimatigtig might have received his basic education in the local convent of his hometown, and then moved on to one of the limited number of secondary schools in Cavite or Bulacan run by native teachers, or *maestro*. He might even have been partly trained for the priesthood. Was he a member of the *principalía*, the local town elite? Perhaps, but he was definitely not aloof from the concerns and thinking of those who were often derisively called the *pobres y ignorantes* (poor and ignorant masses) by the *ilustrados*. He would have been an organic intellectual, someone who could articulate as well as reshape the thinking of 'his people' – in this case, his *kapatid*, or siblings, fighting the Americans. We might thus label Dimatigtig, for want of a better term, a rural *ilustrado*. This category of elites, which played a crucial leadership role during the revolution and the Philippine–American war, is also the least appreciated on its own terms by current scholarship, which has been content with labels such as *patron, cacique* (chief, boss), *principál*, or middle class.[7]

A rural *ilustrado* would have been a 'middle person' in many ways.[8] Writing in Tagalog, in a literary form that could be read aloud or sung, required Dimatigtig to be attuned to the language and sentiments of his popular audience. Yet the content of his awit evidences as well the discourse of Filipino nationhood, a discourse articulated initially by urbanized *ilustrados*, many of whom had lived and studied in Europe. As a poet located 'in the middle,' Dimatigtig was engaged in the activity of translation, comprehending late-nineteenth-century concepts of history and nation through the meaning matrix of Tagalog and rendering them into verses comprehensible to his audience. This was not a one-sided process, however, as 'middleness' implies. The awit evidences, as well, the resistance to and limits of the imposition of notions of modernity in their raw, alien forms. In order for 'history' and 'nation' to make sense, popular ideas of community, of self and others, of the past and the future, and of the interaction of human and divine agency, needed to be articulated and translated into 'modern' yet localized discourses.

The context of this activity of translation was a war with a new imperial power, the United States. Dimatigtig regards the war with the Americans as simply another chapter in the continuing saga of *Las Islas Filipinas*, the nation imaged as a woman or 'mother Filipinas,' who had come into her own on separating from 'mother Spain.'[9] The awit's constant comparisons between the two foreign nations or peoples who have intervened in the life of 'Filipinas' – Spanish in the past and American in the present – can be read as a conventional account of nations engaged in imperial conquest and indigenous resistance. As we shall see, however, the awit story exceeds this simplistic opposition, drawing substantially on notions of kinship, the moral order, and biblical time in its matrix of meaning.

By July 1900, the date of the awit's publication, superior U.S. forces had crushed the regular army units of the Republic in central Luzon. Aguinaldo, president and commander-in-chief, had called for a guerrilla war to be waged. It would take nearly a year before Aguinaldo was captured in the north, and another two years before the last Filipino general surrendered in southern Luzon. One can argue that during the later years of the war formal hostilities between the two armies were of less importance than the war being waged internally, as groups of Filipinos positioned themselves in varying ways vis-à-vis the Americans, who also adopted varying strategies of warfare and attraction. In 1899, as American troops marched toward Aguinaldo's headquarters, President William McKinley had justified the U.S. takeover of the islands as a civilizing and uplifting gesture toward a people stuck in the dark age of Spanish medievalism. The Philippines, as the head of the Philippine Commission put it, would become a 'daughter republic' of the United States in the Pacific. The Americans would give the Filipinos what they had wanted from Spain, *un buen gobierno* (good government), and educate them so that in time they would develop into a modern and progressive nation.[10] These were enticing propositions, indeed, for some leaders of the Republic.

In envisioning a future for the Filipinos, American commissioners in 1899 sought the advice of the Manila-based *ilustrados*, who had been involved in setting up the Republican government but had abandoned Aguinaldo when convinced that the United States army was invincible. The Manila *ilustrado* template for the future of the country was grafted on to the American justification for acquiring the islands, giving U.S. imperialism the spirit of a 'joint venture' with Filipinos rather than an outright grab for a slice of the Orient.[11]

Numerous studies have shown how, since the U.S. conquest, the interests of the Filipino political elite have generally been in harmony with American economic and military aims. But it has also become increasingly clear that at the regional and provincial levels, in particular, the state – whether colonial or national – has not been able to impose its hegemony. Unrest in various forms was a striking feature of twentieth-century Philippine history. To what extent did such unrest stem from the events of the revolution and the traumatic war with the United States? Dimatigtig's awit helps to provide the answer. It regards the war with the United States as an extension of the revolution against Spain. In the awit the war is being waged on two fronts, one against the American army and the other against some Filipinos who have been seduced into serving the Americans' interests. In some ways, as we shall see, the enemy *within* is an even more serious threat to the survival of Mother Filipinas.[12] These are all issues that survived the war itself and continued to be played out in the decades that followed.

Biblical Time, *Historia*, *Nación*

The awit begins with a purely biblical episode:

Dios ama'y nagbilin sa anak niyang tunay
sa kay Jesukristong sumakop sa tanan

kung ayaw ipasakop dimababakuran
sapagka nga't yaon ang hustong katuwiran
At ipinagbilin ng Poong si Cristo
di dapat paraig dyan sa demonyo
at hindi mo pa siya magiging katoto
mahuhulog ka na doon sa infierno

God the father sent word to his true son
to Jesukristo who redeemed mankind
those who shun salvation will remain outside
the pasture, for that is but fair and just.
And Kristo the Lord's message was,
you shouldn't be swayed by the demon
before you can even become his follower
you shall tumble into fiery hell.[13]

God the father sends a message to his son, Jesus Christ (Jesukristo), about the consequences of his redemptive act. Mankind, he warns, will be split into those who 'remain outside' (i.e., those who do not want to be saved) and those who are safely quartered in the enclosure or fenced pasture (*bakuran*). That is *hustong katuwiran* – the right way, the right path. The reference here is to the parable of the lost sheep. The son, Kristo, is the good shepherd who herds the straying sheep into the pasture. The *bakuran* is also associated with the concept of the covenant, the *tipan*, between God and mankind.[14] This is the backdrop for subsequent discussions of *nación*.

If Kristo is the 'true son,' then there must be false Kristos as well. The true Kristo has sent a parting message to his brethren: they should not be seduced by the *demonyo* who is enticing people to join him. Not only is comradeship with him out of the question but one's ultimate destination would be 'fiery hell.' Posing as Kristo, the *demonyo* tries to trick people into joining a community that is, in fact, a 'falling' (*hulog*) into painful hell.[15] What is this false community that competes for allegiance with the true community of the saved?

Dimatigtig also warns that 'we' should not envy those of wicked character. Someone out there is fostering desire. Some of 'us' want to be like them, to have what they have. But what they offer is only an empty promise. The wicked people out there are engaged in *gawang pulítika* (politics), which in Tagalog alludes to the politics of manipulation, whereby all sorts of rewards and spoils are offered to those who change sides. *Pulítika* here is not merely a negative mode of what we would call politics.[16] It *is* politics within the logic of the awit.

The 'them' seducing and enticing 'us' are compared to serpents that continue to move about even though their heads might be twisted and crushed.[17] The allusion here is to the temptation of Adam and Eve by the demon in the form of a serpent. Throughout the awit various creatures from the world of nature are made to represent certain qualities in people, or even certain nationalities. However, it takes a few more sections in the awit before the evil but seductive 'them' are named: they are the Americans who wage war against the Filipinos.

Dimatigtig does not take for granted that his audience understands the 'we' and 'us' as his fellow Filipinos, or that the war raging around them is a resistance movement of all Filipinos against 'them.' The terms *Filipino* and *nación* would have been familiar to this rural *ilustrado* poet but not at this point in history to the villagers who largely made up the guerrilla armies. The religious imagery that suffuses the awit indicates the nature of its intended audience, who would have perceived themselves to belong to the wider world of Christendom – a common theme of nineteenth-century awit.[18] Yet Dimatigtig's awit is not a religious text like the Church-approved *pasyon* and lives of saints in verse form. As its title announces, it is a *pinagdaanang buhay*, a life story, of Filipinas – the name of the Republic at war with the Americans.

Dimatigtig is indebted to the first Filipino nationalists – the late-nineteenth-century *ilustrados* led by Rizal – who had researched and assembled a history of the Filipinos at Spanish contact. By the 1890s separatists among them had combined this picture of a thriving pre-colonial society with a narrative of decline under Spanish rule. This is no doubt what Dimatigtig refers to in stanza 24, when he uses the term *historia* to refer to 'what has been written' about the early Philippines and its relationship with the rest of the world. By 1896 a separatist and largely masonic secret society called Katipunan had incorporated this history into its manifestos and rituals of initiation.[19] When the Republic was formed in late 1898, the Filipinas had a history that led to the inception of the Philippines, or what was formally constituted as the Philippine Republic.

The narrative of the Filipinas past begins in a section of the awit titled 'Ito ay sa mga Tribo' (This Is to the Tribes). The era of tribes begins with Noah, who was saved from the great flood.[20] This is the first of several references in the awit to the repeated threat of drowning and being submerged. In the archetypal deluge, humanity did not totally perish because the Ark carried Noah through the catastrophe.[21] Humanity was given a second lease of life; it got rebuilt. This link of catastrophe (great flood) and community (the Ark) is taken up in later stanzas, for it prefigures the present war and the *nación* that is being formed out of the current turmoil.

Noah's descendants repopulate the world. His three sons beget its three primary spaces: Asia (from the ancestor, or *nunong*, Sem), Greater China (from the ancestor Cham), and Europe (from the ancestor Jafet):

Ang mga tagalog ay kay Sem na ibig
ang kay Cham naman silang mga intsik
ang mga Kastila sa bunsong kay Jafet
na anak ni Nueng amang matandang giliw

Ang sa Nunong Sem ang parte ng Asia
na kasama niya, asawang familia
sa Nunong kay Cham yaong Gran china
sa kay Nunong Jafet ang parting Europa

The Tagalog stem from beloved Sem
those Chinese people from Cham
the Castilians from the youngest, Jafet
all children they are of Noah, beloved elder.[22]

To Ancestor Sem went that part called Asia
he was accompanied by his wife's family
to Ancestor Cham went Greater China
to Ancestor Jafet the part called Europe.[23]

The Tagalogs (the Filipino tribe occupying the region of Manila Bay and the mouth of the Pasig River) are descended from the line of Sem. At this point in the awit the focus is on lineage, on an explication of who 'we' are in terms of origins in the biblical past. Katagalugan (the Tagalog-speaking people and the name Andres Bonifacio gave to his revolutionary comrades and short-lived republic) is aligned with the Christian world. There was wholeness in this world because its 'tribal' elements could claim a common lineage in Noah. This 'clan' is a prototype of a community uniting many *tribos*. Building on this idea, the awit goes on to suggest how the *nación* would be formed: how one part of this world would be defined in terms of an identity beyond Katagalugan but not co-terminous with Christendom – a finite entity, a *nación*, called Filipinas. This is the awit's project.

In stanzas 15 to 17, Dimatigtig makes the connection between biblical time and the time of the Tagalog lineage, or tribe, while announcing the principal reason for the present war:

> Mula niyaon't ngayon nagkawatak watak
> sa dating estado naciones na lahat
> codicia at interes ang siyang sumambulat
> tres mil seiscientos ang nagdaang guerras

> Since that time until today the world has
> disintegrated into a multitude of nations
> desire and profit smashing it to pieces in
> three thousand six hundred years of warring.[24]

The time of the present war is thus merely a continuation of thousands of years of conflict since the disintegration of the age of wholeness. Dimatigtig specifically mentions 'nations' as the basic protagonists in these wars, and then proceeds to identify the warring nations of the present:

> Sa atin desendencia nagbuhat si Kristo
> Hindi sa kanilang idolatriang tao
> saka kung matapos at manalo tayo
> ipatatalastas ang dinaanang tribo

> Kristo descended from our lineage
> not from those idolatrous people
> so when this is over and we are victorious
> the life story of our tribe shall be proclaimed.[25]

The Tagalogs are directly linked to the Kristo of the age of wholeness, when the tribes were all of Noah's family. This crucially differentiates 'us' from the tribe of those idolaters – a reference to the yet-unnamed Americans. So those centuries of warring since the break-up of Noah's clan have reached a head in the current conflict. Will there be another deluge? Will the chosen people be saved from the current catastrophe in the making? Throughout the awit, Dimatigtig calls on his 'brothers and sisters' to think about the past in the present. This past constitutes a suppressed or hidden narrative, however, which the poet gradually reveals through the awit: It is only 'when this [war] is over and we are victorious / [that] the life story of our tribe (*dinaanang tribo*) shall be proclaimed.'[26]

Following his account of the people's biblical origins, Dimatigtig proceeds to the *historia* of the nation proper in a section entitled 'Kay Rajah Matanda' (To Elderly Rajah):

> Itong antigerjes ng panahong una
> tinatawag natin na raja matanda
> salot at panghampas sa boong morisma
> kinasisilawan ng boong Espana

> This ancestor of ours from the earliest times
> whom we call Rajah Matanda
> was a scourge and weapon against the Moors
> but a source of blinding light to Spain.[27]

Rajah Matanda is the first historical personage after Kristo to emerge from Katagalugan. But while Kristo operates in the biblical register, Rajah Matanda belongs to the time of the *nación*. In fact he is a precolonial figure who was resurrected from Spanish colonial accounts by the *ilustrados* and turned into an emblem of the state of wholeness, knowledge, and prosperity that existed before the conquest (or 'fall' into a dark age). *Rajah*, a pre-Hispanic term for ruler used instead of the Spanish *rey*, signifies a political condition – the rule of our own kings – before the Spanish conquest. The elderly rajah is also 'our ancestor,' the head of our lineage, who is closer to the time of Kristo, the source of power.

The figure of Rajah Matanda locates Katagalugan in the time when the world was already divided into contending forces after the break-up of Noah's clan. From the first era (*panahong una*) 'we' of the lineage of Sem and Kristo were already caught up in the archetypal conflict between Christians and Moors. Stories of this conflict, mainly in the Holy Land and Europe, constituted the narrative pool from which most awit literature up to the nineteenth century was derived. Like the story of Christ's passion and death (*pasyon*), awit literature served to prop up Spanish colonial rule. It aligned the Christianized population with the Spaniards against the Moors. The *ilustrados* wrote 'factual' accounts of the Filipinos in the late-nineteenth century precisely in order to combat the popularity of what they regarded as incredible and superstitious awit literature, which kept the native population tied to Spain. Like the *pasyon*, however, awit were also localized and arguably served to bind their readers to each other as well as – or instead of – to Spain. Some writers appropriated the awit form and consciousness of the past and infused it with anticolonial content. A well-known poem by Andres Bonifacio, for example, builds on the famous awit 'Historia Famosa ni Bernardo Carpio,' whose hero is a Spaniard fighting the French invaders.[28]

It is the awit tradition, indeed, that makes Dimatigtig picture Rajah Matanda – the Tagalogs' first 'historical' figure – as 'a scourge and weapon against the Moorish world.' The rajah appears as a blinding source of light (*kinasisilawan*) to Spain. But contrary to conventional awit, he reverses the source and movement of light, power, and knowledge: instead of coming from Europe to Asia, it is the other way around. This is made possible by bringing in Spanish history. Dimatigtig goes back to the time when 'Turks, Moors, and Jews had made [Spain] their home,' a time 'before the Spanish kingdom was baptized,' when the enemies of Christianity had infiltrated and divided it. By contrast, under Rajah Matanda, Asia, the land of Sem, was flourishing. When King Felipe II became king of Spain, he sent an emissary 'to these parts.'[29] The awit posits 'we' as already a flourishing nation even while Spain was struggling to restore its integrity, lost through Moorish occupation. Thus the Filipinos were in a position to help King Felipe.

The original encounter between King Felipe's emissary and Rajah Matanda is described as a form of *pamanhikan*, a stage in the ritual of marriage alliance when the parents of the prospective groom 'go up the steps' of the house of the prospective bride in order to negotiate the union between the two families.[30] Spain is already figured as the groom, but he is the male in the context of an indigenous culture that traces kinship, and therefore rights, cognatically (through any or all of an individual's relatives). The woman's family is the one approached and deferred to, not the other way around. In the awit, the *pamanhikan* takes place between two nations: 'Madrid wanted to join forces with the whole of Luzon,' since Rajah Matanda's power was 'known far and wide.' Spain was 'afraid when threatened with war' and therefore sought the help of Luzon. The world of contending nations – a modern configuration of the globe – is being historically established here. At this point 'Luzon' is used instead of 'Katagalugan' (the culturally homogenous Tagalog people). Luzon not only comprises a multitude of 'tribes' but also delineates a circumscribed space or territory. The *nación* begins to take firmer shape and is read back into 'earliest times.'

So far, nothing has been said in the awit about Spanish conquest and conversion: basic themes of Spanish colonial history. The initial encounter is framed in terms of alliance and marriage. This was, in fact, the way Rizal and other *ilustrado* writers (who were Hispanicized Catholics themselves) framed this early encounter. Spain forged alliances with the native chiefs; there were to be mutual benefits. But the awit's reading of the past is more radical: Spain did not even bring the benefits of Christianity and civilization; Kristo was *already* the king of Katagalugan, whose people were descended from Sem.

The Spanish occupation is narrated in the following manner. Because Rajah Matanda has died, the Spanish envoys decide to stay. They establish a 'tiny government' based on an 'agreement' with the rajah's followers that could be dissolved at any time. One might be tempted to read into this episode a contractual relationship between the Spanish and the inhabitants of the islands, who surrender some of their rights, their individual sovereignty, to the European power. However, here not only is the Spanish state 'tiny' but there is no surrender of sovereignty in the aftermath of 'conquest.' The awit does not admit of colonial domination but instead deploys alternative strategies to incorporate Spain into the narrative.

The national history of the Philippines, as well as of most postcolonial states, begins with a condition of wholeness, abundance, knowledge and sovereignty followed by a 'long, dark night' of stagnation, impoverishment, and ignorance, interrupted by rebellions and forms of resistance. These assertions are localized and inevitable failures until the nationalist movement ejects the usurper and brings the recovered nation into the modern world. Dimatigtig's awit, while clearly producing meanings of this sort, does not bring the past strictly into line with conventional national historiography. This is evident in its treatment of the conquest and 350 years of Spanish rule.

In the first place, the word *conquest*, which designates the event, is considered 'theirs,' not 'ours': 'What *they call* the first conquista.' The so-called conquest is depicted as an almost casual encounter between the conquistador and an old man (*matanda*), accompanied by Luzon. The man could be Rajah Matanda himself, and Luzon seems to prefigure Mother Filipinas. 'The conquistador asked him, what place is this? / The answer was spelled out: Luzon.' And so the Spanish called it Luzon.[31]

The same pattern of events constitutes the so-called second and third conquests. In the second, the Spanish call the place 'Isla Filipina.' In the third, Simon de Anda, King Felipe's emissary, 'declared its name "Isla de Manila."'[32] The Spanish have heard of the place, they arrive, but they are given three different names. Is there a problem with misrecognition here? What are the implications?

> Tatlong daan taon na tinatahanan
> mula niyaot ngayon, di pa maturingan
> walang ginagawa kundi kasalanan
> kaya di matarok ang tunay na ngalan.

> Three hundred years they have lived here
> since then till now they haven't figured it out;
> they do nothing but commit wrongdoing
> and thus cannot figure out the true name.[33]

'Three hundred years they have lived here / since then till now they haven't figured it out,' points to the familiar national history of '350 years of Spanish rule.' In this case, however, it is as if for an extraordinarily long time the groom has been living in the bride's home (*tahanan*), as was the practice, but without getting to know the real 'other.' There is a moral reason for the Spanish failure to learn the secret: 'they do nothing but commit wrongdoing.' In fact, if they had had great power to begin with, they could have known the name without asking. But as pointed out earlier, the locus of power, the source of blinding light, was Rajah Matanda.

Because of the failure to know or 'capture' the name, and thus the essence or inner being of the place, there has not really been a *conquista*. Colonial rule may have resulted in the presence of the Spanish, but an autonomous realm survived throughout those 350 years.[34] What is the true name then? It isn't as if all the 'brothers and sisters' knew it themselves. It is the poet Dimatigtig who holds the secret of the true name, just as he knows the past of the existing *nación*:

> Kung sa inyo ay walang na mapagturing
> lupang Paraiso ang siyang sasabihin
> na pinagdadayo ng sino ma't alin
> kahit anong hirap gumiginhawa rin

> Kaya alisin na ang Isla Filipina
> ang itawag nating Paraisong baga
> kahit hacutan mang maraming gracia
> hindi na papatdan nang ibinubunga

If you yourselves don't know the answer
'land of Paradise' is what you should say
a land that attracts all sorts of people
to relieve them of their every hardship.[35]

So let's do away with 'Isla Filipina'
and simply call it Paraiso
Even if its blessings are carted away
its continues to bear bountiful fruit.[36]

'Isla Filipina' or 'Filipinas' was a name assigned to the islands to honour King Felipe II. It is a superficial name, as the awit points out, so it
makes sense to reject it. But this gesture of defiance does not entail the
recovery of an indigenous name. 'Paraiso' is a Spanish Christian term,
certainly not a name that the revolutionary leadership would have en-
dorsed. Later in the awit, Dimatigtig refers to the land as 'Filipinas,' in
line with the Republican program of appropriating the colonial name.
But at this point he dwells on the nación's 'secret' name, Paraiso, which
associates it with biblical time.

The ilustrados also spoke of their land as paradise, but it was a lost
Eden, to paraphrase Rizal. 'Eden' was the biblical figuration of a nation's lost golden age. In Dimatigtig's awit, however, this land of ours
now is Paradise. It is the centre of the world, 'a land to which all sorts
of people are attracted.' This land beckons because it is beautiful and
abundant, and everyone is welcome to share in its bounty, but that is
precisely why greedy people want to come and take it by force. It was
and still is an Eden, a never-ending source of life, whatever the 'alleged'
history of conquests may suggest. In the context of a difficult war with
the powerful American nation, this knowledge of the true name and its
implications is important for sustaining resistance.

There is nothing in the section 'Conquistadores,' above, to indicate
that the Spanish violently entered Paraiso. There is no suggestion of
invasion and resistance. The coming of Spain is figured as a marriage
alliance, a joining of two nations that, after all, are both Christian and
both opposed to the Moors. In the narration of 'past wars,' i.e., those
that preceded the present war, the threatening Moors were followed by
the English, who managed to gain entry to 'our' land.[37] Then follow attacks by the Dutch and the Chinese 'yet they all failed to seriously over-
power us.'[38] These invasions are all part of Spanish-Filipino colonial
history, when the indios and the Spanish fought alongside each other to

defend the colony. The awit, having dispelled the notion that 'we' were truly conquered by Spain, however, ignores the latter and posits 'us' as defending 'our land' against foreign invaders. In this way, colonial Filipinas can become 'our' *nación*, Filipinas.

There is another difference between the awit and the standard colonial history: the defence of the land succeeded not because 'the people' put up a valiant resistance but because the invaders came with the wrong motives – not as pilgrims but as plunderers: 'Obviously this was pure idolatry / entry was foiled because this is a Holy place.'[39] The interlopers did not succeed because 'our' land had a divine connection. The awit and *ilustrado* narratives do not coincide here because the awit is simultaneously operating in the biblical register.

The defenders of the land would normally be hailed as heroes. The awit instead refers to the 'many saints [who] have come forth from here / [for] Jesus the Lord is the one who rules (*na maraming santos dito ay lumitao / si Jesus na Poon ang siyang may tangan*).'[40] This is a reversal of the origins of saints. To facilitate conversion, Christian saints were substituted for local deities or ancestor spirits. Previously from the outside, as figures introduced by the Spanish missionaries, they are now thought of us emerging from the inside. This is one sense in which saints have, indeed, come from within. As exemplary figures in 'our' land called Paraiso, they anticipate the budding pantheon of anticolonial heroes who are also venerated as saintly figures. There is evidence of this dating from the 1880s, when Father Jose Burgos, one of three reformist Filipino priests martyred in 1872, was reported to be venerated in Samar (in the eastern Visayan islands) as well as in Luzon. Jose Rizal, as is well known, was hailed as a saint shortly after his execution in December 1896.[41] The possibility of martyrdom is conditional on the land being a Holy Land, where 'Jesus the Lord holds sway,' where saints naturally emerge. We have here the ideas of national territory and national heroes, both essential to a nation-state, being mapped on to sacred space and the pantheon of saints introduced by the Catholic church.

After declaring the land to be Paraiso, the awit shifts to an elaboration of *nación* framed in kinship terms. In the section titled 'Ang Mga Kapatid' (The Siblings), the name *Filipinos* is used for the first time:

Sa ibang Filipinos ito'y nangyayari
ang kapalaluan ang siyang umaali
at di asikaso itong pagcaapi
ang pagdadambong din ang nanatili

To some Filipinos this is what is happening:
arrogance has become a diabolic influence
the oppression around them is ignored
and plundering is still rampant.[42]

Quite clearly, on shifting the terminology from 'Tagalogs' and 'true Christians' to the 'Filipinos' in this stanza, the fractures within society immediately reveal themselves. The ideal community of *kapatid* (brothers and sisters, siblings) is far from being realized. Hence the war is also to be fought against divisions within.

It is instructive here to go back to General Aguinaldo's proclamation of independence in 1898. He announced, to the dismay of veterans of the 1896 revolution, that all inhabitants of the islands, whether or not they had participated in the struggle, would be considered citizens of the new nation-state if they pledged their loyalty to it. They would be entitled to the appellation 'Filipino.' Before the revolution, *Filipinos* referred exclusively to Spanish residents of the Philippines, the native inhabitants being pejoratively called *indios*. Having inherited the colonial state from Spain, the revolutionists of 1898 simply appropriated the name. How could this name, reinvented by the state to encompass all citizens, be meaningfully articulated in the context of social and economic relationships and lived experience?[43]

In Dimatigtig's awit the term *Filipinos* names not some primordial condition of unity or an essential identity but a fractured community. It is a microcosm of the world of contending nations that succeeded the oneness of Noah's clan. Greed, pride, and ignorance are what prevent some Filipinos from relating to their *kapatid* as true siblings. They engage in 'plundering' as much as the foreign invaders do. The 'we,' the *kapatid* who are descendants of Sem and followers of Kristo with a history of successfully repelling invaders, are now being destroyed from within: 'We fight amongst ourselves / since there is lack of love for each other.'[44] The lack of national unity is due not to ethnic or linguistic difference but to a lack of love (*kulang ng pagmamahalan*). This lack is caused by the fuelling of desire through the American presence and their techniques of deception.

In this context of internal strife, Mother Filipinas, the personification of the country whose life story is the awit's subject, appears on the scene for the first time. Previously, only Kristo and Rajah Matanda were mentioned as rulers of the Tagalogs. But now that the community has been expanded into a *nación* headed by a Republican government, the emblem of sovereignty is Mother Filipinas, signifying the appropriation of the colonial term *Filipinas*. The mother glances at her children and laments,

> O mga bunso kong ilaw niaring mata
> wala nang naawa't sa inyo't mabalisa
> sa hirap nang isang mapag iwing Ina

> O my young children, so full of promise
> None of you seems to show pity and remorse
> for the plight of your ever-nurturing Mother.[45]

Love, pity, caring – these, rather than some abstract contract between sovereign and people, are what hold the *nación* together. Following this appeal by Mother Filipinas, the story of her life since the coming of Spain is narrated, as if remembering the mother's story would trigger an appropriate response from her children. What is conventionally termed the Spanish colonial period is organized according to the presence or absence of these sentiments of love, pity, and caring.

Spanish colonialism is first treated in a section ironically titled 'Isla de Manila' (one of the incorrect names applied to the country by Spain). Colonial rule is implicitly confined within the limits of the walled city, symbolizing the limits of its control over the thought-world of the wider community. With Spain thus put in her place, so to speak, the awit can elaborate freely on how the *nación* was historically constituted:

> Ang kay Lakandola parteng Kapampangan
> at ang kay Soliman ang lupang Mindanao
> na pulos na ito nga katagalugan
> desendencia ni Sem ang pinanggalingan

> To Lakandola went the Pampangan region
> And to Soliman the land of Mindanao
> all of these were Katagalugan
> the lineage of Sem was their origin.[46]

The meaning of Katagalugan is now made clear: it is co-terminous with Filipinas. The sending of Lakandola to Pampanga, and Soliman to Mindanao, parallel the earlier account of the dispersal of Noah's sons to Europe, China, and Asia to form the Christian world. Lakandola and Soliman, names that emerged from *ilustrado* research into early history, are appropriated and now figure as extensions of the kinship grouping from Luzon to Mindanao. The discourse of blood lineage and divine origins suffuses the new discourse on *nación*, making it comprehensible to the *kapatid* who make up the poem's audience.

The idea of 'our nación' now firmly established, the consequences of domination by another nation can be explored further:

> Kung iba ring nacion ang siyang gogobierno
> sa habang panahon ay alipin tayo
> nailulubog nga ang Ley ni Kristo
> at ang pa iralin yaong sa demonyo

> If another nation should govern us
> forever we shall be slaves
> the Law of Christ drowned forever
> while the demon's [law] holds sway.[47]

The 'Law' is what regulates interaction among humans. When the law of Kristo prevails, the land is holy and there is love among the *kapatid*. But what would it become when the law of the *demonyo* holds sway?

> Sakmal ng salapi at walang kabagay
> codicial, interes at kapalaluan
> siyang maghahari sa ating kalahatan
> kapag mahirap na'y ipagdidiinan

> An unrivalled attachment to money
> cupidity, profit and arrogance –
> these will come to dominate us all,
> the poor will be burdened further.[48]

This is another way of talking about capitalism and its effects on human relations. Colonial rule and capitalist relations are intertwined, and together they undermine love, pity, and caring among the *kapatid*.

The workings of the law of the *demonyo* are made specific in the case of Spaniards: 'When it is a Kastila who commits murder / he cannot be sentenced for that crime.'[49] The law against taking life does not apply to him. Instead the Castilian is quickly sent back to 'their country,' over there. But should he return, 'he has an official posting' (*may katung-kulan*). Murderers can return and even join the Spanish administration. Thus the law of the *demonyo* further entrenches itself.

The awit then pours irony on the Spanish official or judge who invokes the law and the texts that uphold it: 'Then he will declare, *segun articulo* [according to this article] / and gesturing with his hand, *segun capitulo* [according to this chapter].' Worse, they will declare, 'That's what happened in the past' – that is, they will invoke history to justify their claims. But what is this text they invoke? 'The text they read out was the book of the demon [*demonyo*].'[50]

Initially, the criticism of colonial abuses focuses on 'the Castilian,' who could be a government official, a parish priest, or a landowner committing 'bad deeds' against the native inhabitants. However, the reference to the Spaniard, whose 'worst deeds make him pious and revered' points to the friar in particular as an agent of the *demonyo*. This is a serious, and in some ways perilous, suggestion by Dimatigtig. No matter how established was the critique of the 'frailocracy' (the governance by Spanish friars) in late-nineteenth-century nationalist literature, the fact remained that many (some even argue most) lowland Filipinos living on the plantations and in the urban centres at the turn of the century still looked up to their Spanish pastors for spiritual guidance.

It would not have made sense to denounce Christianity itself in a popular awit such as this. The point of Dimatigtig's criticism is to delineate the differences between Christianity as a universal message of salvation and certain of its agents or practitioners who, being human and nation bound (e.g., the Castilian priests), are already caught up in the era of greed and warring among men. Dimatigtig acknowledges that the *kapatid* have been seduced by the Castilian's words and his glittering appearance:

> Natutuwa tayo't mabuting akala
> totoong marikit kita nga ng madla

> We are delighted and think highly of him
> who glistens in the eyes of the masses

But, Dimatigtig retorts,

> ang isinisentir lamang sa gunita
> iginigisa tayo sa atin ding mantika

> what we sense is just the visible [external]
> for he really is frying us in our own lard.[51]

Dimatigtig explains how the law of Kristo was drowned (*inilubog*) by the very system of practices intended to uphold it. The Freilistas (a pro-friar party) even added purgatory to their theology 'because there was profitable commerce in it / everything there was altered for their ends.'[52] We would conventionally classify this issue as a religious problem, but it should be clear by now that the dichotomy between the religious and the secular characteristic of modern thought simply does not operate in the awit. Confession (said to be invented by the Jesuits), doctrine, and prayers (i.e., religious matters) are lumped together with the penal code invented by the lawyers (*Jurista*): 'They are all the same, Freilista.'[53]

How did such awful things happen in the church? Because weak Christians – Spaniards and Filipinos alike – were seduced by the *demonyo*. His perverse law promotes the opposite of what it appears to. Its effect is the inverse of what is true and good. Under the law of the *demonyo*, any sinful act can be made to look good, to go unpunished: 'the worst deeds make one pious and revered.' Our hopes are not pinned on the afterlife; 'rather, in this life on earth one enriches himself.'[54] Arguably, the law of the *demonyo* is also the law of money relations. Money enables almost anything to appear to be what it is not, enables anything one desires to be bought. The appearance of piety can be bought. Salvation can be bought and sold. But this is false salvation, the logic of enrichment in this life brought to the service of the afterlife.

The 'dark age' of colonial rule is depicted in the awit as a time when the law of Kristo was drowned, and when all people thought about was making easy money (*madaling ipagkuwarta*). They found justification for it even in theology, and 'even the word of the Gospel was modified' to justify profit making, but it still appears holy to us.[55] And the Freilistas 'were the ones who set up the miraculous / images of Saints which are objects of trade.'[56] Money and profit infiltrated religious rituals so that our continued church worship was merely a profit-making operation benefiting the Freilistas. Yet we did not see this; the glitter of it all concealed the reality from us.

Superficially this all sounds like a conventional Age of Enlightenment rant against the profiteering Catholic clergy. Quite probably the *ilustrado* texts that Dimatigtig had read were exactly that. But the awit enables us to understand how the separatist movement in 1896 could take off in the political register while maintaining continuity in the cultural realm. According to the awit, 'the cause of it all was bad government (*masamang gobierno*).'[57] This is a crucial statement, because it links the decline in the law of Kristo to the inability of the colonial state to prevent it. This was why the Spanish government, which had been welcomed as an ally in Rajah Matanda's time, was expelled. This description of religio-political corruption makes the poet's narrative of the country's past all the more plausible. The law of Kristo is to be clearly differentiated from the Spanish regime.

With the establishment of a Filipino *nación* bound by kinship or 'blood ties,' what becomes of the status of Spaniards? In earlier sections of the narrative, Dimatigtig made it clear that the Spanish arrival did not amount to a conquest because they failed to capture the true name of 'our' place. However, they did make the land their home (*tinahanan*) for a long time; they were not exactly aliens. The Spanish can be accommodated in the discourse of kinship because the notion of 'blood line' in the awit derives from an episode in the biblical story. Earlier on, the awit traces the origin of 'the baptized' peoples to the piercing of Christ's breast by Longinus. The blood of Christ that trickled forth constituted the magical seven sacraments through which the baptism of all people began.[58] So, in effect, the same blood runs through Spaniards and Filipinos, who, after all, descend from Noah's sons.

In time there came a break between the two siblings. The awit blames it on the fact that 'in speech they [i.e., the Spanish] are extremely able' (*kung sa bunganga ay labis ng galing*). They have the power to seduce with fine words, to make alliances without fulfilling their side of the bargain. Their relationship with the *kapatid* is governed by extreme pride or arrogance (*kapalaluan*) – 'a trait inherited from Lucifer.'[59] Lucifer once belonged to the community of angels, but broke off because of pride and hence became a *demonyo*. The Spaniards could have belonged to the community of *kapatid* (i.e., as in a marriage alliance) but preferred to assert a certain superiority. No wonder, asserts the awit, they painted Kristo in their image: to make us worship a false representation.[60] Instead of love and caring, they practised deceit and domination and thus alienated themselves from 'us.'

The narration of the behaviour of the Freilistas promotes an image of the Spaniards as from 'over there, not here.' The production of a negative 'other' through several contrasts made between 'those from here' (*taga rito*) and 'those not from here, aliens' (*di taga rito*) in turn facilitates the formation of nationalist discourse:

Kapag ang cedula ay hindi taglay mo
ipalalagay ka na masamang tao

kahatulad mo yaong bagamundo
sila nga ang tunay na di taga rito

If you fail to produce your identity card
they consider you a bad person
they liken you to a vagabond [i.e., outsider]
when, in fact, they are the true aliens.[61]

Because the *di taga rito* also happen to be mostly, but not all, Castilian Spanish, a racial difference can be articulated: 'Look, *kabalat*, he has a stone house / and he's even constructing another palace.' Dimatigtig draws the attention of his Filipino audience (called *kabalat*, 'having the same skin type or color') to the visible proof of the concentration of money in the Freilista: 'Where do you think he will get his funds to spend / if not from us poor folks, through all sorts of trickery?'[62] In the last stanza of this section he identifies them clearly as Spaniards:

Masdan mo, kabalat, may mga hacienda
tila baga ang lupa ay taglay nila't dala
tayo'y taga rito; ito'y taga Espana
ang gawa'y manglupig sa ari ng iba

Look, *kabalat*, they have estates
as if they owned and held the land [soil]
we hail from here; they are from Spain
they come to steal what belongs to others.[63]

Dimatigtig speaks in the present tense, even though the reference is to Spaniards who (by 1900) have been forced out by the revolution.

The persistent use of the present tense indicates that the *historia* narrated by Dimatigtig is not a discrete past to be distinguished from the present. This is particularly evident when he dwells on the abuses of the Freilistas and the effects of such on the *kapatid*. The difference between Spanish and American is collapsed, so that the reader or listener of the awit can better imagine the 'true meaning' of the resistance to U.S. occupation. For example, the awit invites listeners to picture the *demonyo* in ways they are familiar with from religious imagery:

Ikaw baga mayroon nakitang demonio
kung nasa pintura, ang makikita mo

walang iba kung di ang mga naciong ito,
and naging kaaway ng poong si Cristo.

Have you ever seen a demon like the one
in the picture, one that you can see for real?
look no further than the people of this nation,
who became the enemy of Kristo the lord.[64]

The reference here could be to the Freilistas, but in fact the *demonyo* whom they can see 'for real' are the Americans. The *kapatid*, followers of Kristo, are asked to imagine their enemy as a national grouping (*mga naciong ito*) that has turned against Kristo. This differential relationship to Kristo was already stated in stanza 17, but now the term *nación* is conspicuously deployed as the biblical conflict is translated into the Philippine–American war – a conflict between nations.

The crucial issue of the war, as far as the awit is concerned, seems to be misrecognition of the enemy, the failure of the *kapatid* to see what is happening to their community as a result of the enemy's clever stratagems:

Di mo baga tanto nating kalahatan
gawang Mericanong masakim sa yaman
na tayo tayo rin ang pinaglalaban
sa hayop na manok doong ibinagay

Don't you – don't we all – realize
what the greedy Americans are up to?
We are being set against each other
turning us into veritable fighting cocks.[65]

'Don't you – don't we all – realize' suggests that many of the *kapatid* are blind to the real intentions of the Americans, who merely 'crave riches' and are not motivated by the high ideals they preach. They are dominated by the same law of money that earlier turned the friars into false representatives of Kristo. Dimatigtig here seems to be aware of U.S. President William McKinley's speech about the white man's burden. He ridicules the civilizing thrust of American policies. Their manifold prohibitions are meant to extract huge fines, their rules of hygiene are money-making gimmicks, yet so many of 'us' are seduced into following 'them.'[66] In this way, they are able to turn us against each other. The real damage they inflict is to undermine the unity of the *kapatid*, turning 'us' into animals: fighting cocks that fight to win or survive without 'thinking' of the implications or rationale of their actions. Fighting cocks are simply the source of gain or loss to their owners and to those who bet on them.

The cure for such blindness, says Dimatigtig in stanza 24, is to 're-flect deeply upon what has been written' – i.e., the history he is narrat-ing as well as the other books that reveal the truth of the past – be-cause this 'lengthy *historia*, if we manage to trace its path' is acting upon the present (*sa panahong ngayon*). By stanza 69, having delineated this *historia*, he can call on his *kapatid* to fight the Americans in repeti-tion of the past:

> O mga kapatid lahing Filipinos
> na pinagtatakhan ng ibang guerreros
> sa panahon ngayon, ano't di idaos
> nang tayo'y ma ibsan sa pagkabusabos

> Oh brothers and sisters of Filipino ancestry
> of whom other warriors once stood in awe
> let us move again in the present era
> to rid ourselves of the misery we bear.

In the awit we are all brothers and sisters of Filipino roots or ancestry. This land is ours, not theirs. We have a glorious past when other war-riors stood in awe of us. Since then we have been carrying a burden of misery on our backs (the cross is alluded to here). Now is the time to lift this burden by moving again as we once did with great success:

> Itong ating Reyno'y di namang talunan
> nang alinma't sinong dito'y sumalakay
> kay Raja matandang pinakamagulang
> ano't lulupigin Mericano lamang

> Our Kingdom was, after all, never vanquished
> by anyone who attacked this place
> that belonged to Rajah Matanda our ancestor,
> how can mere Americans conquer it?[67]

'After all' our kingdom was never vanquished: this 'after all' signifies the new consciousness of the past propagated by Dimatigtig's awit. It is a past in which we had our own kingdom, our own founding king and exemplary ancestor. This kingdom successfully fended off attacks by outsiders. The Americans constitute merely another wave of attackers. They are not special or superior people; they are *Mericano lamang*, 'mere Americans.' How can we be confident of defeating this well-equipped and extremely clever enemy? Because we have rediscovered our hidden source of strength – our connection with Kristo:

> Kahit ibang nación ang siyang pumarito
> hindi papayagan na matalo tayo
> siyang hari nating ang poong si Kristo
> Dios na maykapal sumakop sa tao
>
> Even if another nation were to intervene
> he will not let us be defeated
> he who is our king, the lord Kristo
> the supreme God who redeemed mankind.[68]

The function of the awit is not just to make the audience 'think' of the past and present. It is also to put them in a state of feeling that makes a change of attitude possible. Stanzas such as the following, though ostensibly describing the future, are meant to evoke feeling:

> Sino kaya ama, ang di mahahambal
> mga anak nating pinakamamahal
> sa lagay na yaong ang di manghinayang
> iiwan sa dusa na lulutang lutang
>
> How could any father not feel sadness
> towards our most beloved children,
> how could he not feel regret at
> leaving them afloat in a sea of pain?[69]

Not just any father, but any *kapatid* for that matter, cannot but feel pity and regret at leaving innocent children to fend for themselves in a sea of suffering. But there is still a chance to prevent their drowning. One can still have them aboard the Ark of the *nación* in the current deluge that is swelling.

The narration of the past enables the *kapatid* to locate themselves in a family-*nación* that has its roots at the beginning of time and is sustained by a divine source of power:

Pasalamat tayo sa mag inang Dios
at matatayo na tayong agraviados
kaya ngayon sana magka isang loób
at mayroon na tayong punong naguutos

Let us give thanks to Divine mother and son
because we aggrieved are about to rise up.
So now let us be one in soul and inner being
because we now have a head giving orders.[70]

The 'Divine mother and son' (*mag inang Dios*), of course, signify family
in its purest form, combining divine and human qualities. But the *kapatid* now know that the son Kristo is their king as well. The divine mother has become their mother, Mother Filipinas; her children are little
Kristos ready to die in the war. The revolutionary literature would generate a number of variations on this mother-and-son theme. The discourses of nationalism and religion are so intertwined that one cannot
imagine one without the other. Even Rizal, after his well-known execution, was said to have 'returned to Mother'; his divinity is attributed to
he and the Mother being *mag ina*.[71]

Knowing the basis of the *nación* through the awit leads us back to the
holy mother and son, and ultimately to God. The flow of power from
the divine source is restored and so now 'we,' the aggrieved, can rise
up. What does this rising mean? Fighting the Americans, yes, but all
this warring and bloodshed should also be productive of love and caring among the *kapatid*. In this way, we can have a genuine community,
one cultivated in the *loób*, in the inner being, and not in some relationship of debt or contract.

Being one in the *loób* is also the effect of having 'a leader who gives
commands.' This is not a leader who terrorizes, or who is a big patron, or
who uses seduction to gain a following. The awit defines a new nationalist authority that displaces, not reinhabits (as the rich and educated
leadership was prone to), the space of colonial government vacated by
Spain. The awit has already provided models of leadership in Kristo
who governs through his law, and Rajah Matanda the wise and brave
king. It has already stated repeatedly what bad leaders should not be, for
such leadership destroys community. Who is this leader, then? There is
no mention of a specific person. What is clear is that this leader must
display the qualities of Kristo and that he must protect Filipinas from
disaster: 'Let us attack the enemy camp now, to exterminate them /

Leave it to God to protect (*ampon*) us.'[72] *Ampon* has a double meaning of 'to protect' and 'to adopt as one's children.' Those who die in the holy war against the Americans will return to God, the original father.

Toward the end of the awit, the second stanza is repeated: 'And Kristo the Lord's message was / you shouldn't be swayed by the demon / before you can even become his follower / you shall tumble into fiery hell.'[73] Biblical metaphors can now be connected to real threats. The seductive overtures of the Americans are the work of the *demonyo*. The Americans will never allow the Filipinos to be equal to them, and collaboration with them will only result in more hardship. We, the Filipinos, are blind to the full effects collaboration, which will be felt by our grandchildren. This is the message of Kristo the Lord (or King). We should strive to heed the voice of Kristo rather than that of McKinley.

Dimatigtig's awit started off in the biblical register with the image of the good shepherd and the lost sheep. It appropriately ends in the nationalist register by allegorically summing up the most recent chapter in the 'life story' of Filipinas:

Mula ng magharian haring culig colig
lahat ng kalabaw, nagsisingitngit
na ang haring Leon dito nananangis
sa pinagtago-an nalonod sa tubig

Ever since the Lord of the pigs reigned
the *carabaos* [water buffalo] have all been raging in fury
the king Lion who was weeping here
drowned in his place of hiding.[74]

The allusion to the animal kingdom recalls the *alamat* folk tales, in which the differences in behaviour among beasts are made to illustrate various aspects of the human condition.

Who is the lord of the pigs (*kulig*)? Obviously the Americans under McKinley, whose program of 'benevolent assimilation' is alluded to in many parts of the awit. Pigs are among the most intelligent of animals; they are also much desired in a culinary sense and are the centrepiece of communal meals. They (like the *demonyo*) are extremely clever and can evoke desire in others. On the other hand, they are considered unclean and are sometimes embodiments of the *demonyo*.

The *carabao*, or water buffalo, represents the Filipinos. This animal was mentioned previously when the awit asked,

Hinihintay mo pa na siyang marating
lagyan ta hikaw mga ilong natin
sa habang panahon hihilahilahin
mistulang kalabaw ang siyang kahambing

Why wait for the time
when rings are attached to our noses,
and we are perpetually dragged around
becoming just like the *carabao* [water buffalo]?[75]

The *carabao* is the peasant's source of livelihood, providing labour for tilling the fields, transport, milk and meat. Normally docile, a mad *carabao* can cause a rampage and is much feared.

The king lion is Spain, or the Spanish monarch. The king of the jungle is pictured here as totally subdued, 'weeping' in hiding. He dies by drowning. Images of sinking and drowning are used many times in the awit to refer to the consequences of the rise of the law of the *demonyo*. Goodness is inundated, yes, but a flood can also signal a new beginning, like the original deluge that cleansed the earth so that Noah's tribe could start anew. Who will survive the present deluge that has brought King Lion to grief?

The awit has pictured the war against the United States as a continuation of the revolution, a cataclysmic event that booted out Spain and restored the integrity of Filipinas and her children. The war is, in fact, a repetition of the original deluge that brought forth Noah and his children, who were also the original leaders of a world that was once integrated and peaceful. Now it is the *nación* Filipinas that functions as the Ark that will ensure the survival of the *kapatid* in the future.[76]

Conclusion

Much more can be said about this awit of 1900 but I have chosen to focus merely on how it operates as a form of history buttressing the fledgling nation at war with the United States. While firmly rooted in the traditional awit genre, it is informed by new ways of thinking about community and nation at the beginning of the twentieth century. The poet, Dimatigtig, while obviously a man of some education, narrates a history of Filipinas that partly conforms to the conventional emplotment of nationalist history yet makes no attempt to challenge or correct the myths of biblical origin held by illicit religious sects in the Philippines. On the contrary, Dimatigtig gives them wider currency by stitching them together with the historical knowledge being produced by Filipino scholars of his generation. Most of the Filipino military commanders during the war with the United States belonged to the same social class and had the same mindset as Dimatigtig. Being 'in the middle,' they could frame in culturally meaningful terms their appeals to their soldiers to 'stay the course' in the face of a superior enemy.

Even after the official end of the war on 4 July 1902, armed resistance to the new colonial order continued in many parts of the archipelago. Alongside the more celebrated colonial advances in education, sanitation, and the Filipinization of the bureaucracy must be mentioned the ongoing agitation by radical pro-independence politicians, urban labour unions, and rural peasant associations and religious sects. These activities mostly bore the cultural marks of the so-called spirit of 1896. Somehow, despite attempts to transmute memories of the revolution against Spain and the war with the United States into a narrative of progress and modernity under American tutelage, such memories survived and in some regions were translated into religious-sectarian and political activity.

Dimatigtig's awit is certainly not a one-off text. The patriotic literature of the decades that followed repeats its themes in various ways. We see this in the statements and manifestos that emanated from peasant movements during the colonial era, the most notable being the Sakdal rebellion of 1935, as well as in the post-1946 period. Teresita Maceda has amassed oral evidence showing how the peasant movement of the 1940s and 1950s, called the Huk, was culturally underpinned by discourse stemming from the revolution and the Philippine–American war.[77]

So powerful are the discourses of history and nation of American colonial vintage, however, that educated Filipinos themselves are largely unable to discern the ground of popular radicalism against which Filipino political leaders and American colonial officials formulated their projects. Thus the ease with which competing discourses, where they surface, are dismissed in the name of rationality, modernity and, in the case of the Huks, anti-Communism. Nonetheless, the persistence of seditious movements, and the turmoil that accompanies events such as elections and reform campaigns, indicates that within Philippine society are currents of thought and sentiment that continue to evade the 'normalizing' forces of the nation-state that functions in the shadow of the American empire and global capitalism. What the Philippines has experienced continues to be reproduced in America's other wars, in other places.

NOTES

1 For a multidisciplinary background on the Philippine–American war, including its ongoing effects and contentious representations, see Angel V. Shaw and Luis H. Francia, eds., *Vestiges of War: The Philippine–American War and the Aftermath of an Imperial Dream 1899–1999* (New York: NYU Press, 2002).

2 Located in Manila, Philippine National Library, Philippine Revolutionary Papers, Box I-19. The spelling and punctuation marks in the excerpts I cite in this essay have been somewhat modified to conform to current usage.

3 For an overview of *ilustrado* scholarship see John N. Schumacher's chapter in *Perceptions of the Past in Southeast Asia*, ed. Anthony J. S. Reid and David G. Marr (Singapore: Heinemann Educational Publishers, 1979).

4 Generally regarded as the most accomplished of the late-nineteenth-century *ilustrado* reformists, Rizal and Del Pilar were Spanish-educated Tagalogs who spent most of their careers in Spain. The former wrote primarily in Spanish, and the latter in Tagalog.

5 Reynaldo C. Ileto, *Filipinos and Their Revolution: Event, Discourse and Historiography* (Quezon City and Honolulu: Ateneo University Press and University of Hawaii Press, 1999), ch. 1.

6 I have argued that the language and form of Dimatigtig's revolutionary tracts assume an audience familiar with biblical imagery obtained through vernacular performances of Christ's life story. See Reynaldo C. Ileto, *Pasyon and Revolution: Popular Movements in the Philippines, 1840–1910* (Quezon City: Ateneo University Press, 1979), ch. 3.

7 For a preliminary critique of representations of Filipino political leadership, see part 3 of Reynaldo C. Ileto, *Knowing America's Colony, A Hundred Years after the Philippine War* (Honolulu: Center for Philippine Studies, University of Hawaii at Manoa, 1999).

8 My thinking in this respect follows the general arguments of Partha Chaterjee, who states, 'My problem is that of mediation, in the sense of the action of a subject who stands "in the middle," working upon and transforming one term of a relation into the other' (*The Nation and Its Fragments: Colonial and Postcolonial Histories* [Princeton, NJ: Princeton University Press, 1993], 34).

9 See Ileto, *Filipinos and Their Revolution*, ch. 1.

10 Vicente L. Rafael, *White Love, and Other Events in Filipino History* (Durham, NC, and London: Duke University Press, 2000), ch. 1.

11 See Ileto, *Knowing America's Colony*, part 2.

12 'Philippines' refers to the land. 'Filipinas' refers to the romantic and ideological representation of the people and their spirit.

13 Dimatigtig, 'Awit ng Pinagdaanang buhay ng Islas Filipinas,' stanza 2.

14 Personal communication from Consolacion R. Alaras. See also Alaras, *Pamathalaan: Ang Pagbubukas sa Tipan ng Mahal n Ina* (Quezon City, Philippines: University of Philippines Press, 1988).

15 Dimatigtig, 'Awit ng Pinagdaanang,' stanza 2.

16 There does not appear to be a Tagalog word for 'politics' prior to the appearance of the loan word *pulítika* in late-nineteenth-century texts. The Filipino context for its emergence still needs to be studied. See Anthony Milner's suggestive work, *The Invention of Politics in Colonial Malaya* (Cambridge: University Press, 1995).

17 Dimatigtig, 'Awit ng Pinagdaanang,' stanza 3.

18 As Benedict Anderson would put it, this world is the 'religious community' – an antecedent of the national community; see *Imagined Communities: Reflections on the Origins and Spread of Nationalism*, 2nd ed. (London: Verso, 1991).

19 Ileto, *Pasyon*, ch. 3.

20 The use of the plural term *tribes* already suggests a fragmented world, a precondition for competing nations to emerge.

21 The allusion is not entirely biblical, however, because the basic unit of society was the *barangay*, named after the boats that ferried whole clans from island to island. In a baranganic society, the image of Noah's Ark would have sat comfortably.

22 Dimatigtig, 'Awit ng Pinagdaanang,' stanza 13.

23 Ibid., stanza 14.

24 Ibid., stanza 15.

25 Ibid., stanza 17.

26 Tagalog popular literature often refers to 'secret knowledge' (*lihim na karunungan*) that can be accessed only by the initiated. Dimatigtig offers his audience access to the secret history of his tribe.

27 Dimatigtig, 'Awit ng Pinagdaanang,' stanza 20.

28 See Ileto, *Filipinos and Their Revolution*, ch. 1.

29 Dimatigtig, 'Awit ng Pinagdaanang,' stanza 21.

30 Ibid., stanza 22.

31 Ibid., stanza 25.

32 Ibid., stanza 26.

33 Ibid., stanza 27.

34 This awit view is actually consistent with recent research that has shown the weakness of Spanish control beyond the town centres. Many pilgrimage sites were the scene of 'heretical' practices, as the Spanish priests viewed them. See Ileto, 'Outlines of a Nonlinear Emplotment of Philippine

History,' in *The Politics of Culture in the Shadow of Capital*, ed. David Lloyd and Lisa Lowe (Durham, NC: Duke University Press, 1997).

35 Dimatigtig, 'Awit ng Pinagdaanang,' stanza 28.
36 Ibid., stanza 29.
37 The Tagalog word for the English is *linoóban*, commonly used in reference to bandits raiding a town centre.
38 Dimatigtig, 'Awit ng Pinagdaanang,' stanza 30.
39 Ibid., stanza 31.
40 Ibid.
41 Ileto, *Filipinos and Their Revolution*, ch. 2.
42 Dimatigtig, 'Awit ng Pinagdaanang,' stanza 32.
43 See the discussion in Ileto, *Pasyon*, ch. 4.
44 Dimatigtig, 'Awit ng Pinagdaanang,' stanza 74.
45 Ibid., stanza 37.
46 Ibid., stanza 44.
47 Ibid., stanza 45.
48 Ibid., stanza 46.
49 Ibid., stanza 48.
50 Ibid., stanza 49.
51 Ibid., stanza 51.
52 Ibid., stanza 55.
53 Ibid., stanza 54.
54 Ibid., stanza 50.
55 Ibid., stanza 56.
56 Ibid., stanza 57.
57 Ibid., stanza 57.
58 Ibid., stanza 10.
59 Ibid., stanza 47.
60 Ibid., stanza 8.
61 Ibid., stanza 65.
62 Ibid., stanza 66.
63 Ibid., stanza 68.
64 Ibid., stanza 101.
65 Ibid., stanza 72.
66 Ibid., stanza 96–7.
67 Ibid., stanza 70.
68 Ibid., stanza 88.
69 Ibid., stanza 81.
70 Ibid., stanza 82.
71 Personal communication from Consolacion R. Alaras.

72 Dimatigtig, 'Awit ng Pinagdaanang,' stanza 83.

73 Ibid., stanza 103.

74 Ibid., stanza 107.

75 Ibid., stanza 78.

76 The ark is still a conspicuous motif in contemporary religiopolitical movements. The Philippine Benevolent Missionaries Association, a nationwide movement, considers itself the 'modern Ark of Noah.' Its divine master, Ruben Ecleo, claimed to be a reincarnation in Mindanao of Jesus Christ, Jose Rizal, and Hilario Moncado (an earlier leader). Florio R. Falcon, Religious Leadership in the Philippine Benevolent Missionaries Association, Inc.,' in *Filipino Religious Psychology*, ed. Leonardo N. Mercado (Tacloban: Divine Word University, 1977), 141–69.

77 Teresita G. Maceda, 'Mga Tinig Mula sa Ibaba: Kasaysayan ng Partido Komunista ng Pilipinas at Partido Sosialista ng Pilipinas sa Awit, 1930–1955,' in *Sounds from Below: A History of the Communist Party of the Philippines and the Socialist Party of the Philippines through Songs* (Quezon City: University of the Philippines Press, 1996).

Chapter 10

Telling the Untold: Representations of Ethnic and Regional Identities in Ukrainian Women's Autobiographies

OKSANA KIS

I was eleven when my grandmother Oryna died. I did not know much about her life. She was born in 1899 in the Poltava region in Central Ukraine. She came to western Ukraine immediately after the Second World War and was among thousands of ordinary Communists sent by the Communist Party to establish the Soviet regime there. At that time she married a widower named Mykhailo from western Ukraine. Shortly thereafter, in 1946, his daughter from his first marriage gave birth to my mother, Nina. When she was a baby, her parents perished tragically – they were found shot at night – so Oryna adopted my mother at a very young age and raised her even after Mykhailo's death a few years later. Nina was the only child she had. Oryna never comprehensively recounted her life story either to her stepdaughter or to me, her granddaughter. However, I was able to collect some basic facts about her life from a short newspaper obituary, which suggested that her life was extremely rich and very special.

Indeed, she survived two world wars, the October Socialist Revolution of 1917, the Civil War, the famine of 1932–3 in Ukraine, and periods of collectivization, industrialization, and mass political repressions in the USSR. She witnessed the birth, development, and stagnation of the Soviet regime. She was decorated with several government awards including one 'For Heroic Work on the Home Front.' She obviously went through a lot, but she never spoke about these experiences. Consequently, today I have to avow that I don't know my grandmother's life at all: the details of her childhood and adolescence, her education and professional work, private life and public activities, even her views remain obscure to me. Like many other Soviets, she left no written documents, diaries, or memoirs to cast light on her life story. The line of succession between our generations has been broken because of the silence she kept. Yet nobody was seriously interested in listening to her recollections at that time. As Luisa Passerini has correctly noticed, 'There is nothing left to transmit if nobody is there to receive the message.'[1] For me this has meant the real loss of my foremother's heritage, namely the continuity of memory of women's historical experience that binds the generations together. I believe I could be stronger if I knew whose granddaughter I am.

Academic Context

Since the first passionate appeals of feminist historians in the 1970s and '80s to make women visible in history, historiography has undergone considerable change.[2] Indeed, as Joan Scott has stated, 'The story of the development of human society has been told largely through male agency; and the identification of men with "humanity" has resulted for the most part in the disappearance of women from the record of the past ... Women were ... forgotten or ignored, hidden from history.'[3] As women's studies in history and anthropology became institutionalized in the 1970s, scholars first called for the reinterpretation of classical historical records in order to reveal the real roles women have played in history. But as soon as they realized the inherent androcentrism of the majority of available materials, the elaboration of new empirical sources reflecting the views and historical experiences of ordinary women became the main task of feminist scholarship. Thus various written ego-documents (personal diaries, memoirs, letters, and so forth), which had been considered irrelevant for historical research before, became valuable objects for empirical study. Shortly thereafter, scholars interested in re-establishing women's well-deserved place in world history and in creating a history of their own started paying attention to women's historical voices in not only a figurative but also a literal sense. Oral history has proven to be the most appropriate research method for accomplishing these tasks.

History as a discipline has changed substantially over last few decades as its anthropological dimension has expanded. Recognition of the uniqueness and indisputable value of individual experience for historical reconstructions (and consequently the necessity of interviewing the immediate participants in historical events) has stimulated the rapid development of a new field: oral history. This trend allows the study of the past on the grassroots level. The approach has demonstrated the subjectivity of historical interpretation and the multiplicity of historical truth. It has introduced the possibility of alternative versions of historical events deriving from the perspectives of diverse individuals or social groups. The basic thesis of oral history is the assertion that history is not 'past-in-itself' but present-day interpretations of people's historical experiences. 'Oral history is the history built around people ... It provides a means for radical transformation of the social meaning of history.'[4] Therefore, its main goal is to reveal the way in which individual memories are transformed into the collective memory.

The autobiographical approach, which is often used in oral history research, brings into the centre of the study an individual life, inscribed in its immediate milieu (a micro-environment), so that the subject's personal reflections and social, political, and cultural entourage are in focus simultaneously. At the same time, in-depth autobiographical interviews can shed light on the origins of some people's latent attitudes, thoughts, and deeds even if they are stated either obliquely or not at all. Scott stresses the necessity of studying the past on individual and societal levels simultaneously in order to get the most accurate historical picture: 'To pursue meaning we need to deal with the individual subject as well as social organization and to articulate the nature of their relationships, for both are crucial to understanding how gender works, how change occurs.'[5] And she has proved that a gendered approach allows human society to be studied from different perspectives – structural, cultural, individual. Indeed, women's autobiography provides a multidimensional perspective on history.

The growing importance of qualitative research methods in social studies and the humanities has met the approval of women's studies scholars demanding an alternative way of approaching history. Today, studying the peculiarities of the historical memory of women is one of the most topical trends in women's studies. From its inception, oral history not only offered its methodology and tools to women's history but was also in line with the theoretical goals of the field: to fill the void in historical source material with experiences and perspectives of marginalized people by means of the interview.[6]

Oral history helped to debunk the myth that history is objective and raised questions about the validity of historical records. The notion of intersubjectivity has replaced the older ideas.[7] Indeed, 'over recent years many historians have become acutely aware that any writing about the past is a subsequent reconstruction, and that no history reaches us unmediated.'[8] Leaving aside the long discussion about reliability of a personal interview as a research source,[9] I agree with Daniel Bertaux's statement that the social world is constructed and transformed every minute by actions of ordinary people, who are both observers and agents of reality, and that reality itself consists of the individual experiences of participants in social, economic, political, and cultural processes.[10] Reading autobiography as a social and cultural construct, the researcher is not interested in how true or correct the descriptions of events are. Rather, the meanings attributed to them by the narrator are of primary importance. The person constructs his or her past using the available repertoire of cultural genres, linguistic patterns, discourses, and values that may be identified and extracted from an autobiography afterward and analysed.

Oral history is not only about the reconstruction of events or the documentation of facts by means of individual testimony. 'The first thing that makes oral history different is that it tells us less about *events* than about their *meaning* ... Oral sources tell us not just what people did, but what they wanted to do, what they believed they were doing, and what they now think they did,' Alessandro Portelli has argued.[11] Therefore, oral history research is not undertaken for the sake of any 'historical truth,' which is by definition unknowable. In narrating their life stories, the subjects of autobiographical interviews are talking not so much about events they witnessed as about the meanings those events have produced in the context of their individual life experiences. The researcher's task is to identify the ways in which real biographical facts are transformed into a significant, memorized past. By this means, the personal sense of experienced history is produced.

Feminist scholarship has proved time and again that a thorough study of women's individual experiences, visions, and opinions enriches historical records, making them much more accurate and comprehensive. Although androcentrism has been restrained in social sciences and humanities in the West, it remains a feature of most historical research in Ukraine. As well, the official history of Ukraine has for a long time focused mainly on political, economic, and social changes on the macro level, disregarding ordinary human historical agency.

The history of Ukraine in twentieth century is full of events that altered the political, social, and economic landscape over and over again. And the issue of gender is of special importance in this regard, because Ukrainian women's lives changed dramatically in the twentieth century: they obtained rights and opportunities for self-actualization beyond their families and homes. But women's experience of these historical changes have not been studied properly, inasmuch as the official version of history has marginalized the social reality associated with women. Furthermore, women's participation in and contribution to all national achievements of the twentieth century have been concealed. Women have found themselves underrepresented or even completely excluded from mainstream historical records; their life experiences and practices, views and aspirations remain unknown to scholars and to their younger counterparts. Today Ukrainian women – scholars and activists – are confident that knowledge of our foremothers' lives should be retrieved and their roles in   recent history appreciated. Research in women's oral history is thus perhaps one of the most urgent tasks of feminist scholarship in Ukraine nowadays.

The collapse of the USSR and the disintegration of the socialist bloc in eastern Europe caused a burst of interest in research on post-Soviet issues. Yet over the last decade most publications on the post-socialist era have been dedicated to analysis of Russian cases, whereas articles about Ukraine have appeared in academic collections and journals only occasionally.[12] This situation has compelled Ukrainian scholars to intensify their studies on the history and anthropology of Ukrainian women. Since the 1990s Ukrainian scholars have acquired some familiarity with Western theories and methodological approaches to women's history, which were almost unknown in the USSR.[13] It has resulted in the publication of a number of works on the history of the Ukrainian women's movement of the early twentieth century.[14] Several pieces of popular scientific literature and reference books providing short biographical sketches about women who played important roles in politics, arts, literature, charity, social movements, and so on have come out as well.[15] Only one book, however, has attempted to cover the entire history of women in Ukraine from the Middle Ages to the present.[16] It should also be mentioned that all these publications focus primarily on famous personalities, thus leaving in shadow the everyday lives of the absolute majority – ordinary Ukrainian women.

Over the last sixteen years Ukrainian historiography in general – and Ukrainian women's history in particular – has changed considerably. Although the oral history approach is being used increasingly and several research projects have been conducted over last decade, this field is not deeply embedded in Ukrainian scholarship yet.[17] It is therefore not surprising that despite the obvious urgency, only one project directly related to women's oral history has been carried out in Ukraine so far.[18]

Despite all the complexities of doing oral history in post-totalitarian societies the biographical interview method is being used extensively in
several former socialist countries in research on women's oral history,
and the life history approach has proven to be a relevant and effective
research tool that 'encourages the narrator to shape her own story as
well as to tell it in her own words, and thus puts her at the forefront of
the historical stage.'[19] The quality of the work is also getting higher as
scholars obtain more experience in interviewing. As well as developing
practical skills oral historians have been acquiring greater knowledge
in the theory and methodology of women's oral history owing to several specialized academic publications that have recently appeared in
post-Soviet countries.[20]

Woman's Autobiography: Oral versus Written

Although an impressive body of autobiography has been written by
women worldwide over the course of history the way they represent
female subjectivity is very problematic. Criticizing the highly androcentric character of autobiography as an originally masculine literary
genre, Sidonie Smith, an expert in feminist research on female autobiography, claims that 'women's true autobiography has yet to be written, since women writers have, until recently, only reinscribed male
writing and thereby produced a text which either obscures women or
reproduces the classic representations of women.'[21]

Oral narration of a life story provides a woman with an alternative
mode of self-representation as 'the key point of the life story is to give
people the opportunity to tell their story the way they choose to tell it.'[22]
Indeed, storytelling – even conditioned by certain established cultural
forms and genres – is free from a number of conventions and limitations
peculiar to autobiographical writing. The storytelling is even more informal and liberated when both interlocutors – an interviewer and a
narrator – are women. In her insightful article 'Talking and Listening
from Women's Standpoint,' Marjorie L. Devault adduces a number of
arguments in favour of all-women's talk, which, she argues, generally
results in more thorough recollections on the part of the narrator and a
more accurate understanding of what was said and what was actually
meant on the part of the interviewer. Like many other feminist oral historians she underlines the exceptional role of non-verbal elements of
storytelling (indrawn breath, elongated vowel sounds, and hesitations),[23] which allow a narrator to display her emotions and attitudes.

Because these are not verbalized they will be missing from a written account, thus ultimately distorting its meaning. After a comprehensive discussion of the peculiarities and advantages of feminist interviewing, Marjorie Devault comes to the conclusion that recognizing and employing the distinctively female tradition of 'woman talk' can enrich our research practices.[24]

The oral narration of a life story – even during a prearranged, tape-recorded interview – is not generally perceived as a process of documenting a life. Moreover, the atmosphere and circumstances of a regular biographical interview rarely have an official tinge; it is shaped as a rather private conversation between two women in which one is sharing her experiences with another. In the case of the research project '20th Century Ukraine in Women's Memories,' which informs this chapter, the interviewees are ordinary women who do not regard their life experiences and achievements as exceptional or significant for history. That is why they narrate personal life stories (full of private details, controversies, emotions, conflicts, and the like) rather than part of a 'great history.'

Once autobiography is written, it may be re-read and reinterpreted endlessly, but it cannot be changed. As with any written text, its form is static forever, no matter who the reader is. Autobiography that is spoken, on the contrary, is always flexible and changeable; it takes many forms and can be told in different ways depending on the audience.

Another distinction lies in the differing origins of the impulse to narrate the story. Written autobiography is usually a result of an individual's inner wish and conscious decision to tell his or her life story to other people. Such a narrator regards that life experience as significant for a society. This affects the narrative, determining its form and the repertoire of chosen topics in accordance with the dominant public discourse. Some of the individual's personal attitudes and opinions may thereby be shaded or distorted throughout the written text. In written biographical women's narratives some private issues such as personal relations, emotional problems, sexuality, and the body are covered very poorly, or omitted completely. 'The observance of the principles [of biography] requires [a woman] to exclude of what is "very personal" as something insignificant for History,' concluded Yulia Gradskova in her analysis of the written biography of a Soviet woman.[25] In addition to belonging within a particular literary genre, the written biography is a form of documentation of one's life, and this urges an author to follow certain rules of creation. It implies that the memory must be both intensive and selective at once. The narrator faces the necessity to choose which of her personal life experiences are really valuable in terms of a collective history and deserve to become a part of a historical legacy belonging to generations. 'An androcentric genre, autobiography demands the public story of the public life,' as Sidonie Smith correctly argues.[26]

Once a key event, special experience, or exceptional social role is chosen it becomes a reference point for the whole biographical narrative, which hence is constructed to explain, interpret, legitimize, and generalize it. The recently published autobiography of Maria Savchyn, a Ukrainian woman who participated in the underground national liberation movement against Soviets in western Ukraine in 1944–53, is a good example. 'When I started writing I faced the problem how to delimit my private life from the history of our struggle ... The awareness of the fact that these memories are not my property as they belong to all the friends of mine helped me to overcome the difficulties,' the author admitted in the introduction.[27] She solved the dilemma in favour of history, as the structure of the work testifies, along with its title, *Tysiacha dorih: Spohady zhinky uchasnytsi pidpilno-vyzvolnoi borotby pid chas I pislia Druhoi svotovoi viyny* (A Thousand Roads: Recollections of a Woman Participant of the Underground Liberation Struggle). Although some personal issues, such as romantic relationships and women's friendship, are episodically touched upon, they are still marginalized in the context of a story that is mostly about the struggle itself. Similarly, an autobiography by Anna Polshchikova, who survived a Nazi concentration camp, is entirely shaped by her experience of breastfeeding of numerous babies who survived only owing to her actions. The detailed description of her experiences in the camp and later relationships with her foster children contrasts with a scanty account of her life before and after the war.[28] Thus in a written autobiography the dominant topic actually subdues the others, so some issues are marginalized and others disappear.

Another difference between these two ways of creating autobiography concerns the time it takes. Writing a comprehensive autobiography usually takes months or even years; thus it is exposed to author's ongoing reflections on what she has written: changes in structure, selection of words, polishing of style, and so forth.

The oral presentation of autobiography is often called into being from an outside impulse – either by his/her relatives or an interviewer – and the story is not necessarily produced for public presentation. Therefore, the narrator is not so much focused on its adherence to dominant discourses.

The relation rarely takes more than few hours, and thus represents a more condensed extract of one's life. Inasmuch as a narrator is encouraged to relate her life story in full, from the beginning to the present day, there is less chance that her narrative will be dominated and structured by a single theme, as is usually the case with written autobiographies. Facing the request to tell her entire life story here and now, a narrator must undertake an express inspection of her life, having little time for selection of topics, sequencing the story, and choosing the most appropriate words. The language of her narration is thus more spontaneous and associative, so a life story is less subject to systematic self-censorship than is the case in written memoirs. Natural modes of speech are inherent in informal storytelling. An oral presentation of a life story usually comprises some discrepancies, lapses, reiterations, hesitations, jokes, slang, and so forth. While written autobiographies are usually presented in a linear chronological form, oral ones are often cyclical and digressive. The narrator will return (consciously or not) to certain issues several times in various contexts, as well as approach them from different perspectives. The recurrent themes, repeated expressions, and reiterated topics are perhaps the most important elements of an oral biography when it come to detecting the principal discourses and values that govern a woman's social identity. All these become important elements in the process of analysis, as this chapter reveals.

The most important advantage of the oral autobiography, however, lies in its performative and interactive nature. It provides a range of indirect, non-verbal ways for an interviewee to express (and a researcher to read) her unconscious, latent, or unarticulated thoughts. Discussing the peculiarities of oral sources as compared to written ones, Alessandro Portelli has rightly emphasized that 'the tone and volume range and the rhythm of popular speech carry implicit meaning and social connotations which are not reproducible in writing ... The exact length and position of the pause has an important function in the understanding of the meaning of speech.'[29] Indeed, the speed of speech, facial expressions, posture, and gesticulation can tell us much about the speaker's attitudes and opinions, especially if for some reason it is hard for a respondent to put ideas into words. The interviewer's observations about the narrator's non-verbal messages should be reflected in the transcript and described in a report (a protocol of interview) in order to provide important insights about the unarticulated meaning given to the articulated words. The study on which this chapter is based confirmed the significance of the performative and conversational features of oral biographical narration for further analysis and interpretation.

In post-socialist countries, where many people mistrust written documents and a scholar ought not to trust official records unconditionally , oral history proves to be an indispensable research tool for study of the recent past. The peculiarities and complexities of doing oral history in totalitarian and post-totalitarian societies have been widely discussed among Western scholars in the 1990s.[30] The point is that people were deprived of their individual memories by the state, so often their 'silence gave an illusory unity to collective memory: everyone's experience was made to seem the same.'[31] Similarly, Soviet people over the decades were trained to accept only the official version of history – one for all. It should be remembered that in Stalin's epoch even a political joke was considered a crime and could lead to years of imprisonment. People watched each other in search of so-called national enemies, and nobody trusted anyone – not neighbours, not colleagues, not even relatives. The indiscreetly uttered *word* became the worst enemy of people. 'A chatterer is a boon for a spy!' a propaganda poster of that time said. In this respect children posed a special hazard to their parents since they could blurt out – purposely or not – something they heard at home.

Experiencing enormous pressure from ubiquitous Soviet propaganda and living in an atmosphere of overall terror, ordinary people learned to hold their critical opinions inside.[32] Later, the narrow circle of trusted friends and intimate family members became, perhaps, the only way to discuss public issues during 'the thaw' in the 1960s and 'the stagnation' in the 1970s and '80s. As Nanette Funk correctly remarks, 'The fundamental dichotomy in state socialism was, in fact, between the family and the state. The family thus had a very special and powerful status as the primary institution that stood in opposition to the state ... Rather than being the antithesis to the public sphere, the family became an ersatz public sphere.'[33]

A scholar intending to conduct oral historical research in post-socialist Ukraine has to be aware of the extraordinary complexity involved in motivating people to discuss their personal historical experiences openly and comprehensively. It's especially difficult to get individuals to reflect critically on topics that were taboo in the USSR: political repression, ethnocide, deportation, social stratification, gender inequality, and so on. Yet post-Soviet people sharply distinguish (impersonal) official history from (personal) everyday life, between a national master narrative and an individual story, which quite often considerably diverge from or even contradict to one another. Having little role in decision making in the past, people used to regard themselves as objects – not agents – of history, so for many it is quite a challenge to give any meaning to their individual experiences in the broader context of national history. Taking this into consideration I consider the individual narrative biographical interview as the most advantageous and appropriate method of interviewing in post-Soviet countries.

Project Design

Considering the acute shortage of works in Ukrainian women's history, the need for a serious research project on the topic remains evident and urgent. Participating in the international research project 'Women's Memory: Searching for Lives and Identities of Women under Socialism' is an excellent way to fulfil that academic need. This project was conceived in 1996 in Prague by a group of women from central European countries (the Czech Republic, the Slovak Republic, the former East Germany, Poland, Serbia, Montenegro, and Croatia).[34] Its initial goal was to document women's life experiences under socialism, mainly by recording, archiving, and analysing their autobiographies. Utilizing a common set of interviewing techniques across different countries has facilitated the cross-cultural examination of the materials. In the course of the project, hundreds of interviews have been conducted and are now represented in the impressive international women's oral history archive in Prague, used for research, teaching and publications. From the beginning, the project has enjoyed a great deal of academic interest and public support.

In 2002 the Ukrainian team joined the 'Women's Memory' project. Because each national research team retains relative autonomy, we have been able to shape the priorities of our project to fit Ukraine's particular needs. In addition to covering a number of so-called proper women's issues (the transformation of traditional gender roles and stereotypes, women's gender identity construction, the notion of motherhood, woman's sexuality), this project is also designed to study women's views about the more general social, economic, and political changes they have experienced in Ukrainian socialist and post-socialist society. Comprehensive analyses of the women's life stories sheds light on a number of issues, including: the transformations in women's national/regional/ethnic identities in multinational and multicultural urban environments; the impact of the Soviet regime on women's lives (political repression, the national liberation movement, struggles for civic and political rights); the personal, social, and cultural consequences of forced migration (including deportations of national minorities in the 1940s, the postwar political emigration, repatriation, contemporary labour immigration); strategies devised by women to survive the effects of their historical traumas (especially during the Second World War living in occupied territory, being evacuated, enduring forced labour in Germany, and surviving the battlefront). Women's views and (re)evaluations of the different political regimes under which they have found themselves – Soviet, Nazi, the fledgling Ukrainian nation-state democracy – are of special interest to us. Our initial hypothesis was based on the assumption that women from different regions would have rather different impressions and images of the experienced past. We considered this a given in light of the fact that the respective regions were so diverse in their history, cultural heritage, ethnic composition, and political and economic situation.

Three regions of Ukraine – western, eastern, and southern (represented by the three cities Lviv, Kharkiv, and Simferopol, respectively) – were chosen for field work because of their significant historical, cultural, social, political, and economic differences. The primary task was to interview the oldest generation of women, women born in the 1920s and early 1930s, regardless of their education, occupation, ethnic origin, or religious persuasion. Since age and gender are the only criteria of a respondent's eligibility, all possible channels have been used for recruitment of potential storytellers. They have been identified through a variety of contacts, including personal relations, NGOs, social services for senior citizens, and parish communities. Undergraduate students and women activists, specially instructed for this project, became the interviewers.

In 2003–5 we recorded and transcribed over twenty autobiographical narrative interviews revealing the life experiences of elderly women. Each transcript is accompanied by two compulsory documents. A biogram includes the respondent's principle biographical data: date and place of birth of herself and her parents, grandparents, children, sisters, and brothers; dates of marriage and divorce and birth and death of husband; dates and places of relocations; education; professional experience. This information is extremely useful for the reconstruction and analysis of each segment of a woman's life. Such records help to reveal and interpret the events, people, and places that affected the woman's life, especially if these items are described in detail in the narrative, or, on the contrary, excluded from it. Basic social characteristics such as the respondent's church affiliation and ethnic identity are also indicated in biogram in order to make further comparisons and generalizations possible. The second document – the protocol of interview – is actually a short report written by the interviewer describing the situation of the particular interview: where and how the respondent has been recruited, the setting in which the conversation took place, the interviewer's observations of the interviewee's living conditions, and any difficulties encountered. This information can be extremely helpful for researchers who did not attend the interview as it is an account of the interaction between both interlocutors, the narrator's psychological condition, emotions, reactions and behaviour during the interview; it may thus cast light on the respondent's latent motives for selecting, sequencing, emphasizing, or ignoring topics while constructing her story. It may also help to identify the topics the most important for the respondent herself.

The method of narrative biographical interview used in this project has been elaborated in the works of Gabriele Rosenthal.[35] Here it is used with some minor modifications to fulfil the goals of the study. The interviewers have been trained to follow certain ethical rules and use specific interviewing techniques acceptable for a feminist life story interview.[36] The autobiographical narrative interview aims to sustain a natural, continuous narration and to minimize the interviewer's influence. Each interview consists of several consecutive phases, so the general structure is predictable. The interview begins with an open-ended introductory question, so the respondent can arrange the narration in her own way, guaranteeing maximum freedom of expression. The uninterrupted narrative flow is maintained through a technique of active listening that permits the interviewer to ask only so-called *neutral* questions to stimulate a narrator's talk.[37] After the storytelling is over the next, extremely important, phase of the interview begins with the so-called *internal* questions: they may concern only people, events, and facts directly related to this particular life story. At this time the narrator has an opportunity to immerse herself more deeply in her memories, and many previously omitted details emerge at this time. Some of them may be extremely painful, so maximum sensitivity and tactfulness are required.[38] After all clarifications have been made and the respondent has nothing to add, the interviewer can proceed to the next phase, which consists of so-called *external* questions. Since it is important to reveal the women's opinions about several subjects, this series of focused questions is to be asked at the end of each interview. They are formulated according to the particular academic interests of the researchers involved. Therefore, these questions are not necessarily related to a specific life story but require a respondent to express her reflections on more general social and political issues.[39] The primary analysis of women's biographies then consists of a three-level coding of the narratives, after the methodology elaborated by Anselm L. Strauss and Juliet M. Corbin, which reveals the principal thematic fields and the key categories that frame and structure the women's narratives.[40]

The general success of the enterprise depends heavily on the quality of the interviewer's work, making demands on the interviewer's personality, behaviour, and skills. The interviewer's gender, age, ethnicity, and language are of special importance to the success of the interview. The difference between interviewer and interviewee (gender, age, class, language, education) determines the personal distance between them, and ultimately governs their psychological comfort. This is essential for creation of a trustful, open, and frank atmosphere, so it is advisable for the interviewer to share as much of the interviewee's cultural background as possible in order to understand her verbal and non-verbal messages without difficulty. At the same time, it is better for ethical reasons to avoid any close personal relations between the interviewer and the interviewee, such as being family members, neighbours, or friends.

Historical Background

In what follows, two women's autobiographies are used as case studies – one from Kharkiv, the other from Lviv. These women appear to be quite representative of average city dwellers, and their lives bear several similar features. Both women are currently in their eighties, and each was married only once and is a widow now. Both have children and grandchildren. But more significant is that both were experienced school teachers. That means they took an active part in society but were not engaged in politics as party leaders or even members, or in military service. I tried to analyse the reflections of the two women about inter-ethnic relations in general and about two concrete nations in particular. The women have a shared common historical experience. They lived in the same region (near Lviv) at the same time (right after the Second World War), but they are representative of two opposing sides: local Ukrainians/nationalists on the one hand, and Russian/Soviet newcomers on the other.

The problem of relations between Ukrainians and the other ethnic groups (Russians, above all) who have populated Ukraine for centuries is an important issue in post-socialist Ukrainian society. The recent public debate about Russian as possible second state language has exacerbated problems in Ukrainian–Russian relations in Ukraine. The public discussion on language and cultural distinctions between east and west regions is highly politicized in Ukraine nowadays, especially after the presidential and parliamentary elections of 2004–6.[41]

Some general historical background might be helpful for understanding the main points of tension. Since 1654 a large part of Ukraine to the east from Dnepr River – the so-called Left Bank, including Kyiv, the capital of Ukraine – was under Russian governance. Over centuries the predominantly Ukrainian population of this territory has been exposed to an intensive policy of Russian cultural invasion (known as Russification), especially in big cities. After the October socialist revolution in 1917, this part of Ukraine underwent mass forced collectivization, and tens of thousands of wealthy farmers were murdered or banished to Siberia. This region suffered most in the famine of 1932–3; the majority of churches were destroyed there as well. Indeed, the Ukrainian population of eastern Ukraine has endured the politics of ethnocide in full measure.

The western territories of Ukraine (called Galicia, where the city of Lviv is situated) belonged to Poland (except for the period 1772–1919, when it was a part of Austro-Hungarian Empire) until 1939, when Galicia was incorporated into the Ukrainian SSR. After the Second World War the governments of Poland and the USSR undertook the exchange of population. Poles were forced to leave western Ukraine and move to Poland, and Ukrainians were resettled from Poland to Ukraine. Before, during, and after the Second World War, an underground armed national liberation movement fought against Soviets in this area. In the postwar period masses of locals in the western part of Ukraine were accused of nationalism and collaboration with the Nazis, and a great number of people were imprisoned or banished to Siberia. The local Greek Catholic church was banned completely, and even religiosity became a sufficient reason for discrimination and persecution. At the same time, Russians and eastern Ukrainians working for the Soviet authorities settled throughout Galicia.

A great many Jews lived for centuries in cities and towns all over Ukraine. Although they constituted a large part of the urban population before the Second World War, they were largely exterminated by the Nazis.[42] Living side by side, Ukrainians and Jews never wielded authority over one another. Despite many historically formed prejudices about and distrust of Jews, militant anti-Semitism was never a problem among Ukrainians; generally ordinary people of both ethnicities lived peacefully as neighbours.[43] Jews always tried to maintain good relations with the predominant residential population and usually spoke the local languages.

Obviously, the dramatic historical and political changes that occurred in the three regions of Ukraine not only considerably altered the ethnic composition of the population but also stimulated a number of interethnic tensions. Even though women were active agents of the national liberation movement before and during the Soviet period and played an active role in the process of nation-state building in post-Soviet Ukraine, women's experiences of and opinions about interethnic relations has not yet been studied in depth.[44] It's remarkable that most writing examining the intersection of gender and ethnic identity in the history of Ukrainian women has never been studied from below, through analysis of the attitudes and views of ordinary women.[45] In this chapter I use the two autobiographies to examine how women develop attitudes toward and construct images of other nations. The problem of interethnic relations was touched upon repeatedly in each story, but its representation varied according to the narrator's location and historical experience.

West Ukrainian View: Liuba

The story of Liuba is an appropriate one to begin with.[46] She is Ukrainian and lives in a town in the Lviv region. It is notable that she first discusses a national issue and mentions Jews while speaking about her childhood impressions of the Second World War:

> There was a terrible scream. They were taken out of Sokal and forced to dig a hole, a ditch. Then they were stripped naked and thrown down to the ditches. They were covered by carbide to avoid [the odour] of decay and covered with earth, and evened out. Later, when nobody was there, we children came there to see what happened: the earth was moving and moaning there.[47]

Here she describes the massacre of Jews as an observer; her narration is almost barren of any expression of sentiment. She turned to this topic after a remark that 'a bomb fell on our house and everything burned ... and we were given a Jew's house.' As if justifying why, she began to recall how the Nazis hunted for Jews, and then describes the fate of the Jews in the Sokal ghetto. Then she immediately returns to her recollection of the Second World War; this time she says nothing about her attitudes toward Jews and keeps emotional distance from them. She didn't discuss Jews again until the question 'What do you think about people of various ethnicities living next to you?' was asked at the end of interview. After a preamble moralizing that 'people should be respected regardless of their nationalities,' she recalls horrors of Holocaust again:

> Formerly we despised Germans because of their brutality towards Jews. It was a terrible cruelty ... They could ... A Jewish child could possibly go, and he [the Nazi] could blow out his brains, and there was an end to it. And he stepped over that child, over a human, and went further. We could not comprehend that cruelty.[48]

Then she continues reasoning about how every nation has good and bad representatives, and suggests keeping distance from the latter. Suddenly she recalls her childhood again, arguing for friendly relations among children of different nations:

> When we were children, we were friends with Poles and with Jews. We played in one yard; Jewish children played, and Polish children played. We played all together, until Russians came. All nations played and there was no difference. *All of them tried to speak the Ukrainian language. They adapted themselves to ours.* And a Pole – a boy or a girl – tried speaking our language, even if mixing Ukrainian and Polish words. *And Jews always spoke Ukrainian to us,* although among themselves they babbled in Jewish, so we didn't understand what they said [emphasis added].[49]

She confirms the veracity of this statement and of her sincere goodwill toward Jews in the following story:

> Even during German occupation when all Jewish children were put behind barbed wire, and nobody was allowed to approach, we children took bread and came up to the wires and fed the Jewish children. When a German security guard saw that, he threatened us away and forbade giving them bread. But we threw it to children anyway; I and my brothers,

and neighbour's children, Poles and Ukrainians, went to give [bread] to Jewish children.[50]

This episode is followed by another reinforcing its effect and showing her mother's empathy toward persecuted Jews. It is about a Jew who concealed himself in a barn on their court. Her mother risked her life but did not give him away when a German soldier came hunting for Jews; she didn't even betray him after her barking dog was shot. To convince us that positive attitudes toward other nations are inherent in her family, she adds later, 'My parents never made a distinction between them – is that child a Jewish or Polish child. Mother let us, so we played with them like friends, and understood each other ... They always came because we had a spacious yard.'[51]

Talking about Jews this way, Liuba actually tries to tell us something more. Depicting Jews (and Poles) as cordial friends (a questionable assertion, considering the historical context of their relations), she informs us that xenophobia is not part of the Ukrainian mentality.[52] Why? She probably wants to justify her own (latent) negative attitudes toward another nationality that played a more important role in her life, namely Russians.

Liuba's perception of the Russians is rather ambivalent. On the one hand, she associates them with the Soviet regime, because the Russian-speaking Soviet authorities on all levels, from the military to the school administration, suspected Ukrainians of being nationalists and Nazi collaborators and oppressed them.[53] She dissociates herself from the Soviet regime, which always confronted and dominated her. While she admits that the Soviets offered some concrete benefits (education, housing, work), she does not express positive sentiments toward them.

Russians remain colonialists in her mind: in her recollections they never respected Ukrainians as equals. On the contrary, they were arrogant toward the west Ukrainian population. The national humiliation she experienced from them in adolescence and at a mature age is still traumatic for her:

They paid very little attention to us in school, and it hurt me a lot. It was painful, when I was going to recite a lesson they always said: 'Banderivka[54] Tomchuk is reciting now.' It hurt my child soul very much ... [55] I was, say, persecuted a lot. Some teachers called me banderivka at every step ... It's a kind of humiliation, it was hard for me ... [56] They conferred [the rank of] Honoured Teacher to teachers [coming] from eastern regions. And there was almost nobody [in this rank] from western Ukraine. [They] didn't award us because they perceived us as a kind of dull mass, so-called banderivka.[57]

While these factors naturally resulted in Liuba's negative attitudes toward Russians, her attitude is not directly articulated. Her feelings did not originate solely from the direct offences she suffered long ago, as is made clear through an anecdote she tells about a misunderstanding that took place just after the Second World War, when the Russians came to western Ukraine. At that time neither Ukrainians nor Russians spoke the other's language ('But we didn't know Russian right away') so a play on words sometimes caused a mess. A description of quite a comic situation that took place between her and a neighbouring Russian woman is preceded by a passing remark that this woman 'is about 80 years old now and *still* only speaks Russian, she *does not say a word* in Ukrainian' [emphasis added].[58] At the end of this story Liuba says, 'We lived in friendship. They even helped us when we children were left alone; she was coming, she was speaking Russian, and probably from her I learned to speak Russian well ... *She cannot say a word in Ukrainian, but I have learned speaking Russian from her* [emphasis added].'[59]

This statement may be the key to understanding her attitudes toward Russians. Her negative feelings are rooted in the deep offence to her national dignity that she felt and still feels because of Russian disdain of her native language. Russians represented power, so their language was prestigious, used as the official language and compulsory in schools. But Liuba first learned it voluntarily in order to ease daily communication. Unlike the Poles and Jews, who Liuba considered friends for the efforts they made to speak Ukrainian, the Russians did not volunteer to do the same. Elsewhere Liuba sadly states, 'There was contempt for us; they were saying "You're banderivka, you're zapadenka." Poles didn't respect us, and Russians didn't respect us. Poles called us louts, and Russians called us banderivtsi, and today they still call [me] zapadenka, banderivka ... They felt scorn toward people from western regions of Ukraine. There is nothing more to say.'[60]

This fragment testifies to Liuba's awareness that during the interwar period (as well as centuries ago), when Galicia was a part of Poland, Ukrainians suffered discrimination from the Poles, but because such discrimination was not part of her own life experience she does not develop this theme any further. For her, the period of the Soviet regime and the Ukrainian–Russian relationship is much more personal, so is reflected largely in her life story. The Russian issue comes to the fore throughout her story, although it's silenced in her reflections on different nations. It's important to take into account that after the Second World War the majority of Jews were murdered and the majority of Poles were resettled to Poland, so Ukrainians were left face to face with Russians only. As Liuba herself put it, 'When Russians came, [the situation was] like this: Jews were shot outside Sokal, and all Poles moved to Poland ... Only Ukrainians and Russians were left in Sokal.'[61]

In light of the painful experience of Russian dominance she has reevaluated her attitudes toward and images of other neighbouring nations. This may explain why Poles and Jews have been transformed into friends in her memories; in retrospect, they seem like great friends compared with the Russians she lived with in the following years. Throughout her life she had to deal with Russians who asserted their superiority through minute actions in everyday life. The Russians represented a regime that oppressed west Ukrainians in general and her family in particular. How could she possibly keep goodwill or even neutrality toward them? She could at least pretend to be loyal toward the authorities who had power over her, just like many other survivors of socialism. After years of Soviet oppression, she is well trained to keep her pain hidden, and even today she avoids expressing her feelings openly.[62]

Speaking of nationalities she has never had contact with (Americans and French) as well as Russians, Poles, and Jews, Liuba expresses her overall attitudes: 'People of different nationalities are first of all humans, so we should treat them equally, regardless is he black or white, is he Jew, is he Ukrainian or Pole ... Equal attitude toward all of them, because I guess *he is not at fault to be Russian or Pole, or, say, Negro, or American, or Frenchman* [emphasis added]. What's essential is to be a person.'[63] As a Christian, she wants to maintain impartiality, or at least to convince us (and herself as well) of her unconditional tolerance.[64]

In the protocol the interviewer mentioned that 'she took the interview very seriously ... She was speaking slowly and selecting appropriate words carefully ... She has never forgotten about the tape recorder and tried to speak "polite-correctly."'[65] This suggests that some passing remarks and indirect hints made while speaking may reveal more about her attitudes toward the ethnic/regional other than do her literal statements.

East Ukrainian View: Valentina

The second case study is the story of Valentina from Kharkiv.[66] She defined her ethnicity as Russian, and she is older than Liuba. Her story is of special interest for our study because she had a unique experience – she was a teacher in a rural school near Lviv just after the Second World War. Her recollections provide us with a view of Russian–Ukrainian relations from another perspective.

Her narration has one distinctive feature: she automatically switches from her native Russian language to Ukrainian and back while speaking, even in the middle of a sentence. It happens every time she remembers her life in a west Ukrainian village. Sometimes she switches languages while describing situations that took place in Ukrainian language (university exams, conversation with Ukrainian-speaking people, and so forth).

For Valentina (just as for Liuba) the national question is closely tied to language. She first addresses this issue while talking about her childhood and the advantages of the Soviet educational system over the contemporary one. She returns to this topic time and again in the context of good/Soviet and bad/contemporary education. Being an experienced teacher, she expresses her thoughts as expert opinion:

> They know *neither* Ukrainian *nor* Russian, although they speak Russian but they don't know this language, they make so many mistakes, just like in Ukrainian, *shame on us*! Then we were given a very good education. Currently we talk *a lot* about the Ukrainian language, but children don't know it ... *There is no knowledge* of the Ukrainian language ... It vexes me: you live in Ukraine, you should do something [to know it].[67]

Immediately she underlines her own knowledge of the Ukrainian language to confirm her authority:

> Many parliamentarians from western Ukraine say that Ukrainian was not taught before, but Russian. No, I attended a Russian school, and I can write a dictation together with any zapadnik to show him what I was taught in a Soviet school. I still know this [Ukrainian] language ... I *remember* it. As for me, it's easier for me to speak Russian, *but the Ukrainian language* I know perfectly, that is ... I know the *Ukrainian* language *very* well.[68]

The Ukrainian language is a dilemma for her. She is proud that she has learned Ukrainian and still knows it well. At the same time she understands that she studied Ukrainian not quite voluntarily:

> I remember the vice-dean [at the Lviv Polytechnic Institute] teaching us history, and all [of the students] started complaining that it's in Ukrainian.

And he answered: 'We are preparing teachers for Ukrainian villages, so you have to know everything in Ukrainian. Whoever does not agree – goodbye! ... ' He said: 'I will mark down by one grade those reciting exams in Russian.' We found ourselves ... in western Ukraine ... First time I went [to school], it was my *first* class. They are speaking, but I understand absolutely *nothing*. First, they have the wrong pronunciation, their articulation is somewhat [strange] ... The director told me, 'Don't worry! You'll speak like the others *in a month!*' Precisely so! When we met ... in Lviv our girls from this Ukraine, all of us were jabbering like them. *All of us!*[69]

Valentina also tries to justify why she doesn't speak Ukrainian today, referring to external factors: 'I speak Russian currently because Russians are everywhere I go, *nowhere* can I hear the [Ukrainian] speech, *nowhere* ... Ukrainians ... How can they know it, if there is no Ukrainian speech in Kharkiv – all [people] are speaking Russian here, *all*. Therefore this is a *very* complicated question, *very* complicated, that's it.'[70] Evidently, Valentina's perception of the Ukrainian language is rather ambivalent. But she repeatedly stresses her tolerance of the language; moreover she represents herself as its advocate. Does this attitude apply to Ukrainians as a people? At the end of the interview Valentina articulated her general notion of Ukraine: 'Civil war may happen. Probably it would be better to divide it into three parts: western Ukraine, eastern, and Crimea, that's all. God help us to keep the peace, so everything can go right.'[71]

Thus she articulated her understanding of a deep cultural distance and political difference among the three regions. She leads us to that conclusion through her retrospection of her life in western Ukraine. Valentina begins her 'western story' with an abrupt negative evaluation of west Ukrainians, comparing them to Nazis: 'I'm considering, *who were better – fascist Germans or the west Ukrainians? Honestly*, it was *very* hard [emphasis added].'[72]

This is not a single casual comparison. The slip of the tongue and another little remark about language indicate a rather firm association between west Ukrainians and Germans in her mind: 'There was a normal school in Germany – oops! – not Germany – in western Ukraine. Nobody wanted to go [there]. Their language was far from literary Ukrainian, very far. In their language there are *Romanian* words, and Hungarian, and Polish, something else, and some *German* words ... something related to *German* pronunciation.'[73]

Elsewhere she adds, 'When face to face, they addressed us as "dear lady," but it's [dangerous] if you don't know your *enemy's face* [emphasis added], if he is nice with you, but in reality he's not such a person. That's why sometimes a situation was, say, even worse than under occupation, because [then] you knew that [Nazis] were the *enemy*, unlike them.'[74] Thus in the course of her narration it becomes clear that her answer to who was better, 'fascist Germans' or west Ukrainians, would be the Germans.

Valentina's attitudes toward Germans are formed to a great extent by her experience of war. During the war she lived on occupied territory, and the front line crossed it several times. Her narrative makes clear her emotional ambivalence toward the Germans. On the one hand, the Nazis brought along all of the horrors of war she experienced. On the other, she also experienced positive interactions with Germans: 'Sometimes Germans were different – good and evil ... probably there were good people among them as well.' Valentina concludes after telling a story about a German physician who saved the life of a little boy who was choking.[75] Another episode is about a German officer who prevented her from being taken to Germany as a forced labourer just before the Red Army returned.[76] She told also a story about two Ukrainian girls who were brought to Germany as forced labourers and died by accident there. The Germans gave them a proper burial and took care of their graves.[77] She perceives war as a severe, sudden, and unplanned force that caused hardships and suffering that she described in detail in her autobiography, and she does not hold individual Germans responsible for what happened to her.

Valentina describes extensively the horrors she experienced in western Ukraine, expressing her opinions of west Ukrainians:

How we lived in Western Ukraine and what they did there ... I lived surrounded by criminals ... They came at night to see their people, they offended even them ... They called us ragamuffins, moskali and whatever ... It was terrible and horrible. Teachers disappeared ... I was afraid to say an extra word out of place. There were some incidents: our teacher with some military men went to the district [town] to receive [a salary] for teachers ... Bandery fired at them. I don't remember, I guess all of them were murdered ... We were *afraid* of them, *so afraid* because there was a banderivtsi's hiding place nearby our village ... I know that they [killed] also their own local [people] once they see their sympathy toward the Soviet regime. *If someone got caught by the bandery*, regardless who, he *wouldn't return*, that's true – I lived there, I know, nobody returned. [We] found one dead body, disfigured beyond recognition: eyes stabbed, nose and lips torn, no tongue, ears cut off, outrage done to the genitals – that's a *horror* what they did ... Set on the fire, tied to trees ... *Horror*, it was terrible! After sunset all doors and windows are locked, lights are turned off, and that's all! ... *If you open your mouth* – you won't be here tomorrow![78]

Both Liuba and Valentina mentioned that ordinary people were terrified of both sides: underground nationalists and Soviet authorities. Russian newcomers as well as the local population found themselves in the crossfire: anyone could be accused of relations with either the NKVD or the banderivtsi, so they tried to avoid any contact with either in order to avoid punishment:

It was very frightful when our military men, chekists, came there – we avoid them. God save us from talking to them, [otherwise the banderivtsi] will think that you have reported something to them ... It was *terrible,* horrible ... We learned to pray to God, and we all prayed. Where should we go? Our landlady says, 'You better pray, otherwise [the banderivtsi] will come at night and take you away, and we [will be sent] to Siberia for 10 years. She says this, since the [NKVD] would think that she is related to [banderivtsi].[79]

All of the horrors she depicted occurred in the countryside, whereas the city of Lviv in her narrative represents quite a different, more civilized milieu.[80] As Valentina puts it, 'In Lviv the life flowed *absolutely* otherwise ... because there were more Russians ... It was calmer here, and girls from our Ukraine, from eastern [Ukraine], from our Kharkiv studied in the institute.'[81] It's quite remarkable that Valentina described her life in the west Ukrainian village in Ukrainian, yet she started speaking Russian when speaking of Lviv.

Valentina is quite aware of the hostility that west Ukrainians felt toward Soviets, but she does not understand its origins. So she describes them as thankless, ignorant people time and time again:

When I was in western Ukraine I saw their attitudes ... They all were *uneducated* ... They have not studied, they knew nothing ... They were learning somehow, but they had no knowledge at all ... [We] treated them ... as usual. But *they* treated us very badly, called us sovietki, moskovki, something else ... [They] *hated* us so terribly ... They didn't want Soviet regime, *did not want it* ... We treated them well, with understanding, but they [treated] us badly. We had secondary education, and they learned less in secondary school than we did in a vocational school; [they were] less educated.[82]

The only positive characteristic she found in west Ukrainians was their talent for singing.[83] In Valentina's recollection west Ukrainians looked like barbarians (poor, ignorant, dirty, amoral, insidious, and dangerous), but their indigenous culture was beautiful.[84] Is that not a typical colonizer's attitude toward any dominated people? And does such scornful perception apply to west Ukrainians only? In Valentina's narrative one can find at least two indicative remarks about eastern Ukrainians that imply them to be less moral and intelligent than Russians.[85] Being a representative of the Soviet regime, she felt empowered – at risk of her life – to bring 'enlightenment' to western Ukraine. And she is still proud of that mission, praising the Soviet system of education and health care. In fact, Valentina perceives the Soviet regime as perfect in contrast to the current transitional order.[86]

What about Jews? Just like Liuba, Valentina starts with a short preamble: 'All through my life, in my childhood, we never made [difference] who's a Jew, who's a Ukrainian, who's an Uzbek or what, *no difference*, we all were *of one nation* ... In school we didn't pay any attention to one's ethnicity, and in the institute, too.'[87] Then Valentina immediately narrated a Holocaust story about how her family helped a Jewish boy who had escaped a massacre.[88] It's remarkable that this story preceded her description of west Ukrainians as barbarians. Thus, the story is not an autonomous segment of her life story. It plays a supplementary role in her narration and is used to point out that she is not generally xenophobic, so she can not be biased against west Ukrainians.

Conclusion

The autobiographical narrative interview is an indispensable tool if one wants to reveal women's way of making sense of the past, especially in the post-Soviet countries. After decades of forced silence and denial of historical memory, it is hard for elderly women to express their opinions openly and plainly. We will never know their real views if we ask them only direct questions (usually answered in a 'polite-correct' way). Furthermore, without an end-to-end cross-reading of a woman's autobiography we will never understand her notions of ethnic and regional self and other. This was made apparent through discourse analysis of

both narratives. Passing remarks and seemingly minor (non-verbal) details of the narratives turned out to be extremely important in revealing
subconscious motives, unarticulated feelings, and silenced thoughts.
Often, the women's accounts of various events tell us much more about
their implicit ethnic attitudes than their proclamatory statements do. In
both autobiographies several seemingly separate sentences constitute
discursive units, so each of them is fully understood when considered
in relation to the other.

The awareness of hierarchal relations between (western) Ukrainians
and Russian-speaking people is visible in both stories. The so-called in-
feriority complex of Ukrainians originated centuries ago, but it was
sharpened in the postwar period when Russian-speaking Soviet authorities pacified the Ukrainian national liberation movement. Over decades
the Soviet regime subdued the liberation movement through direct political oppression and latent everyday discrimination against Ukrainians.
The Russian (or Russian-speaking east Ukrainian) newcomers regarded
themselves as civilizers, bringing enlightenment to backward and be-
nighted local Ukrainians, whereas west Ukrainians perceived them as
colonists whose dominance and arrogance deeply offended their national dignity. This resulted in mutual prejudices that still remain (subcon-
sciously) in both women's attitudes today.

Of special interest is the way that both women, despite their different
ethnic backgrounds and mutual biases, resorted to similar discursive
strategies when narrating their life stories. They use the same trope
while arguing for ethnic tolerance. First, each of them stated her positive attitude toward other nations by means of recalling her personal
childhood experiences of interethnic friendship. Then both women offered Holocaust stories – narrated in a very similar way – as evidence
of their inherent feeling of international solidarity (they expressed a
deep empathy toward murdered Jews in general, then related a true
episode about the rescue of a particular persecuted Jew).

Jews and other distinct ethnic groups mentioned in both autobiographies were included in the narratives as a way to explain the women's
perceptions of Russian–Ukrainian relations. Jews are usually perceived
to be the ethnic other for both Ukrainians and Russians. However, in
their stories Jews appear as a kind of contrasting background for the
women's reflections about problematic relations between Ukrainians
and Russians. One might also assume Germans (personified as Nazis)
to be key actors in the women's memories because of their war
experiences, but this was not the case. Like Jews, Germans (and Poles

as well) play a secondary role in the women's narratives, used to attest to their non-xenophobic views in general and their unbiased attitudes toward each other in particular. In short, other ethnicities are used to allude to something untold about Russian–Ukrainian relations, namely the mutual recent resentments and age-old distrust.

In their attitudes toward the Soviet regime and its ideology, both women manifested strong sentiments – either for or against. Although the personal achievements of the two women were more or less equivalent in terms of education, job, marriage, children, and housing, their losses were not. While Liuba came from a middle-class urban educated family, Valentina's parents were poor, illiterate peasants. Liuba's father was repressed, her national sentiments disgraced, her religion persecuted, and her native language devalued by (Russian-speaking) Soviets. As a result, she expresses lifelong opposition to that regime. Valentina, on the contrary, obtained the unique chance to climb the social ladder thanks to the Soviet system, and her ethnicity played a role in this. This may partly explain her strong attachment to the socialist system. The women's regional and ethnic origins have determined their different historical experiences, and consequently shaped their ethnic and regional identities and respective images of the other.

The project '20th Century Ukraine in Women's Memories' is still in progress, so a number of important questions are still to be revealed. What strategies have women used to survive in the most severe circumstances? How did they cope with the economic, social, and political changes that occurred throughout their lives? What significance have family and professional functions had for women of different generations? How have their social roles and views changed in the post-independence years? What factors determined their political views? What are women's notions of post-Soviet nostalgia? How does the current economic, political, and social situation affect and reshape women's senses of the past, present, and future? The answers are embedded in women's life stories. We just have to listen carefully to what is (un)told.

NOTES

I thank the Canadian Institute of Ukrainian Studies, University of Alberta, for the research grant that enabled me to record the interviews used for this study. I am grateful to the organizers and participants of the symposium 'Writing about Talking: Orality and Literacy in the Contemporary Scholarship' for the stimulating questions and comments that assisted considerably my revision. I would also like to express my appreciation to Carolyn Drake who helped me enormously in editing and polishing the final draft.

1 Luisa Passerini, 'Introduction,' in *Memory and Totalitarianism*, ed. Luisa Passerini, *International Yearbook of Oral History and Life Stories*, vol. 1 (Oxford: Oxford University Press, 1992), 1–19.

2 Renate Bridenthal, Claudia Koonz, and Susan Stuard, eds. *Becoming Visible: Women in European History* (Boston: Houghton Mifflin, 1977); Shirley Rowbotham, *Hidden from History* (London: Pluto, 1973).

3 Joan W. Scott, 'The Problem of Invisibility,' in *Retrieving Women's History: Changing Perceptions of the Role of Women in Politics and Society*, ed. S. Jay Kleinberg (Paris: UNESCO, 1988), 5–6.

4 Paul Thompson, 'The Voice of the Past: Oral History,' in *The Oral History Reader*, ed. Robert Perks and Alistair Thompson (London and New York: Routledge, 1998), 28.

5 Joan W. Scott, 'Gender: A Useful Category of Historical Analysis,' in *Feminism and History*, ed. Joan W. Scott (New York: Oxford University Press, 2000), 167.

6 For further discussion on the interconnection and interdependence of oral history and feminist studies, see S. Gluck, 'What's So Special about Women? Women's Oral History' in *Oral History: An Interdisciplinary Anthology*, ed. David K. Dunaway and Willa K. Baum (Walnut Creek, CA: Alta Mira Press, 1996), 215–30; Sherna Berger Gluck and Daphne Patai, eds., *Women's Words: The Feminist Practice of Oral History* (New York and London: Routledge, 1991); Olga Shutova, *Ustnaya i gendernaya istoriya v svete antropologizatsii istoriografii, in Zhenschiny v istorii: vozmozhnost' byt' uvidennymi*, ed. Irina Chikalova (Minsk: BSPU, 2001), 55–74.

7 For further discussion, see H. White, *Metahistory* (Baltimore: Johns Hopkins University Press, 1975); R. Samuel and P. Thompson, eds., *The Myths We Live By* (London: Routledge, 1990); E. Tonkin, *Narrating Our Pasts: The Social Construction of Oral History* (Cambridge: Cambridge University Press, 1992).

8 Selma Leydesdorff, Luisa Passerini, and Paul Thompson, 'Introduction,' in *Gender and Memory*, ed. Selma Leydesdorff, Luisa Passerini, and Paul Thompson, *International Yearbook of Oral History and Life Stories*, vol. 4 (Oxford: Oxford University Press, 1996), 12.

9 For further discussion, see Graham Gardner, 'Unreliable Memories and Other Contingencies: Problems with Biographical Knowledge,' *Qualitative Research* 1, no. 2 (2000): 185–204.

10 D. Bertaux, 'Poleznost rasskazov o zhyzni dlia realisticheskoy i znachimoy sotsiologii,' in *Biograficheskiy metod v izuchenii postsotsialisticheskikh obshchestv*, ed. B. Voronkov and E. Zdravomyslova (St Petersburg: CNSR, 1997), 18.

11 Alessandro Portelli, 'What Makes Oral History Different,' in A. Portelli, *The Death of Luigi Trastulli, and Other Stories: Form and Meaning in Oral History* (New York: State University of New York Press, 1991), 48, emphasis in original.

12 Thus, several special editions devoted to both oral history and women's studies of (post)socialism contained no Ukrainian materials at all, e.g., Barbara Alpern Angel and Anastasia Posadskaya-Vanderbeck, eds., *A Revolution of Their Own: Voices of Women in Soviet History* (New York: Westview Press, 1998); Nanette Funk and M. Mueller, eds., *Gender Politics and Post-Communism: Reflections from Eastern Europe and the Former Soviet Union* (New York and London: Routlege, 1993); and Passerini, *Memory and Totalitarianism*.

13 This became possible when translations of classical feminist texts came out in the former Soviet countries. See, for instance, Liliana Hentosh and Oksana Kis, eds., *Genderhyi pidkhid: istoriia, kultura, suspilstvo* (Gender approach: history, culture, society) (Lviv: Klasyka, 2004) – a reader in feminist history and anthropology.

14 Liudmyla Smoliar, *Mynule zarady maibutnioho: Zhinochy rukh Naddniprianskoi Ukrainy druhoi polovyny 19 – pochatku 20 stolittia* (Odesa: Astroprynt, 1998); Martha Bohachevsky-Chomiak, *Bilym po bilomu: zhinky v hromadskomu zhytti Ukrainy, 1884–1939* (Kyiv: Lybid', 1995). This is the Ukrainian version of Bohachevsky-Chomiak's *Feminists Despite Themselves: Women in Ukrainian Community Life, 1884–1939* (Edmonton: University of Alberta Press, 1988).

15 Oles Kozulia, *Zhinky v istorii Ukrainy* (Kyiv: Ukrainskyi Tsentr Dukhovnoi Kultury, 1993); Oleh Luhovy, *Vyznachne zhinotstvo Ukrainy: istorychni zhyttiepysy* (Kyiv: Dnipro, 1994); Ivan Kuzych-Berezovsky, *Zhinka i derzhava* (Lviv: Svit, 1994); Maria Orlyk, ed., *Zhinky Ukrainy: biohrafichny entsyklopedychny slovnyk* (Kyiv: Pheniks, 2001), which includes about 2,500 entries; Yuriy Khorunzhy, *Shliakhetni ukrainky: eseyi* (Kyiv: Olena Teliha, 2003).

16 Liudmyla Smoliar, ed. *Zhinochi studii v Ukraini: zhinka v istorii ta siohodni* (Odesa: Astroprynt, 1999). For more critical reflections on this work, see Oksana Kis, 'Review of *Zhinochi studii v Ukraini*,' *Ukraina Moderna* 4–5 (2000): 503–11.

17 For example, the following topics have been studied by means of oral history: Church history, by the Institute of Church History, Ukrainian

Catholic University Lviv, 'Fortitude and Flexibility: The Oral History of the Underground Life of the Ukrainian Greek-Catholic Church, 1946–89' (ongoing project); the 1932–33 famine in Ukraine, by J. Mace, ed., *Oral History Project on the Commission on Ukrainian Famine*, vols. 1–3 (Washington, DC: U.S. Government Printing Office, 1990); the Holocaust, by Zh. Kovba, 'Loyalnist u bezodni pekla,' in *Ukraina Moderna,* vol. 1–2 (Lviv: LNU, 1999); political emigration from Ukraine, by Iroida Vynnytska, 'Zhyva istoria ukrainskoi politychnoi emihratsii v Kanadi,' in *Ukraina Moderna,* vol. 4–5 (Lviv: LNU, 2000); collectivization in 1920–30 in Ukraine, by William Noll, *Transformatsia hromadianskoho suspilstva: Usna istoria ukrainskoi selanskoi kultury, 1920–30* (Kyiv: Rodovid, 1999); the forced labour of Ukrainians in Nazi Germany, by Gelinada Grinchenko, ed., *Nevyhadane: Usni istorii ostarbaiteriv* (Kharkiv: Raider, 2004; and by Tetyana Pastushenko, ed., *To bula nevolia: Spohady i lysty ostarbaiteriv* (Kyiv: Instytut istorii NAN Ukrainy, 2006).

18 The gap is not only for academic reasons but above all because of the advanced age of the women who still are able to narrate their recollections of the bygone events in Soviet history. The exception is Halyna Datsiuk, Nadiia Samuliak, and Yaroslava Sorokopud, *Usna zhinocha istoriya: Povernennia* (Kyiv: Zhinochy Tsentr Spadschyna, 2003). The work was a part of a larger international project that included most countries of the former Soviet bloc. Three women activists of different professional backgrounds (Datsiuk, Samuliak, and Sorokopud) led the project, which was devoted to recording biographical interviews with elderly women all over Ukraine. It resulted in the publication of a collection of shortened versions of 28 interviews describing the women's recollections of the most significant events in Ukrainian history of the twentieth century: the forced collectivization of farming and the following famine of 1932–33; the Second World War; the national liberation movement in western Ukraine in the 1940s and '50s; and up to the post-Soviet transition. This pioneering project is of indisputable public importance, but its academic value should not be overestimated. It helps to balance the existing gender disparity in the historical records about the recent Ukrainian past, but its methodological vagueness makes further analysis of the collected materials rather problematic. Evident mistakes in interview documentation along with other transgressions of transcription and archiving rules suggest that project participants were novices in oral history. The relevance of chosen theoretical principles and techniques to the project's goals cannot be assessed as they are not described, and the published materials provide no evidence of a common interviewing strategy or questionnaire for collecting the women's retrospections.

19 Svetlana Shakirova, ed., *Golosa ukhodiashchikh pokolenii: analiz zhenskikh biografii* (Almaty: Tsentr gendernykh issledovanii, 2002); Elmira Arapova, *Yuzhanki: zhenskiye ustnye istorii Elmiry Arapovoy* (Bishkek: Open Society Institute, 2003); Bakhrinisso Kabilova, *Ustnye istorii zhenshchin Tadzhikistana* (Dushanbe: Open Society Institute, 2003); L.V. Miagkaya, *Zhizn kak sudba, ili ustnye zhenskiye istorii* (Dushanbe: Open Society Institute, 2003); L.G. Sarieva, *Vosponinaniya zhenshchin kak otrazhenie sotsialno-politicheskoy i kulturnoy zhizni Azerbaydzhana XX veka: po materialam izucheniya ustnykh istoriy* (Baku: Adilogly, 2004); Krassimira Daskalova, ed., *Voices of Their Own: Oral History Interview of Women* (Sofia: Polis, 2004). Quotation from Barbara Alpern Angel and Anastasia Posadskaya-Vanderbeck, 'Introduction,' in *A Revolution of Their Own*, ed. Angel and Posadskaya-Vanderbeck, 2.

20 Elena Meshcherkina, ed., *Ustnaya istoriya i biografiya: zhenskiy vzgliad* (Moskva: Nevskiy Prostor, 2004); Andrea Peto, ed., *Gendernye issledovaniya: zhenskaya ustnaya istoriya* (Bishkek: Tsentr, 2004); Marina Loskutova, ed., *Khrestomatiya po ustnoy istorii* (St Petersburg: European University, 2003; Daskalova, ed., *Voices of Their Own*.

21 Sidonie Smith, *A Poetics of Women's Autobiography: Marginality and Fictions of Self-Representation* (Bloomington: Indiana University Press, 1987), 18.

22 Robert Atkinson, *The Life Story Interview* (London: Sage, 1998), 9.

23 Marjorie L. Devault, 'Talking and Listening from Women's Standpoint: Feminist Strategies for Interviewing and Analysis,' *Social Problems* 37, no. 1 (1990): 108.

24 Ibid., 112.

25 Yuliya Gradskova, 'Zhenskaya biografiya i "perepisyvanie istorii": sluchay SSSR,' in *Adam i Eva: Almanakh gendernoy istorii*, ed. L.P. Repina, vol. 2 (Moskva: Nauka, 2001), 173.

26 Smith, *Poetics of Women's Autobiography*, 52.

27 Maria Savchyn, *Tysiacha dorih: Spohady zhinky uchasnytsi pidpilno-vyzvolnoi borotby pid chas I pislia Druhoi svotovoi viyny* (Kyiv: Smoloskyp, 2003), 12.

28 Anna Polshchikova, *Deti Osventsima (dokumentalnaya povest)* (Yalta: Tavrida, 1993).

29 Portelli, 'What Makes Oral History Different,', 47–8.

30 Passerini, ed., *Memory and Totalitarianism*.

31 Angel and Posadskaya-Vanderbeck, 'Introduction,' 2.

32 For further discussion on the destructive effects of fear on public remembering in the Soviet Union, see Daria Khubova, Andrei Ivankiev, and Tonia Sharova, 'After Glasnost: Oral History in Soviet Union,' in *Memory and Totalitarianism*, ed. Passerini, 89–101.

33 Nanette Funk, 'Feminism: East and West,' in *Gender Politics*, ed. Funk and Mueller, 323.

34 For general information about the project, its goals, methodology, chronology, and outcomes, see www.womensmemory.net.

35 Gabriele Rosenthal, 'Biographical Research,' in *Qualitative Research Practice*, ed. Clive Seale, Giampietro Gobo, Jaber F. Gubrium, and David Silverman (London: SAGE Publications, 2004), 48–64.

36 For details, see Gluck, 'What's So Special about Women?'; J. Sangster, 'Telling Our Stories: Feminist Debates and the Use of Oral History,' in *The Oral History Reader*, ed. R. Perks and A. Thompson (London: Routledge, 1998), 87–100; A. Oakley, 'Interviewing Women,' in *Doing Feminist Research*, ed. H. Roberts (London: Routledge and Kegan Paul, 1981), 30–6; K. Anderson and D.C. Jack, 'Learning to Listen: Interview Techniques and Analysis,' in *Women's Words*, ed. Gluck and Patai, 11–26; Devault, 'Talking and Listening.'

37 The technique includes sustained visual contact, a mirroring of the interviewee's face and posture, a minimum of looking aside, stimulatory words and gestures, and so forth.

38 For an extensive discussion of the psychological aspects of interviewing, see Gabriele Rosenthal, 'The Healing Effects of Storytelling: On the Conditions of Curative Storytelling in the Context of Research and Counseling,' *Qualitative Inquiry* 9 (2003): 915–33.

39 The external questions are: (1) What did the Soviet regime mean to you? (2) What do you think about people of various ethnicities living next to you? (3) What historical events have influenced your life the most? (4) What did Ukrainian independence mean to you?? (5) What has helped you overcome obstacles in your life?

40 A. Strauss and J. Corbin, *Basics of Qualitative Research: Grounded Theory Procedures and Techniques* (London: Sage, 1990).

41 For a comprehensive discussion of the history of relations between the Ukrainian and Russian languages in Ukraine and the current state of the problem, see Laada Bilanyuk, *Contested Tongues: Language Politics and Cultural Correction in Ukraine* (Ithaca and London: Cornell University Press, 2005).

42 For instance, Jews constituted 30 to 35 percent of Lviv population before 1939; they now constitute only 2 to 3 percent of the population. Yaroslav Hrytsak and Victor Susak, 'Constructing a National City: The Case of Lviv,' in *Composing Urban History and the Constitution of Civic Identity*, ed. J. Czaplicka and B. Ruble (Baltimore: Johns Hopkins University Press, 2003), 142.

43 Prejudice against Jews arose in reaction to their involvement in trade, money lending, and the sale of alcohol. They were perceived to be sly, mercenary and unscrupulous, making profit from Ukrainians.

44 The scale of women's participation in the national liberation movement is represented in the recent biographical reference *Ukrainska zhinka u vyzvol'niy borot'bi, 1940–1950* (Ukrainian Woman in the Liberation Movement), ed. Nadiya Mudra (Lviv: Svit, 2004), which has about 900 entries.

45 Even the work done from historical and sociological perspectives is based on analysis of legislation and public policies concerning women, the activities of women's organizations, mass media publications, and the published biographies of famous women, rather than on the oral accounts of Ukrainian women. See, for example, the recent collection *Gendernye istorii vostochnoy Evropy* (Gendered Stories of Eastern Europe), ed. Yelena Gapova, Almira Usmanova, and Andrea Peto (Minsk: EHU, 2002), which contains two articles on women's issues in contemporary Ukraine, by Tatiana Zhurzhenko and Marian Rubchak. Neither refers to interviews with ordinary women.

46 Institute of Ethnology Archives, Lviv, Ukraine, '20th Century Ukraine in Women's Memories' fonds, file UL2-04, interview with Liuba H. by Oksana Kis, Lviv, 2004. Hereafter cited as Liuba H. interview.

47 Ibid., 58–63.

48 Ibid., 1286–91.

49 Ibid., 1309–18. Emphasis in quotations in original unless otherwise indicated.

50 Ibid., 1322–9.

51 Ibid., 1347–52.

52 It is significant that she mentioned Poles as well: relationships between Ukrainians and Poles were extremely problematic because of the number of historical conflicts. A large part of western Ukraine was under Polish governance up to 1939, and Ukrainians were treated as an inferior people.

53 Liuba's father worked in the post office during Nazi occupation. The Soviet regime accused him (as it did many other west Ukrainians) of collaboration with the Nazis. He was arrested as 'a people's enemy' and banished to Central Asia for ten years; later, he was rehabilitated. Liuba regards that period as the hardest time of her life.

54 The terms *banderivka, banderivtsi,* and *bandery* refer to the followers of Stepan Bandera, the prominent leader of Ukrainian national liberation movement, accused of Ukrainian nationalism and murdered by the KGB in 1959.

55 Liuba H. interview, 1424–7.

56 Ibid., 436–8, 209, 215.

57 Ibid., 1072–4.

58 Ibid., 493–5.

59 Ibid., 509–15.

60 The terms *zapadenka, zapadenets,* and *zapadentsi* literally refer to people of west Ukrainian origin but are associated with the Ukrainian nationalist struggle against the Soviet regime and usually have negative connotations. Liuba H. interview, 1202–15; 1081–2.

61 Ibid., 1344–6.

62 For instance, she uses the more polite word *Russians* instead of *moskali,* which has a negative connotation (used to name Russians as aliens who came to western Ukraine along with the Soviet regime and dominated Ukrainians.)

63 Ibid., 1260–5.

64 Liuba refers to a Christian moral, saying, 'We should treat people the same way as God treats us. We should not offend them, or their dignity, or their beliefs; we should respect people of different nationalities' (1271–3).

65 Protocol of the Liuba H. interview.

66 Institute of Ethnology Archives, Lviv, Ukraine, '20th Century Ukraine in Women's Memories' fonds, file UK1-04, interview with Valentina P., Kharkiv by Lidiia Chesnokova, 2004. Hereafter cited as Valentina P. interview.

67 Valentina P. interview, 201–9, 216–19, 1993–8. Elsewhere she repeatedly states that in Soviet schools the Russian and Ukrainian languages were studied equally (1032–4), which was not the case.

68 Valentina P. interview, 201–9, 216–19, 2017–21, 1986–9. *Zapadnik* is another version of *zapadenka/zapadenets/zapadentsi,* someone from western Ukraine.

69 Ibid., 1109–12, 1122–3, 216–19, 1151–88.

70 Ibid., 2017–21, 1186–8.

71 Ibid., 2372–82.

72 Ibid., 1083–90.

73 Ibid., 1354–5, 1170–5.

74 Ibid., 1509–14.

75 Ibid., 619–33.

76 Ibid., 706–20.

77 Ibid.

78 Ibid., 1385–412, 1454–39, 1505.

79 Ibid., 1533–6, 1544–7, 1515–33. *Chekists* were officers of the Extraordinary Committee, the authority that preceded and had the same functions as the NKVD and KGB did later.

80 She described Lviv as an artistic place full of cultural events (1561–9).

81 Ibid., 1541–50.

82 Ibid., 2313–21, 2338–41, 1354–64.

83 Ibid., 1440–7.

84 'I remember, when I was working in Western Ukraine, children gave [bribes]. God forbid! For us it was such a savagery to take something from a child! But they took ... In Western Ukraine I was working very quietly ... It was very difficult [because of] banderivtsi ... He [said] polite words to you, but he could stab you in the back. They are very tough people' (ibid., 2076–9, 1083–90, 2321–38).

85 First she describes eastern Ukrainians as deserters avoiding the fight against Nazis: 'During the war many Ukrainians stayed at home ... [After escaping from] captivity they didn't look for our [Red Army] troops' (ibid., 725–7). Then she depicts them as unable to speak Russian correctly, so even her two-year-old (Russian) son rebuked a kindergarten teacher who couldn't get rid of her broad Ukrainian pronunciation (ibid., 2460–8).

86 Ibid., 2120–57, 2226–48, 2279–90. Her words suggest that she is even ready to condone the Stalinist regime: 'Today the [image of] Stalin is distorted a lot, distorted a lot. He had something bad, but there was something good, too ... Probably, there was something bad, but you should sift it out, and keep pure grains – they might be always useful' (1195–202, 2248–50).

87 Ibid., 2296–8, 1113–51.

88 Ibid., 2299–312.

Contributors

Gary Arbuckle is an independent scholar living in Vancouver, British Columbia. His research and publications have examined the relationship between orality and literacy and the concept of deity in the era between the Shang and Chou dynasties. His dissertation explored the thought system of the Han dynasty Confucian philosopher Dong Zhongshu (195–115 BCE).

Keith Carlson is a professor of history and director of the Interdisciplinary Centre for Culture and Creativity at the University of Saskatchewan. He has published numerous articles, book chapters, and atlas plates on Coast Salish Aboriginal and Philippine history, and has authored, edited, or co-edited seven books including most recently *The Power of Place, the Problem of Time: Aboriginal Identity and Historical Consciousness in the Cauldron of Colonialism* (Toronto: University of Toronto Press, 2010).

J. Edward Chamberlin is University Professor of English and Comparative Literature at the University of Toronto. He is an internationally recognized scholar in the areas of oral and written cultures, Aboriginal studies and rights, and West Indian poetry. His books are *The Harrowing of Eden: White Attitudes towards Native Americans; Come Back to Me My Language: Poetry and the West Indies;* and *If This Is Your Land, Where Are Your Stories? Finding Common Ground.* He was the Senior Research Associate with the Royal Commission on Aboriginal Peoples, and has worked extensively on Native land claims around the world.

Kristina Fagan is an associate professor in the Department of English at the University of Saskatchewan. She has published many articles on Aboriginal literatures in Canada, theoretical approaches to Aboriginal literature, and the function of oral storytelling in Aboriginal communities. With historian Keith Carlson, she edited a scholarly edition of Henry Pennier's 1972 autobiography under the title *'Call Me Hank': An Aboriginal Man's Reflections on Logging, Living, and Growing Old.*

Twyla Gibson is an assistant professor of culture and technology at the Faculty of Information Studies and a senior fellow at the McLuhan Program, where she teaches courses in the history and philosophy of communication technology, including Media Theory, Information Ethics, and Visual Communication and Culture. Her research focuses on ancient Greek philosophy, communication and media studies, orality and literacy studies, philosophy of literature, and bioethics.

Susan Gingell is a professor in the Department of English at the University of Saskatchewan. She has research interests in Canadian and other decolonizing literatures and textualized oratures, especially those of Anglophone Africa and the Caribbean. She has edited *E. J. Pratt on His Life and Poetry*; the unpublished drama and poetry in part 2 of *Complete Poems*; and *Pursuits Amateur and Academic: The Selected Prose* in the *Collected Works of E. J. Pratt* series. She also edited a special issue of *Essays on Canadian Writing*, 83, Textualizing Orature and Orality.

Reynaldo Ileto is a professor of history and the coordinator of the Southeast Asian Studies Program, National University of Singapore, as well as author of the acclaimed *Pasyon and Revolution; Popular Movements in the Philippines, 1840–1910.* (Quezon City: Ateneo University, 1979, [2003]). Ileto has held the Tañada Chair at De La Salle University (Manila), the Burns Chair in History at the University of Hawaii, and senior fellowships at Kyoto University and Tokyo University of Foreign Studies. His writings have won him the Benda Prize, the Ohira Prize, the Philippine National Book Award, and the Fukuoka Asian Culture Prize 2003.

Oksana Kis (PhD, Institute of Ethnology, National Academy of Sciences of Ukraine) is a Senior Research Fellow at the Institute of Ethnology, National Academy of Sciences of Ukraine (in Lviv); she is also a Director of the Lviv Resarch Center 'Woman and Society' (NGO). She has published over fifty articles relating to women and gender topics and Ukrainian anthropology. Her monograph *Women in the Ukrainian Traditional Culture in the Second Half of the 19th and early 20th Centuries* appeared in Lviv in 2008. Oksana Kis served as a guest editor for special issues of academic journals (*JI, Ukraina Moderna, Narodoznavchi Zoshyty*) and edited volumes devoted to gender issues. She was a Fulbright Fellow at Rutgers University in 2003–4, a Shklar Fellow at Harvard Ukrainian Research Institute in 2007–8, and Petro Jacyk Visiting Professor at Columbia University in 2010.

Natalia Khanenko-Friesen (PhD, University of Alberta) is an associate professor of cultural anthropology and the director of Prairie Centre for the Study of Ukrainian Heritage at St Thomas More College, University of Saskatchewan. Her research interests include transnational and diasporic constructions of identities and communities, letter writing, narrative and oral history, and post-Soviet Ukrainian identity and culture. Her edited collections, articles, book chapters, and reviews have appeared in *Anthropology of Eastern Europe Review, Journal of Canadian Folklore, Ethnologies, Journal of Ukrainian Studies, Rodovid (Journal of Ukrainian Ethnology), Ukraina Moderna, Ukrainian Historical Journal, Slavic and East European Journal, Spaces of Identity, Canadian American Slavic Studies,* and other series. Her monograph *The Other World or Ethnicity in Action: Canadian Ukrainianness at the End of the 20th Century* has just appeared with the Ukrainian publisher Smoloskyp (2011).

Frank Klaassen is an associate professor of history and director of the Classical, Medieval and Renaissance Studies program at the University of Saskatchewan. He teaches and publishes in the area of the late middle ages and early modern Britain and is editor of a new journal *Opuscula: Short Texts of the Middle Ages and Renaissance.* He is also author of the forthcoming *The Transformations of Magic: Illicit Learned Magic 1300–1600,* (University Park: Penn State University Press)

Index